The Law and Practice of
Receivership in Scotland

The Law and Practice of Receivership in Scotland

J H Greene
MA, LLB
Solicitor in Scotland

I M Fletcher
LLB, LTCL, LRAM, ARCO, WS
Solicitor in Scotland
Solicitor of the Supreme Court in England

London
Butterworths
1987

United Kingdom	Butterworth & Co (Publishers) Ltd, 88 Kingsway, LONDON WC2B 6AB and 61A North Castle Street, EDINBURGH EH2 3LJ
Australia	Butterworths Pty Ltd, SYDNEY, MELBOURNE, BRISBANE, ADELAIDE, PERTH, CANBERRA and HOBART
Canada	Butterworths. A division of Reed Inc., TORONTO and VANCOUVER
New Zealand	Butterworths of New Zealand Ltd, WELLINGTON and AUCKLAND
Singapore	Butterworth & Co (Asia) Pte Ltd, SINGAPORE
South Africa	Butterworth Publishers (Pty) Ltd, DURBAN and PRETORIA
USA	Butterworth Legal Publishers, ST PAUL, Minnesota, SEATTLE, Washington, BOSTON, Massachusetts, AUSTIN, Texas and D & S Publishers, CLEARWATER, Florida

© Butterworth & Co (Publishers) Ltd 1987

British Library Cataloguing in Publication Data

Greene, J. H.
  The law and practice of receivership in
Scotland.
  1. Receivers—Scotland
  I. Title   II. Fletcher, I.M.
  344.1106′78   KDC560

  ISBN 0 406 00527 3

Typeset by Latimer Trend & Company Ltd, Plymouth
Printed and bound in Great Britain by Billing & Sons Ltd, Worcester

Preface

The Companies (Floating Charges and Receivers) (Scotland) Act 1972 first introduced into the law of Scotland the concept of receivership. In the years since 1972, this statutory and only form of receivership has been the subject of much discussion and development in the Scottish courts, particularly as a result of the increase in receiverships during the recent severe recession in the Scottish economy.

Despite the comparative novelty and importance of receivership, there has been no legal textbook in Scotland on the subject. This book is an attempt to consider the various aspects of receivership as much from a practical and commercial standpoint as from a legal one. The completion and publication of the book has been greatly complicated by the considerable legislative changes (including two consolidating statutes) which have been taking place recently in the field of insolvency, but it is hoped that the book accurately takes account of all relevant changes affecting the law of receivership in Scotland.

We are indebted to our partners for their patience, encouragement and assistance, to our colleagues in the solicitor profession and at the Bar, whose collective knowledge and wisdom has provoked and stimulated much thought in the preparation of this work and to those of our clients for whom, in their capacity as receivers, it has been our privilege to endeavour to untangle an extraordinary range of complex, diverse and, in some cases, unlikely portfolios of receivership legal problems.

In an age of ever increasing technology, it has been of great benefit to have the manuscript of this book translated efficiently and effectively to a word processor. Our sincere thanks are due to the team of operators who have cheerfully given unstintingly of their time over a considerable period in making our task a great deal easier and providing a readable copy for our publishers.

We are also extremely grateful to Butterworths for agreeing to undertake the publication of this book, for their careful attention to all matters of printing and publishing and, not least, for undertaking the preparation of the tables of statutes, cases and the index. The directors and staff of Butterworths have also provided us with much encouragement, particularly at times when the legislative changes seemed unending.

Last, but by no means least, we have been tremendously encouraged by our wives without whose constant enthusiasm and assistance this book would never have been completed, although it has involved necessarily a diminution in time available for family and other interests.

We have sought to state the law as at 31 July 1986, although we have endeavoured to give effect, when possible, to the subsequent legislative changes, including the new Rules and Regulations made under the Insolvency Act 1986. As these were made after the book went to press a separate commentary on these Rules and Regulations is included.

July 1986   J H Greene

I M Fletcher

Contents

Chapter 3 Powers, liabilities and agency of receiver

Chapter 8 Extent and ranking of securities, guarantees and related matters

Table of statutes

Table of cases

PARA

L

M

N

O

P

References

Throughout this book unless the context otherwise requires the references shall have the meanings ascribed as follows:

the 1972 Act   The Companies (Floating Charges and Receivers) (Scotland) Act 1972

the 1985 Act   Companies Act 1985

Note
The Insolvency Act 1986 came into force on 29 December 1986

Commentary—Rules and Regulations

0.01 Since the main text of this book went to press secondary legislation has been introduced in the form of statutory instruments prescribing Regulations and Rules under the relative enabling provisions of the Insolvency Act 1986,[1] and these Regulations and Rules (in the case of the latter in so far as they apply to receivership) are set out in Appendix 19. In addition new Rules of Court have still to be introduced dealing with the appointment of a receiver by the court and other ancillary procedure. It is perhaps unfortunate that receivers of Scottish companies will require to have regard to three different sets of rules and regulations but this has arisen from the historical framework of the Scottish legislation on receivers in that the statutory provisions in the Insolvency Act 1986 dealing with Scottish receivers arose from the separate Scottish legislation contained in the 1972 Act. Whereas in England the Insolvency Rules will be all embracing, by virtue of the definition of 'prescribed' in section 70 (1) of the Insolvency Act 1986 the matters dealt with in The Receivers (Scotland) Regulations 1986 are those which fell to be prescribed under the provisions relating to receivers in Chapter II or Part III of that Act and accordingly fell to be prescribed by Regulations under that chapter and not by Rules under section 411 of that Act.

1 The Receivers (Scotland) Regulations 1986, SI 1986/1917 (S 141) and The Insolvency (Scotland) Rules 1986, SI 1986/1915 (S 139).

The Receivers (Scotland) Regulations 1986

0.02 As already mentioned these Regulations, which came into operation on 29 December 1986, deal with matters which fall to be prescribed by Regulations under Chapter II of Part III of the Insolvency Act 1986. These matters are as follows.

Forms

0.03 The Regulations contain in a schedule[1] certain forms which, with such variations as circumstances require, are the forms prescribed for the purposes of the provisions of the Act referred to in the forms. These forms are as follows:

Number of form	Nature of form	Section of Insolvency Act 1986 prescribed under
Form 1 (Scot)	Notice of appointment of a Receiver by the Holder of a Floating Charge	53(1)
Form 2 (Scot)	Notice of appointment of a Receiver by the Court	54(3)
Form 3 (Scot)	Notice of the Receiver ceasing to act or of his removal	62(5)
Form 4 (Scot)	Notice of appointment of Receiver	65(1)(a)
Form 5 (Scot)	Statement of Affairs	66(1)

1 Regulation 3 and the Schedule to The Receivers (Scotland) Regulations 1986, SI 1986/1917 (S 141).

Instrument of appointment

0.04   As well as delivering to the Registrar of Companies a notice in the prescribed form the person making such appointment or someone on his behalf also requires to deliver to the Registrar of Companies within seven days of the execution of the instrument of appointment a copy of such instrument of appointment certified in the prescribed manner. The Regulations provide[1] that the certified copy of such instrument of appointment shall be certified to be a correct copy by or on behalf of the person making the appointment.

1 Regulation 4 of The Receivers (Scotland) Regulations 1986, SI 1986/1917 (S 141).

Joint receivers

0.05   The Regulations prescribe[1] that where two or more persons are appointed joint receivers by the holder of a floating charge under section 53 of the Insolvency Act 1986, subsection (6) of that section shall apply subject to the following modifications:

(a) the appointment of any of the joint receivers shall be of no effect unless the appointment is accepted by all of them before the end of the respective business day next following that on which the instrument of appointment is received by or on behalf of each such joint receiver in accordance with Rule 3.1 of The Insolvency Scotland (Rules) 1986; and

(b) their appointment as joint receivers shall be deemed to be made on the day on and at the time at which the instrument of appointment is received by the last of them, as evidenced by the written docquet by or on behalf of such receiver required by paragraph (b) of sub-section (6) of section 53 of the Insolvency Act 1986.

Section 53 of the Insolvency Act 1986 provides that the appointment of a person as a receiver shall be of no effect unless it is accepted by that person before the end of the business day next following that on which the instrument of appointment is received by him or on his behalf and, subject to such acceptance, shall be deemed to be made on the day on and at the time at which the instrument of appointment is so received, as evidenced by a written docquet by that person or on his behalf. While the receiver's acceptance of his appointment need not be in writing, it requires to be intimated to the holder of the floating charge or his agent before the end of the business day following that on which the instrument of appointment was received and a docquet to the effect that it has been so intimated requires to be endorsed on the instrument of appointment as also does a docquet evidencing receipt of the instrument of appointment.

1 Regulation 5 of The Receivers (Scotland) Regulations 1986, SI 1986/1917 (S 141).

Resignation of receiver

0.06 A receiver may resign office by giving notice to that effect in the prescribed manner to such persons as are prescribed.[1] The Regulations provide[2] that a receiver, who wishes to resign his office, shall give at least seven days' notice of his resignation to
(a) the holder of the floating charge by virtue of which he was appointed;
(b) the holder of any other floating charge and any receiver appointed by him;
(c) the members of any committee of creditors established under section 68 of the Insolvency Act 1986; and
(d) the company, or if it is then in liquidation, its liquidator.
The notice requires to specify the date on which the resignation takes effect.

1 Insolvency Act 1986, s 62(1).
2 Regulation 6 of The Receivers (Scotland) Regulations 1986, SI 1986/1917 (S 141).

Report of creditors

0.07 Within three months from his appointment (or such longer period allowed by the court), a receiver must[1] either:
(a) send to all unsecured creditors insofar as he knows their addresses a copy of the report which he now requires to make up; or
(b) publish a notice stating the address to which unsecured creditors should write for copies of the report to be sent to them free of charge.
Where a receiver determines to publish such a notice, the Regulations[2] provide that the notice shall be published in a newspaper circulating in the area where the company has its principal place of business or in such other newspaper as the receiver thinks most appropriate for ensuring that it comes to the notice of the unsecured creditors of the company.

1 Insolvency Act 1986, s 67 (2).
2 Regulation 7 of The Receivers (Scotland) Regulations 1986, SI 1986/1917 (S 141).

The Insolvency (Scotland) Rules 1986

0.08 These Rules, which also came into operation on 29 December 1986, are made under section 411 of the Insolvency Act 1986 and contain all the necessary Rules which require to be prescribed under that Act.

Part 3 of these Rules deals with receivers and contains five chapters which will be dealt with under their headings.

Appointment[1]

0.09   This chapter deals with the appointment of a receiver and in particular the acceptance of his appointment. It provides that:

(1) Where a person has been appointed a receiver by the holder of a floating charge, his acceptance (which need not be in writing) of that appointment shall be intimated by him to the holder of the floating charge or his agent within seven days of the execution of the instrument of appointment and he shall, as soon as possible after his acceptance, endorse a written docquet to that effect on the instrument of appointment.[2]

(2) The written docquet evidencing receipt of the instrument of appointment shall also be endorsed on the instrument of appointment.[3]

(3) The receiver shall, as soon as possible after his acceptance of the appointment, deliver a copy of the endorsed instrument of appointment to the holder of the floating charge or his agent.[4]

This Rule dealing with the acceptance of the appointment applies also in the case of the appointment of joint receivers except that, where the docquet of acceptance is endorsed by each of the joint receivers, or two or more of them, on the same instrument of appointment, it is the joint receiver who last endorses his docquet of acceptance who is required to send a copy of the instrument of appointment to the holder of the floating charge or his agent.[5]

1 Chapter 1 of The Insolvency (Scotland) Rules 1986, SI 1986/1915 (s 139).
2 Ibid r 3.1(1).
3 Ibid r 3.1(2).
4 Ibid r 3.1(3).
5 Ibid r 3.1(4).

Statement of affairs[1]

0.10   Where a receiver decides to require from any person or persons a statement as to the affairs of the company to be made out and submitted to him in accordance with section 66 of the Insolvency Act 1986 he requires[2] to send to each of those persons (a deponent) a notice in the form[3] set out in Schedule 5 requiring the deponent to make out and submit such a statement of affairs in the prescribed form.[4]

The receiver requires to insert any statement of affairs submitted to him in the sederunt book[5] which each insolvency practitioner requires to maintain during his term of office for the purpose of providing an accurate record of the administration of each insolvency proceedings.[6] As regards the expenses of such statement of affairs, a deponent who makes up and submits such statement of affairs is to be allowed and to be paid by the receiver as an expense of the receivership, any expenses incurred by the deponent in so doing which the receiver considers to be reasonable.[7] Any decision by the receiver under this Rule is subject to appeal to the court.[8]

The Rule expressly provides that nothing in it relieves a deponent from any obligation to make up and submit a statement of affairs or to provide information to the receiver.[9]

1 Chapter 2 of The Insolvency (Scotland) Rules 1986, SI 1986/1915 (S 139).
2 Ibid r 3.2(1).
3 Schedule 5, Form 3.1 (Scot).
4 Schedule to The Receivers (Scotland) Regulations 1986, SI 1986/1917 (S 141).
5 Rule 3.2(3) of The Insolvency (Scotland) Rules 1986, SI 1986/1915 (S 139).
6 Ibid r 7.33(1).
7 Ibid r 3.3(1).
8 Ibid r 3.3(2).
9 Ibid r 3.3(3).

The creditors' committee[1]

0.11   The Insolvency Act 1986 contains provisions entitling unsecured creditors in a receivership to establish a committee of creditors. The Rules contain provisions governing the constitution and functions of such a committee and other ancillary matters.

Where it is resolved by the creditors' meeting to establish a creditors' committee, the committee will consist of at least three and not more than five creditors of the company elected at the meeting, any creditor of the company who has lodged a claim being eligible to be a member so long as his claim has not been rejected for the purpose of his entitlement to vote.[2] A body corporate or a partnership may be a member of the committee, but it cannot act as such otherwise than by a representative appointed and authorised under section 375 of the Companies Act 1985 to represent the corporation at a meeting of creditors or contributories.[3] A person so authorised must produce to the chairman of the meeting a copy of the resolution from which he derives his authority and such a copy resolution must be executed in accordance with the provisions of section 36 (3) of the Companies Act 1985 or certified by the secretary or a director of the corporation to be a true copy.[4] Presumably in the case of a partnership a resolution by a majority of the partners will be sufficient authorisation with the copy certified by a partner.

1 Chapter 3 of The Insolvency (Scotland) Rules 1986, SI 1986/1915 (S 139).
2 Ibid r 3.4(1) and (2).
3 Ibid r 3.4(3).
4 Ibid r 3.4(3) and rr 7.20(1) and (2) as applied by r 3.6.

0.12   As regards the functions of the committee it is provided[1] that in addition to the functions conferred on it by the Insolvency Act 1986, the creditors' committee will represent to the receiver the views of the unsecured creditors and shall act in relation to him in such manner as may be agreed from time to time.

1 Rule 3.5 of The Insolvency (Scotland) Rules 1986, SI 1986/1915 (S 139).

0.13   The Rules apply,[1] subject to certain exclusions and modifications, Chapter 7 of Part 4 of the Rules (which deal with the liquidation committee) to the creditors' committee in a receivership and to its members, substituting references to the receiver or to the creditors' committee for references to the liquidator or the liquidation committee and a reference to a creditor for a reference to the creditor member, any references to a contributory member being disregarded. The Rules contained in Chapter 7 of Part 4 which are applied to a creditors' committee in a receivership with the substitution of the necessary references are set out in Appendix 19.

1 Rule 3.6 of The Insolvency (Scotland) Rules 1986, SI 1986/1915 (s 139).

Information from receiver

0.14   Where a committee of creditors is established in a receivership, it may on giving not less than seven days' notice require the receiver's attendance before it at any reasonable time to furnish it with such information as it may reasonably require relating to the carrying out by him of his functions.[1] Where the committee so requires the receiver's attendance, the Rules provide[2] that the notice to him shall be in writing signed by the majority of the members of the committee for the time being or their representatives. The meeting at which the receiver's attendance is required must be fixed by the committee for a business day and shall be held at such time and place as the receiver determines.[3] Where the receiver attends such a meeting, the members of the committee may elect any one of their number to be chairman of the meeting in place of the receiver or any nominee of his.[4]

1 Insolvency Act 1986, s 68(2).
2 Rule 3.7(1) of The Insolvency (Scotland) Rules 1986, SI 1986/1915 (S 139).
3 Ibid r 3.7(2).
4 Ibid r 3.7(3).

0.15   As regards dealings with the company by a member of the committee, membership of the committee does not prevent a person from dealing with the company while the receiver is acting, provided that any transactions in the course of such dealings are entered into on normal commercial terms.[1] The court, however, may, on application of any person interested, set aside a transaction which appears to it to be contrary to the requirements of this Rule and in these circumstances the court may give such consequential directions as it thinks fit for compensating the company for any loss which it may have incurred in consequence of the transaction.[2]

1 Rule 3.8(1) of The Insolvency (Scotland) Rules 1986, SI 1986/1915 (S 139).
2 Ibid r 3.8(2).

Miscellaneous[1]
Abstract of receipts and payments

0.16   Chapter 4 of Part 3 of the Rules deals with various miscellaneous matters.
The Rules provide[2] that the receiver shall—
(a) within 2 months after the end of 12 months from the date of his appointment, and of every subsequent period of 12 months, and
(b) within 2 months after he ceases to act as receiver,

send the requisite account of his receipts and payments as receiver to—
(1) the Registrar of Companies,
(2) the holder of the floating charge by virtue of which he was appointed,
(3) the members of the creditors' committee (if any), and
(4) the company or, if it is in liquidation, the liquidator.
The 2 month period referred to in this Rule may on the receiver's application be extended by the court.[3]
The requisite accounts of the receiver's receipts and payments requires[4] to be in the form of an abstract showing—
(a) receipts and payments during the relevant period of 12 months, or
(b) where the receiver has ceased to act, receipts and payments during the period from the end of the last 12 month period to the time when he so ceased (alternatively, if there has been no previous abstract, receipts and payments in the period since his appointment as receiver).
This Rule as to an abstract of receipts and payments is without prejudice to the receiver's duty to render proper accounts required otherwise than in terms of the Rule and if the receiver makes default in complying with the Rule, he is liable to a fine and, for continued contravention, to a daily default fine.[5]

1 Chapter 4 of The Insolvency (Scotland) Rules 1986/1915 (S 139).
2 Ibid r 3.9(1) and Schedule 5, Form 3.2 (Scot).
3 Ibid r 3.9(2).
4 Ibid r 3.9(3).
5 Ibid rr 3.9(4), (5) and Schedule 4.

Notification on death of receiver

0.17 Where a receiver dies, the holder of the floating charge by virtue of which he was appointed requires,[1] forthwith on his becoming aware of the death, to give notice of such death to—
(a) the Registrar of Companies,
(b) the members of the creditors' committee (if any),
(c) the company or, if in liquidation, the liquidator, and
(d) the holder of any other floating charge and any receiver appointed by such holder.

1 Rule 3.10 and Schedule 5 (Form 3.3 (Scot)) of The Insolvency (Scotland) Rules 1986, SI 1986/1915 (S 139).

Notification on vacation of office of receiver other than by death

0.18 On vacating office on completion of the receivership or in consequence of the receiver ceasing to be qualified as an insolvency practitioner, the receiver requires[1], in addition to giving notice of so doing to the Registrar of Companies under section 62(5) of the Insolvency Act 1986 to give notice of so doing within 14 days thereof to the holder of the floating charge by virtue of which he was appointed and to the other parties specified in paragraphs (b) to (d) of Rule 3.10

1 Rule 3.11 of The Insolvency (Scotland) Rules 1986, SI 1986/1915 (S 139).

VAT bad debt relief[1]

0.19   Section 22(3) of the Value Added Tax Act 1983 was amended by section 32 of the Finance Act 1985 so as to include the receivership of the company within the circumstances in which a company becomes insolvent for the purposes of that section where a person who has been appointed in Great Britain to act as its administrative receiver issues a certificate of his opinion that, if it went into liquidation, the assets of the company would be insufficient to cover the payment of any dividend in respect of debts which are neither secured nor preferential. Rules were first introduced for the issue by an administrative receiver of a certificate of insolvency by a previous statutory instrument[2] and are now embodied in the new Rules. The Rules provide[3] that it is the duty of the administrative receiver to issue a certificate in terms of section 22(3)(b) of the Value Added Tax Act 1983 (as amended) forthwith upon his forming such opinion. The certificate so issued requires[4] to specify:

(a)   the name of the company and its registered number;

(b)   the name of the administrative receiver and the date of his appointment; and

(c)   the date on which the certificate is issued.

Such a certificate requires[5] to be entitled 'CERTIFICATE OF INSOLVENCY FOR THE PURPOSES OF SECTION 22(3)(b) OF THE VALUE ADDED TAX ACT 1983'.

Notice of the issue of the certificate requires[6] to be given by the administrative receiver within 3 months of his appointment or within 2 months of issuing the certificate, whichever is the later, to all of the company's unsecured creditors of whose address the receiver is then aware and who have, to his knowledge, made supplies to the company, with a charge to value added tax, at any time before his appointment. Thereafter the receiver must given notice[7] to any such creditor of whose address and supplies to the company he becomes aware but the receiver is not under any obligation[8] to provide a creditor with a copy of the certificate. The certificate must be retained[9] with the company's accounting records and the provisions of section 222 of the Companies Act 1985 (which relate to the place where and period for which company records are to be kept) apply to the certificate as it applies to these records. On vacating office the administrative receiver has a duty[10] to bring this Rule to the attention of the directors or (as the case may be) any successor of his as receiver.

1 Chapter 5 of The Insolvency (Scotland) Rules 1986, SI 1986/1915 (S 139).
2 The Administrative Receivers (Value Added Tax Certificates) (Scotland) Rules 1986, SI 1986/304 (S 23).
3 Rule 3.12(1) of The Insolvency (Scotland) Rules 1986, SI 1986/1915 (S 139).
4 Ibid r 3.12(2).
5 Ibid r 3.12(3).
6 Ibid r 3.13(1).
7 Ibid r 3.13(2).
8 Ibid r 3.13(3).
9 Ibid r 3.14(1).
10 Ibid r 3.14(2).

Provisions of general application

0.20 Part 7 of the Rules contain provisions of general application in insolvency proceedings. Chapter 1 deals with meetings and its provisions apply to any meetings held in insolvency proceedings other than *inter alia* meetings of a creditors' committee in receivership[1] and so apply subject to any contrary provision in the Insolvency Act 1986 or in the Rules, or to any direction of the court.[2] Amongst the specific matters dealt with in relation to meetings are

(a) Summoning of meetings[3]
(b) Notice of meeting[4]
(c) Chairman of meetings[5]
(d) Quorum[6]
(e) Adjournment[7]
(f) Entitlement to vote (creditors)[8]
(g) Chairman of meeting as proxy holder[9]
(h) Resolutions[10]
(i) Report of meeting[11]

1 Rule 7.1(1) of The Insolvency (Scotland) Rules 1986, SI 1986/1915 (S 139).
2 Ibid r 7.1(2).
3 Ibid r 7.2.
4 Ibid r 7.3.
5 Ibid r 7.5.
6 Ibid r 7.7.
7 Ibid r 7.8.
8 Ibid r 7.9.
9 Ibid r 7.11.
10 Ibid r 7.12.
11 Ibid r 7.13.

0.21 Chapter 2 deals generally with proxies and company representation at meetings of creditors or contributories of the company in insolvency proceedings and in particular—

(a) Definition of 'proxy'[1]
(b) Form of proxy[2]
(c) Use of proxy at meeting[3]
(d) Retention of proxies[4]
(e) Right of inspection[5]
(f) Proxy holder with financial interest[6]
(g) Representation of corporations[7]

1 Rule 7.14 of The Insolvency (Scotland) Rules 1986, SI 1986/1915 (S 139).
2 Ibid r 7.15.
3 Ibid r 7.16.
4 Ibid r 7.17.
5 Ibid r 7.18.
6 Ibid r 7.19.
7 Ibid r 7.20.

0.22 Finally Chapter 3 contains miscellaneous provisions including those dealing with:

(a) Giving of notices, etc[1]
(b) Sending by post[2]
(c) Certificate of giving notice, etc[3]

(d) Validity of proceedings[4]
(e) Evidence of proceedings sat meetings[5]
(f) Confidentiality of documents[6]
(g) Insolvency practitioners' caution[7]
(h) Punishment of offences[8]
(i) Fees, expenses etc[9]
(j) Power of court to cure defects in procedure[10]
(k) Sederunt book[11]

1 Rule 7.21 of The Insolvency (Scotland) Rules 1986, SI 1986/1915 (S 139).
2 Ibid r 7.22.
3 Ibid r 7.23.
4 Ibid r 7.24.
5 Ibid r 7.25.
6 Ibid r 7.27.
7 Ibid r 7.28.
8 Ibid r 7.29.
9 Ibid r 7.31.
10 Ibid r 7.32.
11 Ibid r 7.33.

Forms

0.23   The Rules contain in Schedule 5 certain forms prescribed for use in receivership pursuant to the relative provisions of the Insolvency Act 1986 and the Rules. These forms are as follows:

Number of form	Nature of form	Section of the Insolvency Act 1986 and/or Rules prescribed under
Form 3.1 (Scot)	Notice Requiring Submission of Receivership Statement of Affairs	Section 66(1) and (4) and Rule 3.2(1)
Form 3.2 (Scot)	Receiver's Abstract of Receipts and Payments	Rule 3.9(1) and (3)
Form 3.3 (Scot)	Notice of Receiver's Death	Rule 3.10
Form 3.4 (Scot)	Notice of Authorisation to Dispose of Secured Property	Section 61(6)
Form 3.5 (Scot)	Notice of Receiver's Report	Section 67(1)
Form 4.20 (Scot)	Certificate of Constitution of Creditors' Committee	Rule 4.42 as applied by Rule 3.6
Form 4.22 (Scot)	Notice of Constitution of Creditors' Committe	Rule 4.42 as applied by Rule 3.6

Chapter 1

Appointment of receiver

General introduction

1.01 The Companies (Floating Charges and Receivers) (Scotland) Act 1972 (hereinafter referred to as the 1972 Act) introduced for the first time in Scotland the office of receiver thus enabling the holder of a floating charge (which form of security is available only to incorporated companies and was itself first introduced into the law of Scotland in 1961) to appoint or seek the appointment by the court of a receiver over the property subject to the charge. Between 1961 and 1972 the only remedy available to the holder of a floating charge wishing to realise his security was to have the company placed in liquidation. Whether the whole or only part of the company's property was subject to the floating charge, the person so appointed after 1972 was known simply as a receiver. However, the Insolvency Act 1985 introduced a distinction in such an appointment depending on the extent of the company's property covered by the floating charge. Where a receiver is now appointed by the holder of a floating charge in a case where the whole (or substantially the whole) of the company's property is attached by the floating charge then he is known as an administrative receiver.[1] In any other case he will be known simply as a receiver. This distinction is of importance in relation to administration orders, also introduced for the first time by the Insolvency Act 1985, some new general insolvency provisions contained in Chapter VII of Part II of that Act and to the necessity to report to the Secretary of State on the conduct of directors of insolvent companies but otherwise within the general context of receivership law is not of importance. Accordingly, all references in this book to a receiver or receivers include an administrative receiver or receivers and only where the latter are specifically referred to does it include such administrative receiver or receivers alone. A receiver is appointed when the holder of a floating charge is entitled and wishes to recover the debt secured by the floating charge by realising the property charged under it. Whom can the holder of the floating charge appoint as receiver?

1 Insolvency Act 1986, s 251.

1.02 Until the passing of the Insolvency Act 1985, although there was previously no statutory requirement to do so, the person normally appointed in Scotland to be a receiver of a company was a chartered accountant experienced in insolvency matters. It should be emphasised that the appointment was and still is a personal one. A person who is not an individual is not qualified to act as an insolvency practitioner[1] and a person acts as an insolvency practitioner in relation to a company if he acts as its administrative receiver.[2]

1 Insolvency Act 1986, s 390(1).
2 Ibid s 388(1)(a).

1.03 The Cork Report[1] stated at paragraph 735 that:
'One subject of much criticism is the absence of any requirement that insolvency practitioners should possess some minimum professional qualification. We have received a number of suggestions for remedying this deficiency, in an endeavour to ensure that insolvent estates are administered only by competent practitioners. It is significant that many of these proposals have been put forward by insolvency practitioners themselves.'
The Report[1] recommended at paragraph 756 that:
'... some minimum professional qualification and control is necessary. It is essential that measures are introduced to ensure a high standard of competence as well as integrity in the persons who are eligible for appointment as insolvency practitioners.'

1 Report of the Review Committee on Insolvency Law and Practice (Cmnd 8558).

Qualifications and disabilities for appointment as receiver

1.04 The Insolvency Act 1986[1] now provides that a person who is not an individual is not qualified to act as an insolvency practitioner nor is a person qualified to act as an insolvency practitioner at any time unless, at that time, he is authorised to act as an insolvency practitioner by virtue of being so authorised by a recognised professional body or holds an authorisation granted under section 393.[2] Any person who acts as an insolvency practitioner in relation to a company at a time when he is not qualified to do so is liable:[3]
(a) on summary conviction, to imprisonment for a term not exceeding six months or to a fine not exceeding the statutory maximum or to both;
(b) on conviction on indictment, to imprisonment for a term not exceeding two years or to a fine or to both.

1 Section 390(1),(2).
2 Insolvency Act 1986.
3 Ibid ss 398, 430 and Sch 10.

1.05 Section 390(3)[1] provides that a person is not qualified to act as an insolvency practitioner in relation to another person at any time unless:[2]
(a) there is in force at that time security or, in Scotland, caution for the proper performance of his functions; and

(b) that security or caution meets the prescribed requirements with respect to his acting in relation to that other person.

1 Insolvency Act 1986.
2 The Insolvency (Scotland) Rules 1986, SI 1986/1915 (S 139).

1.06 In terms of section 390(4),[1] a person is not qualified to act as an insolvency practitioner at any time if, at that time:
(a) he has been adjudged bankrupt or sequestration of his estate has been awarded and (in either case) he has not been discharged;
(b) he is subject to a disqualification order made under the Company Directors Disqualification Act 1986; or
(c) he is a patient within the meaning of Part VII of the Mental Health Act 1983 or section 125(1) of the Mental Health (Scotland) Act 1984.

1 Insolvency Act 1986.

1.07 Under the professional rules of The Institute of Chartered Accountants of Scotland,[1] it is improper for a practice, or a partner in or an employee of a practice having, or during the previous two years having had a continuing professional relationship with a company to accept appointment as receiver of a Scottish company or as receiver and manager of a company registered in England. In practice, this means that if a firm of chartered accountants acts as auditors of a company, none of the partners or employees of that firm are eligible to accept appointment as the receiver of the company.

1 Ethical Guide for Members of The Institute of Chartered Accountants of Scotland 1984 Edition paras (28) and (29).

Authorisation of members of recognised professional bodies

1.08 Section 390(2)[1] states that a member of a recognised professional body is authorised to act as an insolvency practitioner if he is permitted so to act by or under the rules of that body. The Secretary of State may by order declare a body which appears to him to fall within section 391(2)[1] to be a recognised professional body for the purposes of section 391 and any such order may be revoked by a further order if it appears to the Secretary of State that the body no longer falls within section 391(2).[2]

1 See Insolvency Act 1986, s 391(1).
2 See ibid s 391(4).

1.09 A body may be recognised under section 391(1)[1] if it regulates the practice of a profession and maintains and enforces rules for securing that such of its members as are permitted by or under the rules to act as insolvency practitioners:
(a) are fit and proper persons so to act;

3

(b) meet acceptable requirements as to education and practical training and experience.

1 See Insolvency Act 1986, s 391(2).

1.10 An order under section 391[1] has effect from such date as is specified in the order and any such order revoking a previous order may make provision whereby members of the body in question continue to be treated as authorised to act as insolvency practitioners for a specified period after the revocation takes effect. Reference to members of a recognised professional body are references to persons who, whether members of that body or not, are subject to its rules in the practice of the profession in question.[2]

1 Insolvency Act 1986.
2 Ibid s 391(3).

Application for authorisation

1.11 An application for authorisation under section 392[1] should contain or be accompanied by such information as the competent authority may reasonably require for the purposes of determining the application and should be accompanied by the prescribed fee. The competent authority is defined by section 392(2)[1] as (a) in relation to a case of any description specified in directions given by the Secretary of State, the body or person so specified in relation to cases of that description and (b) in relation to a case not falling within paragraph (a), the Secretary of State. There are provisions in section 392(4),(6),(7)[1] requiring the applicant to furnish additional information, making clear that directions and requirements given or imposed may differ as between different applications, requiring any information to be furnished to the competent authority, if it so requires, to be in such form or verified in such manner as it may specify and stating that an application for authorisation may be withdrawn before it is granted or refused. Any sums received by a competent authority under section 392(8)[1] other than the Secretary of State may be retained by that authority and any sums received under the same section by the Secretary of State must be paid into the Consolidated Fund.

1 Insolvency Act 1986.

Grant, refusal and withdrawal of authorisation

1.12 In terms of section 393(1)[1] the authority may, on an application duly made in accordance with section 392[1] and after being furnished with all such information as it may require under that section, grant or refuse the application. An authorisation, in terms of section 393(3),[1] unless previously withdrawn, continues in force for such period not exceeding the prescribed maximum as may be specified in the authorisation. The competent authority is empowered to grant the application in terms of section 393(2)[1] if it appears to it from the information furnished by the applicant and having regard to such other information, if any, as it may have:

(a) that the applicant is a fit and proper person to act as an insolvency practitioner; and

(b) that the applicant meets the prescribed requirements with respect to education and practical training and experience.

1 Insolvency Act 1986.

1.13 The competent authority is empowered in terms of section 393(4)[1] to withdraw an authorisation issued pursuant to section 393(1)[1] if the holder of the authorisation is no longer a fit and proper person to act as an insolvency practitioner or without prejudice thereto, the holder of the authorisation has failed to comply with any provision of Part XIII of the Insolvency Act 1986 or of any regulations made under that Part or Part XV or, in purported compliance with any such provision, has furnished the competent authority with false, inaccurate or misleading information. Where the competent authority grants an authorisation it must give notice of that fact specifying the date on which the authorisation takes effect. When the competent authority proposes to refuse an application or to withdraw an authorisation under section 393(4),[1] it must give the applicant or holder of the authorisation written notice of its intention to do so, setting out particulars of the grounds on which it proposes to act.[2] In the case of a proposed withdrawal the notice must state the date on which it is proposed that the withdrawal should take effect[3] and where an application is to be refused or an authorisation to be withdrawn, any such notice must give particulars of the rights exercisable under sections 395 and 396[4] by a person on whom the notice is served.

1 Insolvency Act 1986.
2 Ibid s 394(2).
3 Ibid s 394(3).
4 Ibid s 394(4).

1.14 A person on whom a notice is served under section 394(2)[1] may within fourteen days after the date of service make written representations to the competent authority who must have regard to any representations made in determining whether to refuse the application or withdraw the authorisation, as the case may be.[2]

1 Insolvency Act 1986.
2 Ibid s 395.

Reference to tribunal

1.15 Section 396(2)[1] provides that a person on whom a notice is served under section 394(2)[1] may within twenty-eight days after the date of service give written notice to the competent authority requiring the case to be referred to the Insolvency Practitioners Tribunal in relation to which the provisions of Schedule 7[1] apply. Where a requirement is made in accordance with section 396(2)[1] then, unless the relevant authority within the twenty-eight day period mentioned in section 396(2)[1] decides to grant the application or, as the case may be, decides not to withdraw the authorisation and gives written notice of that fact within seven days to the person by whom the requirement was made, it shall refer the case to the tribunal.[2]

1 Insolvency Act 1986.
2 Ibid s 396(3).

1.16   On a reference pursuant to section 396,[1] the tribunal must investigate the case and make a report to the competent authority stating what would in their opinion be the appropriate decision in the matter and the reasons for that opinion and it is the duty of the competent authority to decide the matter accordingly. The tribunal must send a copy of the report to the applicant or, as the case may be, the holder of the authorisation and the competent authority must serve him with a written notice of the decision made by it in accordance with the report.[2] The competent authority may, if it thinks fit, publish the report of the tribunal.[3]

1 Insolvency Act 1986.
2 Ibid s 397(2).
3 Ibid s 397(3).

1.17   Section 396(1)[1] provides for the continuation of the tribunal established by the Insolvency Act 1985 for the purposes of section 396(2)[1] and the provisions of Schedule 7[1] apply to the operation of such a tribunal. Schedule 7[2] provides for the Secretary of State to draw up and from time to time to revise, firstly, a panel of persons who are barristers, advocates or solicitors in each case of not less than seven years' standing and are nominated for the purpose by the Lord Chancellor or by the Lord President of the Court of Session and, secondly, a panel of persons who are experienced in insolvency matters. The members of the tribunal are to be selected from these panels in accordance with the provisions of Schedule 7.[2] The Secretary of State is entitled out of money provided by Parliament to pay to members of the tribunal such remuneration as may be approved by the Treasury and such expenses as may be approved by the Secretary of State and the Treasury.[3] The tribunal may sit either as a single tribunal or in two or more divisions[4] and their functions require to be exercised in relation to any case referred to them by three members consisting of a legal chairman and two other members experienced in insolvency matters.[5] Any investigation by the tribunal requires to be so conducted as to afford a reasonable opportunity for representations to be made to the tribunal by or on behalf of the person whose case is the subject of the investigation.[6] For the purposes of any such investigation, the tribunal may require any person to attend by notice in writing, to give evidence or produce any books, papers and other records in his possession or under his control which the tribunal considers it necessary to examine for the purpose of its investigation and may take evidence on oath and for that purpose administer oaths. No person is required to go more than ten miles from his place of residence unless the necessary expenses of his attendance are paid or tendered to him.[7] Every person who fails to attend a tribunal without reasonable excuse or who suppresses or refuses to produce any document which the tribunal may require shall be liable to a fine on summary conviction.[8]

1 Insolvency Act 1986.
2 Ibid Sch 7, para 1(1).
3 Ibid para 2.
4 Ibid para 3(1).
5 Ibid para 3(2).
6 Ibid para 4(1).
7 Ibid para 4(2).
8 Ibid para 4(3).

Power of holder of floating charge to appoint receiver

1.18   In terms of section 51 of the Insolvency Act 1986, it is competent under the law of Scotland for the holder of a floating charge (including a floating charge subsisting as such at the commencement of the 1972 Act) over all or any part of the property (including uncalled capital) which may from time to time be comprised in the property and undertaking of an incorporated company (whether a company within the meaning of the 1985 Act or not) which the Court of Session has jurisdiction to wind up, to appoint a receiver of such part of the property of the company as is subject to the charge.

1.19   In most cases the appointment will be as receiver of a company limited by shares incorporated in Scotland under the Companies Acts but section 51 of the Insolvency Act 1986 does state that a receiver may be appointed over the property of any incorporated company which the Court of Session has jurisdiction to wind up. It is, therefore, possible[1] to appoint a receiver over the property of a company limited by guarantee or an unlimited company or an overseas company[2] or a registered friendly society which is subject to the 1986 Act.

1 Insolvency Act 1986, s 120.
2 Ibid s 225.

Power of court to appoint receiver

1.20   In terms of section 51(2) of the Insolvency Act 1986, it is competent under the law of Scotland for the court, on the application of the holder of a floating charge to appoint a receiver of such part of the property of the company as is subject to the charge. It is worth observing that in the years since the 1972 Act came into operation the majority of (if not all) receiverships have resulted from appointments by the holders of floating charges: the authors are unaware of any appointments made by the court. The reason is, of course, that it is much simpler, quicker and less expensive for the holder of a floating charge to appoint a receiver by instrument in writing rather than seeking an appointment by a petition to the court. It is possible that an appointment by the court would be authorised if there was doubt as to whether an appointment by the holder of a floating charge had been validly made or, perhaps, where the court is satisfied that the position of the holder of the charge is likely to be prejudiced if no such appointment is made,[1] or where the holder of the floating charge is unable to make a quick appointment under the terms of the floating charge.

1 Insolvency Act 1986, s 52(2)(a).

1.21   It should be noted that the holder of a floating charge in terms of section 51(1) of the Insolvency Act 1986 has power to appoint a receiver in the case of a floating charge created before the 1972 Act (by which receivers were first introduced into the law of Scotland) came into force and good practice in the years since then has normally involved the holder of a floating charge entering into an instrument of alteration (which incidentally does not require to be registered with the Registrar of Companies provided that it does not affect the ranking of securities or otherwise bring it within the ambit of section 466(3) and 466(4) of the Companies Act 1985 (hereinafter referred to as the 1985 Act)) with the charging company whereby it is agreed that in certain specified circumstances additional to those set out in the Insolvency Act 1986, the holder of the floating charge has power to appoint a receiver.

Form of wording

1.22   The normal form of wording in a typical floating charge giving power to appoint a receiver is as follows:

> 'At any time after any of the sums secured by the floating charge hereby created shall have become due and payable or after the chargee shall have been requested by us in writing so to do, the chargee shall have power by instrument in writing to appoint any person or persons, whether an officer or officers of the chargee or not, to be a receiver or receivers of our property and assets and may in like manner appoint any person or persons to be a receiver or receivers in place of any receiver removed by the court or otherwise who ceases to act'.

1.23   While every floating charge creditor will wish an unfettered right to appoint a receiver in appropriate circumstances, in the majority of cases the charging company requests the chargee to appoint a receiver either at its own instigation or at the suggestion of the chargee. While the chargee (typically a bank) may invite criticism on the grounds that it may wish to avoid the unpleasant task of terminating a relationship with a customer which may have subsisted for many years, there is no doubt that, prior to the enactment of the Insolvency Act 1985, a formal request from the charging company usually indicated a recognition by the charging company that the appointment of a receiver was the practical course to be adopted in the circumstances. Even if such recognition is not forthcoming, the chargee can always take action unilaterally by formally demanding repayment of all sums due to it.

1.24   Prior to the passing of the Insolvency Act 1985, it was considered prudent to specify within the floating charge certain additional powers available to a receiver as there was some doubt whether or not such additional powers could be implied within the statutory framework. An example of the form of wording used is as follows:

'Any receiver so appointed shall, in addition to the powers set out in the 1985 Act, have the following additional powers:

(a) power to make any arrangement or compromise which he may think expedient;

(b) power to call up all or any part of our uncalled capital; and

(c) power to acquire or incorporate another limited company ("the new company") to which may be transferred the whole or any part of the property hereby charged and to carry on or concur in carrying on our business or any part thereof in the name of the new company'.

The Insolvency Act 1985[1] clarified any previous doubts by providing specifically that the foregoing powers are statutorily available to a receiver.

1 Insolvency Act 1985, s 57; see now Insolvency Act 1986, s 55 and Sch 2.

Circumstances justifying appointment by the holder of charge

1.25   The circumstances justifying the appointment of a receiver are set out in section 52 of the Insolvency Act 1986 where it is provided that a receiver may be appointed by the holder of the floating charge under section 51(1) of that Act on the occurrence of any event which, by the provision of the instrument creating the charge, entitles the holder of the charge to make that appointment and, in so far as not otherwise provided for by the instrument, on the occurrence of any of the following events, namely:

(a) the expiry of a period of twenty-one days after the making of a demand for payment of the whole or any part of the principal sum secured by the charge, without payment having been made;

(b) the expiry of a period of two months during the whole of which interest due and payable under the charge has been in arrears;

(c) the making of an order or the passing of a resolution to wind up the company;

(d) the appointment of a receiver by virtue of any other floating charge created by the company.

Circumstances justifying appointment by the court

1.26 A receiver may, in terms of section 52(2) be appointed by the court under section 51(2) of the Insolvency Act 1986 on the occurrence of any event which, by the provisions of the instrument creating the floating charge, entitles the holder of the charge to make that appointment and, in so far as not otherwise provided for by the instrument, on the occurrence of any of the following events, namely:

(a) where the court, on the application of the holder of the charge, pronounces itself satisfied that the position of the holder of the charge is likely to be prejudiced if no such appointment is made;

(b) any of the events referred to in paragraphs (a) to (c) of section 52(1).

Mode of appointment by holder of charge

1.27 Section 53(1) of the Insolvency Act 1986 provides that the appointment of a receiver by the holder of the floating charge under section 51(1) of the Insolvency Act 1986 shall be by means of a validly executed instrument in writing ('the instrument of appointment'), a copy (certified in the prescribed manner to be a correct copy) whereof shall be delivered by or on behalf of the person making the appointment to the Registrar of Companies for registration within seven days of its execution and shall be accompanied by a notice in the prescribed form. If any person without reasonable excuse makes default in complying with the requirements of section 53(1) he is liable to a fine and, for continued contravention, to a daily default fine. It should be noted that failure to lodge the proper particulars with the Registrar of Companies does not affect the validity of the appointment but only renders the person who is responsible for lodging the particulars liable to a fine.

Execution of instrument of appointment

1.28 Under the provisions of section 53(3) of the Insolvency Act 1986 the instrument of appointment is validly executed:

(a) by a company if it is executed in accordance with the provisions of section 36 of the 1985 Act as if it were a contract; and

(b) by any other person, if it is executed in the manner required or permitted by the law of Scotland in the case of an attested deed.

1.29 It would appear that the use of the words 'as if it were a contract' in section 53(3)(a) might indicate that section 36(3) of the 1985 Act which relates to the execution of deeds according to the law of Scotland might not apply to instruments of appointment, but where the holder of the floating charge is a company, it is suggested that section 53(3)(a) would be satisfied if the instrument of appointment was sealed with the common seal of the company and subscribed on its behalf by two of its directors or by a director and the secretary. On the other hand, if the directors of the company wish to appoint a receiver over the assets of a charging company, there would seem to be no reason why such directors should not resolve to authorise any person to sign the instrument of appointment provided that such signature was witnessed in accordance with the law of Scotland. The difficulty about this approach is that it anticipates the provisions of section 53(4) of the Insolvency Act 1986 and accordingly, leaves a doubt as to what is really intended by section 53(3)(a). As already noted, the safer course is for the instrument of appointment to be executed under the seal of the company. If the holder of the floating charge is a person other than a company, the execution should always be in the manner required or permitted by the law of Scotland in the case of an attested deed.

1.30 In terms of section 53(4) of the Insolvency Act 1986, the instrument of appointment may be executed on behalf of the holder of the floating charge by virtue of which the receiver is to be appointed:

(a) by any person duly authorised in writing by the holder to execute the instrument; and

(b) in the case of an appointment of a receiver by the holders of a series of secured debentures, by any person authorised by resolution of the debenture holders to execute the instrument.

It should be clearly noted that the signature of two witnesses signing in the manner required or permitted by the law of Scotland is essential for the purposes of section 53(4).

Demand for payment

1.31 Without prejudice to the statutory provisions, the instrument creating a floating charge will often provide that at any time the holder of a floating charge may on demand require payment of all sums due and failure by the borrower to do so after the expiry of a period of twenty-four hours will entitle the holder of the floating charge to appoint a receiver. Such entitlement to so appoint a receiver is only appropriate where the holder of the floating charge is able to require payment of the debt on demand and would not be appropriate, for example, in the case of a fixed term loan or where the charging company is bound to implement some form of obligation either on its own account or on account of a third party. As to the effect of a demand for payment without specifying a time for payment where the debt is repayable on demand, it has been argued that if a creditor requires payment 'on demand', the debtor, in the absence of a definition of these words in the floating charge, is bound to repay the debt immediately. It is respectfully suggested that a court in construing the meaning of the words 'on demand' would, in all probability, allow the debtor a reasonable opportunity to repay the debt rather than insist on immediate repayment. In the context of a debtor and creditor relationship involving an 'on demand' facility, it is suggested that a period of twenty-four hours from the making of the demand for repayment affords the debtor a reasonable opportunity to repay the debt without serious prejudice to the creditor. Most floating charges in favour of banks state that a simple certificate signed by any one of certain senior officials of the holder of the floating charge (eg director, secretary, manager or other authorised signatory) shall determine the amount of indebtedness of a debtor company at any given time. In all cases, it is very important to ensure that, where a demand for payment is made by the holder of the floating charge, the person signing the certificate falls within the category of persons authorised to do so in terms of the floating charge.

1.32   In one case,[1] the bond and floating charge provided that the notice had to be 'in writing signed by a Managing Director, Deputy Managing Director, Regional General Manager, Secretary or Chief Accountant of the Bank'. The notice sent to the company was signed by the bank's law secretary 'P General Manager JSW' and the company sought to reduce the instrument of appointment of the receiver on the ground that the notice was invalid, it not having been signed by one of the five named officials of the bank. The bank contended that the requirement that the notice be 'signed by' one of the named officials was habile to cover signature by another authorised person. Lord Allanbridge held that:
(1) the wording of the bond was clear and precise and required that the notice be signed by one of the five specified officials;
(2) the list was exhaustive and there was no room for any relaxation of the clear words in the bond by allowing someone else to sign either on behalf of the bank or on behalf of one of the five named officials;
(3) the notice, an essential step in the appointment of the receiver, was invalid; and
(4) consequently, the instrument of appointment was invalid as it proceeded upon an invalid notice.

1 *Elwick Bay Shipping Co Ltd v Royal Bank of Scotland Ltd* 1982 SLT 62.

Notification to Registrar and effective date of appointment

1.33   In terms of section 53(5) of the Insolvency Act 1986, on receipt of the certified copy of the instrument of appointment in accordance with section 53(1), the Registrar is required, on payment of the prescribed fee (currently none is payable) to enter the particulars of the appointment in the Register of Charges and, prior to the enactment of the Insolvency Act 1985, the receiver was regarded in terms of section 496(6) as having been appointed on the date of the execution of his appointment.

1.34   Section 56 of the Insolvency Act 1985 amended section 469 of the 1985 Act which was subsequently replaced, as amended by section 53 of the Insolvency Act 1986. Section 53(6) now provides that the appointment of a person as a receiver shall be of no effect unless it is accepted by that person before the end of the business day next following that on which the instrument of appointment is received by him or on his behalf and, subject to such acceptance, shall be deemed to be made on the day and at the time at which the instrument of appointment is so received, as evidenced by a written docket by that person or on his behalf. Section 53(6) also applies these provisions to the appointment of joint receivers subject to such modifications as may be prescribed[1] and section 251 of the Insolvency Act 1986 defines 'business dayey as meaning any day other than a Saturday, a Sunday, Christmas Day, Good Friday or a day which is a bank holiday in any part of Great Britain.'

1 The Receivers (Scotland) Regulations 1986, SI 1986/1917 (s 141).

1.35 While it is understood that difficulties over the timing of the appointment of a receiver have been experienced in England in the past no such difficulties have as far as the authors are aware, presented themselves in Scottish receivership practice. It remains to be seen whether the amendments introduced by section 56 of the Insolvency Act 1985 will simplify matters and clarify the only apparent uncertainty which related to the precise time at which the receiver's appointment took effect.

Attachment to property covered by floating charge

1.36 In terms of section 53(7) of the Insolvency Act 1986, on the appointment of the receiver under section 53 the floating charge by virtue of which the receiver was appointed attaches to the property then subject to the charge and such attachment has effect as if the charge were a fixed security over the property to which it has attached. A detailed discussion on attachment to the property on the appointment of a receiver is contained in Chapter 2 paragraphs 2.01 to 2.12.

Failure to register floating charge

1.37 Section 410(2) of the 1985 Act provides that certain charges, including floating charges, created by a company are, so far as any security is conferred, void against the liquidator or administrator or any creditor of the company unless registered within twenty-one days of their creation. The reference to an administrator was added by the Insolvency Act 1985.[1] While judicial review of decisions of the Registrar of Companies (eg in issuing a certificate of registration of a charge) is available if he acts beyond his powers, the courts will not hear evidence of whether statutory requirements of registration have been complied with.[2] A charge which has not been registered is not by this section made void against the company[3] but only against the liquidator or administrator or any creditor of the company and as long as the company is a going concern it is only void against and so postponed to claims of creditors who have a security on the property subject to the charge. As far as ordinary creditors are concerned their protection is that an unregistered charge is void against the liquidator or administrator and so in a liquidation or when an administration order has been made the holder of such a charge ranks as an ordinary unsecured creditor.

1 Schedule 6, para 9.
2 *R v Registrar of Companies, ex p Esal (Commodities) Ltd* [1985] 2 All ER 79.
3 *Independent Automatic Sales Ltd v Knowles & Foster* [1962] 3 All ER 27.

1.38   As an unregistered floating charge is valid as between the holder and the company, the appointment of a receiver is otherwise valid as between them but not against the liquidator or administrator or other creditors of the company although a receiver appointed under such a charge may act until a liquidator or administrator is appointed.[1] He would of course be required to account to a liquidator or administrator for any assets in his hands. While such a receiver in these circumstances might be granted an indemnity under section 63(2) of the Insolvency Act 1986, he would almost certainly be reluctant to accept appointment until either the charge is registered after the court had granted an extension of the time for registration or he was granted a satisfactory indemnity from the holder of the floating charge before accepting the appointment.

1 *Bursten Finance Ltd v Speirway Ltd* [1974] 1 WLR 1648.

Rectification of register

1.39   The court on being satisfied inter alia that the omission to register a charge within the prescribed period of time was accidental, or due to inadvertence or to some other sufficient cause, or is not of a nature to prejudice the position of creditors or shareholders of a company or that it is on other grounds just and equitable to grant relief, may, on the application of the company or any person interested, and on such terms and conditions as seem to the court just and expedient, order that the time for registration shall be extended.[1]

1 CA 1985, s 420.

1.40   The effect of such relief will be that the time for registering the charge in question will be extended to allow registration to take place. The Court of Session approved late registration in the unreported case of *Petition of Monklands District Council* (1980). In that case, the district council failed to register a fixed charge and sought relief under the provisions of section 106G of the Companies Act 1948[1] after the company which had granted the charge went into receivership. It was explained to the court that there would be some prejudice to ordinary creditors if late registration was permitted, but the prejudice for the secured creditor if late registration was not permitted was receiving a very small dividend rather than more or less the full repayment of all sums due by the company which had granted the charge. If late registration was not allowed, the addition of the money purportedly secured by the charge would only increase the dividend to ordinary creditors to a minimal extent bearing in mind the large deficiency to ordinary creditors.

1 Re-enacted as CA 1985, s 420.

1.41   A discussion on failure to register a charge within twenty-one days also took place in *Victoria Housing Estates Ltd v Ashpurton Estates Ltd*[1] where a housing association (Victoria) took a legal charge from a borrowing company (Ashpurton) which was a subsidiary of a group of companies. In November 1980 Victoria demanded payment of all indebtedness and when payment was not forthcoming a receiver was appointed on 6 January 1981. On 27 February 1981 Victoria discovered that the legal charge had never been registered with the Registrar of Companies but nonetheless decided to proceed with the realisations rather than apply to the court for an extension of time under section 101 of the Companies Act 1948.[2] Section 101[2] only applied where the court was satisfied that the omission to register a charge within the required period was accidental, or due to inadvertence, or to some other sufficient cause, or was not likely to prejudice the position of creditors or shareholders. On 15 May 1981 the board of Ashpurton decided to call an extraordinary general meeting to consider a resolution to wind up and on 12 June Ashpurton went into voluntary liquidation. Realising its position, Victoria issued proceedings on 4 June 1981 under section 101.[2] If it was successful in these proceedings Victoria would have recovered almost all of Ashpurton's indebtedness, but if it ranked as an ordinary creditor it would only have received about 16p in the pound. The court eventually confirmed a decision of the court registrar to the effect that an extension of time should not be granted both on the ground of lack of evidence of inadvertence by Victoria and on the ground of Ashpurton's impending liquidation. Lord Brightman in his judgment concluded as follows:

'... when an unregistered chargee discovers his mistake, he should apply without delay for an extension of time if he desires to register; and the court, when asked to exercise its discretion, should look askance at a chargee who deliberately defers his application in order to see which way the wind is going to blow.'

It has been held subsequently[3] that, notwithstanding the *Re Ashpurton* decision, the court may make an order pursuant to section 101 to extend the time for registration of a charge in exceptional circumstances even though liquidation proceedings have commenced.

1 [1982] 3 All ER 665.
2 Re-enacted as CA 1985, s 404.
3 *Re RM Arnold & Co Ltd* [1984] BCLC 535.

Avoidance of certain floating charges

1.42 Section 617 of the 1985 Act contained provisions under which on a winding-up certain floating charges could be invalidated in whole or in part. While this section has been repealed, and section 245 of the Insolvency Act 1986 now contains provisions on similar lines, but also applying on the making of an administration order, floating charges created before the coming into effect of the new provisions will not be set aside under them except to the extent that they could have been under the old provisions, assuming for this purpose that any relevant administration order had been a winding-up order.

1.43 Section 617 rendered invalid on liquidation a floating charge created by a company, when insolvent, within twelve months of the winding-up except to the extent of cash paid to the company at or subsequent to and in consideration for the charge.[1] To the extent that a floating charge is so invalidated so also would be the appointment of a receiver by virtue of such charge. Accordingly, the receiver's appointment would be completely invalid if the floating charge was so rendered on liquidation or the making of an administration order. As, however, in the case of an unregistered charge, such appointment would not be void *ab initio* and the receiver could act until liquidation or the making of an administrative order.[2]

1 For further discussion of the provisions of s 617 see Chap 8 paras 8.57 to 8.74.
2 *Bursten Finance Ltd v Speirway Ltd* [1974] 1 WLR 1648.

1.44 Section 104 of the Insolvency Act 1985 (repealed, and replaced by section 245 of the Insolvency Act 1986) introduced new provisions relating to the avoidance of certain floating charges. First of all, floating charges created within certain periods[1] are invalid, except to the extent provided, unless in the case of some such charges the company is and remains on the creation of the charge able to pay its debts. These periods are:
(1) in the case of a charge in favour of a person connected with the company, within two years of either –
　(a) the presentation of a petition for and on which an administration order is made; or
　(b) the date of a commencement of winding up.
For this purpose a connected person is a director or shadow director (ie a person in accordance with whose directions or instructions the directors are accustomed to act) of the company or an associate of either;
(2) in the case of a charge in favour of any other person, within twelve months of either of the events mentioned in (1) above except that in such a case the charge will not be invalid unless at the date of the creation of the charge the company either –
　(a) is unable to pay its debts within the meaning of section 123 of the Insolvency Act 1986; or
　(b) becomes unable to so pay its debts in consequence of the transaction under which the charge is created; and
(3) in the case of a charge in favour of a person whether connected or not, at a time between the presentation of a petition for and the making of an administration order in relation to the company.

1 Insolvency Act 1986, s 245(3).

1.45 Floating charges created within these periods are invalid (with the exception in the circumstances mentioned of charges in favour of unconnected persons) except to the extent of the aggregate of:
(a) the value of so much of the consideration for the creation of the charge as consists of money paid, or goods or services supplied, to the company at the same time as, or after, the creation of the charge;
(b) the value of so much of that consideration as consists of the discharge or reduction, at the same time as, or after, the creation of the charge, of any debt of the company; and
(c) the amount of such interest (if any) as is payable on the foregoing

amount in pursuance of any agreement under which the money was paid or the goods or services supplied.[1]

1 Insolvency Act 1986, s 245(2).

1.46 For these purposes, the value of any goods or services supplied by way of consideration for a floating charge is the amount in money which at the time of their supply could reasonably have been expected to be obtained for supplying them in the ordinary course of business and on the same terms (apart from the consideration) as those on which they were supplied to the company.

1.47 The principal changes introduced by the new provisions are to lengthen the period of potential challenge and to omit the solvency test in the case of floating charges in favour of connected persons, to validate charges otherwise challengeable where not only new money is paid but also where goods or services are supplied, to replace the solvency test by one related to ability to pay debts within the statutory meaning, to open such charges to challenge as gratuitous alienations or fraudulent preferences and to add other challengeable circumstances where an administration order has been made.

1.48 While a floating charge may be completely invalidated under the provisions of section 245 of the Insolvency Act 1986, the charge only is invalidated and not the validity or enforceability of the debt (except on the grounds of fraudulent preference),[1] the repayment of which prior to liquidation by a receiver cannot except on such grounds be attacked.[2]

1 *Re Parkes Garage (Swadlincote) Ltd* [1929] 1 Ch 139.
2 *Mace Builders (Glasgow) Ltd v Lunn* (1985) 129 Sol Jo 573: Court of Appeal upheld original decision – see (1986) Times, 11 October.

1.49 Section 617(3) of the 1985 Act contained provisions to the effect that where a company was being wound up in Scotland, a floating charge created by it was not to be challengeable as an alienation or preference voidable by statute (other than under that section) or at common law on the ground of insolvency or notour bankruptcy. This saving from challenge other than under the provisions of section 617 was not included in section 104 of the Insolvency Act 1985 (now replaced by section 245 of the Insolvency Act 1986) and so it appears that a floating charge may now be challenged not only under section 245 but also as a gratuitous alienation or unfair preference either under sections 242 and 243 of the Insolvency Act 1986 or at common law.

1.50 The consequences of these various statutory provisions relating to the validity of certain floating charges are that any receiver appointed under a charge created within the periods specified, or referred to by reference in sections 242, 243 or 245 of the Insolvency Act 1986, should only act before the expiry of the relative period or periods if satisfied after full enquiry that the charge is valid in whole or in part, or, alternatively, after obtaining a satisfactory indemnity from the holder of the charge. In the case of a floating charge not open to challenge under these statutory provisions, a receiver will also require to satisfy himself that such charge is not open to challenge at common law as a fraudulent preference.

1.51   Prior to the consolidation of the Companies Acts by the 1985 Act, the attachment of a floating charge either on a winding-up or on the appointment of a receiver by the holder of such a charge was specifically made subject to the statutory provisions governing invalidity of a charge as a result of non-registration or creation within twelve months of winding up.[1] The attachment of a floating charge on the appointment of a receiver by the court was not subject to the same provisions.[2] On consolidation, however, the attachment of a floating charge in none of these circumstances was made subject to the equivalent provisions in the 1985 Act.[3] Notwithstanding this fact, the validity or otherwise of a floating charge must remain subject to the provisions of section 410 of the 1985 Act and section 104 of the Insolvency Act 1985[4] (and also sections 615A and B of the 1985 Act) with the effects in so far as the appointment of a receiver is concerned as already described.

1   Companies (Floating Charges and Receivers) (Scotland) Act 1972, ss 1(2) and 13(7).
2   Ibid s 14(7).
3   CA 1985, ss 463(1), 469(7) and 470(6).
4   Now replaced by the Insolvency Act 1986, s 245.

Checking the validity of the appointment

1.52   In checking the validity of a receiver's appointment by the holder of a floating charge, as well as considering the validity or otherwise of the charge in light of the matters discussed in paragraphs 1.37 to 1.51 inclusive, the following documents should be examined:
(a) the memorandum and articles of association of the company which created the floating charge with a view to ascertaining that the principal objects of the company as specified in the memorandum correspond with the actual activities of the company and that as ancillary to the principal objects[1] the company, in the case of a loan, had power to borrow and grant a floating charge in respect of its own indebtedness and also (if applicable to the particular case) indebtedness of other persons and that there are no borrowing restrictions in the articles of association;
(b) a copy of the floating charge (a style of which is given in Appendix 1) to ascertain the property subject to the charge, that the charge has been properly constituted and executed and that the holder had power to appoint a receiver in the particular circumstances;
(c) a copy of the certificate of registration of the charge to ensure that the charge has been registered with the Registrar of Companies within twenty-one days of its date of creation, bearing in mind that in terms of section 418 of the 1985 Act the certificate of the Registrar is conclusive evidence that the requirements as to registration have been complied with;[2]
(d) evidence of the circumstances justifying appointment: for example, where the receiver has been appointed on the written request of the

company, a copy of the board minute of the company resolving to request the appointment of a receiver (a style of which is given in Appendix 2) and a copy of the letter from the company to the floating charge holder requesting such appointment (a style of which is given in Appendix 3) or, where the appointment followed a demand for payment, a copy of the letter of demand from the holder of the floating charge together with evidence that such letter of demand was properly made in terms of the floating charge;[3] and

(e) a copy of the instrument of appointment (a style of which is given in Appendix 4) to check that it has been properly executed in terms of section 53 of the Insolvency Act 1986.

1 As required by *Rolled Steel Products (Holdings) Ltd v British Steel Corpn* [1982] 3 All ER 1057 and on appeal [1984] BCLC 466.
2 *R v Registrar of Companies ex p Esal (Commodities) Ltd* [1985] 2 All ER 79.
3 See *Elwick Bay Shipping Co Ltd v Royal Bank of Scotland Ltd* 1982 SLT 62.

1.53 Although it is the duty in terms of section 53(1) of the Insolvency Act 1986 of the holder of the floating charge or a person on his behalf to deal with the completion of the notice in the prescribed form and to file such notice with the Registrar of Companies, it is prudent for the receiver to check, from the point of view of general publicity, that the correct particulars have been filed with the Registrar of Companies.

1.54 On a matter of practice, it is usually the case that a solicitor acting for a receiver will be invited to examine photocopies of original documents rather than the originals. This really does not matter in the case of some documents such as the memorandum and articles or the certificate of registration but it is clearly important in the case of documents such as the floating charge or the instrument of appointment to examine originals to be certain that such documents have been validly executed.

1.55 In most cases, sight of the instrument of appointment can be arranged easily but in the case of the floating charge itself many holders of floating charges may be reluctant to allow the original document to pass out of their hands. It is for this reason that many solicitors acting for receivers will qualify their confirmation of validity of appointment by the words 'the photocopy documents in my possession bearing to have been validly executed'. The stamp duty payable on a deed of appointment of a receiver prior to 19 March 1985 was 50p and the practice of many holders of floating charges was to use pre-stamped paper. Since the passing of the Finance Act 1985[1] no stamp duty is chargeable in respect of a deed of appointment of a receiver.

1 Section 85(1) and Sch 24.

1.56 A defect in the procedural steps to appoint a receiver may render the appointment invalid but it is a question of degree or of materiality in each case as to whether any such defect may prove fatal to the appointment. It is clear that many of the requirements specified above are subject to the provisions of the general law of Scotland with which it is not proposed to deal in this book and, in the vast majority of cases (particularly, where the lender uses a standard form) a holder of a floating charge will have ensured that requirements of execution and procedure will have been followed at the time of creation of the floating charge. He will almost certainly have checked that the borrower has the power under its memorandum to borrow and to grant securities or charges over its undertaking and assets: otherwise the lender may be at risk by virtue of the ultra vires principle in finding that he has an invalid security.

1.57 For a fuller discussion on the ultra vires principle, reference should be made to the standard textbooks on the subject and to the decision in *Rolled Steel Products*.[1] It is sufficient for present purposes to note that if the objects clause of a company does not include the power to borrow and to grant securities or charges, a general meeting of the members of the company cannot ratify the purported exercise of such powers with retrospective effect.

1 *Rolled Steel Products (Holdings) Ltd v British Steel Corpn* [1982] 3 All ER 1057 and on appeal [1984] BCLC 466.

Borrowing limits exceeded

1.58 Difficult problems can arise in a receivership if the directors' borrowing limits under the company's articles of association have been exceeded. If there is any doubt on such a question, all receivers will wish to be so advised when the validity of the appointment is being checked, but whether or not borrowing limits have been exceeded will not per se affect the validity of the appointment: the security afforded by the floating charge will be valid at least to some extent if not totally. For a fuller discussion on the position where such borrowing limits are exceeded, reference should be made to Chapter 8 paragraphs 8.21 to 8.28.

Mode of appointment by court

1.59 Section 54 of the Insolvency Act 1986 provides that the appointment of a receiver by the court under section 51(2) of that Act shall be by petition to the court which shall be served on the company and in terms of section 54(2) on such application the court shall, if it thinks fit, issue an interlocutor making the appointment of a receiver in such terms as to caution as the court may think fit. The reference to the court in this connection means the Outer House of the Court of Session.[1] It does not appear to be competent to petition the sheriff court. Section 54(3) provides that a copy (certified by the clerk of the court to be a correct copy) of the court interlocutor making the appointment shall be delivered by or on behalf of the petitioner to the Registrar of Companies for registration, accompanied by a notice in the prescribed form within seven days of the date of the interlocutor or such longer period as the court may allow. If any person without reasonable excuse makes default in comply-

ing with the requirements of section 54(3) of the Insolvency Act 1986 he
is liable to a fine and, for continued contravention, to a daily default fine.

1 Rule 218A (a) of Rules of Court 1965 Chap IV as amended by the Acts of Sederunt (Rules
  of Court Amendment No 1) 1973, SI 1973/145: new Rules of Court will be introduced for
  the coming into operation of the Insolvency Act 1986.

1.60   Section 54(4) of the Insolvency Act 1986 provides that on receipt of
the certified copy of the interlocutor in accordance with section 54(3) and
on receipt of a certificate by the appropriate officer of the court that
caution as ordered by the court has been found, the Registrar shall on the
payment of the appropriate fee enter up particulars of the appointment in
the Register of Charges and in terms of section 54(5) the receiver shall be
regarded as having been appointed on the date of his being appointed by
the court. In terms of section 54(6), on the appointment of the receiver
under this section, the floating charge by virtue of which he was
appointed shall attach to the property then subject to the charge and such
attachment shall have effect as if the charge were a fixed security over the
property to which it has attached.

Precedence among receivers

1.61   Section 56(1) of the Insolvency Act 1986 provides that where there
are two or more floating charges existing over all or any part of the
property of the company, a receiver may be appointed by virtue of each
such charge but a receiver appointed by, or on application of, the holder
of a floating charge having priority of ranking over any other floating
charge by virtue of which a receiver is appointed shall have the powers
given to a receiver to the exclusion of any other receiver. Where two or
more floating charges rank equally with one another and two or more
receivers have been appointed by virtue of such charges, the receivers so
appointed shall be deemed to have been appointed as joint receivers.

1.62   The power to the holder of a floating charge and to the court to
appoint a receiver under sections 51(1) and (2) of the Insolvency Act 1986
includes the power to appoint joint receivers and in terms of section 56(3)
receivers appointed or deemed to have been appointed as joint receivers
shall act jointly unless the instrument of appointment or respective
instruments of appointment otherwise provide. In very large receiverships where joint receivers are to be appointed it is advisable that
provision be made in the instrument of appointment for each receiver to
act individually thereby avoiding the necessity of requiring all documents
to be signed by both receivers as otherwise administrative and logistical
problems tend to arise.

1.63   If joint receivers have been appointed to a group of companies the
holding company and some subsidiaries of which are Scottish, but which
also has English subsidiaries, care should be taken to ensure that it is
competent to appoint joint receivers of the English subsidiaries with
power to act individually. The critical test will be the terms of the English

debenture and floating charge giving rise to the appointment: unless power has been specifically taken in the debenture, the appointment of joint receivers with power to act individually may be invalid.

Validity of assignation of floating charges

1.64   From time to time questions have arisen as to the effectiveness or validity of assignation of floating charges. The principal advantage of assigning a floating charge rather than creating a new one is that it may avoid potential challenge under the provisions of the Insolvency Act 1986[1] in the event of the winding up of or the making of an administration order affecting the charging company within certain periods of the constitution of such new floating charge. In the leading case on this subject *Libertas–Kommerz GmbH v Johnson*[2] a Scottish company granted a bond and floating charge over its property in favour of an individual who purported to assign his interest to company A who in turn purported to assign its interest to company B. Company B lodged a claim in the liquidation of the original Scottish company. Lord Kincraig held that the floating charge was assignable.

1   Insolvency Act 1986, s 245.
2   1978 SLT 222.

Competition between receiver and liquidator

1.65   Questions sometimes arise as to priority when a liquidator is either appointed before or after a receiver is appointed. In terms of section 52(1)(c) of the Insolvency Act 1986, the winding up of the company entitles the holder of a floating charge to appoint a receiver and in terms of section 129(2) of the Insolvency Act 1986, a winding up by the court is deemed to have commenced at the date of presentation of the petition to the court. What happens if the liquidator is appointed either prior to or after the receiver?

1.66   The answer is that the receiver acts in the first instance to discharge his statutory duties, prior and preferably to the liquidator.[1] The underlying reason for such an approach is simply that the holder of the floating charge, even in liquidation, should be entitled to exercise his security over the assets of a company and if there is any expectation whatsoever of disposing of a business it is probably in everyone's interests that such a disposal be carried through by a receiver despite possible disadvantageous capital gains tax results following upon the disposal by the receiver of assets of a company in liquidation.[2]

1   *Manley, Petitioner* 1985 SLT 42.
2   David Bertram *Tax Consequences of Receivership and Liquidation* pp3 and 48.

1.67   In *Manley, Petitioner*,[1] the liquidator's appointment preceded the receiver's appointment. In his judgment, Lord Kincraig rebutted the argument that the liquidator had effectually executed diligence and gave effect to the receiver's contention that in terms of section 15(1)(a) of the 1972 Act[2] he was entitled to take precedence over the rights of the liquidator in order to satisfy the debt of the holder of the floating charge. Lord Kincraig also concluded that the receiver was liable for the payment of the secured and preferential creditors of the company but not the costs of the liquidator. In the course of his judgment, Lord Kincraig stated:

> 'The whole scheme of the 1972 Act is to give the receiver precedence over the liquidator in the administration of the whole property of the company, even if appointed after the commencement of the liquidation.'

1 1985 SLT 42.
2 Re-enacted as CA 1985, s 471(1)(a); see now Insolvency Act 1986, Sch 2, para 1.

1.68   It has been held[1] in England that a debenture holder who was contractually entitled to appoint a receiver was free to do so in order to protect his own interests and was under no duty to refrain from exercising his rights on the grounds that to do so might cause loss to the company or its unsecured creditors, or because the appointment of a receiver might be unnecessary in that it merely duplicated the efforts of the liquidator.

1 *Re Potters Oils Ltd (No 2)* [1986] 1 All ER 890.

Chapter 2

Effect of appointment of receiver

Attachment of floating charge

General

2.01 As noted in Chapter 1, a floating charge may be created by a company over all or any part of the property (including uncalled capital) comprised from time to time in its property and undertaking for the purpose of securing any debt or other obligation (including a cautionary obligation) of the company or any other party. Unlike a fixed charge which from the outset attaches to the property subject to it, a floating charge as its name suggests only floats without attachment over the property of the description or class specified in such charge which from time to time belongs to the company. However, on the appointment of a receiver the floating charge by virtue of which he was appointed 'attaches'[1] to the property then subject to the charge. The same result occurs on the commencement of the winding up of the company which created it.[2] In these circumstances, the floating charge ceases to float and instead attaches to the property then subject to it.

1 Insolvency Act 1986, s 53(7).
2 CA 1985, s 463(1).

2.02 Attachment or crystallisation of a floating charge only occurs on the appointment of a receiver under that charge or on winding up: it does not, for example, occur on the appointment of a receiver by the holder of another floating charge, such other charge alone attaching in these circumstances to the property then subject to it. The appointment of a receiver by the holder of a floating charge created by a company, however, entitles the holder of any other floating charge created by the company to appoint a receiver[1] and so effect the attachment or crystallisation of that charge. Where a company has granted more than one floating charge, there is nothing to prevent each holder appointing his own receiver[2] but the usual practice in these circumstances, for obvious practical reasons, is for each holder to appoint the same person.[3] In the event of a different receiver being appointed, the 1985 Act contains provisions regulating precedence amongst such receivers.[4]

1 Insolvency Act 1986, s 52(1)(d).
2 Ibid s 56(1).
3 Ibid s 56(7).
4 See Chap 1 para 1.61 to 1.63.

Effect of attachment or crystallisation

2.03 On the appointment of a receiver, the floating charge by virtue of which he was appointed attaches to the property and assets of the description or class specified in the floating charge as being subject to it and which at the time of appointment belong to the company, as if such charge were a fixed security over such property and assets. A fixed security is defined[1] as, in relation to any property of a company, any security, other than a floating charge or a charge having the nature of a floating charge, which on the winding up of the company in Scotland would be treated as an effective security over that property.

1 Insolvency Act 1986, s 70(1).

Effect of attachment or crystallisation in relation to specific property and assets

2.04 To cover the case of heritable property subject to a floating charge the definition of a fixed security[1] includes a heritable security within the meaning of section 9(8) of the Conveyancing and Feudal Reform (Scotland) Act 1970. Since a security over heritable property in Scotland to be effective must be constituted a real right by recording or registration in the appropriate land register, it is specifically provided[2] that a floating charge shall have effect in relation to any heritable property to which it relates notwithstanding that the instrument creating it is not recorded in the Register of Sasines or registered in accordance with the Land Registration (Scotland) Act 1979.

1 Insolvency Act 1986, s 70(1).
2 CA 1985, s 462(5).

2.05 A floating charge by its nature does not attach to heritable property any more so than it does to any other kind of property from the time of its creation which means the company granting it is, subject to any contractual restrictions undertaken by it to the floating charge creditor, free to deal with such property until the floating charge attaches and in the event of receivership or liquidation the claims of preferred creditors take priority over the claim of the floating charge creditor. Where possible, therefore, a creditor of a company owning heritable property should seek a fixed charge over such property as, unlike a floating charge, such fixed charge will attach from the outset thus restricting the company's ability to deal with the property, the creditor's rights will be capable of exercise without the necessity of appointing a receiver and his claim will not be postponed to those of preferred creditors.

2.06 Corporeal moveable property in the form of plant, equipment and stock often form a substantial part of a trading company's assets and it is over such assets (with or without book debts or other incorporeal moveable property) a creditor more often than not wishes to obtain security. A floating charge affords security over corporeal moveable property contrary to the basic principle of the law of Scotland that security over such property cannot be created without actual or constructive delivery. Prior to 1961 Scottish companies were at a disadvantage compared to their English counterparts in that floating charges were not known to the law of Scotland and consequently, for most practical purposes, it was impossible for a trading company to effectively create a security over corporeal moveables with one notable exception peculiar to Scotland. It was and still is possible to create a fixed security over stocks of Scotch whisky by effecting constructive delivery to the creditor provided they are held in an independent warehouse. The Companies (Floating Charges) (Scotland) Act 1961 however introduced floating charges into the law of Scotland for the first time thus removing the impediment to the creation of charges over corporeal moveable property by Scottish companies. On attachment or crystallisation a floating charge attaches to all such property then subject to the charge and owned by the company as if it were an effective fixed security created by delivery.

2.07   The incorporeal moveable property of a trading company with most value is usually its book debts and a creditor seeking a floating charge will more often than not wish such book debts included. It is of course legally possible in Scotland to create a fixed charge over a book debt by assignation to the creditor followed by intimation to the party owing the debt[1] but the requirement of intimation to the party owing the debt has practical problems against a trading background where both the identity and amount of book debts are constantly changing. On attachment or crystallisation a floating charge accordingly attaches to incorporeal moveable property, such as book debts, as if it were an effective security created by assignation and intimation. The creation of a fixed charge over book debts in England does not have the same practical problems.[2]

1 Transmission of Moveable Property (Scotland) Act 1862.
2 See Chap 8 paras 8.18 to 8.20.

2.08   On attachment or crystallisation a floating charge is accordingly, in effect, converted into a fixed security over the property subject to it. Lord Cameron in one of the first cases[1] to come before the Court of Session on the interpretation of the 1972 Act said:

'I think . . . that when the definition of a "fixed security" in s 31[2] is examined it becomes clear that the intention of the legislature was to provide, in the shape of a floating charge, a form of security over the property of a debtor company which, at the discretion of the security holder, or on application to the court and on the appointment of a receiver, should operate as a fixed security, and that this should be so when the circumstances were appropriate for the secured creditor to be given the right and opportunity to work out his security, without being compelled to proceed into liquidation; the floating charge in these circumstances becomes a valuable and convenient device in the interest both of creditor and company to secure and obtain satisfaction of a debt or claim without recourse to the extreme remedy of liquidation.'

In a more recent case[3] Lord President Emslie stated:

'The intention [of the Act][4] appears to me to be that the holder of the floating charge shall, on the appointment of a receiver, enjoy all the protection in relation to any item of attached property that the holder of a fixed security over that item thereof would enjoy under the general law.'

1 *Lord Advocate v Royal Bank of Scotland Ltd* 1978 SLT 38 at 47 per Lord Cameron.
2 Re-enacted as CA 1985, s 486; see now the Insolvency Act 1986, s 70.
3 *Forth & Clyde Construction Co Ltd v Trinity Timber & Plywood Co Ltd* 1984 SLT 94.
4 The Companies (Floating Charges and Receivers) (Scotland) Act 1972 (consolidated into CA 1985 and amended by the Insolvency Act 1985; the provisions derived from the 1972 Act are now, in part, consolidated in the Insolvency Act 1986).

2.09 The concept of a floating charge being converted into a fixed charge on crystallisation as a result of the appointment of a receiver has given rise to difficulties in relation to book debts due to the company.[1] Paragraph 1 of Schedule 2 to the Insolvency Act 1986[2] bestows on a receiver power to take possession of, collect and get in the property subject to the floating charge from the company or a liquidator thereof or any other person and for that purpose to take such proceedings as may seem to him expedient. In the *McPhail* case,[3] Lord Grieve held in relation to proceedings for recovery of a debt due to the company that as a receiver had power by virtue of the equivalent section of the 1972 Act to raise a claim in his own name to so recover property for behoof of the security holder there were no grounds for holding that the receiver was precluded from recovering property from another person in his own name and that while section 15(1)(f) of the 1972 Act[4] gave him power to bring or defend any action or other legal proceedings in the name and on behalf of the company this was not to be construed as limiting the powers of the receiver in connection with the raising of legal proceedings. Section 15(1)(a) of the 1972 Act[5] accordingly gave the receiver a discretion as to whether to seek to recover such property in his own name or in that of the company.

1 *McPhail v Lothian Regional Council* 1981 SLT 173.
2 Originally the Companies (Floating Charges and Receivers) (Scotland) Act 1972, s 15(1)(a).
3 See n1 above.
4 See now the Insolvency Act 1986, Sch 2, para 5.
5 Ibid para 1.

2.10 In the *Taylor* case[1] however Lord Ross did not follow the *McPhail* decision[2] and held that as under section 15(1)(a) of the 1972 Act[3] the receiver's power was limited to taking possession from the company of a right to debts due to it by others, namely a *jus crediti*, the provisions of that section would enable the receiver to obtain from the company an assignation of those debts but not to sue the debtors for payment of the debts because, at the date of his appointment, what the company owned was not the sums of money due by the debtors but a mere *jus crediti*. Accordingly, the receiver's power under section 15(1)(f) of the 1972 Act[4] was limited to taking proceedings in the name of the company for recovery of debts due to it.

1 *Taylor, Petitioner* 1982 SLT 172; see also 'The Receiver and Book Debts' 1982 SLT (News) 129.
2 *McPhail v Lothian Regional Council* 1981 SLT 173.

3 See now the Insolvency Act 1986, Sch 2, para 1.
4 Ibid para 5.

2.11   In a later case[1] the concept was considered on appeal by the Inner House. The facts of that case were that, on the day after joint receivers had been validly appointed by the holders of a floating charge over the whole property of a company, a creditor upon the faith of a warrant to arrest on the dependence of an action against the company arrested in the hands of Strathclyde Regional Council a sum due by the council to the company under certain building contracts. The company's receivers in the exercise of their powers under section 15(1)(a) of the 1972 Act[2] sought to collect the debt due to the company by the regional council but the creditor, a company which was in liquidation, would not agree to the regional council releasing the sum in question. The receivers accordingly presented a petition for recall of the purported arrestment and were successful both at first instance and on appeal by the respondent creditor. In his judgment, Lord President Emslie (section references being to the 1972 Act) stated:

> 'Upon a proper construction of the words of section 13(7)[3] . . . read together with the definition of the words "fixed security" in section 31(1),[4] in the context of an Act which repeatedly draws a distinction between a fixed security and any diligence, one has to ask, in order to give effect to section 13(7)[5] in the case of a book debt, what kind of security over it (other than a diligence) would be treated by the law of Scotland as an "effective security" over it in the winding up of a company in Scotland. There is only one such security and that is an assignation in security of the right to receive payment of the debt, duly intimated to the debtor.'

On that basis the court held that the regional council's liability to pay the debt to the company for its own behoof had disappeared and so on the date of the purported arrestment the debt was no longer susceptible to arrestment at the instance of a creditor of the company. This decision, it is suggested, looking both to the provisions of what is now section 53(7) of the Insolvency Act 1986 and the other sections of the 1972 Act to which the court referred, gives effect to the overall objective of the legislation. On the appointment of a receiver, while the company remains entitled to recover its book debts, it no longer does so on its own behalf, but on behalf of the holder of the floating charge and the receiver in exercise of his powers will seek to recover these debts in the company's name with a view to satisfying the debt due by the company to the holder of the floating charge within the framework laid down in the legislation.

1 *Forth & Clyde Construction Ltd v Trinity Timber & Plywood Ltd* 1984 SLT 94.
2 See now the Insolvency Act 1986, Sch 2, para 1.
3 Ibid s 53(7).
4 Ibid s 70(1).
5 Ibid s 53(7).

Security for principal and interest

2.12   The attachment or crystallisation of a floating charge on the appointment of a receiver affords security not only for the principal of the debt or obligation in question but also for both pre- and post-receivership interest until payment of the sum due under the charge.[1] A provision in similar terms was first introduced in the 1972 Act to remove any doubt on the matter following a decision[2] to the effect that the holder of a floating charge was entitled to interest from the date of liquidation until payment.

1 CA 1985, s 463(4).
2 *National Commercial Bank of Scotland Ltd v Liquidators of Telford Grier Mackay & Co* 1969 SC 181.

Effect of attachment or crystallisation in relation to diligence

2.13 Powers given to a receiver are made subject to the rights of any person who has effectually executed diligence on property of the company prior to the appointment of the receiver.[1] It has been held[2] on consideration of the equivalent section in the 1972 Act that an arrestment which, prior to the appointment of a receiver, has not been followed by a decree of furthcoming is not 'effectually executed diligence'. On the basis of this decision a poinding which has not been succeeded by a sale prior to a receiver's appointment likewise cannot be effectually executed diligence. This is to be contrasted with the position arising on liquidation where an arrestment or poinding executed more than sixty days prior to the commencement of liquidation is effectual as against the liquidator[3] although, if there exists a floating charge over the assets affected by such diligence, such floating charge crystallises subject to the rights of any person who has effectually executed diligence.[4] An arresting or poinding creditor, who has not proceeded to furthcoming or sale prior to a receiver's appointment, does not have any preference for the expenses of such ineffectually executed diligence which again is to be contrasted with the position on liquidation where a creditor who has arrested or poinded within sixty days of liquidation does have such a preference.[5] An arrestment executed after the appointment of a receiver is also ineffectual.[6]

1 Insolvency Act 1986, s 55(3)(a).
2 *Lord Advocate v Royal Bank of Scotland Ltd* 1978 SLT 38.
3 Bankruptcy (Scotland) Act 1985, Sch 7, para 21.
4 CA 1985, s 463(1).
5 Bankruptcy (Scotland) Act 1985, Sch 7, para 21.
6 *Forth & Clyde Construction Co Ltd v Trinity Timber & Plywood Co Ltd* 1984 SLT 94; see also 'Receivers and Arrestors' 1984 SLT (News) 177.

2.14 The question of whether an inhibition registered before the appointment of a receiver is 'effectually executed diligence' within the meaning of section 55(3)(a) of the Insolvency Act 1986[1] remains an open one.[2] In *Armour and Mycroft, Petitioners*, Lord Kincraig at 455 said:
'It is accordingly unnecessary for me to decide whether an inhibition is an effectually executed diligence within the meaning of s 15 of the said 1972 Act'.

1 Originally the Companies (Floating Charges and Receivers) (Scotland) Act 1972, s 15(2).
2 *Armour and Mycroft, Petitioners* 1983 SLT 453; see also 'Inhibitions and Company Insolvencies' 1983 SLT (News) 145.

2.15 The effect of an inhibition in relation to receivership depends on the date of the inhibition. As an inhibition prohibits inter alia the subsequent granting by the debtor of any security over his heritable property, an inhibition granted before a floating charge will prevail in so far as such charge extends over a debtor company's heritable property. Where, however, a floating charge antedates an inhibition it is unaffected by it and this remains the position when such charge attaches or crystallises on the appointment of a receiver. This was the position in the *Armour and Mycroft* case[1] but, the joint receivers having contracted to sell part of the company's heritable property, the inhibiting creditor refused to discharge its inhibition or to consent to the sale except upon the joint receivers presenting an application to the court under section 21 of the 1972 Act[2] seeking power to sell the property in question free of any security, interest, burden or encumbrance. The court rejected the claim of the inhibiting creditor that its debt should be satisfied before those of the floating charge holders but held that the former's debt should be satisfied from the sale proceeds before satisfaction of any of the claims of ordinary creditors.

1 *Armour and Mycroft, Petitioners* 1983 SLT 453.
2 Re-enacted as CA 1985, s 477 (and amended by the Insolvency Act 1985, s 59); see now the Insolvency Act 1986, s 61.

2.16 Sequestration for rent is the process of diligence available to a landlord for enforcing his hypothec for unpaid rent. It has been held that a receiver's powers prevail over a landlord's right to sequestrate for rent after the receiver's appointment.[1] In *Cumbernauld Development Corpn v Mustone Ltd* a company, Mustone Limited, leased a factory from Cumbernauld Development Corporation. As a result of financial problems, it fell into arrears with rental payments and a receiver was eventually appointed over all its assets. About one month after the receiver's appointment the Development Corporation sequestrated for rent and in another month the company went into liquidation. Both the receiver and the liquidator contested the relevancy of the sequestration proceedings and the sheriff found in the receiver's favour on the grounds that a landlord's hypothec is neither effectually executed diligence in terms of section 15(2)(a) of the 1972 Act[2] nor a fixed security in terms of section 31 of that Act[3] (nor had it been constituted as a real right before the floating charge had attached). Unfortunately, however, the provisions of section 5(2) of the 1972 Act[4] were not brought to the sheriff's attention. That section provides that where all or any part of the property of a company is subject both to a floating charge and to a fixed security arising by operation of law, the fixed security shall have priority over the floating charge. A landlord's hypothec is under the law of Scotland a real right in security which arises by operation of law and section 70(1) of the Insolvency Act 1986 provides that for the purposes of that part of the Act any security that is not a floating charge or of the nature of a floating charge is a fixed security. It is, accordingly, suggested that the *Mustone* decision is open to question.[5] In addition, it is clear that the legislative intention was to give priority to a landlord's right of hypothec.

1 *Cumbernauld Development Corpn v Mustone Ltd* 1983 SLT (Sh Ct)55.
2 See now the Insolvency Act 1986, s 55(3)(a).

3 Ibid s 70(1).
4 CA 1985, s 464(2).
5 See 'Receivership and Sequestration for Rent' 1983 SLT (News) 277 and Journal of the Law Society of Scotland, August 1983 p 352.

2.17 Where a receiver sells or wishes to sell property covered by the floating charge under which he has been appointed and is unable to obtain the consent of a creditor who has effectually executed diligence he may apply to the court for the appropriate authority.[1]

1 See para 2.15 and Chap 7 paras 7.35 to 7.37.

Other effects of appointment of receiver

Powers of directors

2.18 There are no express statutory provisions as to the effect on the powers of the directors of the company on the appointment of a receiver. As however a receiver's powers include power to take possession of the property of the company subject to the floating charge under which he was appointed, the powers of the directors to deal with such property are suspended. In the majority of cases the floating charge extends over the company's whole undertaking and assets and as the receiver's powers include power to carry on the company's business the directors in these circumstances are effectively relieved of all powers of management of the company, its business and assets. The Court of Session in Scotland has ruled that during the receivership the directors have no power whatsoever to deal with property subject to the charge.[1]

1 *Imperial Hotel (Aberdeen) Ltd v Vaux Breweries Ltd*[1] 1978 SLT 113.

2.19 In *Imperial Hotel (Aberdeen) Ltd v Vaux Breweries Ltd*[1] a hotel company had granted a brewery company both a floating charge and a fixed charge in the form of a standard security over the hotel. It had also granted to its bank a floating charge over all its assets. The bank appointed a receiver and at a later date the brewery company called up its standard security and in exercise of its power of sale sold the hotel to another brewery company. The directors of the company in receivership raised an action in the name of the company seeking reduction of the contract for the sale of the hotel on the grounds that the security holder in exercising its power of sale had failed to take all reasonable steps to ensure that the hotel was sold for the best price that could reasonably have been obtained. The court held that where a receiver had been appointed over the whole of the assets of a company, the directors of the company were not entitled to deal in any way with the property of the company during the currency of the receivership. In the course of his judgment (section references being to the 1972 Act) Lord Grieve (at 116) said:

'It would be quite contrary to the object of the Act if a company, all of whose assets were attached to the receiver because all were covered by a floating charge or floating charges could interfere, through its directors, with the exercise by the receiver of his discretion by, for instance, raising actions which the receiver did not consider should be raised. In my opinion it is quite apparent from the terms of the 1972 Act and the nature of the duties which a receiver appointed under it is empowered to perform, that the receiver's primary duty is to the security holder, and that, in order to perform it properly, his discretion is not to be subject to interference by the directors of the company concerned.'

Again (at 117):

'I am quite satisfied that the terms of the Act of 1972 do not empower the directors of a company, whose assets are the subject of a floating charge in connection with which a receiver has been appointed, to deal in any way with assets of theirs which are the subject of such a charge during the currency of the receivership.'

1   1978 SLT 113.

2.20   The decision is to be contrasted with an English Court of Appeal decision in the same year[1] where it was ruled that if directors remain in office after the appointment of a receiver they can continue to exercise their powers in spite of the fact that the receiver has equivalent powers under his instrument of appointment, provided that the directors in exercise of such powers do not thereby impede the proper conduct of the receivership. In that case[1] the directors had raised an action in the name of the company and in the course of its judgment the court said (per Shaw LJ at 819):

'There is not a total extinction of the function of the directors. It is only within the scope of its assets which are covered by the debenture, and only in so far as it is necessary to apply those assets in the best possible way in the interests of the debenture holders, that the receiver has a real function. If in the exercise of his discretion he chooses to ignore some asset such as a right of action, or decides that it would be unprofitable from the point of view of the debenture holders to pursue it, there is nothing in any authority which has been cited to us which suggests that it is not then open to the directors of the company to pursue that right of action if they think it would be in the interests of the company. Indeed, in my view, it would be incumbent on them to do so.'

1   *Newhart Developments Ltd v Co-operative Commercial Bank Ltd* [1978] QB 814.

2.21   The court went on to hold in the *Newhart* case[1] that the appointment of a receiver accordingly did not divest the directors of the company of their power, as the governing body of the company, of instituting proceedings in a situation where so doing did not in any way impinge prejudicially upon the position of the debenture-holders by threatening or imperilling the assets which were subject to the charge. In particular, the directors were entitled to pursue a right of action in the name of the company, provided however that the company was indemnified against liability for costs. It has been suggested that the *Imperial Hotel*[2] and *Newhart*[3] decisions can be reconciled on the basis that in the *Newhart* case[3] the company was not called upon to finance the action out of its own resources and was indemnified against liability for expenses.[4]

1 *Newhart Developments Ltd v Co-operative Commercial Bank Ltd* [1978] QB 814.
2 *Imperial Hotel (Aberdeen) Ltd v Vaux Breweries Ltd* 1978 SLT 113.
3 See n 1 above.
4 R J Reed 'Aspects of the law of Receivership' 1983 SLT (News) 237.

2.22 Since the *Imperial Hotel* and *Newhart*[1] decisions, the question has been considered again in an unreported sheriff court case.[2] In that case the pursuers, a company, itself, both in receivership and liquidation, were suing for loss arising from breach of contract. In the course of the proceedings the defenders had a receiver appointed over their whole property and assets. The pursuers sought to have the receiver of the defenders sisted as a party to the action but the receiver was unwilling to be so sisted, the pursuers being unable to compel him to do so. However, the directors of the defenders decided to continue the defence of the action at their own expense. The pursuers maintained that the effect of the appointment of a receiver over the whole property and assets was to deprive the defenders' directors of any power to continue the defence of the action. The defenders on the other hand argued that they should be allowed to continue the defence as in so doing the defenders' directors were not in any way interfering with the receiver in the exercise of his functions nor eroding the funds available to him since he would incur no liability in respect of any obligations which he had not authorised. The sheriff in reaching his decision had the benefit of considering both the *Imperial Hotel* and *Newhart* decisions[3] and was able to draw a distinction between the facts in the *Imperial Hotel* case and the facts in the case before him.

1 *Imperial Hotel (Aberdeen) Ltd v Vaux Breweries Ltd* 1978 SLT 113; *Newhart Developments Ltd v Co-operative Commercial Bank Ltd* [1978] QB 814.
2 *Hastings Black Construction Ltd v AIR (Air Conditioning and Refrigeration) Ltd* (1984) 4 October (unreported) Glasgow Sheriff Court.
3 See n 1 above.

2.23 The attempt by the directors of Imperial Hotel (Aberdeen) Limited to prevent the sale of property comprised in the receivership was in the sheriff's view[1] a very obvious interference with the receiver in the execution of his functions whereas in the case before him the continuation of the defence to the action did not interfere in any way with the performance by the receiver of his functions. While the sheriff in drawing this distinction overlooks the fact that in the *Imperial Hotel* case[2] the sale was effected not by the receiver but by a heritable creditor in exercise of such creditor's right of sale, the property did form part of the receivership assets over which the receiver's powers extended subject always to the prior rights of the heritable creditor. As section 15 of the 1972 Act[3] contained no prohibition on the directors of a company in receivership from taking any of the actions which a receiver is entitled to take and as the continuation of the defence of the proceedings did not interfere with the exercise by the receiver of his functions, the sheriff found in favour of the defenders. In his judgment while the sheriff states that the major premise of Lord Grieve's reasoning in the *Imperial Hotel* case would appear to be that any actings by the board of directors which could interfere with the exercise by the receiver of his discretion would be illegal, he does express the view that in more borderline cases wherein actings of the directors might or might not be said to so interfere, it might be necessary to consider carefully the meaning and effect of Lord Grieve's statement at 117 of his judgment[4] to the effect that the directors of a company in receivership have no power to deal in any way with assets subject to the floating charge. It is suggested that the sheriff in this unreported case did reach the correct conclusion.

1 *Hastings Black Construction Ltd v AIR (Air Conditioning and Refrigeration) Ltd* (1984) 4 October (unreported) Glasgow Sheriff Court.
2 *Imperial Hotel (Aberdeen) Ltd v Vaux Breweries Ltd* 1978 SLT 113.
3 See now the Insolvency Act 1986, s 55 and Sch 2.
4 See n 2 above.

2.24 In one other reported Scottish case[1] touching on the effect of the appointment of a receiver on the powers of the directors, a case where the court was asked to order a company in receivership to obtemper a decree of specific implement, the Lord Ordinary (Lord Stott) in deciding that a company in receivership could only act through the agency of its receiver said:
'It is plain that the defenders are not in a position to obtemper decree of specific implement through their directors as would normally be the position if the company was not in receivership.

1 *MacLeod v Alexander Sutherland Ltd* 1977 SLT (Notes) 44; but see Chap 4 paras 4.34 to 4.36.

Responsibilities of directors

2.25 While in Scotland, on the basis of the *Imperial Hotel* decision[1] the directors' powers of management over the assets covered by the floating charge cease to have effect, the appointment of the directors as such does not cease nor are they relieved of their statutory obligations. Likewise, the appointment of the secretary of the company does not cease. The directors remain, for example, under obligation to maintain accounting records.[2]

1 *Imperial Hotel (Aberdeen) Ltd v Vaux Breweries Ltd* 1978 SLT 113.
2 *Smiths Ltd v Middleton* [1979] 3 All ER 842.

Remuneration of directors

2.26 It has been held in England[1] that while directors cannot claim remuneration from a receiver unless he employs them, they can nevertheless claim from the company any remuneration to which they are entitled.

1 *Re South Western of Venezuela (Barquisimeto) Rly Co* [1902] 1 Ch 701.

Effect on fixed charges

2.27 The exercise by a receiver in Scotland of his powers are subject inter alia to the rights of the holder of a charge ranking prior to or *pari passu* with the floating charge by virtue of which he was appointed.[1] The rights, however, of the holder of a fixed charge over heritable property in the form of a standard security remain intact on the appointment of a receiver provided that such charge is both intra vires the company and has been validly registered as a charge. The creditor in such a standard security may accordingly, as was done in the *Imperial Hotel* case,[2] exercise all the powers competent to him as heritable creditor including the power of sale. The position is the same in relation to any other validly created form of fixed security over the company's assets.

1 Insolvency Act 1986, s 55(3)(b).
2 *Imperial Hotel (Aberdeen) Ltd v Vaux Breweries Ltd* 1978 SLT 113.

Effect on other floating charges

2.28   If a floating charge covers a company's whole property and under-taking then, on the appointment of a receiver under it, it attaches to or crystallises on all its properties and assets. Any other floating charge granted by the company, whatever its ranking in relation to the floating charge under which the receiver has been appointed, does not automati-cally attach or crystallise on the appointment of such receiver. Any other floating charge only attaches or crystallises on either the appointment of a receiver by its holder or on the winding-up of the company although, of course, the appointment of a receiver by the holder of a floating charge entitles the holder of any other floating charge granted by the company to appoint a receiver.[1]

1 Insolvency Act 1986, 1.61 to 1.63.

2.29   So on the appointment of a receiver by the holder of a floating charge, the holder of any other floating charge in order to crystallise his charge, and generally in his own interests, should likewise appoint a receiver who, unless there is some compelling reason why he should not be so appointed, will normally be the person or persons already appointed by the holder of the first floating charge. As has already been seen,[1] section 56 of the Insolvency Act 1986 contains provisions governing precedence among receivers, the effect of which on the appointment of a different person would be that depending on the ranking of the floating charges in question either only one of the receivers would be entitled to exercise the powers given to a receiver under the Insolvency Act 1986 or, unless the respective instruments of appointment otherwise provided, the receivers so appointed would act jointly in the exercise of such powers. If, on the other hand, a floating charge covers part but not all of a company's assets then, on the appointment of a receiver under it, it attaches or crystallises on these assets alone and the effect on the attachment or crystallisation, or rather non-attachment or non-crystallisation, of any other floating charge over assets other than those covered by the first charge is as described earlier. Accordingly, the holder of any other such floating charge must make his own decision as to whether it is appropriate at that time in his own interests to appoint a receiver under that charge and whether it should be the same receiver as already appointed under the first charge. In these circumstances where the charges cover different assets the provisions as to precedence among receivers do not apply.

1 Chapter 1, paras 1.61 to 1.63.

Extent of security

2.30   On appointment, a receiver, on being satisfied that his appointment has been validly made, requires to investigate immediately the assets covered by the charge under which he has been appointed and, if there are other charges, to investigate at an early date the ranking of the floating charge with any other such charges. The only circumstances in which immediate consideration of the ranking position would be necessary would be if a different person was appointed receiver by the holder of another floating charge, the reason being the provisions relating to precedence among receivers.[1] The question of the assets covered by the floating charge raises no particular problem in the normal course when the charge extends over the company's whole property and assets. It can raise problems, however, where the assets covered are restricted.

1 Insolvency Act 1986, s 56.

2.31   In the receivership of an English manufacturing company whose premises were situated in Scotland the receiver on examination of the floating charge under which he was appointed found that it was granted over the company's property and undertaking with the exception of 'heritable, real and leasehold' property and certain other specified current assets. The intention had been that the floating charge should extend over the company's plant and machinery but as the majority of such plant and machinery was beyond dispute heritable in nature the charge failed to achieve this object because of the exception.

2.32   In another case in practice, involving the receivership of a Scottish company, the floating charge contained in a debenture in favour of an English institution contained general words of charge over its property and undertaking and then proceeded to state that the 'charge hereby created shall be a first fixed charge on the heritable freehold and leasehold property of the company wheresoever situate and the fixed plant fixtures and machinery therein and thereon and a first floating charge as to all other property and assets'. In the absence of a heritable security in statutory form no fixed security existed over the company's heritable property and because of the particular wording of the charge document the floating charge, contrary to the intention, did not extend over such property.

Reduction of unfair preferences and assets acquired after attachment of floating charge

2.33   The question of whether or not a floating charge attaches to the assets resulting from the reduction of an unfair preference (or fraudulent preference as it was formerly described) has never been decided in Scotland. An unfair preference in the case of a company can only be reduced on the company's winding-up and so if a floating charge exists it will have crystallised either on such winding-up or on the earlier appointment of a receiver by the holder of the charge. In an English case[1] the joint liquidators of a company recovered moneys from a creditor who had been fraudulently preferred. The company had granted a floating charge in favour of one of its creditors who claimed unsuccessfully, that such charge attached to the moneys so recovered. The court's decision was that:

(1) at the date of the crystallisation of the charge, the moneys which had been paid to the preferred creditor no longer formed part of the assets and undertaking of the company; and
(2) such moneys recovered by the liquidators were impressed in their hands with a trust for the creditors.

1 *Re Yagerphone Ltd* [1935] Ch 392.

2.34   In the absence of any judicial authority in Scotland, the *Yagerphone* decision[1] is considered by some to be authority for the proposition that in Scotland also the proceeds of assets coming to a company from the reduction of a fraudulent preference or unfair preference are not attached by a floating charge and so become available for the other creditors. This view has been questioned however.[2] There has also been a decision[3] which, while not dealing with the precise point, at least affords guidance.

1 *Re Yagerphone Ltd* [1935] Ch 392.
2 D P Sellar 'Floating Charges and Fraudulent Preferences' 1983 SLT 253.
3 *Ross v Taylor* 1985 SLT 387.

2.35   The facts in the *Ross v Taylor* case[1] were that shortly before the appointment by the holder of a floating charge of a receiver over a company's whole property and assets, certain goods were sold to a loan creditor and the invoiced value of such goods was applied in reduction of the company's indebtedness to such creditor. After the receiver was appointed, he persuaded the creditor (under threat of challenge as a fraudulent preference on winding-up) to return the goods to the company and the question was whether the goods (or the proceeds of their sale by the receiver) fell to be attached by the floating charge or were available for the general body of creditors. The argument for the liquidator was that on the appointment of a receiver the floating charge, in terms of section 13(7) of the Companies (Floating Charges and Receivers) (Scotland) Act 1972,[2] attached to the property then subject to the charge. In the case of new assets coming to the company after the date of appointment of the receiver, as these did not form part of the company's property at the time the floating charge attached to such property, they were not attached by the floating charge. The case of *Re Yagerphone Ltd*[3] was quoted as authority for this proposition.

1 1985 SLT 387.
2 See now the Insolvency Act 1986, s 53(7).
3 [1935] Ch 392.

2.36   The opinion of the court was delivered by the Lord President who stated that the court had found that the case of *Re Yagerphone Ltd*[1] did not afford any reliable assistance in the solution of the problem which was before the court, in that it turned upon its own facts and the particular terms of the debenture in question. In the court's opinion the problem before it fell to be resolved upon a proper construction of section 13(7) of the 1972 Act[2] read together with the scope of the charge as defined in the instrument creating it. The floating charge was expressed to relate to the whole assets of the company, present and future, while the instrument was in force. Accordingly, the true question was not 'what was the property comprised in the company's property and undertaking on the date of the receiver's appointment?' but 'what was the property subject to the charge on the date of the receiver's appointment?' The answer to that question was to be found in the instrument creating the charge. Upon a proper construction of that instrument, the charge was over the whole of the property existing and from time to time emerging and it followed that under the particular provisions of the floating charge, the goods which were re-acquired after the receiver's appointment fell under the attachment of the charge. Any property which came into the company's hands after the appointment of the receiver would be attached and available, if need be, for realisation by the receiver.

1 [1935] Ch 392.
2 See now the Insolvency Act 1986, s 53(7).

2.37   The Lord President in his judgment went on to say that even if the court was wrong in so saying, there was a further reason for holding that the goods reacquired by the company after the receiver's appointment should fall under the attachment of the charge. Counsel for the liquidator had correctly accepted that under section 13(7) of the 1972 Act,[1] the charge did not attach only to the particular items of property held by the company on that date and that goods acquired by the company by purchase or conversion of other goods, while the receiver carried on its business, would fall under the attachment. In the circumstances, the simple position was that items of stock and trade were reacquired by the company on credit terms, in effect by means of an additional loan from the creditor. The powers of a receiver included the power to borrow and, in the court's opinion, no material distinction was to be found between the acquisition of stock in trade by immediate payment and the acquisition of stock in trade on credit terms.

1 See now the Insolvency Act 1986, s 53(7).

2.38   The second question put to the court in *Ross v Taylor*[1] was, if the goods or the proceeds thereof did not form part of the company's assets at the date of appointment of the receiver, on the liquidation of the company would the floating charge recrystallise to the effect that any acquirenda since the date of the receiver's appointment would fall within the assets covered by the floating charge for distribution purposes in such liquidation? The court answered the question in the affirmative on the grounds that the floating charge, on the commencement of a winding up, attached to the property then comprised in the company's property and undertaking and had effect as if it were a fixed security over such property.

1 1985 SLT 387.

2.39   The wording of what are now section 463(1) of the 1985 Act and sections 53(7) and 54(6) of the Insolvency Act 1986 should be contrasted. The first of these sections provides in effect that on winding up, a floating charge created by the company attaches to the property then comprised in its property and undertaking, or any part of the same, whereas the other two sections provide that on the appointment of a receiver, the floating charge attaches to the property then subject to the charge. There is an argument, however, that a company's undertaking includes the right to acquired property.

Ranking of charges

2.40   The ranking of floating charges both amongst themselves and in relation to fixed charges is governed by the provisions of section 464 of the 1985 Act and this topic is dealt with in Chapter 8.

Chapter 3

Powers, liabilities and agency of receiver

Powers contained in charge

3.01 A receiver has, in relation to the property attached by the floating charge under which he is appointed, the powers (if any) contained in the instrument creating the charge in addition to the statutory powers referred to in paragraph 3.02. If a creditor taking a floating charge considers that these statutory powers are likely to be deficient to any extent, then such deficiencies can be remedied by incorporating further powers in the instrument creating the charge. For example, the statutory powers in the 1972 Act did not include the power to call up unpaid capital nor the power to compromise with creditors equivalent to that given to liquidators[1] and it was previously not unusual to include such powers in the instrument creating the charge. As the not infrequent practice of receivers of hiving-down the business (or part of it) prior to its sale to a new subsidiary formed or acquired for the purpose did not fall squarely within any of the statutory powers contained in the 1972 Act (although it is arguable that it is incidental[2] to the power of sale or disposal[3] of property covered by the charge), this led to cautious floating charge creditors incorporating in the charge the specific power to effect such an operation. Such additional powers were often expressed in the following terms:

(a) power to make any arrangement or compromise which the receiver may think expedient;

(b) power to call up all or any part of the company's uncalled capital all in accordance with the power conferred on its directors under and in terms of its articles of association;

(c) power to acquire or incorporate another limited company to which may be transferred the whole or any part of the property charged and to carry on or concur in carrying on the company's business or any part thereof in name of such other company.

Section 471 of the 1985 Act was amended by section 57(f) of the Insolvency Act 1985 and consolidated in section 55 of, and Schedule 2 to, the Insolvency Act 1986 and powers on these lines have now been included among a receiver's statutory powers.

1 CA 1985, ss 539(1)(f), 598(1) and (3).
2 Insolvency Act 1986, Sch 2, para 23.
3 Ibid para 2.

Statutory powers

General

3.02 A receiver has, in addition to any powers contained in the instrument creating the charge, certain statutory powers[1] in relation to the property attached by the charge under which he is appointed in so far, however, as these statutory powers are not inconsistent with any provision contained in such instrument. These statutory powers are summarised in the succeeding paragraphs.

1 Insolvency Act 1986, Sch 2.

To take possession of property

3.03 Power to take possession of, collect and get in the property from the company or liquidator of the company or any other person and to take proceedings as may seem to him expedient for that purpose.

This power lies at the root of the receiver's functions, the primary purpose of which is to realise on behalf of his appointer the assets subject to the floating charge with a view to satisfying the claim of the holder. It enables a receiver to take control and possession of property of the company to which the charge has attached to enable him to satisfy the debt of the floating charge creditor after satisfaction of prior claims in accordance with the statutory scheme of distribution contained in section 60 of the Insolvency Act 1986. It enables him,[1] for example, to collect book debts due to the company by taking proceedings in the name of the company.

1 *McPhail v Lothian Regional Council* 1981 SLT 173; *Taylor, Petitioner*, 1982 SLT 172; *Forth & Clyde Construction Co Ltd v Trinity Timber & Plywood Co Ltd* 1984 SLT 94 and see 'The Receiver and Book Debts 1982 SLT (News) 129, and Chap 2, paras 2.09 to 2.11.

3.04 In the event of a liquidator having been appointed on the winding-up of the company whether before or after the receiver's appointment, the liquidator is required to deliver to the receiver the property covered by the charge by virtue of this statutory power conferred on the receiver.[1] In *Manley, Petitioner* the company in question was ordered to be wound-up by the court (the date of commencement of the winding-up being 15 November 1982) and following his appointment as provisional liquidator Mr Manley was appointed official liquidator on 6 December 1982. On the same date the Bank of Scotland, in whose favour the company had granted a floating charge over its whole property and undertaking, appointed a receiver. Following upon a demand by the receiver on the liquidator in terms of section 15(1)(a) of the 1972 Act[2] to deliver up the property of the company to the receiver, the liquidator presented a petition for directions (1) as to whether the liquidator was obliged to comply with the demand and (2) as to whether the liquidator or the receiver was primarily liable for the payment of the secured and preferential creditors of the company. On the first question, Lord Grieve decided that whether the receiver is appointed before or after the commencement of the winding-up his rights take precedence over the rights of the liquidator and he is entitled to take control of the property of the company in order to satisfy the debt of the holder of the floating charge. The argument put forward by the liquidator was that as the receiver's power to take possession of the company's property was subject to the rights of any person who had effectually executed diligence, this power was subject to the rights of the liquidator being a person who had effectually executed diligence by virtue of the terms of section 327(1)(a) of the Companies Act 1948[3] which rendered the winding-up equivalent to complete and effectual diligences of the forms mentioned in that section. Lord Grieve, however, having taken the view that the purpose of section 327[3] was to cut down and equalise diligences and that the liquidator was not a person who had effectually executed diligence on the property of the company, then went on to state – 'The whole scheme of the 1972 Act is to give him (the receiver) precedence over the liquidator in the administration of the whole property of the company, even if appointed after the commencement of the liquidation'. On the second matter on which directions were sought, namely whether the liquidator or the receiver was primarily liable for the payment of the secured and preferential creditors, Lord Grieve decided the receiver was so liable. The payment of such debts is considered later in this book.[4]

1 *Manley, Petitioner* 1985 SLT 42.
2 See now the Insolvency Act 1986, Sch 2, para 1.
3 Ibid s 185(1)(a).
4 See Chap 9 para 9.13 et seq.

To sell property

3.05 Power to sell, feu, hire out or otherwise dispose of the property by public roup or private bargain, with or without advertisement.
This power gives a receiver a wide discretion as to the method of disposal of the property covered by the charge but in exercising this power the receiver has a duty to take reasonable care.[1] It has been stated obiter[2] that 'in exercising his powers [the receiver] must no doubt, for example, exercise care to see that he does not realise company assets for less than the value which might reasonably be expected to be obtained'. Subject to this duty, a receiver exercises his commercial judgment backed up by whatever professional or other advice he may consider it prudent to obtain in deciding what method to employ in disposing of the company's business and assets either as a going concern or otherwise.

1 See para 3.43.
2 *Forth & Clyde Construction Co Ltd v Trinity Timber & Plywood Co Ltd* 1984 SLT 94 per the Lord President at 97.

To borrow

3.06 Power to raise or borrow money and grant security therefor over the property.
A receiver if he wishes to carry on the company's business almost invariably requires to obtain temporary facilities from a bank, normally the one appointing him and this power enables him to do so. As a receiver

is personally liable on any contract entered into by him, except in so far as the contract otherwise provides,[1] unless expressly agreed with the bank to the contrary, such borrowing becomes the personal liability of the receiver although there is, however, a right of indemnity out of the property attached by the charge.[2] It is a power which requires to be exercised with caution as the property could prove to be insufficient to satisfy such right of indemnity. If a receiver wishes to arrange a bank facility in circumstances where he is unwilling to accept personal liability he should make the position clear to the bank and obtain, if the bank is agreeable, the express written confirmation of or an indemnity from the bank that he will be relieved of personal liability. In view of the provisions of section 57(2) of the Insolvency Act 1986 only with such confirmation or such an indemnity will the receiver be relieved of personal liability should the proceeds of sale of the company's property prove insufficient to meet the indebtedness so incurred to the bank. While in practice it is unusual for a receiver to create a security over the property (save for the case where the receiver procures the creation by a subsidiary of a charge, usually a floating charge over its property following the hive-down to such subsidiary of part or all of the business of the company in receivership), the existence of this power should not be overlooked when acquiring property from a receiver. A small amendment was made to this power by the Insolvency Act 1985 and is now consolidated in section 57(2) of the Insolvency Act 1986 presumably intended to cover the situation where a receiver wishes to raise funds other than by borrowing.

1 Insolvency Act 1986, s 57(2).
2 Ibid ss 57(3) and 60(1)(d).

Appointment of solicitor and other advisers

3.07 Power to appoint a solicitor or accountant or other professionally qualified person to assist the receiver in the performance of his functions. Most receivers in Scotland are accountants and so are more concerned with the appointment of a solicitor to assist in the receivership. As legal problems can arise in the early days of a receivership, particularly in relation to retention of title claims by suppliers and to employee redundancies, it is always advisable and particularly so in major receiverships that in his own interests the receiver should appoint a solicitor as soon as possible after his own appointment. Experienced receivers often ascertain in advance of appointment that a solicitor or one of his partners will be available to assist. As well as being in a position to seek immediate legal advice when confronted by a problem, the receiver is then able to instruct the solicitor so appointed to confirm without delay the validity of his appointment. As in the case of voluntary liquidations, the accounts of solicitors do not normally require to be submitted for taxation.

3.08 In major receiverships, particularly where a group of companies is involved, the sale of the business or businesses is a major undertaking requiring skill and expertise on the receiver's part but which can often only be carried through with the help of adequate back-up staff with insolvency experience and various professional and other advisers. In these circumstances the gathering together at an early date of a team of such persons will hopefully result in a successful outcome to the receivership from the point of view of both the receiver's appointer and also other creditors and employees.

Power to seek directions

3.09   Power to apply to the court for directions.
This could be a very useful power available to a receiver where in the course of carrying out his function he is uncertain as to the validity of any procedural or other step which he is proposing to take. As far as is known however the power has so far rarely been used by receivers. The court means the court having jurisdiction to wind up the company.[1] Prior to the Insolvency Act 1985 the power to seek directions was included in a receiver's powers contained in section 471 of the Companies Act 1985. While this power has been removed from that section it in effect remains, being now covered by the provisions of section 63 of the Insolvency Act 1986. That section provides that the court, on the application of either the holder of a floating charge by virtue of which a receiver has been appointed or a receiver, may give directions to the receiver in respect of any matter arising in connection with the performance of his duties.

1 CA 1985, s 744 and also the Insolvency Act 1986, s 120.

Legal proceedings

3.10   Power to bring or defend any action or other legal proceedings in the name and on behalf of the company.[1]
A receiver in so doing is acting as agent for the company without incurring any personal liability, other than to agents whom he may instruct in this connection without excluding such liability, although, in that event he is entitled to be indemnified out of the property subject to the floating charge. A receiver is not infrequently faced with the problem as to whether or not to continue to defend an action raised against the company prior to his appointment. This is particularly so if, for example, the claim is for substantial damages against which the company may either not be insured at all or only partially insured and on the information then available to the receiver there may be surplus funds after satisfaction of the floating charge creditor's claim. In that event while the claimant in the damages action if successful would only be entitled to an ordinary ranking in the liquidation, the effect of such a claim succeeding might be to substantially reduce the dividend to other ordinary creditors. As, in these circumstances, it is the ordinary creditors who are likely to be affected and not the receiver's appointer, one course open to the receiver is to petition for the company's winding up and to leave the liquidator to take a decision on whether or not the action should continue to be defended. If there are no prospects of surplus funds after satisfaction of the floating charge creditor, the receiver has no interest to see any such action defended. Should, however, the outcome of any such action against the company have a potentially adverse effect on any guarantee obligations of directors, the receiver should take no steps prejudicial to the interests of such persons without their authority and should afford them

the opportunity of continuing the defence of the action. The same considerations apply in the case of proceedings raised against the company after the receiver's appointment.

1 Eg to collect a debt due to the company (*Taylor, Petitioner* 1982 SLT 172) and to recall an arrestment (*Forth & Clyde Construction Co Ltd v Trinity Timber & Plywood Co Ltd* 1984 SLT 94).

Arbitration

3.11 Power to refer questions affecting the company to arbitration.
This is presumably as an alternative to legal proceedings, subject to the agreement of the other party or parties. If the company is party to an agreement which specifically restricts the resolution of disputes to arbitration then in the event of such a dispute arising before or after the appointment of a receiver there is no alternative to arbitration in these circumstances.

Insurances

3.12 Power to effect and maintain insurances in respect of the company's business and property.
It would of course only be prudent for the receiver to ensure that the property subject to the floating charge is adequately insured. In practice, most receivers have special arrangements with insurance companies for block cover immediately upon intimation to the insurance company concerned of the receiver's appointment.

Use of company seal

3.13 Power to use the company's seal.
This is in contrast to the former position in England where a receiver used not to have this power unless where appointed other than by the court, such power was conferred in the debenture under which he was appointed. However, section 48(1) of the Insolvency Act 1985 provided that an administrative receiver shall enjoy the powers conferred by the debentures by virtue of which he was appointed and such powers shall be deemed to include, except in so far as they are inconsistent with any of the provisions of those debentures, inter alia power to use the company's seal.[1]

1 See Insolvency Act 1986, s 42 and Sch 1, para 8.

Execution of deeds

3.14 Power to do all acts and to execute in the name and on behalf of the company any deed, receipt or other document.

Negotiable instruments

3.15 Power to draw, accept, make and endorse any bill of exchange or promissory note in the name and on behalf of the company.

Agents and employees

3.16   Power to appoint agents where appropriate and to employ and dismiss employees.[1]

1 For employees generally see Chap 6.

Work on property

3.17   Power to do everything necessary (including the carrying out of works) for the realisation of the property covered by the charge.

Incidental payments

3.18   Power to make any payment necessary or incidental to the performance of his functions.

Carrying on of business

3.19   Power to carry on the company's business (or any part of it). Whether or not to exercise this power is a decision with which a receiver of a trading company is faced immediately on his appointment and one which he takes after careful consideration of all relevant factors, bearing in mind his potential personal liability if he trades at a loss.

Leases and tenancies

3.20   Power to grant or accept a surrender of a lease or tenancy of any property covered by the charge and also to take a lease or tenancy of any property required or convenient for the company's business.
In exercising any of these powers a receiver will of course require to consider carefully his own position in relation to personal liability.

Arrangements or compromises

3.21   Power to make any arrangement or compromise on behalf of the company.
This power was not previously contained in a receiver's statutory powers having been introduced by the Insolvency Act 1985[1] along with the following powers: to call up uncalled capital, form subsidiaries and transfer to them the business of the company or any part of it and any of the property covered by the charge. The power to make an arrangement or compromise could be useful in that it confers on a receiver a degree of flexibility in dealing with creditors.

1 Section 57(f); see now the Insolvency Act 1986, Sch 2, para 16.

Uncalled capital

3.22   A receiver now has statutory power to call up any uncalled capital of the company.

Establishment of subsidiaries

3.23   A receiver likewise now has statutory power to establish subsidiaries and to transfer to such subsidiaries the whole or any part of the company's business or the property covered by the charge. As already mentioned,[1] these powers are often exercised by receivers in carrying out 'hiving-down' operations as a prelude to the sale of the whole or part of the company's business.

1 Chapter 3 para 3.01.

Ranking in debtors' estates

3.24   Power to rank and claim in the bankruptcy, insolvency, sequestration or liquidation of debtors of the company, to receive dividends and to accede to trust deeds for creditors of any such debtors.

Change of registered office

3.25   Power to change the situation of the company's registered office.[1] This is often necessary in that the receiver frequently sells or vacates the company's premises and this power enables him to alter the company's registered office without reference to its directors.

1 Insolvency Act 1986, Sch 2, para 22.

Winding-up petitions

3.26   Power to present or defend a petition for the winding up of the company.

The most normal circumstances in which a receiver will wish to petition for the company's winding up are where there is a surplus remaining after satisfaction of the floating charge creditor's debt but which is clearly insufficient to meet in full the claims of ordinary creditors. In that event the receiver will present such a petition to the court on the grounds that the company is unable to pay its debts[1] whereupon the court on being satisfied that such is the case[2] will duly make a winding-up order and appoint a liquidator to whom the receiver may then deliver the surplus.[3] The court will normally be satisfied as to the company's inability to pay its debts on the production with the winding-up petition of a statement of assets and liabilities prepared by the receiver revealing such as the position.

1 Insolvency Act 1986, s 122(1)(f).
2 Ibid s 123(1)(e).
3 Ibid s 60(2)(c).

3.27   A receiver may also wish to petition for winding up, having obtained the prior approval of the floating charge creditor if there is unlikely to be sufficient to meet such creditor's debt in full, where it appears that the company has granted an unfair preference or gratuitous alienation. In that event the statutory period or periods within which unfair preferences are rendered invalid should be kept in mind.[1] The question of whether the assets recovered by such proceedings are attached by the floating charge or become available for the ordinary creditors is dealt with elsewhere.[2]

1 Insolvency Act 1986, s 243.
2 See Chap 2 paras 2.33 to 2.39.

3.28 There may also come to the notice of a receiver circumstances which justify the winding up of the company in order to bring into play those sections of the 1985 Act which provide remedies or create offences only in the event of the company's winding up.[1]

1 See also the Company Directors Disqualification Act 1986.

3.29 In one case[1] a receiver of a company's whole assets opposed the grant of the first order for intimation, advertisement and service of a petition presented by an ordinary creditor on the grounds that both this and any subsequent winding-up order would be detrimental to the interests of the secured creditors and sought the summary dismissal of the petition. It was held, however, that where a creditor seeks a winding-up order on the ground that a company is unable to pay its debts, the petition should not be summarily dismissed unless there are compelling reasons for so doing.

1 *Foxhall & Gyle (Nurseries) Ltd, Petitioners* 1978 SLT (Notes) 29; see also Chap 4 paras 4.59 to 4.66.

3.30 Ordinary creditors of a company in receivership, particularly where their claims in aggregate amount to a substantial sum, often used either themselves to petition or fund a petition by the receiver for the company's winding up, even where there was little hope of a surplus after satisfaction of the floating charge creditor's claim, for the sole purpose of obtaining VAT bad debt relief which used not to be available on receivership alone. A receiver had no real grounds for opposing such a petition by ordinary creditors. Such bad debt relief has however been extended to receivership.[1]

1 Finance Act 1985, s 32; the Administrative Receivers Value Added Tax Certificates (Scotland) Rules 1986, SI 1986/304 (s 23) which came into operation on 1 April 1986.

Incidental powers

3.31 Power to do all other things incidental to the exercise of his powers. This gives to a receiver general ancillary powers necessary for the exercise of the specific powers referred to in the foregoing paragraphs.

Powers subject to rights of certain persons

3.32 The powers of a receiver are subject to the rights of certain persons, namely:
(a) any person who has effectually executed diligence on all or any part of the property of the company prior to the receiver's appointment; and
(b) any person holding a fixed security or floating charge over all or any

part of the property of the company ranking prior to or *pari passu* with the floating charge under which the receiver was appointed.[1]

1 Insolvency Act 1986, s 55(3).

3.33   The effect in relation to diligence of attachment or crystallisation of the floating charge on a receiver's appointment has already been discussed.[1] The powers of a receiver are also subject to the rights of any person holding a charge over property of the company ranking prior to or *pari passu* with the floating charge under which the receiver was appointed. The rights of heritable creditors are unaffected by the appointment of a receiver and while another floating charge does not automatically attach or crystallise on the appointment of a receiver other than under it, the holder has then grounds for himself appointing a receiver to enable his charge to attach or crystallise.

1 Chapter 2 paras 2.13 to 2.17.

3.34   Where a receiver sells or wishes to sell property covered by the floating charge under which he has been appointed and is unable to obtain the consent of either a creditor who has effectually executed diligence or who holds a prior or *pari passu* ranking security he may apply to the court for the appropriate authority.[1] Such an application was made by joint receivers where an inhibiting creditor would not consent to the sale of heritable property.[2]

1 Insolvency Act 1986, s 61; see also Chap 7 paras 7.35 to 7.37.
2 *Armour and Mycroft, Petitioners* 1983 SLT 453.

Disposal of interest in property

3.35   Section 61 of the Insolvency Act 1986 consolidated section 477 of the 1985 Act, which in its original form re-enacted section 21 of the 1972 Act. The principal sub-section provides[1] that where a receiver sells or disposes or wishes to sell or dispose of property of the company which is subject to the floating charge by virtue of which he was appointed and, which is subject to the security or interest of a prior, *pari passu* or postponed ranking creditor or is property affected by effectual diligence and the receiver cannot obtain the consent of such creditor or the person entitled to such effectual diligence, the receiver may apply to the court for authority to sell or dispose of the property. The court, on such an application may authorise such sale or disposal on such terms or conditions as it thinks fit.[2]

1 Insolvency Act 1986, s 61(1).
2 Ibid s 61(2).

3.36   Section 61(3) of the Insolvency Act 1986 provides that in the case of an application where a fixed security over the property or interest in question which ranks prior to the floating charge has not been met or provided for in full, the court shall not authorise the sale or disposal of the property or interest in question unless it is satisfied that the sale or disposal would be likely to provide a more advantageous realisation of the company's assets than would otherwise be effected. Section 61(4) further provides that it is a condition of authorisation that (a) the net proceeds of the disposal, and (b) where those proceeds are less than such amount as may be determined by the court to be the net amount which would be realised on a sale of the property or interest in the open market by a willing seller, such sums as may be required to make good the deficiency, are applied towards discharging the sums secured by the fixed security. If there are two or more fixed securities, the above provisions apply in the order of priority of such fixed securities.[1]

1 Insolvency Act 1986, s 61(5).

3.37   Section 61(8) of the Insolvency Act 1986 empowers the receiver to grant to a purchaser an appropriate document of transfer and such document has the effect, or where recording, intimation or registration of such document is a legal requirement for completion of title to the property, then such recording, intimation or registration has the effect, of disencumbering the property of the security and freeing the property from the diligence executed upon it.

3.38   In terms of section 61(6) of the Insolvency Act 1986, the receiver is required to send to the Registrar of Companies within fourteen days of the granting thereof, a copy of the authorisation certified by the clerk of court obtained pursuant to section 61(2). If the receiver fails to do so without reasonable excuse, he is liable to a fine and, for continued contravention, to a daily default fine.[1] Finally, it is expressly provided in section 61(9) that nothing in the section prejudices the right of any creditor of the company to rank for his debt in the winding up of the company.

1 Insolvency Act 1986, s 61(7).

Persons dealing with receiver

3.39   A person who deals with a receiver in good faith and for value is not concerned to inquire whether the receiver is acting within his powers.[1] This does not however relieve such a person from satisfying himself that a receiver has been validly appointed, whether it is a sole or joint appointment and in the latter case whether the joint receivers can act individually or must act jointly.

1 Insolvency Act 1986, s 55(4).

Exercise of powers outwith jurisdiction

3.40   Section 7 of the Administration of Justice Act 1977 replaced section 15(4) of the 1972 Act with provisions to the effect that a receiver and/or manager appointed under the law of any part of the United Kingdom under a floating charge may exercise his powers in any other part of the United Kingdom in so far as their exercise is not inconsistent with the law applicable there. The equivalent provisions in the 1985 Act were contained in section 724 (now consolidated in section 72 of the Insolvency Act 1986). In the table of derivations to the 1985 Act, section 724 was stated to be derived from section 7 of the 1977 Act but the provisions are not reproduced precisely in that there are substituted for the references to the United Kingdom narrower references to Great Britain. Section 7 of the 1977 Act was however not repealed by the 1985 Act. Thus, for example, a receiver of a Scottish company may exercise his powers over property in England provided the exercise of any specific power is not inconsistent with the law of England, on which he would be well advised in the appropriate circumstances to take advice.

3.41   Prior to the repeal of section 15(4) of the 1972 Act the First Division of the Court of Session had occasion to consider[1] the terms of that section which was restricted to extending the powers of a receiver or manager of an English company to property in Scotland in so far as not inconsistent with the law of Scotland. The facts, put simply, were that following the appointment of a receiver over the whole property of an English company a Scottish creditor having obtained decree in Scotland arrested funds in the hands of a Scottish based debtor of the company and followed this up with an action of furthcoming. In dismissing the action the court held that the appointment of the receiver in England had the effect of attaching or crystallising the floating charge as a fixed security over the company's property both in England and Scotland and that as the creditor had not by the arrestment effectually executed diligence prior to the receiver's appointment, such arrestment was of no effect.

1 *Gordon Anderson (Plant) Ltd v Campsie Construction and Anglo Scottish Plant Ltd* 1977 SLT 7.

Duties of receiver

General

3.42   A receiver appointed over the property of a Scottish company operates within the statutory framework of Chapter II (sections 50–71) of Part III of the Insolvency Act 1986. His powers are defined[1] and he is required to distribute moneys received by him in accordance with mandatory directions.[2] However, nowhere in the Insolvency Act 1986 are the duties of a receiver laid down. This is not to say, however, that in exercising his powers a receiver has no duties to any particular party.

1 Insolvency Act 1986, Sch 2.
2 Ibid s 60.

Duty to company

3.43   In the first place a receiver is appointed by or at the instigation of the holder of a floating charge, which charge on the appointment of the receiver becomes equivalent to a fixed charge over the property subject to such charge.[1] This is the only method by which the holder of a floating charge can realise his security for the debt owed to him by the company. The receiver then proceeds to exercise his powers on behalf of the holder of the floating charge whose security by then has become in effect a fixed charge.[1] That being the position it must be assumed that a receiver has duties to the company similar to those which the holder of a fixed security exercising a right of sale has towards the debtor. He must exercise his powers without negligence and generally exercise care in disposing of assets for at least the value which they might reasonably be expected to realise.[2] In England, a receiver has a similar duty of care.[3] It is in addition well established under the law of Scotland that the holder of a heritable security is required to have regard for the interests of both the debtor and postponed heritable creditors[4] and that contractual provisions entitling a creditor to sell security subjects at such price as he might think fit cannot relieve him of the obligation to exercise a power of sale bona fide and with regard to the interests of the debtor and to obtain a fair price.[5] Such contractual provisions might also be open to challenge as being unreasonable in terms of the Unfair Contract Terms Act 1977. In addition, sections 25 and 35 of the Conveyancing and Feudal Reform (Scotland) Act 1970 impose a duty on certain heritable creditors exercising a power of sale.

1 Insolvency Act 1986, s 70.
2 *Forth and Clyde Construction Co Ltd v Trinity Timber and Plywood Co Ltd* 1984 SLT 94, Lord President Emslie at 97.
3 *Re B Johnson & Co (Builders) Ltd* [1955] Ch 634; *Cuckmere Brick Co Ltd v Mutual Finance Ltd* [1971] Ch 949; *American Express International Banking Corpn v Hurley* [1985] 3 All ER 564; *Watts v Midland Bank plc* [1986] BCLC 15.
4 *Beveridge v Wilson* 1829 7 S 279 and *Kerr v McArthur's Trs* 1848 11 D 301.
5 *Rimmer v Thomas & Sons Ltd* 1967 SLT 7.

3.44 It has also been suggested,[1] correctly it is thought, that a duty to take reasonable care would be imposed on a receiver in delict on the basis of a decision[2] which established that a prima facie duty of care arises where there is sufficient relationship of proximity between parties such that, in the reasonable contemplation of the one, carelessness on his part may be likely to cause damage to the other. This view has received judicial support in England.[3]

1 R J Reed 'Aspects of the Law of Receivers in Scotland – The Receiver's Duty of Care' 1983 SLT 261, para 262.
2 *Junior Books Ltd v Veitchi Co Ltd* 1982 SLT 492.
3 *American Express International Banking Corpn v Hurley* [1985] 3 All ER 564 per Mann J at 569.

3.45 A receiver in Scotland is, in addition, deemed to be the agent of the company in relation to the property covered by the floating charge under which he is appointed[1] and may only be removed by the court on cause shown and not, where appointed by the holder of a floating charge, by his appointer.[2] These statutory provisions must, it is thought, imply a fiduciary relationship with consequential duties to the company and other parties whose interests are liable to be affected in the exercise by the receiver of his powers.

1 Insolvency Act 1986, s 57.
2 Ibid s 62(3).

3.46 On the basis of an English Court of Appeal decision[1] it is possible that, in the event of a receiver being considered to be in breach of his duty towards the company, proceedings by the company instituted by the directors would be competent. A derivative action by the directors and majority shareholders would, however, not appear to be competent.[2]

1 *Newhart Developments Ltd v Co-operative Commercial Bank Ltd* [1978] QB 814.
2 *Watts v Midland Bank plc* [1986] BCLC 15.

Duty to guarantor

3.47 While there is no direct Scottish authority on the subject, the court in England has considered on more than one occasion the question of whether a receiver owes a duty of care towards a guarantor of the company's debt. In two earlier decisions[1] the court held that a receiver did not owe a duty of care to a guarantor but these decisions were not followed in a subsequently reported decision.[2] The Court of Appeal held in that later case that a receiver when realising assets owed a duty both to the company and to a guarantor of its debt to take reasonable care to obtain the best possible price which circumstances permit, a decision which has since been followed.[3]

1 *Barclays Bank Ltd v Thienel* (1978) 247 Estates Gazette 385; *Latchford v Beirne* [1981] 3 All ER 705.
2 *Standard Chartered Bank Ltd v Walker* [1982] 1 WLR 1410.
3 *American Express International Banking Corpn v Hurley* [1985] 3 All ER 564.

3.48 The Court of Appeal decision was referred to in a subsequent Scottish case[1] on consideration by the court of whether a creditor realising a security owes a duty to a guarantor. In his judgment Lord Ross reserved at the procedure roll stage a plea to the relevancy of averments that a creditor had acted in breach of a duty of care owed to a guarantor. In considering this question Lord Ross reached the conclusion that the proposition on which the *Standard Chartered* decision was based was not inconsistent with Scottish authorities and that he could not at that stage hold that a creditor in Scotland owed no duty to act reasonably in a question with a guarantor. If a floating charge creditor in Scotland wishes his security realised, this, in the absence of winding up, can only be effected by the appointment of a receiver. Such receiver operates within a statutory framework and although the agent of the company (as was the receiver in the *Standard Chartered* case) exercises his powers on behalf of the holder of the floating charge which by then has become equivalent to a fixed security. It is, accordingly, reasonable to assume that the receiver owes similar duties to those of the creditor on whose behalf he exercises these powers and, if this assumption is correct, it is suggested that the court in Scotland would be likely to reach the same decision as that in the *Standard Chartered* case. In the *Standard Chartered* case it was also held

that the debenture holder might also be attached with responsibility for
the receiver's actions if it were shown that such holder had interfered with
the conduct of the receivership, a view subsequently approved in another
case.[2] It is also suggested that a receiver in Scotland could be liable to a
guarantor in delict on the basis that, in the reasonable contemplation of
the receiver, negligence on his part in disposing of assets could damage
the guarantor.[3]

1 *Lord Advocate v Maritime Fruit Carriers Co Ltd* 1983 SLT 357.
2 *American Express International Banking Corpn v Hurley* [1985] 3 All ER 564.
3 *Junior Books Ltd v Veitchi Co Ltd* 1982 SLT 492.

Duty to creditor other than holder of floating charge

3.49   If it is accepted that a receiver has a duty to exercise his powers
without negligence[1] it is suggested that this duty must extend to any
creditors of the company whose interests are liable to be affected by his
actings. In the *Standard Chartered* case[2] Lord Denning did say (at 1416) –
'The receiver owes a duty not only to the company, but also to the
guarantor, to exercise reasonable care in the disposal of the assets. I say
nothing about creditors. We are not concerned with them today'. If a
receiver, however, disposes of the assets attached by the floating charge in
a way which can clearly be demonstrated resulted in a value being realised
which was less than could reasonably be expected, he has acted negligently and the relationship of the other creditors of the company, is, it is
suggested, in such proximity to him that it must have been in his
reasonable contemplation that lack of care on his part was likely to cause
damage to them.

1 *Forth & Clyde Construction Co Ltd v Trinity Timber & Plywood Co Ltd* 1984 SLT 94.
2 *Standard Chartered Bank Ltd v Walker* [1982] 1 WLR 1410.

Agency and liability of receiver

Agent of company

3.50   A receiver is deemed to be the agent of the company in relation to
the property of the company attached by the charge under which he is
appointed.[1] Accordingly, the receiver in exercising his powers in relation
to such property, providing he makes clear that he does so as receiver of
the company, is acting as an agent for a disclosed principal and both his
liability and that of the company are, subject to the provisions of the
Insolvency Act 1986, governed by the principles and rules of the law of
agency. However, a receiver (including one whose powers are suspended
on the appointment of another receiver under a prior ranking floating
charge) is personally liable on any contract entered into by him in the
performance of his functions, except in so far as the contract otherwise
provides,[2] but, in the event of personal liability not being excluded in
terms of the contract, the receiver has a right of indemnity against the
property covered by the charge.[3] This right of indemnity is postponed to
the rights of fixed charge creditors ranking in priority to or *pari passu* with

the floating charge and creditors who have effectually executed diligence.[4] The provisions of section 473 of the 1985 Act (as amended by section 58 of the Insolvency Act 1985[5] do not limit any right to indemnity which the receiver would have apart from them, nor limit his liability on contracts entered into or adopted without authority nor confer any right to indemnity in respect of that liability. A contract entered into without authority is presumably one outwith the receiver's powers, statutory or otherwise.

1 Insolvency Act 1986, s 57(1).
2 Ibid s 57(2).
3 Ibid s 57(3).
4 Ibid s 60(1)(a) and (b).
5 Now ibid s 57.

3.51 As a result of an amendment introduced by the Insolvency Act 1985, and now consolidated in the Insolvency Act 1986,[1] a receiver is also now personally liable (without the right to exclude such liability) on any contract of employment adopted by him in the carrying out of his functions while at the same time a receiver is not to be taken to have adopted such a contract by reason of any act or omission within fourteen days of his appointment.[2] During such period only a positive act of adoption will, it is assumed, make a receiver personally liable on such a contract but on the expiry of the period if a receiver continues any contract of employment there will, presumably, be an assumption that he has adopted such contract and thus accepted personal liability notwithstanding the provisions of section 57(4) to the effect that a receiver is not by virtue of his appointment alone personally liable on a pre-receivership contract to which the company is a party. This amendment effectively reverses an English Court of Appeal decision.[3]

1 Insolvency Act 1986, s 57(2).
2 Ibid s 57(5).
3 *Nicoll v Cutts* (1985) Times, 20 May.

3.52 The statutory framework of section 57(1) and (2) of the Insolvency Act 1986 appears to be that, in the first place, in relation to the property covered by the charge, the receiver is agent of the company. However, should he enter into any contract in the exercise of his powers, not directly in relation to such property, he is personally liable under such contract unless it provides otherwise and remains so even if his powers are suspended on the appointment of a receiver by the holder of a prior ranking floating charge. He is also personally liable on any employment contract adopted by him. For practical reasons, this is the only way in which a receiver could effectively exercise his powers as third parties and employees would be reluctant to enter into or continue contracts with the receiver (eg for the supply of goods or services) unless there was a reasonable guarantee of payment in full by the receiver undertaking personal liability. Put another way, entering into or continuing a contract with the agent of a disclosed but apparently insolvent principal without such agent accepting personal liability does not make commercial logic. It is arguable that, by virtue of the provisions of section 57(1) of the Insolvency Act 1986, the receiver's personal liability is excluded in respect of the exercise of his powers as receiver directly in relation to the property covered by the charge (eg in selling such property) but it is prudent of a receiver who wishes to exclude such personal liability to expressly so contract to the effect that he does so as receiver and without any personal liability. A receiver incurring personal liability must bear in mind the limitations on his indemnity: namely his right of relief extends to the property covered by the charge alone and then only after satisfaction of the rights of certain other creditors. The maximum value of his indemnity is, therefore, the net value of such property after deducting the claims of such creditors. This point assumes greater importance where the receiver carries on the company's business after his appointment, particularly if this involves carrying on or entering into substantial contracts in, for example, the construction or engineering industries.

3.53   A receiver whose powers are suspended as a result of the subsequent appointment of another receiver by the holder of a prior ranking floating charge is entitled to retain property (including letters or documents) and not to release them to the other receiver until given by him a valid indemnity in respect of any expenses, charges and liabilities he may have incurred in the performance of his functions as receiver.[1] This indemnity is similarly limited and the first receiver should in obtaining such an indemnity take into account the fact that the property in question will cease to be under his control and that its value may decrease under the control of the other receiver.

1 Insolvency Act 1986, s 56(5).

Termination of agency on winding up

3.54   Whereas the office of receiver was only introduced into the law of Scotland in 1972, it has existed in England for over a century with the appointment being capable of being made both by the court and also out of court, the framework of the law being a mixture of common law and statute law. A receiver appointed by the court in England being an officer of the court is neither an agent for the company nor the debenture holder whereas a receiver appointed out of court is usually, in terms of the debenture by virtue of which he is appointed, agent for the company. This agency, in the case of an administrative receiver appointed out of court, is now given statutory authority[1] and is a general agency not restricted to the assets covered by the charge although of course an administrative receiver is defined as a receiver or manager of the whole or substantially the whole of a company's property.[2]

1 Insolvency Act 1986, s 44(1)(a).
2 Ibid s 29.

3.55   In England, it has been judicially established that the liquidation of the company, voluntary or compulsory, terminates the agency of a receiver appointed out of court[1] but not the receivership powers which the receiver remains entitled to exercise in the name of the company,[2] albeit subject to personal liability in that he is then acting as a principal. Statutory authority for the termination of such agency has also now been introduced[3] but at the same time provisions governing a receiver's liability on contracts similar to the equivalent Scottish provisions have also been introduced[4] as have statutory powers which include power to carry on the business of the company.[5] It has also been held in England[6] that on the termination of such agency a receiver who continues to act may in certain circumstances become the agent of his appointer, for example, if his appointer treats him as such. As a result, it was held, in the absence of an express exclusion in the agency contract, that the appointer was entitled to an indemnity from the receiver in respect of negligence on his part.

1 *Gosling v Gashell* [1897] AC 575; *Thomas v Todd* [1926] 2 KB 511.
2 *Barrows v Chief Land Registrar* (1977) Times, 20 October.
3 Insolvency Act 1986, s 44.
4 Ibid s 44(1)(b) and (c).
5 Ibid s 42(1) and Sch 1.
6 *American Express International Banking Corpn v Hurley* [1985] 3 All ER 564.

3.56   The Cork Committee noted[1] that there had been much criticism of the rule that the receiver's agency came to an end on liquidation which they stated caused particular difficulty in the case of a compulsory liquidation since its effect was in general to terminate all contracts of employment with the result that if the receiver decided to retain employees, he became personally liable for their wages and for any redundancy pay if they were later made redundant. As a result some receivers, rather than face the prospect of such personal liability, considered it prudent to close down the business. While an administrative receiver's agency will in England still terminate on winding-up the receiver will be entitled to an indemnity out of the assets of the company in respect of any personal liability incurred on any contract entered into by him in performance of his functions.[2]

1 Report of the Review Committee on Insolvency Law and Practice (Cmnd 8558) para 453 et seq.
2 Insolvency Act 1986, s 44.

3.57   Receivership was introduced in Scotland by the 1972 Act (which was consolidated in the 1985 Act and again in the Insolvency Act 1986) and from the outset all receivers in Scotland, whether appointed by the holder of a floating charge or by the court, have operated within a statutory framework. A receiver in Scotland is agent of the company in relation to the property attached by the charge under which he is appointed and, subject thereto, is, except where otherwise provided, personally liable on contracts which he enters into and is also personally liable without exception on contracts of employment adopted by him. One of the receiver's powers is to carry on the company's business or any part of it. The exercise of this power remains unaffected by the liquidation of the company, his rights whether appointed before or after liquidation taking precedence over the rights of the liquidator.[1]

1 *Manley, Petitioner* 1985 SLT 42.

3.58   The Insolvency Act 1986 does not in Chapter II of Part III (which deals with Receivers in Scotland) include a provision equivalent to that contained in section 44(1)(a) terminating the agency of an administrative receiver in England on the liquidation of the company. That being the case and in the absence of any judicial authority it is not clear whether the statutory agency of a receiver in Scotland is terminated by liquidation. What is clear, however, is that notwithstanding the liquidation of the company he is still entitled to exercise all the powers conferred on him which includes the power to carry on all or part of the company's business and dispose of property subject to the charge. In this connection the provisions of section 127 of the Insolvency Act 1986, which avoid any disposition of the company's property after the commencement of the winding-up, do not apply as the 'disposition' is the charge under which the receiver was appointed.[1] In exercising such powers, however, a receiver must accept personal liability on all contracts entered into by him after liquidation whether or not they relate to the property covered by the charge, unless of course the contract expressly provides otherwise. Against that background he should bear in mind the extent of his indemnity against the property subject to the charge and that his actings will be liable to scrutiny by the liquidator.

1 *Re Park Ward Co* [1926] Ch 828.

Pre-receivership contracts

General

3.59 Any contract entered into by the company prior to the appointment of a receiver continues in force in spite of such appointment, unless the contract specifically provides for termination on receivership. Such provision may render a contract voidable only, entitling the other party to terminate should he so wish. In the event of a contract so continuing, the receiver does not automatically by his appointment alone incur personal liability[1] although it will be a question of fact in each case whether the receiver has by his actings adopted any particular contract so as to incur personal liability unless specifically excluded. As a result of an amendment introduced by the Insolvency Act 1985[2] it is now provided that a receiver is personally liable on any contract of employment adopted by him in the carrying out of his functions.

1 Insolvency Act 1986, s 57(4).
2 See now the Insolvency Act 1986, s 57(2).

3.60 This provision that a pre-receivership contract remains in force does not mean that a receiver must implement the contract as agent of the company and the court will not necessarily force him to do so.[1] In *MacLeod v Alexander Sutherland Ltd* the pursuer had sold ground to a company under and in terms of missives, one of the terms of which was that the purchasing company should perform certain specified building and construction work on the ground. The purchasing company had a receiver appointed over its whole assets before any of this work was carried out and ceased trading. The pursuer raised an action of specific implement against the company and, failing implement, damages. As a matter of fact, implement of the contract was impossible in that having ceased trading the company had no materials or employees. The court refused to grant decree of specific implement, stating that it would be inequitable to grant such a decree against a company which could act only through the agency of a receiver and which, if the receiver should decline to act, would inevitably be in contempt of court in respect of an omission which it would be powerless to remedy.

1 *MacLeod v Alexander Sutherland Ltd* 1977 SLT (Notes) 44.

3.61 Similarly in England the court has refused to grant decree of specific implement.[1] In *Airline Airspares Ltd v Handley Page Ltd* it was held that a receiver appointed out of court was in a better position than the company in relation to current contracts and, having decided not to implement a pre-receivership contract, could not be prevented from following a course of action which would effectively repudiate or frustrate a pre-receivership contract provided this would not adversely affect the company's goodwill or the realisation of its assets.

1 *Airline Airspares Ltd v Handley Page Ltd* [1970] Ch 193.

3.62 The contract in *Airline Airspares Ltd v Handley Page Ltd*[1] obliged the company to pay commission on the sale of a certain aircraft which it manufactured, the action being raised by the plaintiff on learning of the proposed sale by the receiver of such aircraft manufacturing business. These decisions should be contrasted with two subsequent English decisions[2] where the court did make orders for specific performance. However, in the earlier of these cases the contract in question was for the sale of land, the vendor company having been placed in receivership before completion had taken place and in the later the contract involved options over land. These decisions can be distinguished in that the contracts were ones which could have been subject to an order for specific implement whether or not receivership had intervened and in addition there was no question of the receiver having to incur any personal liability as the only alternative to being in contempt of court.

1 [1970] Ch 193.
2 *Freevale Ltd v Metrostore (Holdings) Ltd* [1984] 1 All ER 495 and *Telemetrix plc v Modern Engineers of Bristol (Holdings) Ltd* [1985] LS Gaz R 1561.

3.63 A receiver in Scotland is empowered to carry on the company's business or any part of it[1] and is given wide powers of sale and power to 'do all other things incidental to the exercise' of his powers.[2] It, accordingly, is thought that only in limited circumstances (such as in the *Freevale* case)[3] would the court prevent a receiver in Scotland from taking action which would effectively frustrate a pre-receivership contract.

1 Insolvency Act 1986, Sch 2, para 14.
2 Ibid para 23.
3 *Freevale Ltd v Metrostore (Holdings) Ltd* [1984] 1 All Er 495.

3.64 Failure by a receiver to implement a contract entered into by a company prior to his appointment renders the company liable to damages for breach of contract but any such claim is entitled to an ordinary ranking only. In these circumstances the receiver in the exercise of his powers, in declining as agent for the company to implement a pre-receivership contract, should not have any liability to the other party to the contract for inducing its breach. In considering whether or not to implement a pre-receivership contract a receiver must, nevertheless, exercise reasonable care in reaching his decision to avoid a possible claim on the grounds of breach of duty in that his action had a detrimental effect on the realisation of the company's assets which could have been avoided had he exercised such care. Having decided to implement a pre-receivership contract the receiver in adopting it and carrying it through becomes effectively personally liable although with a right of relief against the assets covered by the charge.

Leases

3.65 One of the commonest pre-receivership contracts encountered is a lease of the company's premises. A receiver of a company occupying premises under a lease is under no obligation to implement the lease and, unless specifically agreeing to do so, he incurs no personal liability for the tenant's obligations. Should the receiver wish to continue the company's occupation for a limited period, for example, until he removes the company's property, he should endeavour to reach agreement with the landlord that he is responsible for rent alone for that limited period from the date of his appointment on the clear understanding that he accepts no personal liability whatsoever for any other of the company's obligations as tenant. More detailed reference to this subject is contained in Chapter 4 paragraphs 4.14 to 4.22.

Effect of suspension of receiver's powers

3.66 As has been seen a receiver who accepts personal liability under a contract entered into by him[1] remains so liable even though his powers are suspended.[2] In addition, any contract entered into by a receiver (whether or not he accepted personal liability), subject always to its terms, continues in force notwithstanding the suspension of the receiver's powers.[3]

1 Chapter 3 para 3.64.
2 Insolvency Act 1986, s 57(2).
3 Ibid s 57(7).

Receiver's liability if appointment invalid

3.67 If a person appointed by the holder of a floating charge to act as a receiver takes possession of and deals with assets of a company and subsequently his appointment is discovered to be invalid, he will incur personal liability. This could arise if the floating charge by virtue of which he was appointed turned out for one reason or another to be invalid because in these circumstances it would not attach to the assets, thereby depriving the person appointed of any right to exercise the powers of a receiver. Some essential step in the appointment might be invalid thus rendering the appointment itself invalid[1] or the instrument of appointment might have been invalidly executed.

1 *Elwick Bay Shipping Co Ltd v Royal Bank of Scotland Ltd* 1982 SLT 62.

3.68 Should however the appointment of a person as receiver by the holder of a floating charge be discovered to be invalid whether as a result of the invalidity of the instrument of appointment or otherwise, the court may order such holder to indemnify the person so appointed against any liability arising solely by reason of the invalidity of the appointment.[1] These provisions only apply in the case of a receiver appointed by the holder of a floating charge and not in the case of a receiver appointed by the court.

1 Insolvency Act 1986, s 63(2).

3.69 Notwithstanding such a provision for indemnity, it is in the interests of every person appointed as a receiver to satisfy himself that the appointment is valid. It is also in the interests of the appointer to ensure the appointment is valid. One basis for challenging the validity of a floating charge is under section 245 of the Insolvency Act 1986.[1] The provisions of section 245 render invalid in certain circumstances floating charges created within specified periods prior to the making of an administration order or the company going into liquidation. Should a person appointed receiver be in any doubt as to the validity of his appointment, whether by reference to these provisions or otherwise, he should consider his position carefully before dealing with the company's assets and whether it might be appropriate to seek an indemnity from his appointer before acting.

1 See Chap 8 para 8.57 et seq.

Chapter 4

Typical legal problems arising on receivership

Contracts

General position

4.01 Although in terms of sections 53(7) and 54(6) of the Insolvency Act 1986 on the appointment of a receiver the floating charge by virtue of which he was appointed attaches to the property then subject to the charge, the appointment per se does not necessarily affect any contract in existence on the date of his appointment. As has been stated in Chapter 3 paragraph 3.59, section 57(4) of the Insolvency Act 1986 goes further by making it clear that any contract entered into by or on behalf of the company prior to the appointment of a receiver continues in force (subject to its terms) notwithstanding that appointment but the receiver does not by virtue only of his appointment incur any personal liability on any such contract. The result is that the receiver has to decide in any circumstances where a contract continues in force whether or not to proceed with the particular contract and, if he decides to do so, he must exclude his personal liability.[1] New rules apply in relation to contracts of employment as a result of the Insolvency Act 1986.[2]

1 Insolvency Act 1986, s 57(2).
2 Ibid s 57(5).

4.02 Some contracts particularly those which have been formally constituted will usually provide a catalogue of events of default (which may or may not include receivership) entitling the innocent party on the occurrence of any one of such events of default to invoke certain remedies. If nothing is said in the contract, the presumption will be that section 57(4) of the Insolvency Act 1986 will apply. An event entitling one party to invoke certain remedies, such as the right to terminate the contract, is to be distinguished from rights arising from a breach of contract which may give rise to a claim for damages or specific implement or rescission of the contract.

4.03 In terms of section 57(1) of the Insolvency Act 1986, a receiver is deemed to be the agent of the company in relation to such property of the company as is attached by the floating charge by virtue of which he was appointed. In terms of section 57(2), a receiver (including a receiver whose powers are subsequently suspended under section 56) is personally liable on any contract entered into by him in the performance of his functions except in so far as the contract otherwise provides. The Insolvency Act 1985 introduced the words 'and on any contract of employment adopted by him in the carrying out of those functions' which fall within the exception.[1] The Insolvency Act 1986[2] also provides that for the purposes of section 57(2) of that Act a receiver is not to be taken to have adopted a contract of employment by reason of anything done or omitted to be done within fourteen days after his appointment. If a receiver continues to employ any employee after the expiry of the fourteen day period the relative contract of employment will presumably be taken to have been adopted.

1 Those words are consolidated in the Insolvency Act 1986, s 57(2).
2 Insolvency Act 1986, s 57(5).

4.04   Hence, it is vitally important in contracts made by the receiver and also in relation to those contracts in existence on the date of appointment which are adopted or ratified by the receiver that the personal liability of the receiver should, where possible, be expressly excluded. Section 57(3) of the Insolvency Act 1986 does provide some relief in that a receiver who is personally liable by virtue of section 57(2) of that Act is entitled to be indemnified out of the property in respect of which he was appointed. However, that Act states that section 57 does not limit any right to indemnity which the receiver would have apart from it, nor limit his liability on contracts entered into or adopted without authority, nor confer any right to indemnity in respect of that liability. A discussion on the receiver's position in relation to personal liability and to contracts in existence on the date of his appointment is contained in Chapter 3 paragraphs 3.59 to 3.65.

Building contracts

4.05   Insolvency (which may or may not be involved on the appointment of a receiver) is not a ground of determination of a building contract unless the contract so provides. Determination is a remedy which is normally only available to an innocent party faced with a material breach of contract on the part of the other party but the parties can previously agree that certain breaches shall be deemed sufficiently material to justify determination. In practice, insolvency of the contractor usually results in a failure on the part of the contractor to perform, ultimately leading to determination on some ground but delay and expense will be incurred by the employer. Clause 25(2) of the Joint Contracts Tribunal Conditions 1963 Edition provides inter alia that, on the appointment of a receiver to the assets and undertaking of a contractor, the employment of the contractor, *not the contract* will be automatically determined forthwith subject always to the possibility of reinstatement on terms to be agreed. The interest of the employer is to get a completed building on time at no extra cost. The interest of the contractor and its receiver is to earn more upon the contract. The employer, failing agreement on reinstatement, has to find another contractor or enter into a new contract with the company and its receiver.

4.06 There have been instances where a receiver of a contracting company has negotiated a new contract on terms that the company accepts no liability for latent defects and the employer keeps the retention moneys but otherwise the company will complete on the same terms and conditions as previously save for an express exclusion of the employer's right of set-off in respect of claims arising from work carried out on the pre-receivership contract. In these circumstances, the company acting by its receiver will be unwilling to agree to complete by a specific date, if at all possible, and, in view of the terms of section 57(2) of the Insolvency Act 1986, an express exclusion of the receiver's personal liability must be provided in the new contract. The employer may well accept such terms and conditions because in this way he should minimise his loss in that the contract should be completed reasonably quickly at no additional cost and, as the employer would rank as an unsecured creditor against the company if it goes into liquidation, his position is not further weakened even if latent defects do appear and there are no funds for unsecured creditors. As part of such arrangements, the employer would normally be entitled to keep the retention money which is reasonable in the circumstances. The benefit to the receiver is additional earnings for the company thus increasing the aggregate realisations. Such additional earnings will arise from work done under the new contract to which can be added earnings due under the old contract, together with sums certified under further certificates for work done under the old contract but not valued as at the date of its determination.

4.07 A deed of novation is the deed under which a contracting company in receivership, subject always to the consent of the employer as *delectus persona* is involved in such contracts, assigns its rights and obligations under a building contract to another contractor who takes over the role of contractor and completes the work. There may also be a side agreement between the contractor acting by its receiver and the substitute contractor as to the terms upon which the contractor in receivership 'sells' the contract and the new contractor 'buys' it. Obviously, if there is no advantage to the receivership in completing or if no one will buy the contract, the receiver simply allows the determination machinery to operate or positively intimates as agent of the company in receivership and without incurring any personal liability that the company will not fulfil the contract. In due course (if appropriate) the employer and also any sub-contractors will be left to make claims in the liquidation (if any) of the company.

Continuing essential contracts

4.08 On his appointment a receiver is immediately faced with normal commercial contracts (principally supply contracts both for goods and for services) which require to be continued, even if only on a short-term basis until the receiver decides whether to carry on the business with a view to its sale. Most receivers within a day or two of their appointment despatch letters (a style of which is given in Appendices 5 and 6) to all known debtors and creditors advising them of the appointment of a receiver. Such a letter to creditors should make it clear that the receiver is acting as agent of the company without personal liability and that debts due by the company in receivership before the appointment of the receiver cannot be set off against debts to become due to the company after such appointment. If the creditor is prepared to continue to deal with the company on such a basis, no difficulty arises.

4.09 However, commercial realities do assume importance in such circumstances and it would be naive to assume that in such situations all creditors will necessarily agree to continue on such a basis. Many creditors will insist on a personal undertaking from the receiver that payment will be forthcoming in respect of goods and services provided to the receiver and if the receiver is prepared to give such an undertaking he is entitled to be indemnified out of the property in respect of which he was appointed in terms of section 57(3) of the Insolvency Act 1986. In these circumstances, most receivers will be prepared to undertake personal liability for goods and services ordered by the receiver or an authorised member of his staff.

4.10 Some creditors, although not statutorily preferential creditors, used to be placed in a very privileged position:[1] monopoly suppliers such as the Electricity Boards, the Gas Boards and British Telecom were, notwithstanding their unsecured status, in a position to force a receiver to settle all pre-receivership arrears otherwise the service would be forthwith discontinued. If the receiver had any hope whatsoever of selling the business as a going concern or even conducting an orderly run-down, circumstances dictated that such creditors were settled at least in some degree. While most receivers were extremely reluctant to be pressurised in such a way, any such action taken in these circumstances required to be capable of being justified to the holder of the floating charge or indeed any other creditor on the grounds that such action was likely to maximise the realisation of the company's assets. Some receivers were sometimes disposed in such circumstances to threaten to publicise the attitude of the particular monopoly supplier in question and link its attitude with a possible loss of jobs or failure to conclude an agreement for the sale of the business to a purchaser. Obviously, such a possible course of action was not a legal matter and was a decision for each individual receiver to consider in the particular circumstances. The government has, however, stated that such monopoly suppliers will no longer be entitled to enjoy their privileged position and section 233 of the Insolvency Act 1986 gives statutory effect to that principle.[2]

1 A very helpful section on this subject appears in the Report of the Review Committee on Insolvency Law and Practice (Cmnd 8558) Chapter 33 paragraph 1451 to 1462 inclusive.
2 See Chap 7 para 7.39.

Leases – company in receivership as landlord

4.11 In cases where the company in receivership is the landlord under a valid lease, there is, save as follows, little change occasioned by the appointment of a receiver. The tenant is entitled to rely on his real right under and in terms of the Act 1449 c17 (whether or not receivership has occurred) and provided the four essentials of a valid lease are present (viz

(1) the lease (if for more than one year) is in writing (2) there is a rent (3) there is an ish or term of expiry and (4) the tenant has entered into possession), the tenant has nothing to fear from the receiver. The only qualification in relation to the tenant's position would be if in granting the lease the landlord had breached an obligation not to grant a lease, referred to in the standard conditions contained in a standard security, in favour of a heritable creditor who had either called up that security or, pursuant to the provisions of a floating charge in his favour, had appointed a receiver with a view to realisation of the property subject to the heritable security whereupon the lease would be regarded as of no effect.[1] Although the point does not appear to have been judicially considered in Scotland, it is suggested that the grant of a lease by a landlord who has created, prior in date to such lease, a floating charge over the whole property and undertaking which contains a prohibition upon such landlord from granting such a lease, would fall to be determined in a manner similar to a breach of the equivalent provision in the standard conditions contained in a standard security.

1 *Trade Development Bank v Warriner & Mason (Scotland) Ltd* 1980 SLT 49, 223; *Trade Development Bank v David W Haig (Bellshill) Ltd* 1983 SLT 107; and *Trade Development Bank v Crittall Windows Ltd* 1983 SLT 107.

Right to receive rent

4.12   Questions sometimes arise as to whether the holder of a standard security or the receiver is entitled to the benefit of rent received from the tenant in the period from the appointment of the receiver until the property in question is finally sold either by the holder of the standard security exercising his power of sale or by the receiver. It is thought that any such rent is properly due for the receivership account unless (a) the holder of the standard security has called up his standard security in terms of section 19 of the Conveyancing and Feudal Reform (Scotland) Act 1970 (the 1970 Act) and in these circumstances any such rent in the period after such holder has taken possession of the subjects will be due to the holder of the standard security; or (b) the holder of the standard security has exercised his rights under the 1970 Act on insolvency of the debtor and obtained an order from the court that such rent is due to him as such holder.

4.13   For the purpose of paragraph 9(2)(c) of Schedule 3 to the 1970 Act insolvency includes the appointment of a receiver. In practice, a receiver, in these circumstances, will usually recognise the rights of a heritable creditor without involving the creditor in the expense of court proceedings.

Leases – company in receivership as tenant

4.14   As previously mentioned in paragraph 4.01, the appointment of a receiver does not per se involve any personal liability on the receiver under any pre-existing contract. For liability to fall on the receiver for the tenant's obligations under a lease, some positive act or acts on the part of the receiver would be required eg the payment of rent or continuance of trading from the premises (as a principal as opposed to an agent for the company).

4.15   On the other hand, the landlord may be entitled to irritate the lease either because of the appointment of the receiver (if there is provision to that effect in the lease) or for non-payment of rent. For this reason, most receivers who wish to continue in occupation of the company's premises even for a relatively short time (often only for the purpose of realising assets) will open negotiations with the landlord and perhaps write to the landlord (a style of which appears in Appendix 7) whereby the receiver undertakes without adopting the lease to pay rent for the period of his occupation but accepts liability for none of the tenant's other obligations. Such an arrangement is normally acceptable to a landlord as at least it guarantees some rental payments thereby minimising his loss pending a new tenant being found.

4.16   It has sometimes been questioned whether a receiver is obliged to enter such arrangements with a landlord in relation to the payment of rent. On a strict legal basis, the receiver is not obliged to pay rent provided he has not taken positive action, by, for example, continuing to trade from the premises or actually paying rent in either case as a principal as opposed to as an agent of the company, thereby rendering himself personally liable. However, against the background of the irritancy rights of landlords as a matter both of goodwill and commercial sense, most receivers will be prepared to pay rent on the basis set out above in the hope of securing the co-operation of the landlord while attempts are made to try to find a purchaser for the business.

4.17   Older leases (ie pre-1972) of property in Scotland are often defective from the landlord's point of view in that the appointment of a receiver is not usually included as a ground for termination of the lease. In these circumstances, provided the receiver reaches agreement with the landlord along the lines previously described and no other breach of the lease has taken place, the landlord cannot normally terminate the lease on receivership.

4.18   The decision in a leading case,[1] which highlighted the principle that a conventional irritancy cannot be purged, was one of the factors which led to less severe irritancy provisions being introduced into leases particularly in relation to the liquidation or receivership of the tenant. In the case in question, the House of Lords refused to allow an irritancy, incurred by the tenant's failure to pay an instalment of rent on the due date required under the lease, to be purged by an offer of payment of the arrears in full made shortly after that date and before the action was raised to irritate the lease.

1 *Dorchester Studios (Glasgow) v Stone* 1975 SC(HL) 56

4.19   As a result, many commercial leases now contain wording qualifying irritancy rights along the following lines:
    'in the case of the Tenants (or the Guarantors, if any) going into

liquidation (other than for the purposes of reconstruction or amalgamation) or in the case of a receiver being appointed over the whole assets and undertaking of the Tenants the Landlords shall not exercise such option of forfeiture on the grounds of appointment of a liquidator or of a receiver unless and until they shall have allowed the liquidator or receiver (as the case may be) a period of six months from the date of such appointment in which to dispose of the Tenants' interest in this lease [and only then if the liquidator or receiver (as the case may be) shall personally accept full responsibility for payment of rent (whether due in respect of a period occurring before or after the date of liquidation or receivership) and for performance of all the obligations on the part of the Tenants under this lease for a maximum period of six months from the date of such appointment (as the case may be) to the expiry of such period or, if earlier, the date of entry under such disposal.]'

4.20   While the inclusion in leases of such provisions restricting the exercise of irritancy rights has helped in receivership situations, few receivers have been enthusiastic about accepting, even for a limited period, personal liability for payment of rent and performance of the other obligations of the tenant. Depending upon the circumstances it has sometimes been possible for the receiver to re-negotiate the irritancy provisions with the landlord on the basis of a personal obligation by him to pay rent without accepting liability for any other obligations. However, the decision varies according to the circumstances and may be affected by, for example, the receiver's desire to dispose of the leasehold property which is secured by way of a standard security to the holder of the floating charge under which he was appointed. Unless he accepts some risk (and, probably, a full indemnity or at least a firm written undertaking from the holder of the floating charge) such standard security may prove to be totally worthless in the event of the landlord if so entitled irritating the lease. The Scottish Law Commission in their report dated 19 November 1982 on Irritancies in Leases[1] formed the view that if the relation of the irritancy to receivership was to be considered it would be more appropriately considered in connection with the law relating to receivers and not as a special case in the law of irritancy as such. Such view follows a suggestion to the Commission from the Institute of Bankers in Scotland to the effect that the particular considerations applicable to receivership might be regarded as justifying special provisions, to prevent an irritancy operating to the disadvantage of a receiver in cases where the company had been a tenant under a lease. The Report stated that it was not really very beneficial in the present economic climate to any of the parties involved if the lease automatically terminated on the appointment of a receiver when one of the objectives of receivership was to ensure the continuance of a business enterprise. It should be emphasised here that a lease does not automatically terminate on receivership and only if the lease entitles the landlord to do so, may he irritate the lease.

1   Scot Law Com No 75.

4.21   The position of tenants generally has however recently been improved by the imposition of statutory restrictions on the exercise of landlords' right of irritancy. Under the provisions of the Law Reform (Miscellaneous Provisions) (Scotland) Act 1985,[1] a landlord cannot irritate a lease if the tenant has failed to pay rent or make any other payment on or before the due date or such later date or within such period as may be provided for in the lease or if such failure is or is deemed by a provision of the lease to be, a material breach of contract unless, after the rent or other payment has become due, he has given the tenant not less than fourteen days' notice or such longer period as may be provided for in the lease requiring the tenant to pay and has stated that the lease will be irritated if he does not do so. The landlord is only entitled to irritate the lease if the tenant has not complied with the requirement specified in any such notice. In the case therefore of a tenant company in receivership the landlord will be unable to irritate the lease on the grounds of failure to pay rent or to realise some other payment alone without giving the requisite notice and then only if the receiver fails to pay within the requisite period. In relation to non-pecuniary obligations,[2] section 5 provides that a landlord is not entitled to rely on a provision in a lease which purports to terminate it, or to enable the landlord to terminate it, in the event of an act or omission by the tenant (other than such a failure as is mentioned in section 4(1)(a)) or of a change in the tenant's circumstances or on the fact that such act or omission or change is, or is deemed by a provision of the lease to be, a material breach of contract, if in all the circumstances of the case a fair and reasonable landlord would not seek so to rely. In the consideration of the circumstances of a case where an act, omission or change is alleged to constitute a breach of a provision of the lease or a breach of contract and the breach is capable of being remedied in reasonable time, regard shall be had to whether a reasonable opportunity has been afforded to the tenant to enable the breach to be remedied.[3]

1 Section 4 which came into force on 1 January 1986.
2 Section 5 which came into force on 1 January 1986.
3 LR MPS Act 1985, s 5(3).

4.22 The parties to a lease are not entitled to disapply for the lease any provision of sections 4 or 5[1] and it is not possible to contract out of these statutory provisions. If a lease entitled the landlord to irritate on the appointment of a receiver over any of the property and assets of a company tenant, this is a provision entitling the landlord to irritate on a change in the tenant's circumstances and so cannot be relied on by the landlord if in all the circumstances a fair and reasonable landlord would not seek so to rely. While the interpretation of these provisions by the courts cannot be anticipated it is thought that, in the absence of any special arrangement negotiated between the landlord and the receiver, if the receiver keeps rental and other payments up to date and procures compliance with the tenant's other principal obligations under the lease then, in these circumstances, a fair and reasonable landlord would not seek to rely on such an irritancy provision.

1 LR MPS Act 1985, s 6.

Receiver as custodian of goods

4.23 From time to time situations can arise where the receiver not only takes possession of the property and undertaking of a company but also acquires possession of goods belonging to third parties which are stored in a building or a factory occupied by the company in receivership. Questions may arise in the context of the exercise of the receiver's power of disposal of the building and assets of the company as to what provision should be made for those goods belonging to third parties.

4.24 One receiver in the authors' experience faced exactly this problem when he was appointed receiver in November of a boat repairing company whose main asset was a boatyard which contained several yachts being stored for the winter. Some, but not all, of the yacht owners had, before the appointment of the receiver, paid storage accommodation charges for the period to the spring of the following year. The receiver had various meetings with the yacht owners to ascertain whether they would be prepared to pay an extra amount over and above the storage charges to defray the costs of running the boatyard over the winter. No agreement could be reached and the receiver indicated to the yacht owners that he intended to write to them, stating that, with a view to the sale of the boatyard, he would be relinquishing responsibility for the yachts. The yachts were insured by the yacht owners and the receiver had no responsibility in that matter.

4.25 It is thought that, in such circumstances, the receiver could effectively exclude any liability for possible damage by writing a letter to the yacht owners (preferably despatched by recorded delivery) indicating that he would no longer be responsible for the safety of the yachts in the boatyard. The receiver would, in these circumstances, however, be well-advised to intimate to the yacht owners that supervision of the yachts would continue for a further reasonable period and would only become unavailable after a certain date (eg say, thirty days from the date of despatch of the letter). What is reasonable notice will obviously vary according to the particular circumstances but it is thought that a period of thirty days for making alternative arrangements to store a yacht is reasonable. On general principles of the law of negligence, the receiver, it is thought, would be obliged to show some degree of care for the yachts in the boatyard, foreseeability being now the general criterion for liability in negligence.[1]

1 *Junior Books Ltd v Veitchi Co Ltd* 1982 SLT 492.

4.26 The contract of storage described above would continue notwithstanding the appointment of the receiver[1] so that the receiver would not render himself liable under the contract unless he took positive steps to personally fulfil the terms of the contract. Specific implement would not necessarily be enforced against a receiver where he would be involved in accepting onerous obligations[2] and the yacht owner's claim if he were to suffer loss would rank as an ordinary claim against the company.

1 See para 4.01.

2 *MacLeod v Alexander Sutherland Ltd* 1977 SLT (Notes) 44; but see *Freevale Ltd v Metrostore (Holdings) Ltd* [1984] 1 All ER 495 and *Telemetrix plc v Modern Engineers of Bristol (Holdings) Ltd* [1985] LS Gaz R 1561.

4.27   The receiver in the circumstances mentioned above considered as an additional remedy taking an action for removal of the yachts, such removal to be effected by the yacht owners themselves or, alternatively, in the event of their failure to do so, by the receiver or his agents. As mentioned above, section 57(4) of the Insolvency Act 1986 protects the receiver provided he does not by some positive act undertake personal liability: however, raising an action for removal would have been a very positive act and the receiver could have been rendered personally liable if any damage to any of the yachts were to result from their removal by him or his agents. An additional problem was that the yachts were stored under and in terms of pre-receivership contracts and at least in some of the cases the yacht owners had paid the full storage charges and so had fulfilled all their obligations under their contracts with the company in receivership. An action against such yacht owners could well have been regarded by the court as being effectively an attempt to ratify a breach of contract on the company's part induced by the receiver and accordingly, any such action, it is thought, would have been unsuccessful.

Bill of lading

4.28   From time to time problems can arise in receivership situations in relation to title to goods delivered from foreign countries in which bills of lading are involved. Suppose, for example, that jute is supplied from India and the company in receivership normally obtained its supplies of jute from the suppliers' agent in Scotland. While a particular consignment of jute is on the high seas, the bill of lading is endorsed by the suppliers' agent in favour of the company prior to its receivership against payment by bank draft at ninety days sight. The receiver is appointed to the company a few days after endorsation of the bill of lading.

4.29   *Bell's Principles* state[1] that 'bills of lading are, by the law and usage of merchants, negotiable instruments passing to onerous bona fide indorsees and other holders untrammelled by any latent claim or exception'. Later on in the same paragraph he states that 'the indorsation and delivery of the bill of lading by custom of merchants passes the property of the goods which it represents'. In the supposed circumstances, title to the jute would pass when the bill of lading was endorsed by the suppliers' agent in favour of and delivered to the company in receivership provided the bill of lading was not marked 'not negotiable' or 'not transferable' and further provided that the contract between the supplier or his agent and the company in receivership did not provide otherwise.

1 Paragraph 417.

4.30   If payment was effected by the company in receivership accepting a bill of exchange when the bill of lading was delivered, then non-payment on maturity date of the bill of exchange by the company would merely give the suppliers' agent the right to sue the company in receivership, a claim which would only be entitled to an ordinary ranking. If payment was effected by bank draft, then the bank in question would be required to meet the obligation.

4.31   A further point should be noted in relation to the position where a consignment of goods is in course of transit and the bill of lading has already been endorsed in favour of and delivered to the company in receivership, thereby transferring the title to the goods. In these circumstances, the receiver could demand delivery from the carrier on presentation of the bill of lading.[1] Therefore, no question of retention would arise in relation to any claims which the suppliers' agent might wish to make but if the original supplier was unpaid, he would have a right of stoppage of goods in *transitu* by virtue of the terms of section 44 of the Sale of Goods Act 1979. Such right would, however, be defeated by a bona fide transfer of the bill of lading for value by endorsement in favour of the company in receivership.[2]

1 *Bell's Principles* para 417.
2 Sale of Goods Act 1979, s 47(2).

4.32   The position arising under the supposed circumstances mentioned above would of course be quite different if the bill of lading was endorsed with the instruction to deliver to the order of the sellers' agent's bank. Even if the company in receivership subsequently acquired possession of the goods, title would still vest in the seller or sellers' agents unless the bank of the sellers' agents authorised unconditional delivery of the goods to the company in receivership.

Intellectual property

4.33   It is not unusual for an inventor whose invention has been patented to enter into an agreement with a company for the future exploitation of that patent. Such an agreement might, in appropriate cases, provide for a lump sum payment to be made to the inventor on execution of the agreement and for royalties on an agreed basis to be remitted to the inventor for a period of time, all in consideration of the beneficial ownership of the patent being immediately transferred to the company subject to the company being obliged, on the happening of the usual events of default occurring (including the appointment of a receiver), to immediately re-transfer such beneficial ownership to the inventor.

4.34   On the appointment of a receiver the floating charge under which he was appointed, if over the whole assets of the company, would attach to the patent in the beneficial ownership of the company and at one time, on the basis of the only Scottish decision in point[1] the court might not in these circumstances have ordered specific implement of the provision for re-transfer of the patent, leaving the inventor with a claim for damages entitled only to an ordinary ranking.

1 *MacLeod v Alexander Sutherland Ltd* 1977 SLT 44.

4.35 However, it is by no means certain, as a result of two subsequent English decisions,[1] that a Scottish court would necessarily decide a receiver's responsibility for contracts in existence on the date of his appointment on the basis of the decision in *MacLeod v Alexander Sutherland Ltd*.[2] In the *Freevale* case,[3] a limited company had entered into a contract to sell land but the transaction was not completed before a receiver was appointed over the property and undertaking of the vendor company. The judge held (at 503) that the mere fact of receivership of the defendants afforded no defence to a claim for specific performance. On the basis of these two decisions the inventor, in the example above, might well be protected by his agreement with the company prior to the appointment of the receiver.

1 *Freevale Ltd v Metrostore (Holdings) Ltd* [1984] 1 All ER 495; and *Telemetrix plc v Modern Engineers of Bristol (Holdings) Ltd* [1985] LS Gaz R 1561.
2 1977 SLT 44.
3 See n 1 above.

4.36 It is thought that the decisive factor in assessing a receiver's position in such circumstances will be the nature of the contract in question. If the receiver is required to implement a contract which will involve him in no costs or personal liability of any materiality, it is suggested that the receiver will require to implement such a contract. If, on the other hand, the receiver is, for example, required to implement a major building or engineering project, it is thought that the court would not order specific implement on the receiver. The subject is, however, considered in more detail in Chapter 3 paragraphs 3.60 to 3.64.

Hire-purchase and leasing contracts

4.37 In almost every case, a receiver finds that the company has entered into hire-purchase and leasing contracts relating in some instances to some of the most valuable items of plant and machinery used by the company. In all of such contracts, title will remain (in the case of leasing contracts at all times) with the finance house until all payments due under the contract have been made. The floating charge does not accordingly attach to such items but the continued use of such items by the receiver may be vital if he is to continue the business and sell it as a going concern. The receiver, bearing in mind the provisions of section 57 of the Insolvency Act 1986, will, therefore, require to make early arrangements to continue the payments under such contracts pending the sale of the business unless, of course, the contracts specifically entitle the owner to terminate them on the appointment of a receiver and such right is exercised. If no sale of the business is envisaged, the receiver, acting as agent of the company in receivership and without incurring personal liability will usually request the owner of such plant and machinery to remove it.

4.38 It is not unusual to find where there are a number of hire-purchase contracts with a particular hire-purchase company, that under one of such contracts almost all the payments have been made to the hire-purchase company leaving a substantial equity value available to the company on payment of the outstanding balance. However, the hire-purchase company will often have included provisions in all such contracts with the company to the effect that if there is a substantial debit balance on one account, such debit balance may be offset against an account on which there is an equity value. It is important to check in every case the precise terms of each such hire-purchase contract.

4.39 If the receiver is successful in finding a potential purchaser for the company's business, he will in all probability, as agent of the company endeavour to reach some form of settlement with the finance houses involved so that the company will be in a position to sell as beneficial owner or assign to the purchaser its interests under hire-purchase or leasing contracts relating to its plant and machinery. A more advantageous settlement is often achieved if negotiated directly by the potential purchaser. The receiver is not in a good negotiating position in that his only interest is to dispose of the business and assets whereas a purchaser is in a better position in that he will be a potential source of ongoing business and will relieve the hire-purchase or leasing company from the necessity to make arrangements for the removal of the plant and machinery in question.

Right of third parties against insurers

4.40 A creditor of a company in receivership may find himself in a more favourable position than normally would be the case where a liability to such creditor is established, being a liability which has been insured against by the company. The Third Parties (Rights against Insurers) Act 1930 (the 1930 Act) provides that where, under any contract of insurance, a company is insured against liabilities to third parties which it may incur, then in the event inter alia of a receiver being appointed if any such liability is incurred by the insured, the rights of the insured against the insurer under the contract in respect of the liability shall, notwithstanding anything in any Act or rule of law to the contrary, be transferred to and vest in the third party to whom the liability was so incurred.[1]

1 Third Parties (Rights against Insurers) Act 1930, s 1.

4.41 The 1930 Act applies to Scotland and the word 'receiver' is also used in the English law sense of 'receiver or manager of a company's business or undertaking' although, when the 1930 Act was enacted, the appointment of a receiver was not, of course, competent under the law of Scotland. The 1930 Act covers the situation where, for example, a few days before the appointment of a receiver, the driver of one of the company's lorries negligently collides with a stationary private motor car belonging to a third party. If the company was adequately insured for such an eventuality, then the company's rights against the insurer would be automatically transferred to the owner of the private motor car.

4.42   One aspect of the 1930 Act is that an obligation is placed on a receiver by the terms of section 2(1) of the 1930 Act to give, at the request of any person claiming that the company in receivership is under a liability to him, such information as may reasonably be required by him for the purpose of ascertaining whether any rights have been transferred to and vested in him by the 1930 Act and for the purpose of enforcing such rights and any contract of insurance under the 1930 Act. If such information is given in terms of section 2(1) of the 1930 Act and discloses grounds for supposing that there may have been transferred to him rights against any particular insurer that insurer is subject to the same duty as is imposed on a receiver. There is also a duty in terms of section 2(3) of the 1930 Act to allow all contracts of insurance to be inspected and copies thereof to be taken.

Liens and hypothecs

Liens

4.43   In many receiverships the exercise of a lien is claimed by some person or other: it can range from a carrier of goods for his charges to a solicitor in respect of unpaid fees. In every case, it is essential to establish clearly the circumstances under which the alleged right of lien came into being. A right of lien exists where one person has goods in his possession for some purpose at the instance of another person and the first person declines to part with possession of such goods until his charges for work transacted or services rendered have been fully satisfied. Absolutely central to the existence of a valid lien is actual or constructive possession legally obtained and if such possession is lost, the lien ceases to exist.

Special lien and general lien

4.44   A distinction should be drawn between a special lien and a general lien. A special lien exists where the goods are in the possession of one party who is entitled to withhold delivery of such goods until satisfaction of his charges in respect of the particular contract relating to work done on the goods. An example of a special lien is where garage owners repair a vehicle belonging to a company over whose assets a receiver is subsequently appointed. The garage owners would be entitled to exercise a valid special lien over the vehicle for settlement of the costs of the particular repair. In the absence of contractual provisions to the contrary, it would not be competent for the garage owners to seek settlement of a whole series of accounts relating to other vehicles or, indeed, to earlier repairs to the particular vehicle.

4.45 On the other hand, a general lien exists where the person in possession of the goods can competently seek satisfaction of all outstanding claims arising out of a contractual arrangement or course of dealing and not simply be restricted to claims under the particular contract in question. Examples of general liens almost always arise from custom of certain trades and professions or from contract express or implied: viz the standard terms and conditions of the Road Haulage Association provide that a general lien will exist over goods in the possession of the carrier in respect of all outstanding claims against the party despatching such goods. On being met by a claim to such a lien, a receiver if he is satisfied that such a term has been incorporated into the contract of carriage and that a general lien can validly be claimed, will require to settle the outstanding claims to effect release of the goods. By so doing, he should be able to ensure that the carrier will complete the particular delivery or deliveries, the customers should be satisfied and also the receiver will have retained a great deal of goodwill which will be important if the receiver has any reasonable expectations of selling the business as a going concern.

4.46 What happens if the person claiming the lien factored his own debts? Can the lien be validly exercised? It is thought that a lien cannot in such circumstances be validly exercised because the sums due by the company in receivership are not actually owed to the person exercising the lien, provided the assignation of the debt to the factoring company has been duly intimated to the company in receivership. It is possible, but doubtful, that the benefit of the lien could be assigned to the factoring company by delivery of the goods held by the person claiming the lien but it is suggested that in these circumstances, as the exercise of the lien by the factoring company would take place after the appointment of the receiver, the company in receivership could not possibly be held to have consented to the assignation of the lien. On the other hand, as the right of lien arises by operation of law, it should not be necessary for the company to consent to the assignation of the lien. If the factoring company took possession of the goods before the appointment of the receiver, the factoring company would be able to argue with some prospects that a valid lien had been established. If possession is transferred to the factoring company after the appointment of the receiver, it must be considered doubtful whether a valid lien can be established by the factoring company. The rights of the various parties must be established as at the date of appointment of the receiver and the factoring company would, in addition, find it difficult to rebuff the argument of bad faith. It is understood that the position in England in such circumstances is that the lien is certainly capable of being assigned but there is considerable doubt as to whether a subrogated right in equity to the lien can be maintained unless with the consent of the company in receivership. However, for commercial reasons, it may be more advantageous for the receiver in the long term to recognise the lien to protect the business rather than rest on the legal position and risk expensive and lengthy delay to the detriment of the receivership.

4.47 From time to time, the solicitor who acted for the company prior to the appointment of the receiver seeks to enforce a lien over the miscellaneous documents, title deeds and other papers which he holds against settlement of his fees and outlays. The solicitor's lien is based on professional usage and is not enjoyed, for example, by accountants who are entitled only to exercise a right of lien for work transacted by them on a particular matter for which the papers were specifically given. Since the introduction under the Conveyancing and Feudal Reform (Scotland) Act 1970 of extracts as acceptable alternatives to original titles, the value of a solicitor's lien over title deeds in his possession is negligible and extends to the cost of obtaining appropriate extracts. However, there can be occasions when speedy delivery and examination of title deeds is vital to a successful quick sale of the business: and the receiver requires again to carefully consider his priorities. The importance or otherwise of any other papers will depend largely on the circumstances of the particular case. It should also be remembered that urgent and detailed assistance can often be obtained from the solicitor claiming the lien if some form of speedy settlement of his claim is agreed.

Maritime lien

4.48 Three types of lien may be involved where a receiver either finds a vessel in his custody or seeks to recover possession of a vessel from a third party on which work was carried out prior to his appointment. In the normal case, such a lien may be very critical in either recovering amounts due from the owner of the vessel or in ascertaining the net value of the vessel if in either case the vessel is subject to the rights of a mortgagee. In these situations, the types of lien could be (1) maritime lien or (2) statutory lien or (3) a possessory lien.

4.49 A maritime lien is restricted to claims for salvage, seamen's wages, damage caused by a vessel and the master's wages and disbursements. The right of maritime lien does not extend to repairs to a vessel.

4.50 A statutory lien arises out of the Administration of Justice (Scotland) Act 1956 which in itself was passed following two Brussels Conventions of 1952. Part V of that Act enumerates nineteen separate claims which may be classified as statutory liens and these categories include maritime liens. A statutory lien like a maritime lien is enforced by way of an action *in rem* but the attachment of the vessel for the purposes of the claim does not arise until either the action *in rem* has formally been raised or the vessel has been arrested. The statutory lien would be defeated in the event of a sale in good faith to a purchaser unless the action *in rem* was served before the date of sale. It is thought that a statutory lien competently secured by an action *in rem* would cover the cost of repairs to a vessel.

4.51 A possessory lien is available to a custodian of a vessel if repairs have been carried out to the vessel but payment has not been made. In order to enforce the lien, it is necessary that possession of the vessel should be withheld and therefore an action *in rem* as previously described would be the normal route. An action *in personam* is also competent to enforce a possessory lien and has been described in *McMillan's Scottish Maritime Practice* as a 'petitory action with arrestment of the ship [and] with conclusions for judicial sale'.

Copyright on drawings

4.52 A receiver may find a property development included in the assets attached by the floating charge which is perhaps in the early stages of construction or, although all necessary planning and building consents have been obtained, no actual construction has taken place. The receiver will have to decide the most beneficial course of action but bearing in mind his personal liability as receiver and the general potential liabilities hanging over a project of such magnitude, he will probably decide to dispose of the project on the most advantageous terms to the receivership. It is more than likely that architects, in particular, and other advisers will be owed substantial fees for work and services carried out prior to the date of appointment of the receiver. If the receiver decides to dispose of the project in its original form using the plans and documents already prepared, he should carefully consider that if he does so, he may be liable for breach of copyright.

4.53 It is, therefore, prudent in such circumstances for the receiver to engage independent and skilled project management advisers to assess the viability of the original proposals and comment upon alternative approaches. Obviously, if the project has already commenced, such assessment may not be possible and in these circumstances, if the original professional team is not to be re-engaged by the purchaser, some form of settlement may require to be arranged with them.

Hypothec and sequestration for rent

4.54 In many receiverships a receiver will find that the business of the company is conducted from premises on lease from a landlord to whom substantial pre-receivership arrears of rent are due. On the appointment of the receiver, the landlord may wish to secure his position rather than awaiting the disposal of the business to a purchaser who may or may not wish the lease assigned to it, a condition of consent to such assignation being normally payment of rental arrears. The landlord's common law remedy is to claim landlord's hypothec which secures one year's rent only and which extends to all corporeal moveable items situated in the premises and used for the purposes of the company's business. Such items as ordinary equipment, furniture, stock and finished goods are covered by a landlord's hypothec.

4.55 Until recently, it was thought that the right of hypothec was unaffected by the attachment or crystallisation of a floating charge and that the only (in many cases, decisive) qualification on the exercise of hypothec was the requirement under section 64 of the Taxes Management Act 1970 to pay off one year's outstanding tax as a preferential claim before enforcing the hypothec. Section 64(1) of the Taxes Management Act 1970 provides that:

'No moveable goods and effects belonging to any person in Scotland, at the time any tax became in arrear or was payable, shall be liable to be taken by virtue of any poinding, sequestration for rent, or diligence whatever, or by any assignation, unless the person proceeding to take the said goods and effects pays the tax so in arrear or payable . . .'

4.56 The words 'sequestration for rent' refer to the ordinary diligence of sequestration for rent.[1] In that case, Lord Kinnear, in interpreting a similar provision in section 7 of the Revenue Act 1884 said that the landlord was put in exactly the same position as other creditors in that his right to enforce payment of rent should not be disturbed by the privilege given to the collector of taxes. It has been established that the Crown[2] (in respect of taxes) and the rating authority[3] (in respect of rates) take precedence over the landlord's hypothec.

1 *Sinclair v Edinburgh Parish Council* 1909 SC 1353.
2 *County Council of Lanark v Hamilton's Trustees* 1934 SLT (Sh Ct) 51.
3 *Campbell v Edinburgh Parish Council* 1911 SC 280.

4.57 In many cases, the landlord took the matter no further on learning of the extent of one year's preferred tax or rates outstanding but it was still usual for a receiver, confronted by sheriff officers on the premises of the company ready to sequestrate for rent, to settle all outstanding arrears of rent rather than permit possible irritation of the lease and the expenses of resisting sequestration proceedings.

4.58 The right of hypothec, following upon the appointment of a receiver, has been affected by a decision of the sheriff court[1] in a case where a receiver was appointed over the whole assets and undertaking of a company. A month after the appointment of the receiver, the landlord of the leased premises occupied by the company sequestrated for rent. The receiver contended that as the floating charge had crystallised over the whole assets and undertaking of the company the action was irrelevant on the grounds that hypothec was not a fixed security in terms of the equivalent section of the 1972 Act (prior to the enactment of section 486 of the 1985 Act, now section 70 of the Insolvency Act 1986) nor an effectually executed diligence in terms of the equivalent section of the 1972 Act (prior to the enactment of section 471(2) of the 1985 Act, now section 55(3) of the Insolvency Act 1986). The landlords argued that they were doing no more than preserving their position in a competition with creditors of the company other than the holder of the floating charge. The court upheld the receiver's case and accepted the arguments that hypothec is neither a fixed security nor an effectually executed diligence. The decision has attracted some adverse comment and reference is made to articles in the Journal of the Law Society of Scotland 1983 at page 352 and in 1983 SLT 277 and also to Chapter 2, paragraph 2.16.

1 *Cumbernauld Development Corpn v Mustone Ltd* 1983 SLT (Sh Ct) 55.

Threatened winding-up petition

General

4.59 A receiver who wishes to sell a business as a going concern must do so in the expectation that a liquidator is not appointed on or prior to the date of sale. The appointment of a liquidator may, subject to certain exceptions relating to employees in some forms of liquidations, terminate all contracts and such an appointment is clearly unhelpful from the point of view of the sale of business, particularly in relation to taxation.[1]

1 Chapter 7 para 7.51.

4.60 However, it has long been accepted in practice that if a receiver has been appointed and is still acting as such, the appointment of a liquidator does not preclude the receiver from continuing to realise assets of the company with a view to satisfaction of the floating charge. To support this proposition, reliance is placed on the terms of Schedule 2 to the Insolvency Act 1986 which makes it clear that the receiver enjoys not only a power of sale but also the power to take possession of, collect and get in the property from the company or a liquidator thereof. The courts have also approved such proposition.[1] The practical and legal position is, therefore, that although a liquidator may have been appointed and the agency of the receiver may technically have been terminated, the receiver will continue to realise assets of the company in satisfaction of the charge while the liquidator will only be entitled to take possession of any assets remaining after the floating charge creditor has been fully satisfied or any assets which fall outwith the scope of the floating charge.

1 *Manley, Petitioner* 1985 SLT 42; and see Chap 3 para 3.58.

4.61 Most receivers, certainly in the early stages of a receivership will wish to avoid the appointment of a liquidator on the grounds that such an appointment would: (a) be prejudicial in the context of a sale of the business as a going concern when such a sale might be more advantageous to the creditors as a whole; (b) cause unnecessary confusion and anxiety in the minds of employees of the company and unhelpful publicity when attempts are being made to sell the business; and (c) cause adverse taxation problems when, for example, large parcels of land still remain unsold involving substantial capital gains tax.[1] However, as will be noted in paragraph 4.66 the receiver cannot prevent the appointment of a liquidator if valid grounds to do so exist.

1 See Chap 7 para 7.51.

4.62 In this context the form of liquidation envisaged is liquidation by the court. Members' voluntary liquidation will usually be quite inappropriate as the company is almost certainly, but not necessarily, insolvent and a creditors' voluntary liquidation requires action by the company to convene meetings under section 98 of the Insolvency Act 1986. It is thought that any actions by the directors which might interfere with the conduct of the receivership will not find favour with the courts in Scotland and in the particular circumstances, it is thought that action by directors to cause the appointment of a liquidator may be deemed to be prejudicial.[1]

1 Chapter 2 paras 2.18 to 2.25.

4.63 Ordinary creditors whose expectations in receivership today are unenviable used to seek the appointment of a liquidator to recover value added tax already paid to HM Customs & Excise under the bad debt relief provisions. In many cases, several creditors agreed to fund the cost of the liquidation where it was clear that there would be no dividend for ordinary creditors. The position was altered by the Finance Act 1985 and the introduction of the Administrative Receivers (Value Added Tax Certificates) (Scotland) Rules 1986[1] which came into operation on 1 April 1986.[2] Under the new arrangements a receiver now has a duty for the purposes of section 22 of the Value Added Tax Act 1983 to issue a certificate in the terms of paragraph (b) of the said section 22 forthwith upon his forming the opinion that the company is deemed to be insolvent. It should be noted that these new arrangements apply to all new receiverships commencing after 1 April 1986 and to all receiverships existing as at that date. Where a receiver has completed his duties and resigned, it would appear that no VAT bad debt relief can be claimed without petitioning for the liquidation of the company.

1 1986/304 (S 23).
2 Superseded by The Insolvency (Scotland) Rules 1986, SI 1986/1915 (S 139), rr 3.12 to 3.14.

4.64 Under the old rules for VAT bad debt relief, a receiver used to brace himself to deal with ordinary creditors of the company many of whom were suppliers and customers on whom the receiver was dependent for the continuance of the business prior to its sale. While ordinary creditors will normally still feel aggrieved at the appointment of a receiver, the new arrangements for VAT bad debt relief should remove some of the immediate pressure for the appointment of a liquidator. Consequently, one of the first steps to be taken by a receiver in receiverships of any significance will be still to lodge caveats in the Court of Session and in the sheriff court jurisdiction in which is located the registered office of the company. Suggested styles of caveat are contained in Appendix 8. The caveats will normally be very general and will seek to cover both the possible appointment of an unwelcome liquidator and an interdict by a creditor who claims retention of title. It should be noted that in some jurisdictions the sheriff court will accept a form of joint caveats to cover both liquidation and interdict but in other cases it is safer to lodge separate caveats for both eventualities as, in the larger sheriff courts, interdict processes and liquidation processes are handled by different departments and sometimes at different offices.

4.65 The effect of lodging caveats is no guarantee of protection to the receiver but at least the receiver is entitled to be heard in any court proceedings before an order is made by the court. This is of particular benefit in resolving retention of title disputes. It should be borne in mind that, however convincing the arguments of the receiver may seem, the court will normally take the view that if sections 122 and 123 of the Insolvency Act 1986 apply and the debt is not disputed, the granting of the first order in the liquidation process is the proper course of action.[1]

1 *Foxhall & Gyle (Nurseries) Ltd, Petitioners* 1978 SLT (Notes) 29.

Prevention of liquidator's appointment

4.66   In the *Foxhall & Gyle (Nurseries)* case,[1] Lord Kincraig allowed a petition for liquidation to proceed to the first order and dismissed the submissions of the receiver regarding the adverse consequences of the granting of such first order. Lord Kincraig stated that where a creditor seeks a winding-up order on the ground that a company is unable to pay its debts, the petition for winding up should not be dismissed unless there are compelling reasons for it. It would therefore seem that it will only be in exceptional circumstances that the court will decline to grant the first order in a winding-up process.

1 *Foxhall & Gyle (Nurseries) Ltd, Petitioners* 1978 SLT (Notes) 29.

Set-off

General

4.67   Set-off or compensation of one debt against another with the result that each such debt is *pro tanto* extinguished was originally introduced by statute.[1] Its elements are principally that there must be *concursus debiti et crediti*: namely that the parties must be in the same capacity and at the same time debtor and creditor. Set-off must be pleaded and it is only competent in general as between liquid debts save for cases of insolvency where the debtor may defend himself against a present demand by setting off a debt that is future or contingent although the time of payment is after insolvency.[2] No guidance from the courts is available as to whether the right of set-off opens up upon the appointment of a receiver as it does upon insolvency but it is submitted that while the appointment of a receiver need not coincide with insolvency, in most instances it does so.

1 The Act 1592 c 143.
2 Bell's Commentaries 122.

4.68   Set-off in the context of receivership has been the subject of judicial consideration. This has arisen principally from two cases namely *McPhail v Lothian Regional Council*[1] and *Taylor Petitioner*,[2] the conflicting decisions in which have caused uncertainty as to the correct legal position. The subsequent case of *Forth & Clyde Construction Co Ltd v Trinity Timber & Plywood Co Ltd*,[3] although not concerned with set-off, has to some extent clarified the position in its application to book debts.

1 1981 SLT 173.
2 1982 SLT 172.
3 1984 SLT 94.

4.69 Section 53(7) of the Insolvency Act 1986 states that on the appointment of a receiver, the floating charge by virtue of which he was appointed attaches to the property then subject to the charge; and such attachment has effect as if the charge was a fixed security over the property to which it has attached. Fixed security is defined by section 70 of that Act in relation to any property of a company as security, other than a floating charge or a charge having the nature of such, which on the winding-up of the company in Scotland would be treated as an effective security over that property. Thus, in the case of a book debt due to a company it would include a security created by an assignation of such debt duly intimated to the debtor.[1] Set-off is subject to the legal principle *assignatus utitur jure auctoris*, the effect of which is that a debtor on receiving a claim for payment of the debt can competently plead against an assignee of the debt any defences which would have been competent against the cedent. Such defences would include the right of set-off[2] but they would require to have been competent before the assignation was intimated. If it is accepted that on the appointment of a receiver the attachment of the floating charge to the company's book debts is equivalent to a completed assignation in security in favour of the holder it follows that a debtor wishing to plead set-off would require to have been in a position to counter claim prior to the receiver's appointment. If the counter claim is only competent in respect of a debt arising after the receiver's appointment, the principles of *assignatus utitur jure auctoris* and *concursus debiti et crediti* will not apply. According to Bell,[3]

'the right to compensate passes against assignees, if once vested against the cedent by a proper concourse before assignation. But if a debt be assigned, and the assignation intimated before the counter-debt arises, the concourse is prevented, and there is no compensation'.

Bell[4] also states that, in cases of insolvency, a future or contingent debt, even although the time of payment is after insolvency, may be set-off against a due debt. Receivership does not necessarily involve insolvency although frequently the company is in fact insolvent.

1 *Forth & Clyde Construction Co Ltd v Trinity Timber & Plywood Co Ltd* 1984 SLT 94.
2 *Shiells v Ferguson, Davidson & Co* 1876 4 R 250.
3 II Bell's Commentaries 138.
4 Bells Commentaries 122.

4.70 The facts in the *McPhail* case[1] were that the receiver of a company appointed under a floating charge over the whole property of the company raised an action in his own name in his capacity as receiver to recover from the statutory successors of a local authority a sum admittedly due to the company under a contract between it and the authority's predecessors. The defenders argued that the receiver had no title to sue in his name and contended, furthermore, that they were entitled to apply set-off in respect of a debt due by the company before the appointment of the receiver to the predecessors of the defenders. The receiver rejected the set-off argument on the ground that there was no *concursus debiti et crediti* although as a result the defenders maintained that if that was so the receiver should have raised a plea as to the competency of the counter claim.

1 *McPhail v Lothian Regional Council* 1981 SLT 173.

4.71   Lord Grieve held in the Outer House that the receiver, in terms of the equivalent provisions in the 1972 Act to those contained in paragraph 1 of Schedule 2 to the Insolvency Act 1986, had power to recover property of the company in his own name and his powers were not to be limited by such provisions to raising proceedings in the name of the company. His Lordship also accepted the argument that as the counter claim did not justify a decree because the averments were based on a claim to set-off which was unsound in law a plea to the relevancy of the counter claim had been legitimately taken. As the action had been raised by the receiver in his own name, there was no *concursus debiti et crediti* and the counter claim was dismissed.

4.72   The facts in *Taylor, Petitioner*[1] were that a receiver who was appointed over the whole property and undertaking of a company sought to recover sums due from debtors who, subsequently to his appointment, had assigned to them by a creditor debts due to such creditor by the company, in one case for full value and in the other case for certain good and onerous causes. Both assignations had been properly intimated to the company. The receiver sought a declaration from the court that he was entitled to recover the debts in terms of the equivalent provisions in the 1972 Act to those contained in paragraphs 1 and 5 of Schedule 2 to the Insolvency Act 1986 and secondly that set-off by the debtors was inappropriate. The receiver argued in relation to set-off that as he was entitled to recover the debts under the relevant statutory provisions, the debtors were not entitled to set-off since this would be contrary, amongst other things, to insolvency law and that similar rules applied to receivership as to bankruptcy. Once the floating charge had crystallised, a fixed security was thereby created. Accordingly, *concursus debiti et crediti* would require to have existed prior to his appointment and as the assignations of the debts post-dated his appointment, the plea of compensation should be repelled.

1 1982 SLT 172.

4.73   Lord Ross held that the receiver's rights under the equivalent provisions in the 1972 Act to those contained in paragraph 1 of Schedule 2 to the Insolvency Act 1986 were limited to taking possession of a right to debts, a mere *jus crediti*, as on the appointment of the receiver the company owned not the sums of money due by debtors but only the right to recover the debts. Secondly, his Lordship held that the receiver, unlike *McPhail*'s case[1] only had the power to take proceedings in the name of the company for payment of the debts and consequently the creditors to whom the debts had been assigned were entitled to set-off against the company's claim against them the debts due by the company which had been assigned to them. It was considered such action would not be prejudicial to the security holder's security over the *jus crediti* of the company, the principles of law relative to insolvency having no application to cases of receivership and there being no justification upon grounds of equity or public policy for introducing any such exception into the law.

1 *McPhail v Lothian Regional Council* 1981 SLT 173.

4.74 Following upon the decision in *Taylor, Petitioner*[1] it was considered necessary by some receivers and their advisers for the company
immediately upon the appointment of a receiver to assign all of its book
debts to the receiver thereby, hopefully, overcoming the difficulty posed
by the decision in *Taylor, Petitioner*.[1] On further consideration, some of
those receivers and their advisers abandoned the idea of such an assignation. Quite apart from the burden of *ad valorem* stamp duty on the
aggregate value of the book debts which in most cases would be very
substantial, it was considered that a *jus crediti* was effectively assigned by
the terms of the 1972 Act[2] and the receiver had, in terms of the *Taylor,
Petitioner* decision, the right to take proceedings in the name of the
company. An assignation of the book debts would not really achieve any
particular purpose. In view of the implications of the decision in the case
in so far as it related to set-off the advice given to receivers faced with
similar circumstances was that no intimation of assignation of a debt due
by the company in receivership should be accepted.

1 1982 SLT 172.
2 Now re-enacted as part of the Insolvency Act 1986.

4.75 While many receivers were unhappy with the *McPhail* decision,
the *Taylor, Petitioner* decision[1] offered no real comfort. It is suggested
that the principal defect of the decision in *Taylor, Petitioner*[1] was that
neither the effect of the equivalent provisions of the 1972 Act to those
contained in sections 53(7) and 54(6) of the Insolvency Act 1986 (crystallisation of a floating charge) nor the question of possible bad faith in
assigning post receivership were properly argued in court.

1 1982 SLT 172.

4.76 The question of whether the attachment of a floating charge to a
book debt, upon the appointment of a receiver could be regarded as a
fixed security (as defined in the equivalent provisions in the 1972 Act to
those contained in section 70 of the Insolvency Act 1986), notwithstanding that the only way to so constitute an effective fixed security was to
assign in security the right to receive payment of the debt and to intimate
such assignation to the debtor, was considered by the First Division in
Forth & Clyde Construction Co Ltd v Trinity Timber & Plywood Co Ltd[1]
In that case, an arrestment was served on Strathclyde Regional Council
the day after the appointment of joint receivers in respect of a debt due by
the petitioners to the company. The court held that the attachment of the
book debt in question by the floating charge must have had effect as if on
the date of appointment of the joint receivers there had been duly
intimated to the third party debtor by the petitioners an assignation
thereof in security in favour of the holder of the floating charge.

1 1984 SLT 94.

4.77 In his judgment in the case[1] the Lord President stated, in relation
to the attachment of the debt:

'the intention appears to me to be that the holder of the floating charge shall, on the appointment of a receiver, enjoy all the protection in relation to any item of attached property that the holder of a fixed security over that item thereof would enjoy under the general law.'

and later in his judgment:

'It follows, accordingly, that in the case of an attached book debt one can only reasonably discover the effect of the attachment by treating it as if there had been granted in relation to it the only relevant "effective security" known to the law, namely an assignation in security, duly intimated. To adopt any other approach would in my opinion deprive the holder of the charge of the advantages which he was intended to enjoy, namely the advantages which would be enjoyed by the holder of an "effective security" recognised by the law, over each and every form of property attached by the charge. It could also result in frustrating a receiver in the exercise of his powers in the interests of the holder of the floating charge who has appointed him. It is, of course, the case that the 1972 Act has not expressly provided that the book debts shall be regarded as having been assigned in security to the holder of the floating charge on the date upon which it attaches to them but the language of section 13(7)[2] makes it quite clear that the attachment is to have effect "as if" such an assignation in security had been granted and intimated by the company. From the date of appointment of a receiver the company, no doubt, retains the title to demand payment of the debt but no longer for its own behoof. The interest in the recovery of the debt is that of the holder of the floating charge, and a receiver who seeks recovery in the name of the company does so in order to secure the application of the recovered sum towards the satisfaction of the company's debt due to the creditor in the floating charge.'

1 *Forth & Clyde Construction Co Ltd v Trinity Timber & Plywood Co Ltd* 1984 SLT 94.
2 See now the Insolvency Act 1986, s 53(7).

4.78 The effects of the *Forth & Clyde* decision[1] may be summarised as follows:

(a) on the appointment of a receiver, a book debt is deemed to be assigned in security to the holder of a floating charge and duly intimated to the debtor as if it were a fixed security (as defined in section 70 of the Insolvency Act 1986);

(b) the receiver only is capable on behalf of the company in receivership of recovering the debt even though the beneficiary of the proceeds of the debt is the holder of the floating charge;

(c) the debtor may not be able to set-off debts due by the company in receivership which he acquired by assignation duly intimated to the company in receivership after the appointment of the receiver. This would be contrary to the decision in *Taylor, Petitioner*[2] which with its concept of *jus crediti* is at variance with the fixed security concept of the *Forth & Clyde* decision.[3]

1 *Forth & Clyde Construction Co Ltd v Trinity Timber & Plywood Co Ltd* 1984 SLT 94.
2 1982 SLT 172.
3 See n 1 above.

4.79 The question of set-off in receivership can by no means be regarded as settled. The courts will, however, it appears, be prepared to accept that set-off is competent after a company becomes insolvent in the circumstances set out in *Gloag on Contract* (2nd edn) at 626. Gloag states that the rule that a demand for a liquid debt is not relevantly met by a defence founded on an illiquid or unascertained claim does not hold where the pursuer is bankrupt or where it is averred that he is insolvent. He continues that on the principle of retention or, in Bell's words, of balancing accounts in bankruptcy, the party who is sued on a claim which he admits to be payable may put forward in defence claims which are not yet due, which involve only a contingent liability or which are disputed and require to be established by proof.[1]

1 *McPhail v Cunninghame District Council* 1985 SLT 149.

Crown set-off

4.80 From time to time, the right of the Crown or some other person to claim set-off against the other has arisen judicially. The statutory provisions relating to Scotland governing such right are contained in section 50 of the Crown Proceedings Act 1947 and state:

'(2) The following provisions shall apply as regards proceedings in the Court of Session or the sheriff court:

(a) where decree in absence has been granted against the Crown the decree shall not be operative without the leave of the court obtained on an application of which notice has been given to the Crown;

(b) a person shall not be entitled to avail himself of any set-off or counter claim in any proceedings by the Crown for the recovery of taxes, duties or penalties, or to avail himself in proceedings of any other nature by the Crown of any set-off or counter claim arising out of a right or claim to repayment in respect of any taxes, duties or penalties;

(c) a person shall not be entitled without the leave of the court to avail himself of any set-off or counter claim in any proceedings by the Crown if the subject matter of the set-off or counter claim does not relate to the Government department on whose behalf the proceedings are brought;

(d) the Crown, in any proceedings against a Government department, or against the Lord Advocate on behalf of a Government department, shall not, without the leave of the Court, be entitled to avail itself of any set-off or counter claim if the subject matter thereof does not relate to that department.'

4.81 The leading Scottish case on the matter is *Smith v Lord Advocate (No 2)*[1] where the pursuer, as liquidator of Upper Clyde Shipbuilders (UCS), sued the Lord Advocate as representing the Ministry of Defence in Scotland. The liquidator of UCS sought payment of a substantial sum in respect of the construction and repair to certain naval vessels. The liability to pay was not disputed by the Lord Advocate but he claimed the right to set-off this liability against (a) the amount of a loan due by UCS to be paid to the Secretary of State for Trade and Industry (b) an amount of unsecured loan stock due for repayment to the Secretary of State for Trade and Industry (c) an amount in respect of national insurance contributions due to the Secretary of State for Health and Social Security and (d) an amount due by UCS to the Department of Inland Revenue.

1 1980 SLT 105.

4.82   As noted in paragraph 4.80, section 50(2)(d) only allows set-off with the leave of the court, if the subject matter does not relate to that department.[1] The court held that by virtue of section 50, government departments were to be regarded as separate legal entities from the Crown so far as set-off and counter claim were concerned and that sub-section (d) of section 50 applied to the circumstances of the case.[2] Lord Kincraig considered at 109 that the court should be furnished with facts and circumstances to enable it to come to a decision as to whether, viewing the issue judicially, leave should be granted or not. His Lordship, having accepted the pursuer's submission that set-off should not be allowed unless circumstances are put before it to enable it to exercise its discretion in favour of set-off by the Crown, made reference to two earlier Scottish cases[3] in which in neither case was evidence heard, the parties evidently wishing the court to decide the issue on the averments in the pleadings. Lord Kincraig considered that, in the present case, the defenders' averments of the circumstances which should be regarded as relevant to the granting of leave were not significant and he, accordingly, refused leave.

1 Crown Proceedings Act 1947.
2 *Smith v Lord Advocate (No 2)* 1980 SLT 105.
3 *Atlantic Engine Co (1920) Ltd v Lord Advocate* 1955 SLT 17; *Laing v Lord Advocate* 1973 SLT (Notes) 81.

Chapter 5

Retention of title

Background

5.01 The seller of goods on credit, where possession and ownership has passed to a customer who goes into liquidation (other than a members' voluntary winding up) or has a receiver appointed over its property and undertaking before payment, ranks as an ordinary creditor for the price. The credit made available in this way by suppliers may well have enabled the customer to continue trading when practically insolvent and when bankruptcy intervenes the claims of the preferential and secured creditors will often swallow up most, if not all, the available assets resulting in such suppliers receiving little, if anything, by way of dividend on their claims. The position of such suppliers has been made worse over the years by the increasing range of preferential debts (a trend now reversed to some extent by the Insolvency Act 1986) and, in Scotland, by the ability since 1961 of incorporated companies to create floating charges over all or any of their assets. It is hardly surprising, therefore, that suppliers of goods have looked for ways of protecting their interests in the event of a customer's insolvency and one method of doing so, namely by retaining title to goods sold on credit until payment of the price, was highlighted by a celebrated English case[1] which has become so well known that contracts of sale containing retention of title provisions are now commonly known as 'Romalpa Clauses'. The normal practice of most major suppliers to now include such provisions in their Standard Conditions of Sale stems to a large extent from the wide publicity given to the decision in that case. While such provisions apply whether or not insolvency occurs, the event against which they are primarily intended to protect the supplier is the insolvency of the customer. As a result, the supply of goods subject to such conditions to a company which goes into receivership often presents the receiver, at least in the early stages, with significant practical and legal problems. For this reason, the topic deserves special attention.

1 *Aluminium Industrie Vaassen BV v Romalpa Aluminium Ltd* [1976] 2 All ER 552.

5.02 It should be made clear at the outset that, because of differences between the legal systems of Scotland and England, the treatment of such conditions by the Scottish and English courts has not been the same. A receiver of a Scottish company is more likely to be concerned with the position under the law of Scotland in relation to goods in the company's possession situated in premises in Scotland at the time of his appointment but, if the company has premises in England, could also be concerned with the position under the law of England.

5.03   Before discussing retention of title in a receivership context, it is necessary to understand what it is. Put simply, it is when possession but not title passes. In the case of the sale of goods, the position under the law of Scotland, prior to the Sale of Goods Act 1893 was that, in the absence of agreement to the contrary, title passed on delivery to the buyer whether or not the price had been paid. The seller and the buyer could, however, agree that while possession would pass, title would not until some condition had been fulfilled, eg payment of the price. Underlying this aspect of the law was the distinction derived from Roman law between a real and a personal right and thus, in this context, the distinction between title and possession.

5.04   The Sale of Goods Act 1893 introduced a uniform statutory code for both England and Scotland governing the sale of goods. This Act remained in force until re-enacted with some amendments in 1979. Scottish lawyers have experienced difficulty in applying these statutory provisions in so far as they relate to the passing of possession as opposed to title because of the absence in the law of England of a clear distinction between title and possession. Section 17(1) of the Sale of Goods Act 1979 provides that, where there is a contract for the sale of specific or ascertained goods, the property in them is transferred to the buyer at such time as the contracting parties intend it to be transferred. Section 18 then sets out five rules for ascertaining the intention of the contracting parties where the contract is silent on such intention. The 1979 Act does not refer to the transfer of title or ownership but to the transfer of property and with one qualified exception contained in rule 5(2) none of the rules points to property passing at the time of delivery. It is suggested that, for the purposes of the law of Scotland, property must be assumed to mean title or ownership. Section 19(1) of the 1979 Act provides that, where there is a contract for the sale of specific goods, the seller may, by the terms of the contract, reserve the right of disposal of the goods until certain conditions are fulfilled: and, in such a case, notwithstanding delivery to the buyer, the property in the goods does not pass until the conditions imposed by the seller are fulfilled. This statutory provision effectively restates the law of Scotland prior to 1893 in that the seller of goods can impose a condition that title to the goods will not pass until, for example, the price is paid. That is the present basis for the imposition by a seller of goods of a retention of title condition.

Practical application

5.05   On appointment, a receiver will almost certainly discover that, included in the company's stock, will be goods in respect of which unpaid suppliers are claiming retention of title and, failing payment in full of the invoice price, are threatening proceedings for re-delivery and perhaps also interdict against the receiver dealing with the goods. The alleged condition may go further than simply retaining title until the price of the goods in question is paid but the efficacy or otherwise of such conditions will be dealt with later. As the receiver will in most cases wish to continue the company's business at least until he has completed a preliminary financial investigation, he will wish to avoid interdict or other proceedings which might prevent his using or disposing of the company's stock-in-trade or finished goods. The receiver must, therefore, as a matter of urgency, discover whether there are goods in the company's possession the price of which is unpaid and which have been obtained from a supplier who is claiming retention of title. If so, the receiver must then ascertain whether a valid retention of title condition does form part of the contract for the sale of these goods.

5.06 It is, therefore, recommended that, at the earliest possible stage and preferably on the first day of the receiver's appointment, a physical stocktaking of goods likely to be the subject of retention of title claims be taken and a careful note of the stock physically located should be made against unpaid invoices of the suppliers maintaining or likely to maintain valid retention of title clauses. The establishment by the supplier of a valid claim to retention of title is made much more difficult where goods cannot be differentiated by any distinguishing mark and it is reasonable to insist on a supplier matching an unpaid invoice against particular goods located in the company's possession. If the goods in question have a serial number or other similar distinguishing mark, the task of the supplier is rendered easier but it clearly depends on the circumstances of the particular case as to whether a supplier can substantiate his claim.

Incorporation in contract

5.07 The receiver must first ascertain whether any retention of title condition has been incorporated into the contract for the sale of the goods. This can be a question of fact or a mixed question of fact and law. The terms of all relevant documentation require to be examined, eg quotations, offers, orders, order acknowledgments or acceptances, delivery notes, catalogues, price lists, invoices etc and any standard or other conditions referred to in any of such documents. Generally speaking, the earlier any such condition is imposed the more likely (in the absence of the attempted imposition by the other party of a contradictory condition) it is to be effective. For example, an attempt to impose such a condition by direct or indirect reference in a delivery note or invoice, particularly if there has been no previous course of dealing between the parties, is unlikely to be successful in that the terms of a contract are established prior to delivery of or payment for the goods.

5.08 If the supplier appears to have included such a condition in the contract, the receiver should investigate whether the company has effectively rebutted such condition by imposing a contrary condition. In such circumstances, the rules which apply are those generally relating to offers and acceptances and each such case must be examined in light of the facts and the law. It has been held[1] in England that a party wishing to rely on a term incorporated into a standard form contract must show that the term was brought to the notice of the party sought to be bound before or at the time the contract was made. If that party was aware that the contract contained any particular term or if he was unaware that any such term was contained in the contract but the other party had done all that was reasonably sufficient to bring the term to his notice, then he would be bound by such term.

1 *John Snow & Co Ltd v DBG Woodcroft & Co Ltd* [1985] BCLC 54.

Course of dealing

5.09   Where a particular condition, such as one of retention of title is not *ex facie* incorporated into the contract documents, it is sometimes possible for a supplier to rely on a regular course of dealing between the parties over a period of time and to maintain that the purchaser knew that the supplier's terms and conditions of business applied to the contract as these had been accepted by the purchaser over a period of time. Reliance on such terms and conditions on the course of dealing argument is not nearly so satisfactory from the supplier's point of view as the specific incorporation in the contract documentation of such terms and conditions.

5.10   For an interesting consideration of the course of dealing argument, reference is made to *Grayston Plant Ltd v Plean Precast Ltd*[1] where an English company with a place of business in Scotland hired out to manufacturers of prefabricated units a twelve ton telescopic lorry-mounted crane on the basis of a verbal contract with the hirers. The crane overbalanced during the period of the hire and the owners of the crane sued the hirers for the loss. The owners averred that the contract of hire, which inter alia provided that any damage to the crane was the responsibility of the hirer, incorporated the general conditions of hire established by the Contractors' Plant Association of which the hirers were members. After a proof was allowed, it was established that when the contract was made verbally, an acknowledgment of order form, stating that the order was accepted subject to such general conditions of hire, was sent by post to the hirer by way of confirmation. It was further established that in a period of two years, the hirers had hired from the owners plant on some eleven or twelve occasions although proof was not established as to whether the hirers had accepted such general conditions of hire. The court held that the onus of proving that the hirers were aware of such general conditions of hire was upon the owners, that the owners had not discharged such onus and decree of absolvitor was granted.

1 1976 SLT 74.

5.11   Lord Robertson in the course of his judgment in the *Grayston Plant* case[1] reviewed a number of English cases, namely *Hardwick Game*

Farm v Suffolk Agricultural and Poultry Producers' Association.[2] *Hollier v Rambler Motors (AMC) Ltd*[3] and *British Crane Hire Corpn Ltd v Ipswich Plant Hire Ltd.*[4] In the *British Crane* case, both parties were experienced in the hiring of cranes. The owners sent a printed form to the hirers for their signature but before the form was despatched the crane, due to no fault of the hirers, was damaged. Under the conditions which were the same as those used in the plant hire business, the hirers were liable to indemnify the owners for any damage. The owners relied on the course of dealing argument by referring to two previous transactions some months before the present transaction. Lord Denning concluded that the course of dealing argument could not be sustained but he held that since the parties were of similar bargaining strength, the owners were entitled to conclude that the hirers had accepted the conditions because of their wide usage in the plant hire business.

1 *Grayston Plant Ltd v Plean Precast Ltd* 1976 SLT 74.
2 [1966] 1 WLR 287 and [1969] 2 AC 31.
3 [1972] 2 QB 71.
4 [1974] 1 All ER 1059.

5.12 Lord Robertson in the *Grayston Plant* case[1] then continued:
'In my opinion, the mere counting of occasions when a similar transaction has previously been entered into between the parties and thereby obtaining a sufficiently high score, is not all that is required in cases such as this in order to justify the conclusion that a written condition has been incorporated into a verbal contract. The state of knowledge of the defenders is important (see Salmon LJ in *Hollier*);[2] so, too, is their status and professional experience (*British Crane Hire*).[3] "The judicial task is not to discover the actual intentions of each party; it is to decide what each was reasonably entitled to conclude from the attitude of the other" [Lord Reid in *McCutcheon v MacBrayne Ltd*].[4] It is therefore relevant to consider what steps were taken by the owner to bring to the notice of the hirer the conditions alleged to be incorporated into the contract.'

1 *Grayston Plant Ltd v Plean Precast Ltd* 1976 SLT 74.
2 *Hollier v Rambler Motors (AMC) Ltd* [1972] 2 QB 71 at 78.
3 *British Crane Hire Corpn Ltd v Ipswich Plant Hire Ltd* [1974] 1 All ER 1059.
4 1964 SC (HL) 28.

5.13 Reference is made to two further cases involving incorporation of terms into standard form contracts and the statutory test of 'reasonableness' specified in the Unfair Contract Terms Act 1977 (for the purposes of paragraph 5.14 referred to as 'the 1977 Act') and the Sale of Goods Act 1979.

5.14 In *McCrone v Boots Farm Sales Ltd,*[1] the defenders relied on their general conditions of sale to exclude their liability for an alleged breach that a quantity of weedkiller supplied by the defenders was not fit for the purpose for which it was sold. The defenders also averred that the contract was neither a 'consumer contract' nor a 'standard form contract' within the meaning of section 17 of the 1977 Act. Lord Dunpark held (1) that the defenders' averments were insufficient to establish that the general conditions of sale had been imported into the contract by implication; and (2) in any event, that the term 'standard form contract' within the meaning of section 17 was wide enough to include any contract which included a set of fixed terms applied by their proponer to contracts of the kind in question. His Lordship approved the decision in the *Grayston Plant* case[2] and confirmed the previous tests as to whether general conditions of sale could impliedly be included in a contract. On the question of a standard form contract his Lordship stated:

'Counsel for the defenders referred to section 24(1) of the 1977 Act which limits the circumstances relevant to the "reasonableness" test to those which were, or ought reasonably to have been, known to or in contemplation of the parties at the same time when the contract was made. So he argued, ingeniously but fallaciously, this contract was concluded as an oral contract and it could not be transformed into a standard form contract by the addition of the defenders' written general conditions. The fallacy, in my opinion, is that these general conditions were added to the contract after its conclusion. Not so. The basis of the defenders' case that these conditions were incorporated in this particular contract is that the pursuer knew that the defenders always inserted these conditions in their contracts of sale and that the reasonable inference from this knowledge is that the pursuer impliedly accepted them as included in this particular contract at the time it was concluded. The defenders have no averments which even suggest that their contract was modified after its conclusion by the addition of their general conditions. Accordingly, it follows from the assumption that the general conditions were part of this contract, that it was a standard form contract.'

1   1981 SLT 103.
2   *Grayston Plant Ltd v Plean Precast Ltd* 1976 SLT 74.

5.15   In *George Mitchell (Chesterhall) Ltd v Finney Lock Seeds Ltd*[1] where the defendants relied on an exclusion clause to avoid liability under a contract, Parker J stated that it was making commercial nonsense of the contract to suggest that either party intended it to operate where what had been delivered was wholly different in kind from what had been ordered and agreed to be supplied. The Court of Appeal held that it would not be 'fair or reasonable' within the meaning of the Sale of Goods Act 1979[2] to permit reliance upon conditions of sale which had not been the subject of prior discussion before the contract was concluded and which in practical terms were not vigorously applied.

1   [1982] 3 WLR 1036.
2   Section 55(4) and Sch 1, para 11.

Resolution of dispute

5.16   Where there is a potential dispute over a retention of title claim the receiver or his solicitors frequently write a standard form of letter indicating that in the receiver's view the company in receivership has title to the goods in question and that, as part of the receiver's general powers of sale, it is his intention to dispose of the goods in the normal course of business or otherwise. It is, clearly, important from the receiver's point of view to put on record his general intentions so that the supplier, if he feels that he has a reasonable case to put forward, can take suitable proceedings to protect his interests. In many cases, where the supplier feels so justified, interdict proceedings are commenced under which the supplier seeks interim interdict preventing the receiver from disposing of the goods in question pending a resolution of the disputed retention of title claim, either by negotiation or by the court. As mentioned in Chapter 4[1] where there are suppliers claiming retention of title, the receiver usually lodges caveats in the Court of Session and the appropriate sheriff court to prevent such suppliers obtaining interim interdict without the receiver having an opportunity of being heard.

1 Paragraphs 4.64 and 4.65.

5.17   It is often the case that where a real dispute does exist, a practical short-term solution is negotiated along the lines of the receiver:
(1) either giving some form of written undertaking that if it should be established by the court that the goods in dispute are subject to a valid retention of title clause, then he will return the goods or pay for them at their invoice value; or
(2) reaching some other form of extra-judicial settlement with the supplier which avoids further delay and expense in resolving the dispute.

Validity of retention of title conditions and trusts over funds

5.18   Suppliers of goods in attempting to gain the maximum protection for their interests have imposed retention of title conditions in varying terms and, as part of such conditions or independently, creditors have purported to establish trusts over moneys held by or on behalf of the company all of which have been subject to review by the Scottish courts in recent years. As a result the following principles appear to have emerged in relation to the validity or otherwise of such conditions and/or trusts:
(1) A simple clause of retention of title which is separable from other ancillary clauses related to retention of title will be effective but if the retention of title provision is included as part of a larger clause incorporating other concepts which are unacceptable under the law of Scotland, then the whole clause will be ineffective.[1]
(2) Any attempt to secure the payment of all outstanding moneys to a supplier by a retention of title over particular goods will be unenforceable under the law of Scotland.[1]
(3) Trust moneys credited to a bank account, without notice being given to the bank of the existence of a trust, may be protected if such moneys are clearly distinguishable from other moneys of a company[2] and a condition imposed on a purchaser to set up a trust fund for any

moneys received by that purchaser in the event of a further sale will not be effective unless positive steps have been taken by the purchaser to place the trust proceeds outwith the purchaser's control and so to set up a valid trust.[3]

(4) If a purchaser acquires materials from a supplier and uses these to create a new species of goods from them, then the ownership of the new goods vest with the purchaser under the doctrine of specification.[4] The manufacturer, however, of the new goods must have acted in good faith.[5]

(5) A supplier of goods will have no rights against a receiver of the purchaser if the purchaser prior to the receiver's appointment sells the goods to a sub-purchaser, on the grounds that the law of Scotland does not recognise the doctrine of tracing in the case of sale proceeds being received either before or after such appointment.[6]

(6) Where goods are sold by a person who is not their owner and who sells them without the authority or consent of the owner, the buyer acquires no better title to the goods than that of the seller unless the owner of the goods is by his conduct precluded from denying the seller's authority to sell.[7]

(7) Where goods with the owner's consent are in the possession of a party other than the owner and such party disposes of such goods to a third party, the third party without notice of a retention of title clause will obtain a good title to such goods.[8]

(8) The *lex situs* governs the interpretation of a retention of title clause expressed to be subject to the law of a foreign jurisdiction.[9]

1 *Emerald Stainless Steel Ltd v South Side Distribution Ltd* 1983 SLT 162; *Deutz Engines Ltd v Terex Ltd* 1984 SLT 273; *Hammer and Sohne v HWT Realisations Ltd* 1985 SLT (Sh Ct) 21.
2 *Smith v Liquidator of James Birrell Ltd* 1968 SLT 174.
3 *Export Credits Guarantee Dept v Turner* 1981 SLT 286; *Clark Taylor & Co Ltd v Quality Site Development (Edinburgh) Ltd* 1981 SLT 308.
4 *International Banking Corpn v Ferguson Shaw & Sons* 1910 SC 182; *Armour v Thyssen Edelstahlwerke AG* 1986 SLT 452.
5 *McDonald v Provan of Scotland Street Ltd* 1960 SLT 231.
6 *Michelin Tyre Co Ltd v Macfarlane (Glasgow) Ltd* 1917 2 SLT 205.
7 Sale of Goods Act 1979, s 21(1); and the *Liquidator of Brechin Auction Co Ltd v Reid* 1895 22 R 711.
8 Sale of Goods Act 1979, s 25(1); *Thomas Graham & Sons Ltd v Glenrothes Development Corpn* 1968 SLT 2; and *Archivent Sales & Development Ltd v Strathclyde Regional Council* 1985 SLT 154.
9 *Hammer & Sohne v HWT Realisations Ltd* 1985 SLT (Sh Ct) 21; *Armour v Thyssen Edelstahlwerke AG* 1986 SLT 452; but see *Zahnrad Fabrik Passau GmbH v Terex Ltd* 1986 SLT 84.

5.19   The facts in *Emerald Stainless Steel Ltd v South Side Distribution Ltd*[1] were that suppliers sold certain goods under terms and conditions of sale which the parties agreed had been validly incorporated into the contract. The suppliers raised an action against the company in receivership and the joint receivers for delivery of the goods, failing which payment of the value thereof and, they also sought interdict to prevent the receivers from disposing of the goods. The relevant conditions on which the suppliers founded were as follows:

'8.1 – Title to each item of goods sold or agreed to be sold shall remain vested in the Company [ie the suppliers] until the full purchase price and all additional charges relating to that item and all or any other moneys for the time being owing by the customer to the Company shall have been paid in full to the Company and pending such payment all such items of goods held by the customer (and all products into which such items come to be converted or incorporated) shall be and remain the property of the Company and shall be held by the customer as trustee for the Company but with liberty for the customer to pass title as the Company's agent on a sale or other disposal of such items by the customer on its own account (but subject to 8.2 below) bona fide for full value in the normal course of the customer's trading.

8.2 – All and any sale and other disposal proceeds received by or on behalf of the customer in respect of any item of goods, title in which is reserved to the Company or which is otherwise property of the Company shall be received by or on behalf of the customer as trust moneys for the Company's account and shall be promptly remitted to the Company.'

1 1983 SLT 162.

5.20 Lord Ross, in the Outer House of the Court of Session, stated in his opinion:

'Having considered the terms of Condition 8.1, I am of the opinion that it cannot be construed merely as a clause of retention of title but that it is truly an attempt to create a security without possession in which the machinery of a trust under Scots law is sought to be employed. It is significant that security is sought not only for the purchase price of the goods but also for "all and any other moneys for the time being owing by the customer to the Company". So far as the reference to trust is concerned, I am quite satisfied that no valid trust under the law of Scotland could be created by the language used in this Condition.

It falls that Condition 8.1, in my opinion, is wholly ineffectual. The pursuers' Counsel submitted that even if the decision in *Clark Taylor*[1] applied, there was no reason why the earlier part of the Condition reserving title should not be treated as having effect. In my opinion, however, Condition 8.1 cannot be broken down in this way and it is in reality an attempt to obtain security without possession, using the machinery of a trust. The attempt is not well-founded in law and, in my opinion, is ineffectual.'

1 *Clark Taylor & Co Ltd v Quality Site Development (Edinburgh) Ltd* 1981 SLT 308.

5.21 The relevant clause of the General Conditions of Sale in the *Terex* case[1] stated as follows:

'13. Until all sums due from the Buyer to the Company in respect of the goods or equipment sold or otherwise shall have been paid in full:
(1) the title to such goods or equipment shall remain vested in the Company and in the case of goods or equipment purchased for re-sale or incorporation in any other equipment for re-sale until conclusion of a legally binding contract for re-sale; thereafter, such goods

and equipment shall stand surety for full payment of all sums due to the Company and until payment such goods and equipment shall be retained by the Buyer for the Company in its capacity as fiduciary owner thereof.

(2) All goods and equipment supplied shall be at the Buyer's sole risk in all respects.

(3) If any payment due in respect of the goods shall not be made when due or if the Company shall cancel the order under the Special Conditions of Sale or these General Conditions the Company may without notice at any time retake possession of the whole or any part of the goods or equipment and for this purpose may enter upon any premises occupied by the Buyer without prejudice to any other remedy of the Company.'

Lord Ross had little difficulty in holding that the clause appeared to be seeking security without transfer of possession by the debtor which, except in certain special circumstances, is not permitted by the law of Scotland. He then drew attention to the contention of counsel for the pursuer who had stated that the first part of Condition 13 could be read separately and because of the punctuation could be distinguished from the *Emerald Stainless Steel* case.[2] His Lordship then continued:

'It is true that Condition 13(1) here does contain punctuation which was not present in the provision under consideration in *Emerald Stainless Steel Limited*, but Condition 13(1) must be read along with the opening words of Condition 13 which refer to "all sums due". Moreover, even if Condition 13(1) down to the semi-colon is read as a whole it goes far beyond a mere reservation of title in respect of the goods delivered, and purports to alter the law of Accession and Specification in that title is to be reserved by the seller even when the goods have been purchased for re-sale or incorporation.

For present purposes I am prepared to assume that the words which precede the semi-colon in Condition 13(1) should be read as one, and that for present purposes one may disregard the words which follow the semi-colon. If, however, these words are considered, then the reference to "surety" and "fiduciary owner" would suggest to me that, like *Emerald Stainless Steel Ltd*, an attempt was being made to obtain security without possession using the machinery of a trust.'

1 *Deutz Engines Ltd v Terex Ltd* 1984 SLT 273.
2 *Emerald Stainless Steel Ltd v South Side Distribution Ltd* 1983 SLT 162.

5.22 In *Smith*'s case,[1] some months prior to its liquidation, a company received the proceeds of certain policies of assurance which had been arranged under a pension and life assurance scheme for the benefit of its employees. The scheme was being discontinued and the sums were received by the company for behoof of its employees. The company paid the proceeds of the policies of assurance into a No 2 account with its bank but the bank was not on notice of the trust affecting the proceeds. At all times, from the date when the proceeds were credited to the No 2 account until the date of liquidation, there was always a sum in excess of the amount received under the policies of assurance and, at the same time, the company's No 1 account was continuously overdrawn to an amount in excess of the funds in the No 2 account. The court held that the proceeds received in respect of the assurance policies were clearly distinguished and capable of being disentangled from the company's own funds and that such sum should be credited for behoof of the company's employees.

1 *Smith v Liquidator of James Birrell Ltd* 1968 SLT 174.

5.23 In the case[1] of *Export Credits Guarantee Dept* (ECGD), ECGD guaranteed repayment to a bank of advances made by the bank to a company against invoices for goods exported by the company to overseas customers. The relevant clause in a recourse agreement regulating the terms of business between ECGD and the company provided as follows:

'The Exporter [ie the company] hereby acknowledges and declares that all sums received by the Exporter or by any person on its behalf in respect of any transaction which is the subject of a Guaranteed Advance shall, unless repayments of that Guaranteed Advance shall have previously been made by the Exporter to the Bank, be received and held in trust by the Exporter for the Guarantor until the Exporter has made such repayment to the Bank or has paid to the Guarantor the amount of any demand made by the Guarantor in respect of that Guaranteed Advance.'

1 *Export Credits Guarantee Dept v Turner* 1981 SLT 286.

5.24 The liquidator admitted the claim of ECGD to an ordinary ranking in the liquidation but ECGD claimed that the delivery of the recourse agreement to them as sole beneficiaries set up an irrevocable trust. It maintained that all sums received by the company or its liquidator and the right to all debts incurred by overseas customers as soon as these were constituted were caught by the terms of the trust and that all such moneys were truly held for behoof of ECGD. The court held[1] that a trust had not been constituted prior to the liquidation by the delivery of the recourse agreement since intimation, where necessary to constitute the trust, would require to take place simultaneously with the coming into existence of a trust fund and no such trust fund was in existence at that time. There was only a contractual obligation on the company to hold payments in trust and such an obligation was not binding on the liquidator.

1 *Export Credits Guarantee Dept v Turner* 1981 SLT 286.

5.25 The facts in *Clark Taylor & Co Ltd v Quality Site Development (Edinburgh) Ltd*[1] were that Clark Taylor sold bricks to Quality Site subject to the terms of a condition in the following terms which had been validly incorporated into the contract between the parties:

'In the event of the buyer re-selling or otherwise disposing of the goods or any part thereof before the property therein has passed to him by virtue of clause 11(a) hereof, then the buyer will, until payment in full to the seller of the price of goods, hold in trust for the seller all his rights under such contract of resale or any other contract in pursuance of which the goods or any part thereof are disposed of or any contract by which property comprising the said goods or any part thereof is or is to be disposed of and any money or any other consideration received by him thereunder.'

1 1981 SLT 308.

5.26 Quality Site used the bricks sold by Clark Taylor in carrying out a number of contracts and, in due course, payment in respect of the bricks supplied by Quality Site was duly made by the ultimate customer. As soon as each payment was received by Quality Site, it was immediately remitted to the current account of Quality Site with the Bank of Scotland. The issue in the case was solely concerned with the sub-clause which purported to create the obligation to 'hold in trust' all their rights under any contract of free sale and any other contract in pursuance of which disposal of the bricks was involved.

5.27 The First Division of the Court of Session held[1] firstly, that Condition 11(b) purported to secure the freezing of the defined subjects regardless of their value under an alleged trust which gave no beneficial interest to the supposed beneficiary until they received the price of the bricks which they sold to Quality Site; the essential ingredients of a trust were entirely lacking and condition 11(b) was no more than an attempt, under the guise of an alleged trust, to keep valuable assets of the company out of the hands of its other creditors. Secondly, where the truster and trustee are the same persons, there must be in existence an asset, there must be a dedication of the asset to defined trust purposes, there must be a beneficiary with defined rights in the trust estate, and there must also be delivery of the trust deed or subject of the trust or a sufficient and satisfactory equivalent to delivery, so as to achieve irrevocable divestiture of the truster and investiture of the trustee in the trust estate. Finally, a contractual obligation to constitute a trust is not sufficient to have the effect of constituting a trust in favour of one contracting party, particularly where the party undertaking the obligation is himself to discharge the office of both truster and trustee. Clearly, some form of delivery was essential before a valid trust could be created.

1 *Clark Taylor & Co Ltd v Quality Site Development (Edinburgh) Ltd* 1981 SLT 308.

5.28 The facts in *International Banking Corpn v Ferguson Shaw & Sons*[1] were that oil had been stolen and sold to the defenders who were bona fide purchasers and as such, converted the oil with other materials into lard or cooking fat. The lard or cooking fat was then sold to customers in the ordinary course of business. The court held that this was a proper example of specification; the defenders had the exclusive right of property in the lard but had to account to the pursuers for the value of the oil which had been used.

1 1910 SC 182.

5.29 In the case of the *Armour v Thyssen Edelstahlwerke AG*[1] the issues of specification and *lex situs* were fully considered. In the case, the joint receivers of Carron Company Limited sought a declarator that a quantity of steel amounting to 67,423 kilograms, for which no payment had been made and which was delivered to the company's premises prior to the date of appointment of the joint receivers by the defenders, belonged to the company and could be sold by the joint receivers. Alternatively, the proportion of steel which had been cut into pieces before the appointment and could not be returned to its original state belonged to the company in accordance with the principle of specification. The defenders relied on the defenders' general conditions of delivery and payment which expressly provided that the law of the Federal Republic of Germany was to be applied to the contracts between them and the company.

Clause I No 3 of the general conditions of delivery and payment stated:
'Reservation of Ownership (Retention of Title)

(1) All goods delivered by us remain our property (goods remaining in our ownership) until all debts owed to us, including any balances existing at relevant times – due to us on any legal grounds – are settled. This also holds good if payments are made for the purpose of settlement of specially designated claims. Debts owed to companies, being members of our combine, are deemed to be such debts.

(2) Processing of the goods remaining in our ownership is effected on our behalf as manufacturer, according to section 950 of the Civil Code, but without putting us under any obligation. Goods so processed are deemed to be goods remaining in our ownership according to paragraph (1).'

1 1986 SLT 452.

5.30 There were in fact eleven separate sub-clauses under Reservation of Ownership which came before the court but the quoted sub-clauses are essentially the critical ones for the purpose of the issues raised. The above translation from the German was agreed by a joint minute to be an accurate translation into English. It was maintained by the joint receivers that property in all steel strip passed to Carron at latest on delivery of such strip to their premises in Scotland. There was no dispute that delivery was actually carried out and invoices were produced. It was maintained by the joint receivers that the provisions of the defenders' general conditions of delivery and payment had no bearing on the ownership of the steel strip once it had been delivered to Carron's premises by the defenders. The joint receivers maintained that the steel strip was situated in Scotland thereafter and the parties' property rights in it were governed by Scots law. They therefore maintained that Clause I No 3 of the defenders' general conditions was invalid under Scots law in that it was an attempt to create security over moveable property in circumstances where Scots law did not recognise such a security. The defenders, on the other hand, maintained that Clause IV No 5 of the said conditions provided that the law of the Federal Republic of Germany should apply and under such law Clause I No 3 was valid as a simple retention of title.

5.31 The Lord Ordinary decided at procedure roll that a proof before answer was appropriate on the grounds that there had been no agreement as to translation from German to English in relation to the various documents; that the defenders sought to prove that the law of the Federal Republic of Germany applied and that it was appropriate that there should be investigation into the averments to specification. At the conclusion of the proof, the joint receivers' counsel maintained his plea to the relevancy and sought decree. Alternatively, he submitted that the evidence on the law of the Federal Republic did not support or, at any rate, sufficiently support the conclusion that Clause I No 3 was a simple retention of title clause. Further, and in any event, the property in a portion of the steel had passed to Carron when it was converted into manufactured goods under Scots law relating to specification. It was averred that after cutting the steel, it was impossible to return the steel strip to its original state. Having heard the evidence of three witnesses involved in the steel trade, the court concluded that once the steel was cut it was not easily resaleable and, in any event, only in a different market. Similarly, when the steel was cut into shapes. On melting, the resulting steel changed in its chemical composition and was not in its original state and would only command scrap value. Lord Mayfield in his review of the authorities on specification considered the authorities, namely *Wylie & Lochhead v Mitchell*,[1] *International Banking Corpn v Ferguson Shaw & Sons*[2] and *McDonald v Provan*.[3] Reference was also made to *Bell's Principles* and *Erskine's Institutes*. His Lordship stated that he found the rules difficult to apply to modern industrial and manufacturing processes. The evidence, however, led him to the view that, as a result of cutting, and if melting were carried out, the result would be steel in a different form. After melting, the steel would be in a different form because of the change in chemical composition. Its state was altered and to return it to its former state an element would have to be added. His Lordship, therefore, concluded that the evidence suggested a recognition by the steel trade that the steel, in fact, was in a different form and thus, in a manufacturing sense, a new species.

1 1870 8M 552.
2 1910 SC 182.
3 1960 SLT 231.

5.32   In *McDonald v Provan*,[1] the front part of a stolen motor vehicle including half the chassis, the engine and the gears was welded to the rear portion of another similar motor vehicle. The composite vehicle was then sold to a third party who acquired it bona fide before they, in turn, resold it. Three months after the resale, the police removed the motor vehicle from the possession of the eventual purchaser who raised an action of damages for breach of warranty against its seller. The court held that the doctrine of *specificatio* (pleaded by the seller) can only be invoked where there was absolute bona fides on the part of the manufacturer and could not be applicable where part of the composite subjects was constructed from stolen property.

1 1960 SLT 231.

5.33 The facts in *Michelin Tyre Co Ltd v Macfarlane (Glasgow) Ltd*[1] were that tyres were supplied to Macfarlane who were motor agents by Michelin under what might be termed a simple retention of title clause. On Macfarlane's liquidation the question which arose was whether Michelin were entitled to recover the moneys in respect of tyres sold by Macfarlane (but not paid for) to customers before the appointment of the liquidator. It was conceded by Michelin that they were not entitled to recover, except as ordinary creditors, the moneys received by Macfarlane prior to their liquidation and Macfarlane's liquidator conceded that Michelin were entitled to recover tyres remaining unsold as at the date of liquidation. This left the question of the moneys received by the liquidator after the commencement of the company's winding up. The House of Lords were clear in their judgments: the Lord Chancellor said that the suggestion that Michelin should be entitled to the sale proceeds by virtue of the doctrine of surrogation in respect of a notional property in the goods remaining in Michelin after the actual property had passed to a purchaser from Macfarlane was untenable.

1 1917 2 SLT 205.

5.34 In the *Brechin Auction* case,[1] a purchaser of cattle agreed with an auction company who paid for the cattle and therefore acquired title thereto that title to the cattle would pass to the purchaser whenever he should choose in the future. The purchaser was in possession of the cattle and thereafter he sold the cattle to a third pary without informing the auction company. In an action by the liquidator of the auction company against the sub-purchaser, the court held that the liquidator was personally barred by what is now section 21 of the Sale of Goods Act 1979.

1 *Liquidator of Brechin Auction Co Ltd v Reid* (1895) 22R 711.

5.35 The *Thomas Graham*[1] case which was approved in the subsequent *Archivent*[2] case both involved the supply of materials to a building company which sold those materials in the case of *Thomas Graham* in the construction of houses and garages and in the *Archivent* case, subject to a retention of title clause for the purposes of building a school. When in the *Thomas Graham* case, the contractor went into voluntary liquidation and in the *Archivent* case, the contractor went into receivership, the supplier in each case sued direct the eventual purchaser. In both cases, the defenders argued and succeeded in showing that the circumstances fell within the provisions of section 25 of the Sale of Goods Act 1979 (or, in the earlier case, the equivalent section of the Sale of Goods Act 1893) and in each case, the court held that property in the materials had been transferred by the contractor as a mercantile agent under the Factors Act 1889 to the respective purchaser in good faith.

1 *Thomas Graham & Sons Ltd v Glenrothes Development Corpn* 1968 SLT 2.
2 *Archivent Sales & Development Ltd v Strathclyde Regional Council* 1985 SLT 154.

5.36 In the *Hammer and Sohne* case,[1] the pursuers founded on a contractual provision which purported to allow them to retain title to the goods until all the defenders' liabilities to the pursuers had been discharged. As part of these conditions, the law governing the conditions was stated to be West German law. The defenders who were in receivership argued that the clause in question was an attempt to create a security over moveables which was unacceptable under the law of Scotland and, in any event, while the proper law of the contract might be West German, the proper course was to apply the *lex situs* of the present location of the goods in question, namely Scots law. It was recognised that if Scots law applied to the transaction, the clause would be rejected on the grounds already clearly established in the *Emerald Stainless Steel* case[2] and the *Deutz Engines* case.[3]

1 *Hammer & Sohne v HWT Realisations Ltd* 1985 SLT (Sh Ct) 21.
2 *Emerald Stainless Steel Ltd v South Side Distribution Ltd* 1983 SLT 162.
3 *Deutz Engines Ltd v Terex Ltd* 1984 SLT 273.

5.37   The learned sheriff in the *Hammer & Sohne* case[1] said at 22:
'In *Cheshire and North on Private International Law* (Tenth Edition) Page 195, the expression "the proper law of the contract" is referred to as being "a convenient and succinct expression to describe the law that governs many of the matters affecting a contract". Determination of this may depend on ascertaining whether or not the parties have expressed any choice of system within the terms of their contract and/or whether the contract is most closely associated with a particular system of law. On such criteria, I would not be disposed to question whether West German law is the "proper law" in that restricted sense and in the circumstances of the present case. In my belief, however, that is not the appropriate way by which to approach the present issues – at least not initially. I consider that the course is rightly charted by *Cheshire and North* (Supra at Page 195), where it is said:
"the correct inquiry is not – what law governs a contract question? It is – what law governs the particular question raised in the instant proceedings?"
for, as was was said in *Re United Railways of Havanna and Regla Warehouses Ltd* [1960] Ch 52 at Page 92 (quoting *Cheshire* 5th Edition), "the fact that one aspect of a contract is to be governed by the law of one country does not necessarily mean that that law is to be the proper law of the contract as a whole".'

1 *Hammer & Sohne v HWT Realisations Ltd* 1985 SLT (Sh Ct) 21.

5.38   The learned sheriff then considered whether the particular clauses in question would be acceptable and valid under the law of Scotland and concluded on the basis of *Emerald Stainless Steel*[1] and *Deutz*[2] that they would not, on the grounds that there was an attempt to create a security over moveables. The learned sheriff then referred to the principle established in *Mitchell v Burnett & Mouat*[3] which stated the principle that the *lex situs* governs the creation of securities over moveables and he, therefore, considered that the same case made it plain that the effectiveness or otherwise of the security falls to be determined by the law of the place where the goods in question are actually located. As a result, the learned sheriff decided that Scots law applied to the transaction and as the clauses in question were ineffective under the law of Scotland the action was dismissed.

1 *Emerald Stainless Steel Ltd v South Side Distribution Ltd* 1983 SLT 162.
2 *Deutz Engines Ltd v Terex Ltd* 1984 SLT 273.
3 (1746) Mor 4468.

5.39 It may, however, be wrong to regard the *lex situs* as being an inflexible corpus of law. In another case,[1] the pursuers' Terms and Conditions provided inter alia that contracts were subject to German law. The judge drew a distinction between the interpretation of personal contractual rights as opposed to proprietary rights: the case being concerned with the latter. His Lordship approved a passage from an opinion of Lord Chancellor Herschell in *Hamlyn and Co v Talisker Distillery Ltd*[2] as follows:

'I should be prepared to admit that an agreement which was opposed to a fundamental principle of the law of Scotland founded on conditions of public policy could not be relied upon and insisted upon in the Courts of Scotland . . .'

1 *Zahnrad Fabrik Passau GmbH v Terex Ltd* 1986 SLT 84.
2 (1894) 21R (HL) 21 at 23.

5.40 Lord Davidson concluded in the case[1] that there was no reason why one of the parties should not incorporate into a contract one or more provisions of a foreign legal system subject always to the qualification that if such provisions were opposed to a fundamental principle of the law of Scotland, there could be a challenge. However, any such challenge would not be successful if the difference was one of degree and could not be regarded as fundamental.

1 *Zahnrad Fabrik Passau GmbH v Terex Ltd* 1986 SLT 84.

5.41 In the *Carron* case,[1] Lord Mayfield in his consideration of the *lex situs* issue reviewed a number of the authorities[2] and concluded that there was clear authority that the *lex situs* governs the creation of real rights in corporeal moveables. He considered it was also clear that whether or not a security has been created the effectiveness or otherwise has to be determined by the law of the place where the goods are actually located. In his view, that finding was supported by *Mitchell v Burnett & Mouat* and subsequent authorities.[2] Accordingly, if a security has been created, then the law of Scotland governs the matter. Counsel for the defenders submitted that the primary question was one of title rather than the creation of a security. Lord Mayfield held, however, that that was not the approach taken by Lord Ross in *Emerald Stainless Steel*[3] and *Deutz Engines*.[4] In these cases, it was agreed that the particular conditions provided that the property and goods were not to be transferred to them until all sums due by them had been paid in full. His Lordship came to the conclusion that he should adopt the same approach.

1 *Armour Ltd v Thyssen Edelstahlwerke AG* 1986 SLT 452.
2 *Mitchell v Burnett & Mouat* (1746) Mor 4468; *Hamlyn v Talisker Distillery* (1894) 21 R (HL) 21 and *Hammer and Sohne* 1985 SLT (Sh Ct) 21.

3 *Emerald Stainless Steel Ltd v South Side Distribution Ltd* 1983 SLT 162.
4 *Deutz Engines Ltd v Terex Ltd* 1984 SLT 273.

5.42   One area which has not yet been mentioned is the difficult one where goods supplied have been inmixed with other goods. Due to the fairly strict attitude of the Scottish courts in relation to retention of title clauses, it is thought that the Scottish courts would be unlikely to uphold a retention of title clause which purported to retain ownership in a seller of materials until the price had been paid once such materials had been inmixed with other goods. However, there may be certain circumstances where the supplier of materials converted into manufactured goods which contain various materials inmixed may have some protection under the law of Scotland.

Specification

5.43   Specification is the creation of a new *res* with materials belonging to another and stems from the original Roman law concept of specification. An obvious example of specification would be grapes turned into wine: the *res* cannot be changed back into its original state.

In *Bell's Principles* (10th edn) at para 1298(1), the rules for determining ownership are set out as follows:

'That, if the materials, as a separate existence, be destroyed in bona fide, the property is with the workman, the owner of the materials having a personal claim for a like quantity and quality, or for the price of the materials; that, if still capable of restoration to their original state, the property is held to be with the owner of the materials, a claim against him for work and indemnity in quantum lucratus being competent to the workman.'

As has already been noted the rules quoted by Bell were followed in the *International Banking Corpn* case[1] and the *Carron* case.[2]

1 *International Banking Corpn v Ferguson Shaw & Sons* 1910 SC 182.
2 *Armour v Thyssen Edelstahlwerke AG* 1986 SLT 452.

Confusion

5.44   Confusion is the mixing of liquids and commixtion is a mixing of solids. An example of confusion might be the mixing of motor oils and an example of commixtion might be the mixing of bricks of the same type.

5.45   In *Bell's Principles* at para 1298(2), the rules for determining ownership where liquids or solids belonging to different persons are inmixed are set out as follows:

Confusion or commixtion 'raise a common property, if the commodities be of the same kind; and of such property *pro indiviso* the shares are in proportion to quantity and value; where either the union is by common consent, or where, having been made by accident or without fault, the commodities are inseparable. The property is unchanged if the articles be capable of separation. If the union be of substances different, so as to create a *tertium quid,* the property is (according to the rule in specification) with the owner of the materials, or with the manufacturer, according to the possibility or impossibility of restoring the original substances.'

5.46 The general result is that if the liquids or solids may be separated into their original properties, then the property rights are unchanged but if the various materials are inseparable, then the new *res* may be regarded as common property and the supplier's share would be calculated on the basis of his contribution to the new *res*. If an entirely new *res* has been created, then the specification rules referred to above will apply.

5.47 There is a further set of circumstances which is worthy of consideration, namely where the item which has been manufactured or is in the process of manufacture cannot be regarded as falling within the rules applicable to specification, confusion or commixtion. In the case of *Wylie & Lochhead v Mitchell*[1] the defender had contracted to build a hearse for a firm of undertakers. Wylie & Lochhead supplied a number of the materials but the defender became bankrupt before completion of the hearse. The court held that the hearse was the result of neither specification nor confusion. The materials, skill and labour of the contributions were voluntarily and inseparably combined and the court applying general principles of equity said that the parties were joint proprietors of the subject produced in proportion to the value of their respective contributions.

1 1870 8M 552.

5.48 In recent times there has been much discussion on the whole topic of retention of title in the context of the law of Scotland and of the judicial decisions in the cases which have come before the courts. It is not intended in this book to comment on the articles which have been written, the references to which appear below, but it may be useful for these articles to be listed.

1 D J Cusine 'The Romalpa Family visits Scotland' The Journal of the Law Society of Scotland April and May 1982.
2 Letter from Mr C N McEachran 1983 SLT 102.
3 K G C Reid and G L Gretton 'Retention of Title in Romalpa Clauses' 1983 SLT 73.
4 T B Smith 'Retention of Title: Lord Watson's Legacy' 1983 SLT 105.
5 W A Wilson 'Romalpa and Trust' 1983 SLT 106.
6 K G C Reid and G L Gretton 'Retention of Title for all sums: a Reply' 1983 SLT 165.
7 Eleanor Sharpston 'Retention of Title' The Journal of the Law Society of Scotland June 1984.
8 W J Stewart 'Romalpa Clauses – Choosing the Law' 1985 SLT 149.
9 John M Halliday 'Romalpa Again – The Trust Device' 1985 SLT 153.

The English position

5.49 The preceding paragraphs on retention of title reflect the position in Scotland where the courts have looked generally with disfavour on other than simple provisions of retention of title. The more sophisticated forms of retention of title clauses have, however, found greater acceptance with the courts in England. In particular, tracing and trust arguments have found more favour there whereas these arguments have been rejected by the Scottish courts unless, in the case of trust, the essential requirements for the establishment of a trust are satisfied. However, it may be useful to consider briefly the main aspects of English cases since *Romalpa*.

Principles established in English courts

5.50 From recent English judgments, the following principles seem to have emerged:

(1) An attempt to secure the payment of all outstanding moneys to a supplier by a retention of title over particular goods will be enforceable in England in certain circumstances[1] although to be effective as a security it is necessary that title should first pass to the buyer[2] and as the clause creates a charge, it should be registered with the Registrar of Companies.[3]

(2) A clause retaining only equitable and beneficial ownership rather than full legal ownership will be invalid.[4]

(3) A clause similar to the Scottish concept of specification will not be recognised in England unless a charge is created and registered with the Registrar of Companies,[4] but it is likely that if the goods could be separated and restored to their original state the court would uphold the clause.[5]

(4) An attempt to trace the proceeds of sale by virtue of a fiduciary relationship established between the buyer and the seller is unlikely to be successful unless treated as a charge which has been registered with the Registrar of Companies.[6]

(5) Where goods are sold by a person who is not the owner thereof and who does not sell them under the authority or with the consent of the owner the buyer acquires no better title to the goods than the seller had unless the owner of the goods is by his conduct precluded from denying the seller's authority to sell.[7]

(6) Where goods are in the possession of one party and with the owner's consent, such party disposes of such goods to a third party, the third party without notice of a retention of title clause will obtain a good title to such goods.[8]

1 *Aluminium Industries Vaassen BV v Romalpa Aluminium Ltd* [1976] 2 All ER 552; *Borden (UK) Ltd v Scottish Timber Products Ltd* [1979] 3 All ER 961; *Clough Mill v Martin* [1984] 3 All ER 982.
2 *Clough Mill v Martin* above.
3 *Re Bond Worth Ltd* [1980] Ch 228.
4 *Borden (UK) Ltd v Scottish Timber Products Ltd* above; see also *Clough Mill v Martin* above.
5 *Hendy Lennox (Industrial Engines) Ltd v Grahame Puttick Ltd* [1984] 2 All ER 152.

6 *Aluminium Industries* above; *Borden (UK) Ltd* above; *Re Peachdart Ltd* [1983] 3 All ER 204; *Re Andrabell Ltd* [1984] 3 All ER 407.
7 Sale of Goods Act 1979, s 21(1); *Yorkshire Joinery Co Ltd* (1967), 111 Sol Jo 701.
8 Sale of Goods Act 1979, s 25; *Four Point Garage v Carter* (1984) Times, 19 November.

5.51 The *Romalpa* case[1] while primarily concerned with the proceeds of sale of goods sold by a buyer, nevertheless laid the foundations for the premise that an 'all sums due' clause could be effective under English law. In the *Borden* case,[2] which is more particularly considered in paragraph 5.55, Templeman LJ gave further authority for the proposition when, in the course of his judgment at 972, he stated that:

'In my judgment, when resin was sold and delivered *the property* in the resin *could be retained by the sellers*, and *was retained, only as security for the payment of the purchase price and other debts incurred, and to be incurred*, by the buyers to the sellers in respect of supplies of resin.'

1 *Aluminium Industries Vaassen BV v Romalpa Aluminium Ltd* [1976] 2 All ER 552.
2 *Borden (UK) Ltd v Scottish Timber Products Ltd* [1979] 3 All ER 961.

5.52 The facts in *Clough Mill*[1] were that yarn was sold to the buyer under four contracts which were subject to certain terms and conditions. The retention of title clause stated that the ownership of the yarn would not pass until full payment had been received by the seller but the Court of Appeal held that such a clause ensured that the title to the yarn was never actually transferred to the buyer and accordingly did not create a charge in favour of the seller. *Romalpa*,[2] *Borden*[3] and *Clough Mill*[4] have also demonstrated that if a charge is created it will be void unless registered pursuant to section 95 of the Companies Act 1948.[5]

1 *Clough Mill v Martin* [1984] 3 All ER 982.
2 *Aluminium Industries Vaassen BV v Romalpa Aluminium Ltd* [1976] 2 All ER 552.
3 *Borden (UK) Ltd v Scottish Timber Products Ltd* [1979] 3 All ER 961.
4 See n 1 above.
5 Re-enacted as CA 1985, s 395.

5.53 The facts in *Re Bond Worth Ltd*[1] were that the suppliers despatched synthetic fibre to the purchasers who used it in the manufacture of carpets. The contract for the sale of the synthetic fibre provided that the equitable and beneficial ownership of the fibre was to remain with the sellers until full payment had been made for the fibre delivered or until prior resale, in which case the sellers' beneficial entitlement was to attach to the proceeds of sale and, further, if the fibre became a constituent of, or was converted into, other products, the sellers were to have equitable and beneficial ownership in those products or the proceeds of resale thereof. The fibre, in due course, was spun into yarn as part of the buyers' manufacturing process with other fibre and the yarn was then processed and woven into carpets. On the appointment of a receiver to the buyers, there was little raw fibre on that date but substantial stocks of yarn and finished carpets were within the premises of the buyers. It was argued for the receivers that the purpose of the retention of title clause was to create a security which should have been properly registered under section 95 of the Companies Act 1948.[2] The sellers contended that they were to be regarded as beneficiaries under a trust or, alternatively, that if a charge had been created, it was done so by the sellers reserving to themselves payment of the purchase price and, therefore, did not come within the scope of section 95.[2]

1 [1980] Ch 228.
2 Re-enacted as CA 1985, s 395.

5.54 The court held that the rights conferred on the sellers were merely by way of an equitable charge over the fibres supplied since the buyers' equity of redemption was inconsistent with the existence of a trust under which the entire beneficial interest in the fibre or proceeds of sale remained in the sellers. On a true construction of the contract, the equitable charge in favour of the sellers was created by the buyers by way of an implied grant back to the sellers after the whole of the property in the fibre had first passed to the buyers and not by the sellers reserving or accepting to themselves an interest out of the property passing to the buyers. As such, the charge could only be construed as a floating charge and not as a specific charge over specific assets which was clearly registrable under section 95 of the Companies Act 1948[1] and as the charge had not been registered, it was void against the creditors of the buyers.

1 Re-enacted as CA 1985, s 395.

5.55 The facts in *Borden (UK) Ltd v Scottish Timber Products Ltd.*[1] were that the sellers supplied resin to the buyers under a contract which provided that property in goods supplied was to pass to the buyers when full payment had been made for those goods and all other goods supplied up to the date of payment. It was well known to the sellers that the buyers used the resin as an ingredient in the manufacture of chipboard within two days of it being supplied, the resin thereafter becoming an inseparable component of the chipboard. On the appointment of a receiver to the buyers, the Court of Appeal held that as the buyers had used the resin in the manufacture of chipboard, the resin ceased to exist as resin and there was nothing which the sellers could trace. The retention of title clause simply reserved title to the sellers so long as the resin was unused. Secondly, it was held that there was no fiduciary relationship between the buyers and the sellers such as to entitle the sellers to trace the resin supplied by them into the chipboard manufactured from it or into the proceeds of sale of such chipboard. Thirdly, any rights enforceable by the sellers could only be sustained by way of a registered charge and, as the charge was unregistered, it was void under section 95 of the Companies Act 1948[2] as against the liquidator and other creditors.

1 [1979] 3 All ER 961.
2 Re-enacted as CA 1985, s 395.

5.56 The court in *Hendy Lennox (Industrial Engines) Ltd v Grahame Puttick Ltd*[1] decided that where goods supplied by a seller can be separated from a finished product, a retention of title clause will be effective. In the case, it emerged that the sellers supplied engines for incorporation by the buyers in diesel generating sets and it was intended that the buyers would then sell to sub-purchasers. As in all such cases, the critical issue was to assess whether the process of incorporation physically changed the engines. In *Hendy Lennox* the court held that there was no such change. The engines were attached to the generators by bolts but remained identifiable by serial numbers. Secondly, although a seller of such goods may not be entitled to the proceeds of sale of such goods to sub-purchasers, if his claim for the return of the goods is changed during the proceedings to a claim for the proceeds and provided title to the sub-purchasers has not passed the seller's position may still be tenable.

1 [1984] 2 All ER 152.

5.57 In the *Romalpa* case, the plaintiffs sold aluminium foil to the defendants who subsequently went into liquidation but it was established that there existed the proceeds of sale to third parties of some of the aluminium foil. The plaintiffs claimed successfully to be entitled to trace the aluminium foil into the proceeds of sale. At first instance Mocatta J held the clause showed an intention to create a fiduciary relationship between the parties and that the plaintiffs were entitled to follow the proceeds of the sub-sales. In the Court of Appeal, Roskill LJ stated:

'It seems to me clear . . . that to give effect to what I regard as the obvious purpose of the clause one must imply into the first part of the clause not only the power to sell but also the obligation to account in accordance with the normal fiduciary relationship of principal and agent, bailor and bailee. Accordingly, like the judge I find no difficulty in holding that the principles in *Re Hallett's Estate, Knatchbull v Hallett*[1] are of immediate application, and I think that the plaintiffs are entitled to trace these proceeds of sale and to recover them, as the learned judge has held by his judgment.'

1 (1880) 13 Ch D 696.

5.58 The facts in the *Borden* and *Clough Mill* cases are set out in para 5.55 and 5.52 respectively, but it is clear from the judgments in *Borden* that to be effective the retention of title clause purporting to give a right to the proceeds of sale requires to be registered as a charge under section 395 of the Companies Act 1985, always assuming that the necessary fiduciary relationship between the seller and the buyer has been established.

5.59 The facts in *Re Peachdart Ltd*[1] were that the seller supplied leather to the buyer (manufacturer of handbags) subject to a condition that title to the leather, including the right of resale if payment was overdue, and the right to trace any proceeds of sale by virtue of the fiduciary relationship established between the buyer and the seller were all reserved to the seller. On the appointment of the receiver to the buyer, the court held that an intention had been contemplated by the parties once the leather had been appropriated into the handbag-making process for the seller, whether as bailor or unpaid vendor, to cease to have exclusive title to the leather but in lieu thereof to enjoy the benefit of a charge over the completed and uncompleted handbags, including any proceeds of sale and, accordingly, as the charge had not been registered pursuant to section 95 of the Companies Act 1948,[2] it was void against the liquidator and other creditors.

1 [1983] 3 All ER 204.
2 Re-enacted as CA 1985, s 395.

5.60 The next case to come before the courts in respect of the right to proceeds was *Re Andrabell Ltd (In Liquidation): Airborne Accessories Ltd v Goodman.*[1] In that case the relevant clause provided that ownership of travel bags would not pass until payment had been made in full. The buyer obtained supplies of travel bags from the seller in the ordinary course of business and, without carrying out any further work on the travel bags, sold them as part of its retail and export business of selling travel bags. The proceeds of such sales were paid into the buyer's bank account but no distinction was made between moneys representing such proceeds and other moneys representing other transactions. The court held that whether or not there was a fiduciary duty to account for the proceeds of sale depended on the facts of each case and in this case no fiduciary duty was established. The court also specified various elements which would be required to establish a fiduciary relationship (eg an obligation to store the goods separately or to account for the proceeds of sale or an express acknowledgement of the relationship or an obligation to keep the proceeds of sale of the travel bags separate from other moneys of the buyer). In addition, no term could be implied into the simple clause of retention of title used in this case to impose a duty on the buyer to account for the proceeds of sale.

1 [1984] 3 All ER 407.

5.61 Reference is made to section 21 of the Sale of Goods Act 1979 in the context of goods sold by a person who is not the owner thereof and who does not sell them under the authority or with the consent of the owner and questions of title of the buyer arising therefrom.

5.62 Similarly, where the buyer acquires goods from a person who is not the owner but who disposes of such goods with the owner's consent, the buyer without notice of a retention of title clause acquires a good title.[1] In the case of *Four Point Garage Ltd v Carter,*[2] such a principle was reinforced.

1 Sale of Goods Act 1979, s 25.
2 (1984) Times, 19 November.

Chapter 6

Receivership as it affects officers of company and its employees

Effect on officers of company and their powers

6.01 The appointment of a receiver does not affect the position of the officers of the company, namely its directors and secretary. Their tenure of office as such is not terminated by the receiver's appointment and accordingly they remain subject to their statutory duties. While there is nothing to prevent any director or the secretary subsequently resigning office as such, this does not, for example, necessarily relieve the person resigning from his obligations in relation to the statutory statement of affairs to be submitted to the receiver.[1] Tenure of office as a director or secretary is to be distinguished from executive employment however and, as regards the latter, the effect of the appointment of a receiver is no different from that on other employees.[2] As regards remuneration it has been held in England[3] that while directors cannot claim remuneration from a receiver unless he employs them, they can nevertheless claim from the company any remuneration to which they are entitled.

1 Insolvency Act 1986, s 66.
2 See para 6.07.
3 *Re South Western of Venezuela (Barquismeto) Rly Co* [1902] 1 Ch 701.

6.02 The powers of the company's officers as such are, however, affected by a receiver's appointment. While they can still exercise certain powers, such as the power of the directors to convene a general meeting of the company, for example, to place the company in voluntary liquidation their general powers of management and to deal with the assets covered by the charge are suspended. It has been held[1] that where a receiver has been appointed over the whole assets of a company the directors of the company were not entitled to deal in any way with the property of the company comprised in the receivership. In the course of his judgment Lord Grieve stated:

> 'I am satisfied that the terms of the Act of 1972 do not empower the directors of a company, whose assets are the subject of a floating charge in connection with which a receiver has been appointed, to deal in any way with assets of theirs which are the subject of such a charge during the currency of the receivership. In particular it is not competent for the directors to raise actions in connection with such property.'

1 *Imperial Hotel (Aberdeen) Ltd v Vaux Breweries Ltd* 1978 SLT 113.

6.03 While the general principle is accepted that, on the appointment of a receiver, the directors' powers to deal with the company's assets are suspended, it is thought that to extend this principle to exclude the right of the directors to raise actions in relation to the company's property is too wide an interpretation of such a principle particularly in light of the reasoning behind a Court of Appeal decision in England[1] subsequent to that in the *Imperial Hotel* case.[2] It was held in the Court of Appeal decision that a provision in a debenture empowering the receiver to bring an action in the name of the company whose assets were charged was merely an enabling provision, investing the receiver with the capacity to bring such an action, and did not divest the company's directors of their power to institute proceedings on behalf of the company, provided that the proceedings did not interfere with the receiver's function of getting in the company's assets or prejudicially affect the debenture holder by imperilling the assets. The court went on to hold that the directors were under a duty to bring an action which was in the company's interest because it was for the benefit of creditors generally, and to pursue that right of action did not amount to dealing with the company's assets so as to require the receiver's consent or concurrence. Any request for such consent or concurrence would have presented the receiver with certain difficulties in that the action instigated by the directors in the name of the company was against the debenture holder who had appointed the receiver.

1 *Newhart Developments Ltd v Co-operative Commercial Bank Ltd* [1978] QB 814.
2 *Imperial Hotel (Aberdeen) Ltd v Vaux Breweries Ltd* 1978 SLT 113.

6.04 The effect of a receiver's appointment on the powers of directors in relation to proceedings in the company's name and behalf has been considered in an unreported sheriff court case[1] which is referred to in more detailed discussion of this topic in Chapter 2.[2] It is suggested that the powers of the directors to take or continue such proceedings may only be exercised if in doing so there is no interference with the performance by the receiver of his functions. To deprive them of any right to raise actions in connection with the property covered by the charge could effectively prevent them from instituting proceedings on the company's behalf against the receiver himself for breach of duty.

1 *Hastings Black Construction Ltd v ACR (Air Conditioning and Refrigeration) Ltd* (1984) 4 October (unreported) Glasgow Sheriff Court.
2 See Chap 2 paras 2.18 to 2.24.

6.05 Where a floating charge does not extend over the whole assets of a company, the powers and duties of the directors in relation to the excluded assets (including assets held in trust) remain intact.

Position of employees

6.06 The general rule is that, except in certain special circumstances mentioned below, the appointment of a receiver does not of itself terminate then existing contracts of employment between the company and its employees.[1] The special circumstances in which the appointment of a receiver results in termination of such contracts were enunciated in an English decision[2] involving the appointment out of court by holders of a debenture of a receiver and manager to act as agent of the company and are as follows:

(1) the appointment was accompanied by the sale of the business of the company; or

(2) simultaneously with, or very soon after, the appointment, the receiver entered into a new agreement with a particular employee which was inconsistent with the continuation of his previous contract of service; or

(3) the continuation of a particular employee's employment was inconsistent with the role and function of the receiver and manager.

1 *Re Foster Clark Ltd's Indenture Trusts, Loveland v Horscraft* [1966] 1 WLR 125; *Re Mack Trucks (Britain) Ltd* [1967] 1 WLR 780; *Griffiths v Secretary of State for Social Services* [1974] QB 468; *Nicoll v Cutts* (1985) Times, 20 May.
2 *Griffiths v Secretary of State for Social Services* above.

6.07 That case[1] involved the company's managing director and in relation to the last of these special circumstances it was held that the mere fact that he held such position did not mean that his continued employment in that capacity was inconsistent with the role and function of the receiver in that, firstly, he had, in fact as well as in theory, been under the fairly stringent control of the Board and, secondly, the receiver had not been appointed to work full-time in the conduct of the company's business but merely to exercise supervision and control over the way in which the company's business was run with particular regard to the financial implications.

1 *Griffiths v Secretary of State for Social Services* [1974] QB 468.

6.08 The general rule in relation to employees' contracts of service as stated by the court in England is consistent with the statutory provision[1] that any contract entered into by or on behalf of the company prior to the receiver's appointment shall, subject to its terms, continue in force notwithstanding such appointment. As a practical matter, however, if the receiver wishes to continue any such contract (or for that matter enter into new contracts of employment) he will in order to maintain the employee's goodwill ensure that the employee is paid as such payments will be a proper expense of the receivership. The effect of the general rule as to pre-receivership contracts of employment is that the employees in question have, for the purposes of the Employment Protection (Consolidation) Act 1978 continuity of employment.

1 Insolvency Act 1986, s 57(7).

6.09 Prior to the coming into effect of section 58 of the Insolvency Act 1985 (now consolidated in section 57 of the Insolvency Act 1986) a receiver incurred no personal liability merely by continuing to employ existing employees of the company.[1] This was thought by the government to put at risk the interests of such employees and that section accordingly made amendments to the statutory provisions governing the agency and liability of a receiver for contracts so as to render a receiver personally liable for contracts of employment adopted by him[2] although he is given a fourteen day period of grace to decide whether or not to adopt any such contract.[3]

1 *Nicoll v Cutts* (1985) Times, 20 May.
2 See now Insolvency Act 1986, s 57(2).
3 Ibid s 57(5).

Rights of employees on receivership

Preference for wages

6.10   Where a receiver is appointed, debts which would have ranked as preferential debts in a winding up require to be paid from the assets in the receiver's hands in priority to the floating charge creditor's debt provided such preferential debts have been intimated, or otherwise become known to him, within six months of advertisement by him for claims in the Edinburgh Gazette and a local newspaper.[1] While section 59(1) of the Insolvency Act 1986 provides for such priority where a receiver is appointed 'and the company is not at the time of the appointment in course of being wound up' this does not necessarily preclude the payment of these debts by the receiver even where his appointment is subsequent to the commencement of a winding up.[2]

1 Insolvency Act 1986, s 59(1) and (2).
2 *Manley Petitioner* 1985 SLT 42.

6.11   The debts which rank as preferential debts in a winding up are those which so rank under sections 175 and 386 of the Insolvency Act 1986 and Schedule 6 to that Act (read with Schedule 3 to the Social Security Pensions Act 1975) and there is a right of relief in respect of any such debts so paid from the assets of the company available for the payment of ordinary creditors. These debts include inter alia:
(1)   so much of any amount which is owed by the company to an existing or past employee and is payable by way of remuneration in respect of the whole or any part of the period of four months up to the receiver's appointment, subject to such maximum amount prescribed by order of the Secretary of State;[1] and
(2)   any accrued holiday remuneration in respect of any period of employment prior to the receiver's appointment owed to an employee whose employment has been terminated before or after the receiver's appointment.[2]

1 Insolvency Act 1986, Sch 6, para 9 and s 387(4)(b): the present limit is £800.
2 Ibid para 10 and s 387(4)(b).

6.12   An amount is payable by way of remuneration if it is paid as wages or salary whether for time or piece work or earned wholly or partly by way of commission.[1] It does not include remuneration payable to a director by way of fees. Holiday remuneration is deemed to have accrued if, notwithstanding termination of employment, it would have so accrued had such employment continued until the holiday entitlement arose and remuneration in respect of a period of holiday is deemed to be wages or salary for such period and includes sums which for social security purposes would have been treated as earnings for such period.[2] Likewise, remuneration in respect of absence from work through sickness or other good cause is deemed to be wages or salary for the period of absence.[3]

1 Insolvency Act 1986, Sch 6, para 13(1)(a).
2 Ibid paras 14(2) and 15(b).
3 Ibid para 15(a).

6.13   In addition certain other entitlements of employees principally under the employment protection legislation, each of which are dealt with later in this chapter, are deemed to be wages in respect of the periods for which they are payable.[1] These are:
(1) guarantee payments;
(2) remuneration on suspension on medical grounds;
(3) payments for time off work for trade union activities, looking for work etc or ante-natal care;
(4) statutory sick pay; and
(5) remuneration under a protective award.
These entitlements are deemed to be wages in respect of the period for which they are payable. As a result there is a problem in the case of protective awards as to how such awards in so far as relating to a period after a receiver's appointment should be treated. This problem is in practice resolved by the payment of such an award being made to the employee by the Secretary of State for Employment out of the Redundancy Fund.[2]

1 Insolvency Act 1986, Sch 6, para 13(1)(b), (2).
2 Employment Protection (Consolidation) Act 1978, s 122(3)(d) and see para 6.25.

Entitlements under employment protection legislation

6.14   In addition to the preferential statutory rights on receivership in respect of arrears of wages, or salary etc, employees also have other statutory entitlements introduced by the employment protection legislation which, while generally unaffected by the receivership of their company employer, are paid not by the receiver, but by the Secretary of State for Employment out of particular statutory funds. Before dealing with the treatment of such entitlements on receivership it is necessary to describe them. As it is not within the scope of this work to describe these comprehensively the descriptions in the following paragraphs are of necessity brief and reference should be made to the relative statutory provisions for more detail.

Redundancy payments

6.15 An employee made redundant is entitled to a redundancy payment calculated in accordance with Schedule 4 to the Employment Protection (Consolidation) Act 1978 (referred to hereafter as 'the 1978 Act'). In most cases the calculation is based on 1 week's pay for each year's service under the age of forty-one and 1.5 weeks' pay for each year's service over the age of forty-one with a maximum of twenty years' service being allowable. Thirty-five per cent of a redundancy payment is normally recoverable by the employer from the statutory Redundancy Fund. It has been announced that redundancy rebates are to be discontinued with effect from 1 October 1986 except for firms employing fewer than ten employees.

Notice

6.16 While at common law employees have always been entitled to contractual notice where so provided by the contract or reasonable notice in the absence of a contractual provision, section 49 of the 1978 Act now lays down statutory minimum periods of notice which may be summarised in most cases as one week's notice for each year of service up to a maximum of twelve. Under Schedule 3 to the 1978 Act employers are obliged to pay employees during the statutory notice period.

Protective award

6.17 There are statutory requirements laid down in Part IV of the Employment Protection Act 1975 for handling redundancies where certain descriptions of employees are represented by independent trade unions recognised by the employer. These requirements are, shortly, that an employer must consult with the union or unions in question about proposed redundancies at the earliest opportunity and not later than 30 days before the first redundancy in the event of between 10 and 99 employees being involved in such redundancies and not later than 90 days in the event of 100 or more employees being so involved. Failure to fulfil these requirements entitles the relevant union (not the individual employees) to apply to an industrial tribunal for an award as a protective award and, in the absence of special reasons justifying failure to consult, such an award will be made. The award, if made, entitles the employees to payment during the protective period which will be a period of up to 30 days in the case of 10–99 redundancies; up to 90 days in the case of 100 or more redundancies and 28 days in other cases. The protective period commences on the day on which the first dismissals by reason of redundancy take effect. The entitlement of any employee included in such an award is abated by any remuneration actually received or due for services rendered by the dismissing employer and by payments in lieu of notice. In the case of receivership for obvious practical reasons, it is more often than not impossible for the receiver to comply with these statutory requirements as to consultation, but in this connection it should be noted that insolvency or the appointment of a receiver is not of itself a special reason under section 101(2) of the Employment Protection Act 1975 justifying failure to comply with these statutory requirements[1] as the events leading to insolvency and/or the appointment of a receiver will generally be foreseeable by the company. There have, however, been circumstances which, in conjunction with insolvency, have been considered to be special reasons.[2]

1 *Bakers Union v Clarks of Hove Ltd* [1978] IRLR 366.
2 *Association of Patternmakers and Allied Crafts v Kirwin Ltd* [1978] IRLR 318 and *Union of Shop, Distributive and Allied Workers v Leancut Bacon* [1981] IRLR 295.

Maternity pay

6.18   Qualifying female employees (generally those with more than two years' service) who become pregnant are entitled to up to a maximum of six weeks' maternity pay calculated in accordance with section 35 of the 1978 Act, namely 9/10ths of a week's pay less the amount of the Social Security Maternity Allowance. This payment is normally recoverable by the employer from the statutory Maternity Pay Fund.[1]

1 Employment Protection (Consolidation) Act 1978, s 37.

Unfair dismissal

6.19   If an employee is found to have been unfairly dismissed he or she is entitled under the employment protection legislation to an award assessed under one or more of the following headings:
(a) Basic award[1]
   This is calculated in a similar way to a redundancy payment.
(b) Compensatory award[2]
   This is assessed on actual or anticipated loss but subject to a maximum amount of £8,000.[3]
(c) Enhancement on failure to obey a tribunal order to reinstate or re-engage.[4]
   In the ordinary case this amounts to an extra 13 to 26 weeks' pay.
(d) Dismissal related to trade unions or refusal to join same:
   (i)   a minimum basic award of £2,200;[5]
   (ii) where no order for reinstatement, or re-engagement, is made an additional 104 weeks' pay, subject to a minimum of £11,000 and a maximum of £22,000;[6]
   (iii) where such an order is not complied with, an additional 156 weeks' pay subject to a minimum of £16,500.[7]

1 Employment Protection (Consolidation) Act 1978, s 73.
2 Ibid s 74.
3 Unfair Dismissal (Increase of Compensation Limit) Order 1984, SI 1984/2020.
4 Employment Protection (Consolidation) Act 1978, s 7(2).
5 Ibid s 73(4A) and Unfair Dismissal (Increase of Limits of Basic and Special Awards) Order 1985, SI 1985/2033.
6 Ibid s 75A and Unfair Dismissal (Increase of Limits of Basic and Special Awards) Order 1985, SI 1985/2033.
7 Ibid.

Guarantee payment

6.20   Employees who are laid off are entitled to a guarantee payment calculated in accordance with section 14 of the 1978 Act, this payment being subject to a maximum of £10.70 per day and 5 days' pay in any period of 3 months.[1]

1 Employment Protection (Consolidation) Act 1978, s 15 and the Employment Protection (Variation of Limits) Order 1985, SI 1985/2032.

Suspension on medical grounds

6.21   Employees suspended from work to comply with any enactment or instrument or to comply with the Health and Safety at Work etc. Act 1974 are entitled to a week's pay for each week's absence up to a maximum of 26 weeks.[1]

1 Employment Protection (Consolidation) Act 1978, ss 19 and 21.

Time off for trade union activities

6.22   Employees who are union officials are entitled to what may simply be described as usual remuneration when engaged in carrying out their duties as such officials or in relevant training.[1]

1 Employment Protection (Consolidation) Act 1978, s 27.

Time off to look for employment or arrange training

6.23   Employees who are under notice of redundancy are entitled to be paid for absence from employment either to look for alternative employment or arrange training.[1]

1 Employment Protection (Consolidation) Act 1978, s 31.

6.24   Where in the foregoing entitlements reference is made to a 'week's pay', this is calculated in accordance with Schedule 14 to the 1978 Act. A 'week's pay' is presently subject to a maximum limit of £155.[1]

1 The Employment Protection (Variation of Limits) Order 1985, SI 1985/2032.

Treatment of employees' claims including statutory preferential rights and employment protection entitlements on receivership

6.25   The claims of employees in respect of unpaid salary or wages (as defined for this purpose) and their entitlements under the employment protection legislation may be dealt with in the three following ways, each of which may overlap the other:

(1) If it is a claim for wages or salary or for deemed wages and/or for accrued holiday pay it is entitled, within the statutory limits, to a preferential ranking.

(2) It may be paid by the Secretary of State for Employment out of the Redundancy Fund or other appropriate fund.

(3) To the extent that it is not paid out as a preferential claim or by the Secretary of State, it will be entitled to an ordinary ranking in the liquidation of the company if any surplus assets are available for ordinary creditors. For example, a compensatory award for unfair dismissal is only entitled to an ordinary ranking. As regards payments by the Secretary of State he will on receivership pay such claims from the Redundancy or other appropriate fund where all or part of the claim in question is due to the employee on the later of:

(i) the date of insolvency which includes the date of the appointment of the receiver;[1] or

(ii) the date of termination of employment; or

(iii) in the case of a Protective Award or a basic award for unfair dismissal, the date of the award.[2]

1 Employment Protection (Consolidation) Act 1978, s 127(2).
2 Ibid s 122 as amended by the Employment Act 1982, Sch 3, para 3.

6.26 The claims which will be so paid, the limits of the payments and the Fund from which they are payable are as follows:

PAYMENTS BY SECRETARY OF STATE

Out of Redundancy Fund	*Maximum Amount*	*Maximum Period*	*Section of the 1978 Act*
Arrears of pay*	£155 pw	8 weeks	122(3)(a)
Holiday pay in respect of the 12 months immediately preceding the relevant date, including pay for accrued holidays and pay for holidays taken but for which no payment has been made by the employer	£155 pw	6 weeks	122(3)(c) 127(3)(a) 127(3)(b)
Pay in lieu of notice[1]	£155 pw	12 weeks	122(3)(b)
Basic award of compensation for unfair dismissal			122(3)(d)
Reimbursements of the whole or part of a premium or fee for an apprentice or articled clerk	Reasonable amount – such amount as receiver admits being deemed to be reasonable		122(3)(e) 122(8)

*It should be noted that 'arrears of pay' includes all the items in the deemed to be 'wages' category referred to earlier (section 122(4) of the 1978 Act)

Out of the Maternity Fund
Maternity pay – no maxima – section 40 of the 1978 Act.

1 This item is damages and is subject to mitigation by other earnings and by employment benefit. *Westwood v Secretary of State for Employment* [1985] AC 20 and [1984] IRLR 209, HL.

121

Occupational pension schemes

6.27   Included amongst preferential debts in a winding up and so in the preferential debts which a receiver must pay in priority to the floating charge creditor's debt is any sum owed by the company to which Schedule 3 to the Social Security Pensions Act 1975 applies, namely contributions to occupational pension and state scheme premiums.[1]

1 Insolvency Act 1986, Sch 6, para 8.

Sale of the business and hiving down

6.28   The receiver of a company's whole undertaking and assets in order to maximise his realisations will normally endeavour to dispose on a going concern basis of the company's business or parts of it or, where the company has several businesses, some of them. If a receiver were to sell a business as a going concern and either took no positive steps to terminate the contracts of the employees engaged in the business or only did so with effect from the effective date of transfer of the business to the purchaser the effect on the employees, whether or not offered re-employment by the purchaser, would be:

(1) the employees would cease to be employed by the company in receivership;

(2) the employees would become employed by the purchaser, subject to immediate dismissal in the case of those not offered re-employment;

(3) the employees would have continuity of employment for all purposes, and all rights which they had against their previous employer, namely the company in receivership, would be transferred against the purchaser;

(4) the employees not offered re-employment would be entitled to claim a redundancy payment[1] (subject to having the necessary qualifying service) and other usual claims including claims for notice and unfair dismissal (dismissals because of a transfer or connected with it being automatically unfair subject to certain provisos) against the purchaser who would alone be liable for such claims;

(5) the employees offered re-employment by the purchaser on terms no less favourable than those previously enjoyed with the company in receivership could not claim redundancy.

1 *Gorictree Ltd v R T Jenkinson* [1984] IRLR 391 and *Anderson v Dalkieth Engineering Ltd* [1984] IRLR 429.

6.29   These consequences flow from the combined effects of the provisions of sections 84 and 94 of the Employment Protection (Consolidation) Act 1978 and regulation 5 of the Transfer of Undertakings (Protection of Employment) Regulations 1981[1] and have obvious disadvantages from the point of view of the purchaser of the business. Employees with qualifying service who are re-engaged by the purchaser, while not entitled to such, might be disappointed at not receiving any redundancy payments although for this and other purposes their continuity of employment would be preserved. The receiver for his part would be relieved of the administrative work of processing employees' claims against the Redundancy Fund but otherwise no advantage would accrue to him or to the preferred creditors and floating charge holder in that had the employees' claims against the purchaser fallen upon the company they would either have been met from the Redundancy Fund or been ranked as ordinary claims.

1 SI 1981/1794.

6.30   For these reasons a receiver and a prospective purchaser from him of a business usually reach agreement on steps to be taken prior to the transfer of the business in relation to the persons employed in it. Before the introduction of the 1981 Regulations[1] the usual procedure was that the receiver, prior to the transfer of the business dismissed all the employees to avoid the purchaser having to take over their accrued redundancy rights and the purchaser would then offer to employ only those employees he wished to retain in the business. All the employees who held the qualifying service would be paid redundancy payments by the Department of Employment from the Redundancy Fund under section 106 of the 1978 Act. The department would rank as an ordinary creditor for the employer's proportion of these payments. While those employees re-engaged by the purchaser would start again for the purposes of redundancy entitlement, they would otherwise have continuity of employment under the provisions of Schedule 13 to the 1978 Act if they were employees at the time of the transfer (paragraph 17(2) of Schedule 13). The expression 'at the time of the transfer' was considered in an English Court of Appeal case[2] and it appears that the expression may be interpreted in various different ways. However, an employee who is re-engaged by the new owner of a business will generally have continuity of employment except for the purposes of redundancy if a redundancy payment was received.

1 SI 1981/1794.
2 *Teeside Times Ltd v Drury* [1980] ICR 338.

6.31   A receiver frequently 'hives down' the company's business or part of it to a new wholly owned subsidiary formed specially for that purpose prior to taking steps to dispose of it. The principal reasons for now doing so are that the receiver can then continue the business with the benefit of limited liability and it forms a very marketable package for a prospective purchaser although to avoid the build up of liabilities in the subsidiary and the consequential necessity to grant warranties and indemnities to a purchaser the hive-down operation is often not completed until a purchaser for the business has been found without necessarily a contract having been entered into for its sale. In a hive down operation the employees should remain employed by the company in receivership so as to ensure that any claims they may ultimately have for redundancy, payment in lieu of notice, or unfair dismissal are only entitled to an ordinary ranking. Another reason for hiving down, namely to facilitate the carry forward of tax losses, is only now relevant if the company is solvent.[1] The employees themselves do not suffer any material disadvantage in that the bulk of such claims will be met by the Department of Employment which will similarly rank in their place. Were the employees to be transferred with the business when the hive down to the subsidiary is carried through they would become in effect pre-preferential creditors which would only be of advantage to the Department of Employment but of distinct disadvantage to the preferential creditors and the holder of the floating charge. As in the case of a direct sale of the business to a purchaser the procedure followed in the sale of a hive down subsidiary prior to the introduction of the 1981 Regulations[2] was normally for the receiver to dismiss all the employees.

1 Finance Act 1986, s 42 and Sch 10.
2 Transfer of Undertakings (Protection of Employment) Regulations 1981, SI 1981/1794.

6.32   The introduction of the 1981 Regulations,[1] in spite of prior fears to the contrary, has not in practice inhibited the sale of businesses by receivers through potential additional liabilities in respect of accrued employment rights falling on purchasers nor has it altered to any material degree the normal pre-1981 Regulations procedure. Trade unions and employees generally also viewed the introduction of the 1981 Regulations with concern in that it was thought they could result in employees re-engaged by the purchaser on the sale of a business by a receiver being denied the right to claim redundancy although the normal pre-1981 Regulations procedure was followed.

1 SI 1981/1794.

6.33   To understand the apprehension with which the introduction of these Regulations was viewed it is necessary to consider their principal provisions. Regulation 5(1) provides:
'A relevant transfer shall not operate so as to terminate the contract of employment of any person employed by the transferor in the under-taking or part transferred but any such contract *which would otherwise have been terminated by the transfer* shall have effect after the transfer as if originally made between the person so employed and the transferee'.
For the purposes of the Regulations a 'relevant transfer' is a transfer from one person to another of an undertaking situated immediately before the transfer in the United Kingdom or a part of one which is so situated and any reference to a person employed in an undertaking is a reference to a person so employed *immediately before the transfer*.

6.34   The provisions of these Regulations of primary relevance in the context of a receivership situation are, with the exception of the special provisions to cover transfers by receivers and liquidators referred to later, those which refer to a person employed in an undertaking or any part of it *immediately before* its transfer under a contract which, *but for the provisions of the Regulations*, would be terminated by the transfer of the undertaking or its relative part. In the first place what does the expression 'immediately before' mean in this context? The Regulations in question were made in implement of Council Directive No 77/187/EEC[1] and that Directive refers to contracts of employment or an employment relationship 'existing on the date of the transfer'. Considerable confusion caused by conflicting decisions of the Employment Appeal Tribunal have been resolved, as this work goes to press, in a Court of Appeal decision[2] which approves of the decision in *Premier Motors (Medway) Ltd v Total Oil Great Britain Ltd*[3] and holds that the Regulations were intended to relate only to a contract of employment that was subsisting at the moment of the transfer of the undertaking. It follows that the Regulations would not apply to employees dismissed prior to the moment of the transfer. The Regulations apply, it should be noted in passing, to the transfer of undertakings and not simply to the transfer of assets.[4]

1 EEC Direction Notice 3(1).
2 *Secretary of State for Employment v Spence* (1986) Times, 2 June.
3 *Premium Motors (Medway) Ltd v Total Oil Great Britain Ltd* [1983] IRLR 471.
4 *Melon v Hector Powe Ltd* [1980] IRLR 80.

6.35   As already mentioned the 1981 Regulations[1] contain special provisions, introduced by Parliament as a result of representations made by or on behalf of insolvency practitioners in the United Kingdom, relating to transfers by receivers and liquidators against the background of the practice in the United Kingdom of hiving down by such receivers or liquidators. The effect of the provisions in question, which are contained in Regulation 4, is, in the event of the transfer by inter alia a receiver of a company to a wholly owned subsidiary, to postpone the transfer until immediately before either the subsidiary ceases, otherwise than by liquidation, to be such a subsidiary or the undertaking (or relevant part) is transferred by such subsidiary to a third party. These provisions put the receiver in the same position had he sold the undertaking (or relevant part) directly to a purchaser and so should he hive down the business or any part of it he can follow the procedure described in relation to the prior dismissal of employees.

1 SI 1981/1794.

6.36   It is generally accepted that the law with regard to employees' rights where businesses are transferred is in a most unsatisfactory state. The present confusion is compounded by certain recent decisions of the European Court which has held that Council Directive 77/187 which the Transfer Regulations are intended to implement does not extend to 'the transfer of an undertaking, business or part of a business where the transferor has been adjudged insolvent and the undertaking or business in question forms part of the assets of the insolvent transferor although the Member States are at liberty to apply the principles of the Directive to such a transfer on their own initiative'.[1]

1 Judgment of the European Court dated 7 February 1985 in Case 135/83 *HBM Abels and the Administrative Board of the Bedrijfsverenigin voor de Metaalindustrie en de Electrotechnische Industrie.*

Chapter 7

Sale of receivership assets

Introductory considerations

7.01   One of the most urgent matters for consideration by a receiver after his appointment is the investigation and evaluation of the business carried on by the company and its saleability as a whole or in parts. If he is fortunate, the receiver will have had an opportunity of considering a financial report prepared prior to and resulting in his appointment in which in all probability valuations will have been specified either on a going concern basis or a break-up basis. One of the unfortunate consequences of receivership is that valuations on a going concern basis in the recent economic climate are for practical purposes of limited value in a receivership context. As a very rough guideline, sales by a receiver at approximately one-third to one-half of a going concern valuation have not been unusual and, while most receivers will endeavour to sell more advantageously, a receiver will probably be reasonably satisfied with the consideration if, firstly, it reflects the best value which the receiver could reasonably have hoped to achieve in the circumstances and secondly, such consideration is equal to an amount in excess of an estimated break-up figure. It is emphasised, however, that each sale by a receiver carries with it different problems and characteristics and there is no such thing as a 'standard' sale of a business or its individual assets. In assessing whether the consideration properly reflects the best value which a receiver could reasonably hope to achieve, account will be taken of the extent of advertisement of the business or assets in the press and specialist publications and also of the general market conditions both as regards the general location of the business and assets and the state of the particular trade nationally and internationally.

7.02   There are, in practice, two principal courses open to a receiver in disposing of assets belonging to a company in receivership: he can either sell the business or separate businesses with their assets on a going concern basis in whole or in part or he can dispose separately of individual assets without continuing the trade. A combination of both is, of course, possible in the appropriate circumstances. It has been suggested[1] that a receiver can arrange to sell the issued share capital of the company in receivership on a basis which ensures creditors are taken on and which leaves something for the shareholders or arrange for a scheme of reconstruction but it is respectfully submitted that it will only be in exceptional circumstances that either of these courses of action will be either appropriate or possible.

1 *Tolley's Receivership Manual* (2nd edn) para 7.1.

7.03 Depending on the size and type of business, the receiver may decide to prepare and circulate an information brochure about the activities and particulars of the company including, for example, details of the latest accounts and trading results, the business itself and employees and information about the fixed assets and stock and work-in-progress. Most receivers who prepare such an information brochure will normally insert a disclaimer of liability in relation to any matters contained therein. Such a disclaimer will be in a form similar to the following:

'The following particulars are set out as a general outline only for the guidance of intending purchasers or their advisers and do not constitute either in whole or in part an offer or contract.

All references to descriptions, dimensions, references to condition and necessary permissions for use and occupation and other details, while given in good faith and believed to be correct should not be relied upon as statements or representations of fact by intending purchasers or their advisers all of whom should satisfy themselves by inspection or otherwise as to the accuracy of all such references. No warranty or representation whatsoever is given as to the accuracy of any such references. The Receiver acts only as agent of the company and without personal liability.'

Duties of receiver

7.04 Turning briefly to the duties of a receiver, it is generally accepted that the primary duty of a receiver is owed to the holder of the floating charge by whom he was appointed to realise the property subject to the charge with a view to satisfying such holder's secured claim. In preparing his information brochure the receiver should be very careful to avoid offering securities for sale, for example in the case of the issued share capital of a hive down subsidiary, as he may commit an offence under the Prevention of Fraud (Investments) Act 1958. The duties of a receiver are considered more fully in Chapter 3 but in relation to the disposal of assets generally, a receiver has a duty to exercise reasonable care in their disposal.[1]

1 *Standard Chartered Bank v Walker* [1982] 3 All ER 938; *Forth & Clyde Construction Co Ltd v Trinity Timber & Plywood Co Ltd* 1984 SLT 94; *American Express International Banking Corpn v Hurley* [1985] 3 All ER 564.

Form of agreements

7.05 There are set out in Appendices 9 and 10 of this book suggested forms of hive down agreement and agreement for the sale of a business and the first point to emphasise is that a clear and concise definition of the constituent elements in the particular business is essential. For ease of discussion, the meanings ascribed in such forms of agreement are used in the following paragraphs of this chapter.

7.06   A typical definition of a particular manufacturing business may include the business and undertaking of the Vendor relating to the manufacture, distribution and sale of space invaders and associated products carried on by the Vendor at Pitlochry including (without prejudice to the generality of the foregoing) the following:

(i)   all plant and machinery, vehicles, (including all unexpired periods of taxation licences), office furniture, fixtures, fittings and equipment all more particularly specified in Part [   ] of the Schedule and other equipment owned and used by the Vendor in connection with the Business (but, for the avoidance of doubt, shall exclude assets of the Vendor which are subject to leasing agreements or hire purchase or contract hire or otherwise encumbered);

(ii)   the stock, work-in-progress, raw materials and finished goods of the Business (excluding finished goods manufactured and sold to customers by the Vendor prior to the Transfer Date) and, if required, photocopies of each of the customer list, the order books, all other books and records of the Business and, the benefit of all rights and obligations under all contracts, orders and engagements relating to the Business current at the Transfer Date;

(iii)   the Premises; and

(iv)   all patents, designs, copyrights, trade marks, trading names (including in so far as the Vendor can grant the same the exclusive right for the Purchaser to use any particular trade name), know-how (including without limitation all technical or confidential information) or similar industrial or intellectual property rights (whether registered or not) used in or necessary to the production, marketing and sale of products manufactured by the Vendor in connection with the Business.

Difficulties in definition

'Owned and used'

7.07   The words 'owned and used' in the context of plant and machinery are deliberately inserted to exclude assets which are leased or on hire purchase. When, for example, a company in receivership possesses three or four fork lift trucks, two or three lorries, four or five private motor cars, a computer and photocopying equipment all on lease or hire purchase, it is fundamentally important to differentiate between items owned and items used but not owned. It is sometimes provided as a double precaution that an exclusion of all items subject to leasing agreements or hire purchase or contract hire or otherwise encumbered should be inserted. As often as not, the practical solution is that the receiver or, more probably, the purchaser may negotiate terms with the leasing or hire-purchase company for the continued use by the purchaser of such items. Opinions vary as to the desirability of including a schedule of plant and machinery which is owned by the company in receivership as there is a risk in preparing such a schedule that some equipment may be omitted or that equipment may be included which is leased or on hire purchase. In many cases, the plant and machinery and other assets will be quite obvious to the parties so that the need for a schedule is not so necessary. It is suggested (if time permits in the transaction) that, at least, a list of both the principal items which are owned and those which are leased or on hire purchase should be specified but the circumstances of the particular case will often dictate the best approach.

Basis of valuation

7.08 In some transactions the parties will have agreed an aggregate consideration for the Business or various individual assets and the necessity for valuations of, for example, stock and work-in-progress will not arise: however, in other cases this is not the position. If a valuation of such assets is required, it will be necessary for a stocktaking to be carried out at or as near as possible to the Transfer Date (normally the opening or close of business on a particular date) by representatives of the receiver and the purchaser. It is vitally important that the basis of valuation should be clearly specified whether in terms of standard accounting principles or otherwise eg the lower of cost or net realisable value using the principles and bases of accountancy consistent with those used in the preparation of valuations for the balance sheet of the company in receivership over the previous two or three years. It is often provided (but depends on the circumstances) that no account shall be taken of, or direct allowances made for, obsolete, damaged or slow-moving stock.

7.09 As one would expect those involved in stocktakings to be both experienced and responsible one would always hope that the provision of some firm basis of valuation (such as described) would prevent disputes arising between the parties. However, it is prudent to provide that in the event of a dispute arising as to any aspect of the stocktaking and/or the valuation, the same should be referred to an arbiter, acting as an expert and not as an arbiter and appointed by agreement between the parties or, failing agreement, as nominated by the holder of some office such as the President for the time being of the Institute of Chartered Accountants of Scotland whose decision shall be final and binding on the parties. There should also be provision for payment of the arbiter's fees and outlays either in the reference to arbitration or as may be directed by the arbiter.

7.10 Finally on valuations, it is recommended (if acting for a receiver) that a clause be inserted in the agreement to the effect that the parties will all use their best endeavours to ascertain the valuation of such stock and work-in-progress as soon as practicable and within a reasonable and definite period: otherwise a purchaser may delay completion of the stocktaking for his own benefit.

Status of finished goods

7.11 Questions sometimes arise as to the status of finished goods: for example, whether some items form finished goods sold to customers and, therefore, are not included in the sale or whether they form other unsold finished goods or work-in-progress and are so included. It is suggested that items which have been completed through all their manufacturing and production processes and are clearly identifiable as goods already sold to a particular customer (even although still physically within the company's premises) should always be regarded as finished goods sold to customers and not included in the sale: in other words, finished goods are goods which are in a deliverable state and in this context have already been sold.[1] Problems can arise, particularly in relation to sales for an agreed aggregate consideration, where over-zealous receivers produce and sell finished goods immediately prior to the Transfer Date, thereby diminishing the value of stock and work-in-progress. It is obvious that the agreement should endeavour to be clear and precise on such matters to avoid misunderstanding and dispute.

1 See the Sale of Goods Act 1979, s 61(5).

Assignation of rights and obligations under contracts

7.12 In certain receiverships the assignation or transfer of the rights and obligations under contracts will be vitally important as the rights and obligations under such contracts may form a significant element of the Business for which the purchaser is paying. In other types of receivership, contracts will be essentially short-term and formal assignation will not be necessary. Care should be taken to check the text of all contracts of any importance to ensure that the appointment of a receiver does not allow or result in automatic termination of any such contracts or otherwise adversely affect their value. If an assignation is required and is duly executed both by the company in receivership and the purchaser, it will, to be effective, require to be intimated to the third party in terms of the Transmission of Moveable Property (Scotland) Act 1862. As a practical consideration, if the contracts are a vital element of the business, the purchaser will not proceed unless at the very least he has reached an informal understanding with the third party or parties whereby agreement is reached with the purchaser taking over the particular contracts in question.[1]

1 For a general discussion on assignation of contracts reference should be made to David M Walker *The Law of Contracts and Related Obligations in Scotland* paras 29.18 et seq.

7.13 It should be borne in mind that contracts forming part of the Business often carry with them a strong element of *delectus personae* and a third party may not be agreeable to the assignation of the rights and obligations under a contract. Indeed, in certain cases, the contract may specifically prohibit assignation of rights without the prior permission of the third party. One of the areas where this problem commonly arises is building and other construction contracts: although most receivers will be reluctant to become involved in such contracts for obvious reasons of general personal liability and liability for defects, circumstances do arise where, in the early stages of a receivership, a receiver will see an opportunity to collect a substantial amount of money if he can assign the rights and obligations under one or more contracts to another construction company. A deed of novation is often entered into in these circumstances between the company in receivership, the employer and the new contractor. At the same time, a side agreement is usually entered into between the parties to deal with such matters as moneys lying in the hands of the employer, retention moneys and the exclusion by the company in receivership and the receiver of all liability for latent defects. The receiver will obtain a payment from the new contractor, the employer will have his contract performed more quickly and less expensively and the new contractor will collect the balance of sums due on the contract, presumably on terms advantageous to him.

Supplies on or about the Transfer Date

7.14 It is usual to provide that pre-payments made by the Vendor prior to the Transfer Date in respect of goods to be supplied to the Business but not delivered prior to the Transfer Date and not forming part of the Business at the Transfer Date shall be refunded by the purchaser within a period (normally seven days) after delivery of such goods.

7.15 The agreement should also make it clear that the purchaser will assume and fulfil all debts, liabilities and obligations relating to the Business arising or accruing after the Transfer Date and will take over all outstanding contracts, engagements and orders relating to the Business disclosed to it at or prior to the Transfer Date. A receiver should obtain an indemnity from the purchaser in respect of all losses arising out of the purchaser's failure to perform these obligations. Care should be taken to cover the position where goods are due to be supplied after the Transfer Date but which are delivered early by the supplier on or prior to the Transfer Date. In these circumstances, the purchaser should be responsible for payment but in a case where valuations of stock and work-in-progress are required, the early arrival of goods could involve the purchaser in paying twice. Accordingly, such goods should be excluded from any valuation of stock.

Books and records of the company

7.16 The beneficial ownership of the books and records of the company is usually retained by the company in receivership and if required, photocopies of such books and records are usually made available to both the receiver and the purchaser although physical delivery of such books and records has already been made to the purchaser. The possibility should always be covered of the appointment of a liquidator who in terms of section 144 of the Insolvency Act 1986 takes into his custody or under his control all the property of the company to which the company is or appears to be entitled. If the books and records have been delivered by the receiver to the purchaser and the beneficial ownership of such books and records also transferred to the purchaser, the liquidator would not be in a position to recover them. In addition, the receiver or the liquidator may require the books and records of the company to deal with creditors generally or in connection with possible offences by officers of the company. It should be noted that, in terms of section 33 of and Schedule 7 to the Value Added Tax Act 1983, where a business carried on by a taxable person is transferred to another person as a going concern, the Commissioners can require any records relating to the business which under Schedule 7 are required to be preserved, to be preserved for any period after the transfer not exceeding three years.

Patents and trade marks

7.17 In acquiring rights to patents and trade marks, a purchaser will require a formal assignation of all such rights and will thereafter require to apply to the Patents Office or Trade Mark Registry (in the case of registered marks) to complete the appropriate registration formalities.

Premises

7.18 In relation to heritable and leasehold property being acquired by the purchaser the normal conveyancing procedures will obviously require to be carried out but this aspect is considered at paragraphs 7.64 to 7.77.

Book debts

7.19 As a general rule, the definition of the Business will not include the right to collect all book debts up to and including the Transfer Date. Most receivers will wish to retain the right to collect outstanding debts of the company in receivership and will only be interested in selling physical assets. However, circumstances may arise where the purchaser wishes to maintain sole contact with customers as a result of his purchase of the Business and it may be convenient for the receiver to allow the purchaser to collect on his behalf as agent certain or all of the outstanding book debts, on the basis of a commission (incorporating expenses incurred) being charged by the purchaser to the receiver.

7.20 Again, arrangements of this nature may form part of a total package with the purchaser and the only warning note which might be sounded relates to the financial standing of the purchaser. It would be ironical, indeed, for a receiver to appoint the purchaser to act as his agent and for the purchaser, during the period of the engagement, to go into receivership or liquidation or become bankrupt, without clearly establishing a valid trust over the funds collected on behalf of the receiver and remitting such funds into a separate account as required pursuant to the decision in *Clark Taylor & Co Ltd v Quality Site Developments (Edinburgh) Ltd.*[1] It is obviously a question of judgment for the receiver in the particular circumstances. A suggested form of letter regulating the terms of any such agreement for the collection of debts is given in Appendix 11.

1 1981 SLT 308.

Liabilities prior to the Transfer Date

7.21 The purchaser will be anxious to ensure that he does not take over or in any way become responsible for any of the debts and liabilities of the Business incurred by the company in receivership prior to the Transfer Date. As the purchaser is acquiring only assets, the purchaser will not normally in any event be concerned with debts and liabilities except perhaps in the case of liabilities to employees.[1] The purchaser should, if he can, however, obtain an indemnity from the company in receivership and the receiver from and against all such debts and liabilities.

1 Transfer of Undertakings (Protection of Employment) Regulations 1981.

Goodwill

7.22 Goodwill is rarely included as part of the constituent elements in the sale by a receiver of the business. It is, of course, a very intangible asset in the case of solvent businesses and even more so in a receivership context. For that reason a value is rarely placed on the goodwill of the business of a company in receivership and if it is included as an asset, its value will usually be nominal. In a sale, goodwill also suffers from the disadvantage of attracting *ad valorem* stamp duty on the value attributable to it as part of the consideration payable by the purchaser.

Early transfer of the Business

7.23 It will be readily appreciated that although agreement in principle may have been reached quickly between the receiver and the prospective purchaser, there are many and detailed arrangements to be discussed before a formal agreement can be finally concluded between the parties. Many solicitors engaged in insolvency work experience some anxiety when it is suggested by the purchaser and the receiver that notwithstanding the wording of a formal agreement has still to be concluded, they wish to enter into some form of interim arrangement pending completion of such an agreement whereby the purchaser takes over the effective management and operation of the business. From a commercial point of view, such a course of action may be sensible for the future success of the Business in the hands of the purchaser but the encapsulation of a suitable form of wording may create problems. In the final analysis, such an arrangement can really only be contemplated where the receiver is satisfied with the good faith and standing of the purchaser, financial and otherwise. A suggested form of wording is given in Appendix 12 but it is emphasised that such wording is an outline only and requires to be adapted to suit the particular circumstances of the case.

Mechanics of sale of the Business-form of sale

7.24   There are basically two methods of disposing of a business. It can be implemented either (1) by way of an agreement for the sale of the business between the company in receivership and the purchaser (a suggested style of which is given in Appendix 10) or (2) by way of a hive down agreement between the company in receivership and a new subsidiary of the company in receivership followed, after an interval of at least a few days, by a share purchase agreement between the company in receivership and the eventual purchaser for the sale to the purchaser of the issued share capital of the new subsidiary (suggested styles of which are given in Appendices 9 and 13).

Missives

7.25   While consideration will be given principally to formal agreements, there is nothing to prevent the sale of the Business or of individual assets being effected through an exchange of missives between the solicitors for the respective parties. However, all solicitors involved in missives of this nature should be encouraged to agree the form of words between them prior to delivering holograph letters: otherwise the process of comprehending five or six letters constituting missives can become very tedious and cumbersome. In general, where the particular business is of some substance, it would be more usual practice for a formal agreement to be concluded between the parties.

Designation of vendor and liability of receiver

7.26   Before dealing with the main clauses of these types of agreement, a few words should be said about the designation of the company in receivership. Any sale of a business or its individual assets is essentially a sale by the company albeit that the receiver negotiates, authorises and effects any such sale under the power given to him in terms of Schedule 2 to the Insolvency Act 1986: the receiver having been appointed by the holder of the floating charge acts in terms of section 57(1) of that Act as an agent of the company in realising the assets attached by such floating charge. It is often helpful, however, to design the company in receivership as the vendor acting by its receiver followed by the designation of the receiver (thereafter defined as 'the receiver') because certain obligations may fall to be performed by the vendor and the receiver will wish to ensure that as few obligations as possible fall upon him. Nonetheless, it seems clear that if a company in receivership has undertaken an obligation, such an obligation would be enforceable against the company in receivership and recoverable from the assets caught within the floating charge under and in terms of section 60(1)(d) of the Insolvency Act 1986.

7.27 All receivers will seek to exclude completely personal liability (bearing in mind the provision of section 57(2) of the Insolvency Act 1986 which states that a receiver is personally liable on any contract entered into by him except in so far as the contract otherwise provides) but if compelled to grant some personal obligations a receiver will wish a clause inserted to the effect that he will only be liable to the extent of any free proceeds available after all categories of persons described in section 60(1) of the Insolvency Act 1986 (which includes the holder of the floating charge by virtue of which he was appointed) have been satisfied. If any liability falls upon the receiver in terms of such a clause, the receiver, by virtue of section 57(3) of the Insolvency Act 1986, is entitled to be indemnified out of the property in respect of which he was appointed. The effect of these provisions is that if a claim is competent against the receiver personally out of the free proceeds available to the liquidator, the provision for the receiver's liabilities under section 60(1)(d) of the Insolvency Act 1986 will be increased by the extent of such claim. As liquidation may follow at an early date there is a strong case for inserting a time limitation of, say, six months for the intimation of any claim under the agreement against the receiver otherwise the receiver may not be in a position to release all the surplus funds to the liquidator.

Terms of agreement for sale of business

7.28 The main clauses of an agreement for the sale of a business (not previously considered) are set out below.

Recital

A recital is normally included which sets out the provisions of the floating charge by virtue of which the receiver was appointed and details of his appointment. If acting for the purchaser, a copy of the receiver's appointment should be obtained together with copies of the floating charge under which the receiver was appointed and the certificate of registration of the charge. Attention is drawn, however, to the former rules set out under the provisions of section 471(3) of the 1985 Act which stated that a person transacting with a receiver should not be concerned to inquire whether any event has happened to authorise the receiver to act. It is submitted that the section relieved the purchaser, for example, from the obligation of ascertaining whether in relation to the appointment of a receiver pursuant to section 469 of the 1985 Act (now section 53 of the Insolvency Act 1986) an event of default had arisen in terms of the floating charge causing the floating charge holder to appoint a receiver or whether the company, where the floating charge so provided, requested the appointment in terms of its provisions. It did not relieve the purchaser from checking that the receiver had actually been appointed by the floating charge holder pursuant to the floating charge. However, section 55(4) of the Insolvency Act 1986 now provides that a person dealing with a receiver in good faith and for value shall not be concerned to inquire whether the receiver is acting within his powers. It appears, therefore, that a purchaser in dealing with a receiver is under no obligation to inquire into the regularity or otherwise of a receiver's appointment or whether he is acting within his powers and it will only be in cases where the purchaser is on notice of an irregularity in the receiver's appointment or restraint in his powers that the onus will shift to the purchaser to satisfy himself further, otherwise he will be deprived of the benefit of the protection of section 55(4).

Interpretation

7.29 An interpretation clause should contain definitions of the business (encompassing the principal assets) or of the assets (in the case of a sale of assets), the Transfer Date and normally a completion date if different from the Transfer Date.

Consideration

7.30 The consideration in the agreement will either be a fixed aggregate amount or a variable amount depending, for example, on the result of a stocktaking. In either case it is advisable to have a proper allocation of the consideration as against particular assets. From the point of view of the receiver, he will wish to ensure that the allocation compares favourably with any valuations obtained by him of assets such as heritable property and plant and machinery and that such allocations will stand scrutiny by a liquidator who will wish to see an allocation in excess of break-up. The figure for any heritable property will also be important in determining the amount to which a holder of a standard security over such property is entitled although the prior approval of the heritable creditor to such allocation is not only advisable but essential if such creditor's claim will not be satisfied in full from the amount allocated to such heritable property. From the point of view of the purchaser, he will wish to see sensible values taking into account, principally, possible stamp duty on the conveyance of heritable property, capital allowances on fixed assets (though this is less important since the changes to the structure of capital allowances) and also the availability of possible government assistance in respect of fixed assets.

Exclusion of warranty

7.31 A useful clause if acting for a receiver is one stating that the purchaser, having inspected the assets comprised in the Business as they stand, shall take the same in the condition in which they are and no warranty or assurance is given or implied as to the condition, quality or fitness of such assets.

Good title

7.32 It is normal in a clause dealing with completion of the sale to insert wording that the vendor shall deliver full and free possession of the Business free from all liens, restrictions, options, encumbrances, mortgages and charges of any kind. In this connection if any of the parties have knowledge of a retention of title claim, suitable arrangements should be made in case the claim is upheld. If the purchaser proceeds without knowledge of a particular claim, there is a strong argument that he has purchased in good faith and obtained a good title,[1] thereby giving to the supplier, in the event of the retention claim being upheld, a claim in damages against the receiver. As a practical solution where a retention of title claim has been intimated but not accepted, the receiver can attempt to negotiate with the supplier for an amount equal to the invoice value of the goods the title of which is in dispute to be placed in a separate bank account pending resolution of the dispute or can arrange for the supplier to buy back the goods in dispute at a discounted figure (probably the likely realisation figure at an auction). If the latter method is employed, then if the supplier is successful in his claim, he will obtain full payment of the value of the original goods irrespective of any arrangements made for the return of the goods at a discounted figure. If he is unsuccessful, at least he will have obtained the return of the goods at the discounted figure. Most receivers will procure that they have an unchallengeable title to the assets which they are purporting to sell and will normally make some arrangements with suppliers who are maintaining a retention of title claim.

1 Sale of Goods Act 1979, s 25(1); *Thomas Graham & Sons Ltd v Glenrothes Development Corpn* 1968 SLT 2; and *Archivent Sales & Development Ltd v Strathclyde Regional Council* 1985 SLT 154.

Miscellaneous provisions

VAT

7.33 It should be borne in mind that VAT may be payable on the sale of certain assets unless it can be shown that a business or a part of a business is being sold. Where the purchaser is taking over a business or is substantially carrying on such business hitherto carried on by the company in receivership, liability for VAT is avoided by reliance on the Value Added Tax (Special Provisions) Order 1981.[1] In cases of doubt, where prior clearance from HM Customs and Excise cannot be obtained, it is recommended that VAT should be charged and should be recovered at completion from the purchaser. In addition, it is advisable to state that the consideration is exclusive of VAT (if any) otherwise the purchaser may seek to claim that the consideration was VAT inclusive and thereby leave the receiver with a potential liability for an apparent VAT element on the sale. If VAT is payable, the receiver will require to deliver to the purchaser a VAT invoice to enable the purchaser to recover the VAT in due course. It has recently been held[2] in the context of insolvency that the ultimate intentions of the transferee as to the type of goods or services that it would supply were irrelevant for VAT purposes as was the transferor's insolvency. The vital consideration was whether the transferee had been put in possession of a going concern business at the time of transfer.

1 SI 1981/1741.
2 *Customs and Excise Comrs v Dearwood Ltd* (1986) Times, 16 June.

Stamp duty

7.34   Stamp duty at the current *ad valorem* rate will normally be exigible as follows, based on the value of the following assets comprised within the Business: namely, conveyances of heritable and leasehold properties, goodwill and assignations of patents and trade marks. Stamp duty is also payable on the consideration for book debts if these are included in the assets comprised within the Business. It may in certain circumstances be necessary for the agreement for the sale of the business to be adjudicated by the Stamp Duty Office. Stamp duty is, in the absence of any agreement to the contrary, payable by the party wishing to enforce the agreement.

Section 61 petition

7.35   What happens if a standard security holder refuses to grant a discharge because he will not receive the full amount of indebtedness due to him or as happened in the petition of *Armour and Mycroft*[1] the company in receivership is inhibited prior to the appointment of the receiver and the inhibitors refuse to discharge the inhibition? The answer is that the receiver requires to petition the court pursuant to section 61 of the Insolvency Act 1986 for the discharge of the security or encumbrance. Fortunately, the number of occasions when difficulties of this nature arise are thought to be infrequent and the *Armour and Mycroft* petition[1] was the first reported case which invoked the provisions of section 21 of the 1972 Act.[2]

1 1983 SLT 453.
2 See now the Insolvency Act 1986, s 61.

7.36   The facts in the *Armour and Mycroft* petition[1] were that the petitioners as the joint receivers of Carron Company Limited were about to sell the first of the Carron businesses when it was discovered that a creditor, Buccleuch Engineering Limited, had, on the day before the appointment of the joint receivers, raised an action for payment of a debt and had inhibited on the dependence of the action. The practical short-term solution involved the payment into court of an amount equal to the debt and the execution by Buccleuch of a partial discharge of the inhibition in relation to the heritable property forming part of the Carron business about to be sold together with an application by the joint receivers under section 21 of the 1972 Act.[2] As was appreciated at the time, the joint receivers were likely to be selling various businesses and properties over the immediately following weeks and months thereafter and a motion to the court for further partial discharges of the inhibition as and when required was felt to be impractical. It was, therefore, agreed by the parties concerned that an application should be made pursuant to the provisions of section 21.[2] On the application being heard, Buccleuch contended that authority for the sale should only be given on condition that their debt was satisfied before that of the floating charge holders or, alternatively, that they should be paid before the company received any part of the proceeds of sale.

1 1983 SLT 453.
2 See now the Insolvency Act 1986, s 61.

7.37 The court held (1) that except in exceptional circumstances the court should not impose conditions on a sale whereby creditors who had not effectually executed diligence – such as the respondents – would obtain the same favourable treatment as if they had; but (2) that it was equitable that the respondents should be paid before the company, since by their inhibition they could have successfully prevented the company from selling its heritable property but for the intervention of the receivers; and the approval of the sales was authorised subject to this condition.

Hive down agreements

7.38 A few observations in general should be made about hive down agreements.

Nature of hive down agreements

In relation to a business, a hive down agreement itself is essentially an agreement between a company, including one in receivership and a new wholly owned subsidiary for the sale of the Business to that new subsidiary, the reasons for which are more fully set out in paragraph 7.39. The consideration is normally stated as an inter-company loan repayable on demand. It used to be very important for tax reasons from the eventual purchaser's point of view that the new subsidiary should carry on the same trade, normally for a few days, under the control of the receiver before the next stage was reached: namely, the sale by the company in receivership to the eventual purchaser of the issued share capital of the subsidiary. It was equally important that during the whole stages of hive down and subsequent sale there should be a continuity of ownership of the trade.[1] For more detailed discussion of this subject reference should be made to a specialist publication.[2] However, the taxation advantages of hive downs in receivership situations have been severely curtailed by the provisions of the Finance Act 1986[3] and it remains to be seen in practice whether hive downs will be used as a convenient receivership vehicle in the future.

1 Income and Corporation Taxes Act 1970, s 177.
2 David Bertram *Tax Consequences of Receivership and Liquidation* Butterworths.
3 Finance Act 1986, s 42 and Sch 10.

Reasons for hive down agreement

7.39   The main reasons for hiving down used to be as follows but as a result of changes[1] in the law effected by statute only the reason given in paragraph (2) following is likely to remain relevant:

(1)   To preserve the tax benefit of trading losses available to be carried forward under section 177 of the Income and Corporation Taxes Act 1970 so as to enhance the value of the business to the purchaser although the hiving down had to involve the whole of the particular business and undertaking of the company and had to be completed before a written agreement was concluded with the eventual purchaser.[2] Obviously, the earlier the hiving down took place the easier it was to show that such hiving down had not taken place with a view to a sale to an eventual purchaser.

(2)   To avoid the consequences of liquidation by transferring the whole of the business to a separate legal persona, thereby avoiding uncertainties in respect of (a) the receiver's position as agent of the company in receivership, (b) his ability to carry on the Business and (c) his liability on contracts entered into after the appointment of a liquidator.

(3)   To avoid arguments with such utilities as the gas, electricity, water and telecommunications authorities whose status respectively is not and was not preferential in respect of accounts unpaid as at the date of appointment of the receiver or in any circumstances and who are obliged to supply a new consumer although it is understood that, in England, where such arguments used to be more prevalent, such authorities used to decline to operate the same terms as offered to the company in receivership. However, such utilities, if requested by or on behalf of inter alia an administrative receiver to supply the service in question, are now prohibited by statute[3] from making it a condition of the giving of a supply or doing anything which has the effect of making it a condition of the giving of a supply that any outstanding charges in respect of a supply given to the company before the relevant date are paid, the relevant date being defined to include the date on which the administrative receiver was appointed.

1 Finance Act 1986, s 42 and Sch 10; Insolvency Act 1986, s 233.
2 Otherwise, there would be no carry forward of trading losses as the beneficial ownership of the 75 per cent of the issued share capital of the subsidiary as required by the Income and Corporation Taxes Act 1970, s 252 would have passed: *J H & S (Timber) Ltd v Quirk* (1972) 48 TC 595.
3 Insolvency Act 1986, s 233.

Requirement of wholly owned subsidiary

7.40   The new subsidiary, normally a ready made company, was usually for taxation reasons, before the impact of the Finance Act 1986, a wholly owned subsidiary of the company in receivership[1] and normally as there are usually only two shares of the new subsidiary in issue, one share is registered in the name of the company in receivership and the other in the name of the receiver who should sign a deed of declaration of trust indicating that he holds the share as a nominee of the company in receivership. The directors and secretary are normally the receiver and one or two of his partners. From the point of control over the assets hived down to the subsidiary, it is not advisable to appoint as directors and secretary either employees of the receiver's firm or more especially directors of the company in receivership. The registered office will normally be the receiver's own office.

1 To satisfy the rule under the Income and Corporation Taxes Act 1970, s 252 that at least 75 per cent of the issued share capital of the subsidiary was beneficially owned by the company in receivership.

Hive down but no purchaser

7.41 It sometimes happens in practice that following upon a hive down of the Business, the receiver is unable to find a purchaser who wishes to continue the Business as a going concern. While it is theoretically possible that the receiver in these circumstances might appoint a receiver himself by virtue of the floating charge in favour of the original company in receivership[1] over the assets and undertaking of the subsidiary rather than petition for liquidation of the subsidiary, no responsible receiver would ever contemplate such a course which would enable him to enjoy a secured creditor status as his personal reputation inter alia depends on honouring obligations to creditors of the hive down subsidiary. It is much more probable that the receiver will either 'hive up' the Business to the company in receivership (if this is practically possible) or, if the receiver has ceased trading, transfer the title to the various assets of the hive down subsidiary back to the company in receivership in either case proceeding on the basis that the hive down never took place. However, it may not be very easy on a practical basis or tidy to 'hive up' the Business or its individual assets and the more sensible course may be for the receiver to realise the assets at their best value in the hive down subsidiary, settle all creditors of the hive down subsidiary and remit the net amount of the realisations to the company in receivership by way of full settlement of the inter-company loan account.[2]

1 Paragraph 7.44.
2 Paragraph 7.45.

Main clauses of hive down agreement

7.42 The main clauses in a hive down agreement are fairly similar to those in an agreement for the sale of a business (as previously described) save for the following.

Consideration

The consideration is normally specified as such amount as the vendor and the purchaser may agree or such amount as may be certified by the receiver's firm acting as experts and not as arbiters. In practice, the amount agreed is the eventual consideration agreed with the ultimate purchaser.

Book entry as inter-company loan

7.43 No consideration actually passes between the parties but, as soon as the eventual consideration is known, in the books of account of both the company in receivership and its subsidiary an entry is made showing the consideration as an inter-company loan repayable on demand and on such terms as the parties wish to insert.

Floating charge by way of security

7.44 A valuable safeguard is to arrange for the new subsidiary to grant a floating charge in favour of the company in receivership, such floating charge being discharged on repayment of the inter-company loan. Such a safeguard is of particular benefit if the subsidiary continues to trade and if for any reason the sale to the ultimate purchaser does not proceed although the considerations set out in paragraph 7.41 are very relevant in this context.

7.45 If the receiver were to exercise his rights to appoint a receiver over the assets and undertaking of the hive down subsidiary, it is quite likely that other creditors of the hive down subsidiary would petition for its liquidation with a view to challenging the validity of the floating charge under the provisions of section 245 of the Insolvency Act 1986. As the hive down subsidiary prior to the hive down would have no assets and liabilities and on completion of the hive down would own assets the value of which was reflected by its own liability, namely the inter-company loan it is thought that a challenge under section 245 is unlikely to succeed. For discussion of the provisions of section 245, reference should be made to Chapter 1 paragraphs 1.42 to 1.51.

Miscellaneous provisions

VAT

7.46 If the subsidiary is registered for VAT purposes with effect from the Transfer Date, no VAT will be chargeable in terms of the 1981 Statutory Instrument[1] but, as previously observed, it is advisable to state that the consideration is exclusive of VAT (if any). Any liability for VAT will be for the account of the purchaser otherwise the eventual purchaser may seek to claim that the consideration was VAT inclusive and thereby leave the receiver with a potential liability for any VAT element on the sale.

1 Value Added Tax (Special Provisions) Order 1981, SI 1981/1741.

Stamp duty

7.47 The stamp duty position will normally be as previously described in connection with an agreement for the sale of a business except for the possible availability of section 42 relief.[1] Very occasionally, circumstances can arise where a receiver hives down a business (which comprises inter alia heritable property) where he is confident that he will find an eventual purchaser. In such circumstances, subject to proper statements being made in a statutory declaration to the effect that the receiver may as part of his statutory functions sell or otherwise dispose of the subsidiary, an application may be made under section 42[1] as amended by the Finance Act 1967 for relief from stamp duty on the basis that the company in receivership and its subsidiary company are associated. It is emphasised that the situations where section 42 applies are very strict: relief cannot be obtained and should not be sought if any arrangement has been reached with an eventual purchaser.

1 Finance Act 1930, s 42.

Insurance

7.48 It is vital to draw to the receiver's attention, following upon a hive down having taken place, the necessity of insuring the assets comprised in the Business in the name of the subsidiary.

Trading by receiver in control of subsidiary

7.49 To maintain the trading losses[1] when this was a material consideration, it used to be essential that the receiver should trade in control of the new subsidiary for a few days at least and despatch several invoices in the name of the new subsidiary before moving on to the next stage of the sale of its issued share capital to the eventual purchaser.

1 Income and Corporation Taxes Act 1970, s 177.

Legal and accounting expenses

7.50 As the hive down agreement was in many cases entered into with a view to preservation of the tax losses, it used to be thought (generally by receivers) that the subsidiary should bear all legal and accounting expenses in connection with the hive down. Such expenses would cover stamp duty and other outlays as well as a provision for accountancy assistance in the future in connection with agreeing the tax losses with the Inland Revenue. Normally, all such expenses were added to the amount of the inter-company loan which was ultimately paid by the eventual purchaser. In other words, the consideration payable by the eventual purchaser was appropriately increased.

7.51   There is normally included within the definition of 'the Business' any heritable property owned and occupied for the purpose of carrying on the Business by the company in receivership as, generally, although one of the principal purposes of hive down agreements used to be to transfer a trade for tax purposes, such heritable property will require to be included as part of the eventual purchaser's requirements. It should be appreciated, however, that when the hive down company ceases to be a wholly owned subsidiary of the company in receivership a capital gains tax liability may arise in the hands of the hive down subsidiary under section 278 of the Income and Corporation Taxes Act 1970. For this reason, heritable property is sometimes not transferred to the hive down company but is subsequently sold direct by the company in receivership to the eventual purchaser. The benefit of this method is that any capital gains tax liability falls on the company in receivership and will not be preferential in the subsequent liquidation of the company.

Main clauses of share purchase agreement

7.52   Having successfully hived the Business down to a new subsidary and having found an eventual purchaser, the company in receivership will then enter into an agreement with the purchaser for the sale of the issued share capital of the subsidiary. The normal provisions to be included in such an agreement (save as otherwise covered) are contained in the following paragraphs.

Consideration

7.53   On the assumption (as is the usual case) that two shares are in issue the consideration for the issued share capital will be stated to be £2 but there will also be an obligation on the purchaser as soon as it is in control of the subsidiary to procure the repayment of the inter-company loan.

Sale of shares

7.54   A clause will provide for the sale of the shares and on the completion date for transfers in respect of such shares to be executed and delivered by the vendor in favour of the purchaser or his nominee.

Directors' meeting to approve transfers

7.55   An obligation will be imposed on the company in receivership to procure that a meeting of the directors of the subsidiary will be held at which the transfers will, subject to stamping, be approved for registration in the books of the subsidiary.

Appointment of purchaser's nominees

7.56   A clause is normally inserted to deal with the appointment of the purchaser's nominees to the board and the resignation of the receiver's nominees as directors and as secretary.

Repayment of inter-company debt and discharge of floating charge

7.57   An obligation will be imposed on the purchaser to procure the subsidiary to repay the amount of inter-company indebtedness, and as soon as the repayment has been made, the company in receivership will, where the subsidiary has given it a floating charge, grant a discharge of such floating charge.

Exclusion of receiver's liability

7.58   As is normal in all such agreements, the exclusion of the personal liability of the receiver should be covered expressly as previously described in paragraph 7.27.

Management buy-outs

7.59   Reference should also be made to the fact that the sale of the Business (or part of it) may take the form of a management buy-out. The usual scenario involves three or four directors of the company in receivership or in larger receiverships a group of middle managers who are well acquainted with the manufacturing and production aspects of the business but who normally lack financial experience. Frequently, these are the vital personnel who perform a very important role in advising and assisting the receiver on a day to day basis particularly in the early days of receivership and, if they indicate a wish to purchase the Business, the receiver will normally encourage the managers to seek independent professional advice. It should be emphasised that, however anxious the receiver may be on a personal level to sell the Business to the managers, he must bear in mind his duties and properly advertise and expose the Business for sale to ensure that the optimum realisation is attained.

Preparation of financial package

7.60   Accountancy and general financial advice is readily available nowadays to a prospective management buy-out group from the accountancy profession and they, in suitable cases, are in a position to present to suitable institutions a financial package incorporating projected capital expenditure, working capital and cash flow requirements as well as marketing trends within the particular industry. Institutions such as the merchant banks, the clearing banks, Investors in Industry plc and the Scottish Development Agency are frequently involved and the managers, if properly advised, can normally hope to obtain grant assistance from bodies such as the Industrial Development Unit, if operating within its area, and the Highlands and Islands Development Board. The institutional investment often takes the form of part loan and part equity and frequently involves participating preference shares which may, at the option of the institution concerned, be converted into equity capital. In the case of loans, the institution will normally wish some security in the form of standard securities and/or floating charges or, if the managers are prepared to grant them, personal guarantees.

Finalising documentation

7.61   If acting for a team of managers, the importance of speed and professionalism in putting together all the parts of a complex jig-saw cannot be over-estimated. The solicitor acting for the managers must be negotiating and settling the form and content of the documentation with the institution's solicitors as well as dealing with the receiver's solicitors on the form of the agreement for the sale of the Business whether on the straightforward basis or through the hive down route. It is not appropriate in this book to deal in any detail with the documentation required by an institution but usually a form of subscription agreement will be settled whereby the institution takes up ordinary shares or preference shares as the case may be in the shelf company which will have been acquired by the managers. The form of the subscription agreement will be largely regulated by the terms of the offer letter issued to the managers by the institution.

Employees

7.62   The position of employees is considered in detail in Chapter 6. It is sufficient here to restate the broad principles relevant to the sale of a business. The 1981 Regulations[1] will apply to a sale of a business unless all the employees being transferred are dismissed some time prior to the effective date which, on the basis of a recent decision, means that the Regulations will apply only to a contract of employment that was subsisting at the moment of the transfer of the undertaking.[2]

1 Transfer of Undertakings (Protection of Employment) Regulations 1981.
2 *Secretary of State for Employment v Spence* (1986) Times, 2 June.

7.63   In a hive down transaction, the effective sale date is the date when the company in receivership ceases to be registered as the holder of the entire issued share capital of the subsidiary – it is not the effective date of the hive down. During the period from the effective date of the hive down to the date of acquisition of the share capital of the subsidiary by the purchaser, the employees should remain the employees of the company in receivership and should be sub-contracted by the company in receivership to the subsidiary, the subsidiary normally being obligated in terms of the hive down agreement to indemnify the company in receivership in respect of wages, PAYE, national insurance contributions and like obligations.

Property matters

7.64 Consideration will now be given to the conveyancing formalities involved in the sale of heritable property forming part of the Business before giving consideration to the question of letters of obligation to be given by the vendors' solicitors. It is recommended that the obligations of the receiver in relation to detailed property matters (including letters of obligation) should be discussed and agreed before any agreement is executed. In the case of a disposition of heritable property, it is suggested that the narrative should describe the company in receivership as 'Galaxy Products Limited incorporated under the Companies Acts and having its registered office at 10 Heavenly Mansions, Pitlochry acting by Frederick Galileo, Chartered Accountant, Saturn House, Pitlochry, as receiver thereof conform to instrument of appointment in his favour dated 11th November 1983.' The warrandice clause *quoad* the receiver should be qualified to fact and deed only and it is submitted that there should be inserted *in gremio* a clause excluding the personal liability of the receiver. The safe course is to make provision for these terms in the agreement for the sale of the Business. In terms of paragraph 8 of Schedule 2 to the Insolvency Act, 1986 the receiver has power to use the company's seal and adhibiting the seal together with execution by the receiver in the presence of two witnesses constitutes a probative execution. If there are joint receivers, the signature of both receivers is required unless, in terms of section 56(3) of the Insolvency Act 1986, the instrument of appointment permits them to act individually in which event the signature of one receiver is sufficient.

7.65 If the receiver of a Scottish company is selling property situated in England, the accepted mode of execution in England (provided there are friendly directors available) was formerly the normal two directors or one director and the secretary together with the company seal and the signature of the receiver in the presence of one witness. The reason for such a mode of execution was because of a receiver's former lack of capacity under English law to use the company seal. If there were no friendly directors available, the signature of the receiver appeared to suffice. However, section 42(1) of and paragraph 8 of Schedule 1 to the Insolvency Act 1986 provide that except in so far as may be inconsistent with the debenture by virtue of which he was appointed, the receiver is now specifically entitled to use the company's seal. Previously, it was understood that HM Land Registry took the view that a disposition executed by a receiver in the name and on behalf of the company could properly be accepted for registration (even though the company was in liquidation) provided the receiver had express power to effect such a disposition as he did in Scotland under the 1972 Act.

Power of execution by receiver after appointment of liquidator

7.66 From time to time, the question arises as to the competency of a receiver executing a disposition of heritable property after a liquidator has been appointed. Cautious conveyancers have been known to seek the consent (either by separate letter or *in gremio* of the disposition) of the liquidator. While the agency of the receiver may have been terminated by the appointment of a liquidator, it is submitted that it is still valid and competent for the receiver to dispose of property subject to the floating charge including heritable property, without recourse to the liquidator for the following reasons:

(1) under paragraph 2 of Schedule 2 to the Insolvency Act 1986, the receiver has the power to sell heritable property provided he is still the receiver; and

(2) under paragraphs 8 and 9 of Schedule 2 to the Insolvency Act 1986, the receiver has power to use the seal and execute any deeds on behalf of the company.

In addition, section 127 of the Insolvency Act 1986 (avoidance of dispositions of property after the appointment of a liquidator) does not apply to a sale by a receiver because in granting the charge the company disposed of the property and as was explained in the case of *Barrows v Chief Land Registrar*,[1] the rights and powers given to the receiver were those specified in the debenture and as such the property of the debenture holder rather than the company. The receiver's power in Scotland to deal with the property is not affected by the liquidation.

1 (1977) Times, 20 October.

Letters of obligation

7.67　All firms of solicitors in Scotland are engaged almost daily in giving their personal obligations to deliver or exhibit clear searches and the historical development of letters of obligation and their necessity in settling property transactions in Scotland is well known. What is, however, increasingly being realised is the fact that in the context of receivership where the receiver normally excludes his liability totally, his solicitor may well undertake personally an unduly burdensome liability relating to some matter which may well have occurred some time prior to the appointment of the receiver. Against the background of a sale of heritable property by a receiver, an unguarded and unqualified letter of obligation in respect of heritage may read as follows:

'With reference to the settlement of this transaction today and provided that the disposition in favour of your clients is recorded within 7 days of today's date, we hereby undertake to deliver to you within 6 months of this date Search in the Property, Personal and Companies Charges Registers brought down in terms of the Memorandum adjusted between us and showing the records clear of all incumbrances and diligences prejudicial to our clients' title.'

The wording is considered as follows.

Personal obligation

7.68　The obligation is the personal obligation of the selling solicitors. Occasionally, the form is encountered . . . 'On behalf of our clients [Name and Designation of clients], we hereby undertake . . .'. In these circumstances, the law of agency ensures that the principal will be bound where the agent is acting for a disclosed principal.[1] If it is desired to enforce the obligation against the selling solicitors the words 'on behalf of our clients etc . . .' should be deleted.

1 *Bell's Principles* 224A; *Miller v Mitchell* (1860) 22 D 833.

Property, Personal and Charges Registers

7.69 It is probably accepted that on a settlement date, the Property Register may be as much as three months in arrears, while the Personal Register can be checked up to 10 am on that date and the Companies Charges Register can be checked right up to the last moment. What happens, however, if unknown to the receiver's solicitors, the company some weeks pre-receivership disponed to a neighbouring proprietor part of the property which the receiver is purporting to sell and the disposition has not yet been recorded or does not appear in the Property Register? What happens, firstly, if the company pre-receivership or secondly, post-receivership, was inhibited and this fact is only discovered after conclusion of a contract but before settlement or thirdly, if the company in receivership is inhibited the day after settlement but before the disposition in favour of the purchaser is recorded? What happens if a floating charge (apart from the floating charge under which the receiver was appointed) already on the Register crystallises the day before settlement but intimation in the Register is not given of the appointment of a receiver until several days after settlement? Consideration of these matters is given in the succeeding paragraphs.

Our client's title or our clients' title

7.70 A great deal of potential trouble could be avoided by carefully specifying for which client the granter of the obligation is acting viz the company in receivership or simply the receiver. It is obviously very much easier to control the activities of the receiver than a company in receivership which in all probability faced financial problems in the period immediately preceding receivership with consequent inhibitions, arrestments and other forms of diligence.

Proposals

7.71 It is suggested that in the case of transactions involving receivers the following matters may be considered as qualifying the extreme limits of the typical letter of obligation to which reference has already been made.

Property Register

So far as the Property Register is concerned, the position will be known down to the latest date disclosed by the interim report. In cases involving property subject to registration of title, less difficulty is encountered as the Land Register reports are very much more up to date. In a typical receivership, the receiver's solicitors will normally have taken delivery of title deeds and other documents from the company's solicitors and in these cases the company's solicitors, although by no means obliged to do so, will probably provide a report of the company's transactions including recent transactions up to the time of the receiver's appointment. Although there is a theoretical possibility that some of the company's property may have been conveyed prior to the appointment of the receiver without as yet an entry appearing on the Property Register, it is suggested that the risk of the receiver's solicitors being unaware of that fact is, in the normal course of events, minimal. It is therefore proposed that, notwithstanding the point made in paragraph 7.67 and pending change in Scottish legal practice in this area, an undertaking by the receiver's solicitors to provide a clear search in respect of the period from the date of the interim report to the date of settlement could normally be given in the usual terms.

Personal Register

7.72   So far as the Personal Register is concerned, the receiver's solicitors should not conclude any agreement involving heritable property until a search in the Personal Register has been carried out: otherwise a purchaser, on finding an inhibition, could decline to proceed (*Dryburgh v Gordon*).[1] Any inhibition prior in date to the date of creation of the floating charge under which the receiver was appointed will have to be cleared before a purchaser can receive a good title and, consequently, before any moneys are paid out in terms of the floating charge. If the inhibition is registered after the date of creation of the floating charge, then on the *Armour and Mycroft*[2] principle, a sale can only proceed if the inhibitor is paid the amount of his debt after the floating charge creditor but before the claims of ordinary creditors. An inhibition registered after the date of appointment of a receiver will be ineffective in a question with the receiver on the ground that the floating charge has already crystallised on the assets of the company and has become a fixed security in terms of section 70 of the Insolvency Act 1986.

1 1896 24 R 1.
2 1983 SLT 453.

7.73   It is suggested that it would be appropriate for the receiver's solicitors to undertake to deliver a clear search in the Personal Register but subject to any rights of inhibitors who have inhibited firstly, prior to the date of creation of the floating charge (which inhibition will rank before the floating charge) and secondly, prior to the appointment of the receiver. Such a course may be unsatisfactory to the purchaser's solicitors but the alternative, in the case of a pre-floating charge inhibition, involves either a discharge of the inhibition (if one can be obtained) to free the heritable property from the scope of the inhibition or depending on the amount due to the inhibiting creditor a partial discharge of the inhibition releasing the heritable property the receiver wishes to sell provided other heritable property exists to safeguard the inhibiting creditor's position and/or a section 61 petition under the Insolvency Act 1986. None of the alternatives is very attractive from the point of view of speed. If the inhibition is past the date of creation of the floating charge but pre-dates the date of appointment of the receiver, it is, nevertheless, suggested that the purchaser's solicitors should seek a partial discharge or failing that insist on a section 61 petition and settle the transaction based on present law viz *Armour and Mycroft*.[1] If practical in the scale of value of the transaction, at the same time there should be placed on deposit receipt an amount equal to the debt owed to the inhibitor pending the result of the section 61 petition. This latter suggestion may of course be impractical in that the amount of the debt owed to the inhibitor may exceed the consideration payable by the purchaser. It is accepted that in view of the *Armour and Mycroft*[1] decision the receiver may decide to petition for the immediate appointment of a liquidator with the prospect of cutting down an inhibition in terms of section 185 of the Insolvency Act 1986. An early appointment of a liquidator is, however, often unhelpful to a receiver in his general conduct of the receivership and can be very disadvantageous from the point of view of taxation.[2]

1 1983 SLT 453.
2 See David Bertram *Tax Consequences of Receivership and Liquidation*: Butterworths, ch 5.

Companies Charges Register

7.74   From time to time certain solicitors will require a clear search in the Companies Charges Register. Such a requirement is usually impossible because (A) the floating charge creditor may never be fully satisfied and (B) full satisfaction is rarely achieved immediately following the sale of one particular property. There is a school of thought that insists that a memorandum of partial or full satisfaction should be executed to release the particular property from the charge on the ground that the floating charge has become equivalent to a fixed security in terms of section 70 of the Insolvency Act 1986 and it is, therefore, necessary for the floating charge holder to discharge such fixed security in a similar way as a heritable security would be discharged under and in terms of the Conveyancing and Feudal Reform (Scotland) Act 1970. The argument by the receiver is that he has been appointed by the holder of the floating charge to realise on his behalf the property subject to the charge and that as in terms of Schedule 2 to the Insolvency Act 1986 he has full power of sale over such property, it is not necessary either for a discharge to be given by the floating charge creditor or for the receiver to provide a clear search in the Companies Charges Register. In relation to any prior ranking floating charge which has not crystallised, it is suggested that a letter of non-crystallisation is obtained from the holder of such prior ranking floating charge and delivered to the purchaser.

7.75   For practical purposes, it is suggested that the purchaser's solicitors should rely exclusively on the receiver's statutory power of sale. Any other floating charges do not automatically crystallise by the appointment of a receiver but can do so by the operation of section 52(1)(d) of the

Insolvency Act 1986 or of a provision in the floating charge, or any ancillary documents to that effect, entitling the holder thereof to appoint a receiver and such holder in these circumstances appointing a receiver. Accordingly, it should not be necessary to require a Companies Charges obligation from the receiver's solicitors.

7.76   From what has been said, it will be readily appreciated that a clear understanding between the receiver's solicitors and the purchaser's solicitors should be reached before any sale agreement relating to or including heritable property is concluded. It is much easier to agree the form and content of a letter of obligation before concluding an agreement than at a later stage.

7.77   In recent years there has been considerable legal comment on various aspects of the consideration involved in the sale of heritable property in the context of insolvency. While it is not intended in this book to consider the articles, the references to which appear below, it may be useful for these articles to be listed.

1 G L Gretton 'Diligence, Trusts and Floating Charges' (1981) Journal of The Law Society of Scotland 57, 102.
2 G L Gretton 'Inhibitions and Company Insolvencies' 1983 SLT (News) 145.
3 JADH 'Inhibitions and Company Insolvencies: a Contrary View' 1983 SLT (News) 177.
4 A J Sim 'The Receiver and Effectually Executed Diligence' 1984 SLT 25.
5 G L Gretton 'Delivery of Deeds and the Race to the Register' (1984) Journal of The Law Society of Scotland 400.
6 A J McDonald 'Bankruptcy, Liquidation and Receivership and the Race to the Register' (1985) Journal of the Law Society of Scotland 20.
7 G L Gretton 'The Title of a Liquidator' (1984) Journal of The Law Society of Scotland 357.
8 G L Gretton and K G C Reid 'Insolvency and Title' (1985) Journal of The Law Society of Scotland 109.

Pension matters

7.78   As part of the overall arrangements for the sale of a business, the purchaser, if an established company of any size, in all probability will wish to make suitable arrangements to transfer the benefits (if it is possible to do so) of the pension scheme of the company in receivership to the pension scheme operated by the purchaser. Since it is usually impossible to finalise the pension aspects of the sale before completion it is sometimes agreed that if the trustees of the pension scheme of the company in receivership are agreeable and subject to the purchaser becoming an 'employer' for the purposes of such scheme within a period of not more than twelve months from the completion date, then subject to Inland Revenue approval, the trustees of such pension scheme will discuss with the trustees of the purchaser's pension scheme appropriate transfer values for those employees being transferred to the purchaser's pension scheme. Although a receiver is not really affected by such pension arrangements, it is usual to arrange for the receiver to consent in a formal deed of adherence for any right, title and interest he may have thereto. A suggested form of deed of adherence is given in Appendix 14.

Change of name

7.79 In many receiverships and particularly larger cases, the company name will be perceived by a purchaser as a valuable asset in an ongoing business. For this reason, arrangements are often made as part of an agreement for the purchaser to be entitled to use the name of the company in receivership.

7.80 Taking as an example Galaxy Products Limited (Galaxy), a holding company of several subsidiaries and Rococo Cocoa Co Limited (Rococo), its principal trading subsidiary, the following points should be noted:

(1) Any change of name of Galaxy will require the members of Galaxy to pass an appropriate special resolution and the cost of convening the necessary extraordinary general meeting may or may not be an acceptable cost to a purchaser who would normally be expected to meet such cost. In the case of a public listed company in receivership the cost is unlikely to be acceptable.

(2) On the other hand, the prospective purchaser of the business of Rococo will probably only wish the use of the corporate name of Rococo and if Rococo is a wholly owned subsidiary of Galaxy it should in most cases be possible for the receiver acting as receiver of Galaxy to require Rococo to change its name while at the same time the purchaser passes a special resolution to change its name to Rococo. In most cases the costs involved in changing names, while a matter for negotiation, will be borne by the purchaser.

(3) As the main function of a receiver is to realise assets, it has become customary in many cases to change the name of the company in receivership to a name embodying the function of realisation. In normal circumstances Rococo could expect to become RCC Realisations Limited. Difficulties have sometimes been experienced in a subsequent liquidation when creditors of the old Rococo do not recognise in statutory liquidation notices the name RCC Realisations Limited. The practice has therefore developed in many instances of showing the former name of RCC Realisations Limited while at the same time to avoid embarrassment to the purchaser of the business of the old Rococo, inviting such purchaser, at his own cost, to insert an intimation beside any such statutory liquidation notice making it clear that the purchaser is not associated in any way with the company in liquidation.

Chapter 8

Extent and ranking of securities, guarantees and related matters

General position

8.01 It is advisable in all receiverships that as soon as possible after the appointment of the receiver, detailed enquiries should be made by carrying out a search at the Companies Registry as to any existing fixed securities and other floating charges and their respective rankings. As regards ranking of floating charges, section 464(1) of the 1985 Act provides that, subject to section 464(2), the instrument creating a floating charge over all or any part of the company's property may contain:

(a) provisions prohibiting or restricting the creation of any fixed security or any other floating charge having priority over, or ranking *pari passu* with, the floating charge: or

(b) provisions regulating the order in which the floating charge shall rank with any other subsisting or future floating charges or fixed securities over that property or any part of it.

8.02 Section 464(2) provides that where all or any part of the property of a company is subject both to a floating charge and to a fixed security arising by operation of law, the fixed security shall have priority over the floating charge. This means, it is suggested, that a fixed security arising by operation of law such as a landlord's hypothec would rank prior to a floating charge but case law does not necessarily support that view.[1] It should also be noted that the rights and remedies of the holders of fixed securities such as standard securities are unaffected by the appointment of a receiver and such holders while in many cases working in co-operation with the receiver are nonetheless free to exercise their rights independently. In the absence of any agreement with regard to the ranking of various securities, section 464(4)(a) of the 1985 Act provides that a fixed security, the right to which has been constituted as a real right before a floating charge has attached to all or any part of the property of the company, shall have priority of ranking over the floating charge. Floating charges rank with one another according to the time of registration in accordance with Chapter II of Part XII of the 1985 Act.[2] In addition, floating charges which have been received by the Registrar of Companies for registration by the same postal delivery rank with one another equally.[3]

1 *Cumbernauld Development Corpn v Mustone Ltd* 1983 SLT (Sh Ct) 55; see Chap 2 para 2.16.
2 CA 1985, s 464(4)(b).
3 Ibid s 464(4)(c).

Ranking agreements and related problems

8.03   In practice, where a number of securities have been constituted by the borrowing company, the normal course is for a formal ranking agreement to be concluded between the borrowing company and its various secured creditors so that the order and extent of ranking of all such securities is clearly laid down. A style of a typical ranking agreement is set out in Appendix 15 but it is emphasised that various ranking permutations are possible and the style is merely intended to highlight the principal general clauses.

Running account

8.04   Difficulties can arise in relation to section 464(5) of the 1985 Act in the case of a clearing bank or other secured creditor having a floating charge over the assets and undertaking of the borrowing company and which has made available a running account overdraft or otherwise to the borrower. Section 464(5) provides that where the holder of a floating charge, in such circumstances, has received intimation in writing of the subsequent registration in accordance with Chapter II of Part XII of the 1985 Act of another floating charge over the same property or any part thereof, the preference in ranking of the first mentioned floating charge shall be restricted to security for (a) the holder's present advances; (b) future advances which he may be required to make under the instrument creating the floating charge or under any ancillary documents; (c) interest due or to become due on all such advances; and (d) any expenses or outlays which may reasonably be incurred by the holder. As a result, all clearing banks and other creditors holding securities from a borrowing company in respect of a running account normally always insist on a 'fluctuating advances' clause being agreed with the borrowing company and other such creditors. A form of 'fluctuating advances' clause is set out in clause 5 of Appendix 15 but its effect is to protect the ranking of the holder of a floating charge in terms of the ranking agreement notwithstanding that such holder may advance further moneys to the borrower after intimation of the registration of another floating charge, the effect of which would normally cause such holder to be restricted in his preference in ranking to security for the sums specified in section 464(5).

Interest and additional interest

8.05   From time to time, questions have arisen as to the right of loan creditors to charge certain additional interest on amounts outstanding by a borrower. Normally, the documentation setting up the loan facilities will provide for interest to be fixed, for example, in accordance with the particular lender's rates for the time being with power to the lender to give a certificate indicating the amount due together with interest at any particular time. A problem may arise where a lender inserts in loan documentation that in certain circumstances the borrower will, in addition to all other interest chargeable in terms of the loan facility, also be required to pay, for example, one year's interest on the amount of the loan then outstanding. The point arises as to whether the additional interest is validly chargeable by the lender or whether it is to be regarded as a penalty and so unenforceable.

8.06 In considering the question of additional interest charges in these circumstances, careful examination of the precise wording in the loan documentation is very important. If the documentation states that such additional interest will be payable on the happening of certain events none of which involves a breach of contract, the provision for additional interest will be enforceable.[1] In that case Lord Keith reviewed the authorities and concluded:

'I am unable to accept that the law about penalty and liquidated damages has any application in a case which is not a case of breach of contract and I consider that *Bell Brothers (HP) Ltd v Aitken*[2] is authority binding upon me for the view that it has no application.'

On the other hand, if the additional interest is stated to be payable in the event of a breach of contract, the clause in the loan documentation to that effect will be subject to the tests set out in the leading case on the subject.[3] Lord Roskill summarised the position in a recent case[4] as follows:

'... one purpose, perhaps the main purpose, of the law relating to penalty clauses is to prevent a plaintiff recovering a sum of money in respect of a breach of contract committed by a defendant which bears little or no relationship to the loss actually suffered by the plaintiff as a result of the breach by the defendant. But it is not and never has been for the Courts to relieve a party from the consequences of what may in the event prove to be an onerous or possibly even a commercially imprudent bargain.'

1 *Granor Finance Ltd v Liquidator of Eaststore Ltd* 1974 SLT 296.
2 *Bell Bros (HP) Ltd v Aitken* 1939 SC 577.
3 *Clydebank Engineering and Shipbuilding Co v Castaneda* 1904 7F (HL) 77.
4 *Export Credits Guarantee Department v Universal Oil Products Co* [1983] 1 WLR 399.

8.07 It is sometimes the case that the additional interest provisions in loan documentation refer to other provisions which set out the circumstances in which the additional interest becomes payable and/or circumstances constituting a breach of the loan agreement. Clearly, careful drafting of the loan agreement will avoid ambiguity but in the final analysis the enforceability of additional interest provisions may depend on the severability of the provisions relating to the breach from those under which the additional interest becomes payable.

Wages preference

8.08 Consideration requires to be given to the situation where a floating charge holder has a claim for a wages preference and a ranking agreement exists with other floating charge holders. The usual situation involves a clearing bank having made available to the borrowing company an overdraft facility on current account and also operating a separate wages account. On the appointment of a receiver, the clearing bank will be due a certain amount on current account overdraft as well as a further amount which may be entitled to a preferential ranking as sums advanced for the payment of wages. In the absence of any discussion (save for a standard form of ranking agreement providing for *pari passu* ranking to some extent) with another secured creditor, who perhaps has made available a fixed loan secured also by way of a floating charge, what is the position with regard to the clearing bank's claim for preferential ranking in the company's overall aggregate indebtedness?

8.09 Firstly, the clearing bank would be entitled to a preferential ranking in respect of its wages account, subject to the receiver being satisfied that its claim qualifies for a preferential ranking under and in terms of section 386 of the Insolvency Act 1986 as applied by section 59 of that Act and also to the limits imposed from time to time by statutory instrument. The more difficult question is whether, in the absence of previous written agreement between the parties, in the *pari passu* ranking between the clearing bank and the other lender, the amount of the admitted wages preference should be deducted from the overall indebted-ness to the clearing bank or should the clearing bank be entitled to argue that the aggregate indebtedness due by the borrowing company is the figure which should be fixed insofar as the *pari passu* ranking is con-cerned? It is thought that the amount of any claim to preferential ranking must be deducted from the total aggregate indebtedness of the clearing bank on the basic principle that a creditor cannot rank more than once. When the clearing bank has been paid the amount of its preference, the clearing bank and the other lender are in the position that there is still an aggregate total indebtedness, albeit that in the case of the clearing bank the amount of the wages preference has already been paid.

Option in loan documentation to heritable creditor

8.10 A heritable creditor may attempt to improve his position by the use of an option arrangement whereby on the happening of certain events (eg the sale of the security subjects) such creditor is entitled to exercise an option to purchase part of the security subjects for a consideration specified in the original loan agreement. To further protect his position, the standard security over the security subjects in favour of the heritable creditor will have specified that the security being granted is 'in respect of all sums due or to become due and in respect of all obligations contained in the loan agreement'. In a question with a receiver who has been appointed over the whole property of the borrowing company, is the option arrangement valid?

8.11 As a general rule, obligations such as those specified above are not usually enforceable against a receiver.[1] However, for the following reason, it is thought that such an option arrangement may be binding on a receiver. If the standard security states that all obligations contained in the loan agreement are secured, in the absence of acceptance by the receiver of the option arrangement, the heritable creditor would be justified in withholding its consent to a sale to a third party and in declining to deliver an executed discharge of the standard security. The obligations to grant consent to the sale in exchange for an acceptance by the receiver that he will honour the option arrangement are interdependent. If the receiver wishes the sale to proceed to the third party, he may be required in practice to honour the option arrangement otherwise, in the absence of an executed discharge of the standard security, the sale cannot proceed.

1 *MacLeod v Alexander Sutherland Ltd* 1977 SLT (Notes) 44; but see *Freevale Ltd v Metrostore (Holdings) Ltd* [1984] 1 All ER 495 and *Telemetrix plc v Modern Engineers of Bristol (Holdings) Ltd* [1985] LS Gaz R 1561 and Chap 4 paras 4.34 to 4.36.

8.12 It could be argued that the provisions of section 61 of the Insolvency Act 1986[1] could be invoked to deal with the situation where the receiver wishes to sell a heritable property which is subject to a secured obligation. However, it is suggested that the court, on hearing an application under section 61, would reject the receiver's case on the ground that a valid, binding and secured obligation existed and that the heritable creditor would be entirely justified in refusing to discharge a standard security where an option arrangement clearly formed part of the secured obligations of the company in receivership. The receiver could hardly be said to be unable to obtain the consent of the heritable creditor: on the contrary, in most cases, the heritable creditor would give his consent provided his rights under the option arrangement were preserved.

1 Further consideration of this section is given in Chap 3 paras 3.35 to 3.38 and Chap 7 paras 7.35 to 7.37.

General duty to guarantors

8.13 In the context of ranking of securities and guarantees, serious consideration should be given to the position of guarantors in the light of the decision in *Standard Chartered Bank Ltd v Walker*.[1] A detailed discussion of the position of guarantors is contained in Chapter 3 paragraphs 3.47 to 3.48.

1 [1982] 3 All ER 938.

Position of inhibitions in ranking

8.14 The petition of *Armour and Mycroft*[1] has been the subject of much discussion in the general context of diligence and reference is made to Chapter 2 paragraphs 2.14 to 2.15.

1 1983 SLT 453.

8.15 What principles derive from both the general law and in particular the *Armour and Mycroft* decision[1] as regards the ranking of inhibitions in relation to floating charges? It is thought these are as follows:

(1) An inhibition which pre-dates the creation of a floating charge ranks prior to any claim by the holder of the floating charge.

(2) an inhibition which post-dates the creation of a floating charge but pre-dates the receiver's appointment is not thought to be an effectually executed diligence and on the basis of *Armour and Mycroft*, such an inhibiting creditor is entitled to be paid out after the floating charge has been satisfied but before the claims of ordinary creditors.

(3) An inhibition taken out after the appointment of a receiver is completely ineffective *quoad* the receiver on the ground that the floating charge will already have crystallised on the assets of the company and become a fixed security in terms of section 70 of the Insolvency Act 1986.[2]

(4) Faced with the circumstances of *Armour and Mycroft*,[3] a partial discharge should be obtained (if possible). Counsel for the inhibitors in *Armour and Mycroft*[3] refused to allow a full discharge in exchange for a payment into court of the whole amount of the debt due to the inhibitor on the ground that such an arrangement might not be binding on a liquidator. Liquidation might well be a convenient route in appropriate cases to nullify an inhibition by virtue of the provisions of section 185 of the Insolvency Act 1986. However, it is appreciated that the immediate appointment of a liquidator can be unhelpful to a receiver in his general conduct of the receivership and can in certain circumstances be disadvantageous from the point of view of taxation.

1 1983 SLT 453.
2 See also *Forth and Clyde Construction Co Ltd v Trinity Timber and Plywood Co Ltd* 1984 SLT 94.
3 See n 1 above.

8.16 The practical realities of the circumstances with which the receivers were faced in *Armour and Mycroft*[1] are also relevant. As has been stated,[2] whatever the strengths of the receivers' position in a question as between them and the inhibitors as a matter of strict law, the fact remained that there was an inhibition standing on the register and the purchasers to whom the receivers were anxious to sell certain properties were not being offered a clear title. It is well settled in law that a title which is subject to an inhibition is not a title which a purchaser is bound to accept.[3] If no agreement can be reached then the only remedy is to petition the court under section 61 of the Insolvency Act 1986 although as a speedy remedy it is not attractive. Therefore, as a practical matter, some form of arrangement must, if at all possible, be negotiated with an inhibiting creditor.

1 1983 SLT 453.
2 JADH 1983 SLT (News) 177.
3 *Dryburgh v Gordon* 1896 24 R1.

Position of arrestors in ranking

8.17 What is the position if a receiver is appointed over the whole assets and undertaking of a company and the day after the receiver's appointment, a creditor of the company arrests funds in the hands of a third party? It could be argued on the one hand that the arrestment falls to be settled on the basis of the decision in the *Lord Advocate v The Royal Bank* case[1] and, in any event, the charge has crystallised over the assets of the company before the arrestment was made. Reference is made to the opinion of Lord Cowie in *Forth and Clyde Construction Co Ltd v Trinity Timber and Plywood Co Ltd*[2] which case was the subject of an appeal to the First Division of the Court of Session who upheld the interlocutor of the Lord Ordinary. Lord Cowie decided in the Outer House that a receiver had power by virtue of section 15(1)(a)[3] to ingather the property attached by the floating charge and if that property consists of the whole property of the debtor the receiver cannot be prevented from exercising his power by an arrestment whether or not the value of the company's other assets exceeds the company's total liabilities; and the arrestment was accordingly recalled. Reference is also made to Chapter 2 paragraph 2.13.

1 *Lord Advocate v Royal Bank of Scotland Ltd* 1978 SLT 38.
2 1984 SLT 94.
3 See now the Insolvency Act 1986, Sch 2, para 1.

Fixed charge by an English registered company over book debts

8.18 Consideration should also be given to the position where an English registered company with a place of business in Scotland has granted in favour of the holder of a floating charge also a first fixed charge over book debts. It is submitted that unless a valid assignation of each and every debt had taken place and after being duly stamped, has been intimated, in terms of the Transmission of Moveable Property (Scotland) Act 1862, to each debtor, no valid security over the book debts of the company would have been created under the law of Scotland. In England, the following wording, as it is understood the law in England now stands, should provide an effective assignation of all book debts of the company:

> 'The Company as beneficial owner and to the intent that the security shall rank as a continuing security for all indebtedness and liabilities from time to time due and to become due hereby charges by way of a first fixed charge all book debts both present and future (and the proceeds of realisation thereof) due or owing to the Company.'

However, there is a clear line of authority[1] suggesting that to be effective, such a clause should ensure that not only is there an obligation on the company to open a separate account to deal solely with receipt of book debts but also there should be an express obligation on the company that such an account be used for no other purpose.

1 *Siebe Gorman & Co Ltd v Barclays Bank Ltd* [1979] 2 Lloyds Rep 142; *Re Armagh Shores* [1982] NI 59; *Re Keenan Bros Ltd* [1984] 2 ILT 205.

8.19 It is generally accepted that it is the *lex situs* which governs questions relating to securities over incorporeal moveable property which includes debts and that the *situs* of a normal contract debt will be the place where the debtor resides.[1] It therefore appears that a charge over book debts created by an English registered company with a place of business in Scotland will be valid without intimation in respect of debtors residing in England but, on a strictly Scottish basis, will be invalid in respect of debtors residing in Scotland unless followed by intimation to each and every debtor.

1 See Chap 5 paras 5.18(8) et seq.

8.20 However, attention is drawn to the Civil Jurisdiction and Judgments Act 1982[1] which provides that a person domiciled in a Contracting State, may, in another Contracting State, be sued in matters relating to a contract, in the courts for the place of performance of the obligation in question. In these circumstances, it would appear as a result of that Act (when it comes into force) to be possible for a Scottish debtor to be sued in England and for the proceeds thereof in a question between the receiver and the liquidator of the company in receivership to be caught within the floating charge.

1 Schedule 1, art 5.

Directors' borrowing limits exceeded

8.21 In this chapter, it is also relevant to consider the position of a secured creditor who has made a loan to a company but who may or may not have realised that in making such a loan, restrictions imposed on the directors of the company as to the limits of borrowing of the company may thereby to some extent have been exceeded. The question, therefore, may arise as to whether the debt in question or the security is to some extent invalid.

8.22 Regulation 79 of Table A of the Companies Act 1948 stated that the directors might exercise all the powers of a company to borrow and to charge the undertaking of the company as security for any debt. The proviso to Regulation 79 (which was frequently deleted in modern articles of association of a private company incorporated prior to the repeal of Table A to the Companies Act 1948) stated that:

'the amount for the time being remaining undischarged (apart from temporary loans obtained from the company's bankers in the ordinary course of business) shall not at any time, without the previous sanction of the company in general meeting, exceed the nominal amount of the share capital of the company for the time being issued, but nevertheless no lender or other person dealing with the company shall be concerned to see or inquire whether this limit is observed. No debt incurred or security given in excess of such limit shall be invalid or ineffectual except in the case of express notice to the lender or the recipient of the security at the time when the debt was incurred or security given that the limit hereby imposed had been or was thereby exceeded.'

No problems arose if in articles of association adopting Regulation 79 the proviso to it was deleted without further addition but a number of matters required consideration by a receiver if a proviso to the borrowing powers of the directors in these or similar terms was incorporated in articles. Although the new Table A[1] contains no provisions on the lines of the old Regulation 79 empowering the directors to borrow with or without ristruction articles of association of new companies may still incorporate such special provisions even if the articles are based on the new Table A and, in the case of old companies, their articles are likely to adopt Table A to the Companies Act 1948 (or earlier Companies Acts) and may, therefore, contain such provisions. The articles of association of public listed companies will contain such provisions and are likely to do so even if unlisted.

1 Contained in Companies (Tables A–F) Regulations 1985, SI 1985/805.

Method of calculation of borrowings

8.23   As a fact, have the borrowing powers been exceeded? In all cases, a company will either have contained its borrowings within the limit specified in its articles or it will have exceeded such limit. How is the question resolved, however, if borrowings are to include the aggregate of borrowings of a holding company and all subsidiaries of such holding company and at the same time temporary loans obtained in the ordinary course of business are to be excluded? Furthermore, for the purpose of calculation of such borrowings, are the articles specific and definite as to how aggregate indebtedness is to be ascertained, whether by reference to the last preceding accounting date of the holding company and its subsidiaries, or the date of constitution of such indebtedness or the date of appointment of the receiver or some other basis?

8.24   In most cases, a company, while it may have obtained fixed term loans or other long-term loans, will usually also operate under an overdraft facility with its bankers. *Palmer on Company Law*[1] states that incurring an overdraft is a form of borrowing and, as such, counts for the purpose of calculating whether a company has exceeded any limit on its borrowing. Although there appears to be no judicial authority for the proposition, it is thought that an overdraft will normally be regarded as a 'temporary loan' within the meaning of that expression as previously used in Regulation 79 of the former Table A,[2] bearing in mind that in nearly every case an overdraft facility is repayable on demand. Having isolated moneys properly regarded as temporary loans, consideration should then be given as to whether the figure which represents all other loans at the relevant date breaches the limits set out in the articles. Careful analysis of the precise wording of borrowing restrictions for other types of borrowing is required in each particular case to answer the questions postulated in the preceding paragraph for it should be possible to reconstruct the longer term borrowing position as at the relevant date and evaluate accordingly. In most cases, the relevant date will be stated to be either the date or dates when the borrowing was constituted or the aggregate amount of borrowings as at the date of the last preceding accounting date.

1 Twenty-third edition para 42–09; *Looker v Wrigley* (1882) 9 QBD 397.
2 Companies Act 1948, Sch 1.

Possible protection to lender

8.25   What is the effect of the provision in the articles of a company that a lender or other person dealing with the company shall not be concerned to see or inquire whether a borrowing limit has been exceeded? It is suggested that such words provide a very considerable protection to a lender: it means that a lender is under no duty to inquire. Suppose, for example, that an audited consolidated balance sheet was despatched to the lender within a short time after the last accounting date as a matter of normal commercial practice and the lender is in possession of an up-to-date copy of the memorandum and articles of the company. This does not really alter the position, it is submitted, because the lender is under no duty to examine the audited consolidated balance sheet or the memorandum and articles nor is the lender under a duty to inquire as to whether or not the previous sanction of the company in general meeting had been given should the limitation be exceeded. The only variation to this general rule might arise where the lender is given express notice that the borrowing limit has been or could be exceeded and then if this express notice was given at the time when the debt was incurred. However, if the fact that the borrowing limitation had been or would be exceeded, could only be discovered by a process of research (which could well be difficult to establish in the case of a group of companies whose accounts are consolidated), then it is submitted that the test of 'express notice' would not be satisfied.

Rule in *Royal British Bank v Turquand*

8.26   Does the rule in *Royal British Bank v Turquand*[1] assist a lender? It is suggested that the rule provides protection to a lender because an outsider need only be aware that the directors of a company are empowered by the memorandum and articles to enter into the transaction in question but only if certain conditions are fulfilled or if a specified procedure is followed: it does not impose a duty on the lender to inquire whether such conditions were fulfilled or if the specified procedure was followed. The rule would apply if directors are empowered to borrow no more than a specified total amount on their own initiative and also to borrow in excess of that amount if a general meeting consents. In this situation, a lender may assume that any necessary consent has been given even after he knows that the directors have already borrowed up to the limit set for them personally:[2] otherwise, a third party has no means of

ensuring that conditions or procedure prescribed by the memorandum
and articles have been implemented.

1 (1856) 6E & B 327.
2 *Re Hampshire Land Co* [1896] 2 Ch 743.

Section 35 of the 1985 Act

8.27   Can section 35 of the 1985 Act[1] add further protection? It is
suggested that it can indeed add further protection because the section
provides that if a company enters into a transaction which has been
decided on by its directors and the transaction infringes a limitation on
the powers of the directors contained in the memorandum and articles of
association, the other party to the transaction may nonetheless treat the
company as bound by it if he enters into it in good faith. *Pennington's
Company Law*[2] states that it is uncertain whether 'good faith' means an
outsider must not know or suspect that a limitation on the directors'
powers is being exceeded or whether he may act in good faith despite such
knowledge or suspicion if a transaction is otherwise fair and reasonable.
However, the First EEC Directive on Harmonisation of the Company
Laws of Member States under which this statutory rule was enacted does
not permit national legislation to deprive an outsider of protection
because he is aware that the directors are exceeding limitations imposed
by the company's memorandum and articles of association as it does in the
case of ultra vires transactions.

1 Formerly the European Communities Act 1972, s 9.
2 Fourth edition p 101.

Conclusion on borrowing limits

8.28   Complex questions can arise in connection with the possible breach
of borrowing limits which involve detailed investigation by receivers but
it is hoped that the more important aspects of such questions for receivers
have been highlighted. The facts and circumstances in every individual
case, where there is a possibility of a breach of borrowing limits, must be
carefully examined and considered. It is thought that the only circumstances in which real problems are likely to arise are in cases of a lender
having 'express notice' of borrowing limits having been exceeded or some
irregularity in procedure on which the lender failed to take any action. In
such circumstances the validity of the loan debt and the security will be
open to question.

Ultra vires and the implication of *Rolled Steel Products*

8.29   Reference is made to the *Rolled Steel Products*[1] decision in connection both with borrowings and the granting of joint and several unlimited guarantees. The decision in that case has raised a number of issues of far reaching importance and has caused the majority of lenders to reassess established lending practices.

1 *Rolled Steel Products (Holdings) Ltd v British Steel Corpn* [1982] 3 All ER 1057 and on appeal [1984] BCLC 466.

8.30 The court held in the *Rolled Steel* case[1] that individual objects of a company were not to be construed independently but that objects permitting lending and the giving of guarantees should be regarded as ancillary to and in furtherance of the principal object of the company. If a company purported to lend money and to give guarantees contrary to the authority granted by its memorandum of association, any such activity would be ultra vires the company. In the case in question, the court did not consider that the granting of a guarantee and creation of a debenture in security thereof could be construed as being in the company's interest to enter into such transactions.

1 *Rolled Steel Products (Holdings) Ltd v British Steel Corpn* [1982] 3 All ER 1057 and on appeal [1984] BCLC 466.

8.31 It is, therefore, of great importance in each case to establish that any borrowing or giving of a joint and several unlimited guarantee by a company can be said to be in its interests. There should not normally be any problem in relation to the borrowing capacity of a company if the borrowing was required to further its principal object. What is more likely to create problems is establishing that the granting of a joint and several unlimited guarantee in respect of the obligations of a third party can be said to be in the best interests of the company. The duty of directors in this context is to act bona fide in the best interests of the company. It is their decision rather than a decision of a lender as to what is and what is not in the best interests of the company.[1] It is thought that the decision of the directors should be assessed on the basis of the opinion of an intelligent and honest man being faced with the circumstances as to whether or not the proposed transaction was for the benefit of the company.[2] The fact that the directors act in breach of their responsibilities will not affect the enforceability of a joint and several unlimited guarantee unless the lender was aware of some irregularity in its constitution.

1 *Re Smith and Fawcett Ltd* [1942] Ch 304.
2 *Charterbridge Corpn v Lloyds Bank Ltd* [1970] Ch 62 at 74.

8.32 Problems have arisen where a lender provides a borrowing facility to a group of companies on condition that the lender receives floating charges and a joint and several unlimited guarantee in respect of the obligations of the group executed by all companies in the group. Does the fact that a company carrying on a wine importing business in the South of England and a company manufacturing space invaders in Pitlochry, both subsidiaries of the same holding company, have both executed jointly and severally an unlimited guarantee to the lender in respect of the group indebtedness, matter in the context of a transaction being in the best interests of the respective companies? It is thought that a borrowing facility offered on a group basis, on condition that floating charges and a joint and several unlimited guarantee be executed by each of the subsidiaries, will satisfy the test particularly if it can be shown that each of the subsidiaries requires facilities from its holding company to carry on its normal trading business. If, however, there is a suggestion or suspicion of pressure on the directors of a subsidiary company or that the granting of a joint and several unlimited guarantee by each subsidiary of the group in respect of the group's indebtedness will render the subsidiary insolvent and such suggestion or pressure or insolvency is known to the lender, the commercial justification for the execution of a joint and several unlimited guarantee will be called into question and, depending on the circumstances, may result in the subsidiary not being bound by the terms of the unlimited guarantee. The effect on other guarantors is uncertain, but it is conceivable that the unlimited guarantee may be found not to be binding on the other guarantors for similar reasons of not being in their best interests or on the basis of the rule that by relieving one joint guarantor from obligations, the others are automatically released.[1]

1 Mercantile Law Amendment (Scotland) Act 1856, s 9.

8.33 To what extent should a receiver check the steps taken by a lender to protect the borrowing from challenge under the ultra vires doctrine as enunciated in the *Rolled Steel* case? It is suggested that the following checklist of points should be considered according to the circumstances of each particular case although failure by the lender to have done so, in relation to any one or more of the following, may not be fatal to the validity of the transactions:

(1) The memorandum and articles of each of the borrowing and guaranteeing companies should always be examined to establish that there is in each case power to borrow and power to guarantee (both on its own account and for the obligations of other parties and, if appropriate, in each case power to grant security). It has to be recognised that in adopting such a practice, the lender will almost certainly be denied (in relation, for example, to breaches of borrowing limits specified in the articles) the benefit of protection under the rule in *Royal British Bank v Turquand*[1] and section 35 of the 1985 Act but, in view of the *Rolled Steel* decision, the importance of constituting an effective security probably outweighs the possible protections afforded by not doing so.

(2) Assuming the requisite authority is contained in the objects clause, the proposed transaction should contain commercial justification to enable the directors of the guarantor company to state that such transaction is in the best interests of the guarantor. If the commercial justification is absent, or on any reasonable assessment the directors should have reached that view and these facts are known or ought to be reasonably known by the lender, the proposed granting of a joint and several unlimited guarantee will almost certainly be ultra vires. In any event, it may assist the lender if the shareholders of the guarantor company were to pass a special resolution approving specifically the granting of a joint and several unlimited guarantee in favour of the lender in respect of another company's obligations.

(3) Where some of the directors of a guarantor company are also directors of the borrowing company, there should be a quorum of other directors on the board of the guarantor who ought to be in a position more objectively to state whether the granting of a joint and several unlimited guarantee is in the best interests of the guarantor company. At the very least, any directors who are on the boards of both companies, and assuming these companies adopt Regulation 85 of Table A, should identify their interest and declare it before a meeting of the respective directors of each company.

1 (1856) 6E & B327.

Unlimited guarantees and letters of set-off

8.34   As mentioned in the preceding paragraphs, a floating charge creditor lending money to a number of companies in a group normally insists at the outset that each of the borrowing companies execute a joint and several unlimited guarantee in respect of its own borrowings and those of any other company in the group. In addition, it is also usual for each of the borrowing companies to execute a letter of set-off which entitles the lender to apply any sums at credit of any accounts in the name of any of the borrowing companies against any debt of whatsoever nature owed by any of the other companies in the group. Examples of a form of a joint and several unlimited guarantee and a letter of set-off are contained in Appendix 16 and Appendix 17 respectively. It is important for a receiver to check that all such forms of joint and several unlimited guarantee and letters of set-off have been validly executed by each of the borrowing companies, otherwise the guarantors may not be bound under their terms.

Suggested approach of receiver

8.35   As to how a receiver should deal with a situation where there are joint and several unlimited guarantees and letters of set-off, the following is a typical example of the outcome of the receivership of a group of companies. It is assumed that there are five companies in the group:

Galaxy Products Limited	(the holding company)	(Galaxy)
Rococo Cocoa Co Limited	(a trading subsidiary of Galaxy)	(Rococo)
Rococo Cocoa Co (Scotland) Limited	(a trading subsidiary of Galaxy)	(Rococo (Scotland))
Orinoco Cocoa Co Limited	(a trading subsidiary of Galaxy)	(Orinoco)
Orinoco Cocoa Co (Scotland) Limited	(a dormant subsidiary of Galaxy)	(Orinoco (Scotland))

8.36   Shortly before the appointment of the receiver, if the holder of the floating charge executed by each company in the group (for the purposes of the remainder of this chapter known as 'the lender') applied the terms of a letter or letters of set-off while at the same time consolidating all the accounts of Galaxy and its subsidiaries, the result would have been that at the date of the appointment of the receiver only Galaxy to the extent of £2.75 million was indebted to the lender. The reason for such setting-off and consolidation might be on account of the desire of the lender to treat the indebtedness of Galaxy as a group facility for the purpose of strengthening some of the arguments specified in paragraph 8.32. In fact, the letters of set-off were only applied by the receiver to the extent that there were credit balances in some of the bank accounts after his appointment. The indebtedness of the companies to the lender on the receiver's appointments secured over the respective property and assets of each company in the group is as follows:

Company	Amount
	£
Galaxy	1,500,000
Rococo	250,000
Rococo (Scotland)	75,000
Orinoco	Nil
Orinoco (Scotland)	Nil

8.37   Let it also be assumed that Galaxy is hopelessly insolvent and not able to pay off any of its indebtedness to the lender, that Rococo and Orinoco have substantial assets (most of which have been realised, realisations to date being in the case of Rococo £1.5 million and being in the case of Orinoco £1 million) and that Rococo (Scotland) is in a position to pay off some £50,000 of its own total indebtedness of £75,000, although not able to contribute to group indebtedness. Orinoco (Scotland) has no assets or liabilities.

8.38   Galaxy owns heritable properties in Pitlochry which were acquired shortly before the appointment of the receiver and before the lender could take standard securities from Galaxy and which, at the date of the first distribution by the receiver, remain unsold. While the value of such properties cannot be accurately assessed, it is likely on the basis of valuations provided to the receiver that an aggregate figure in the region of £100,000 might be achieved. Orinoco owns heritable property and moveable plant and machinery in Edinburgh which is, as yet, unrealised but is thought to have a value in the region of £50,000, the heritable property being subject to a standard security in favour of the lender and all such property also being subject to a floating charge in favour of the lender. Given these facts, how should the receiver allocate the realised assets against the respective liabilities?

8.39   The indebtedness, realisations to date and liabilities of the various companies as at the date of the first distribution by the receiver are as follows:

Indebtedness at date of first distribution

	Galaxy	Rococo	Rococo (Scotland)	Orinoco	Orinoco (Scotland)
	£	£	£	£	£
Indebtedness	1,500,000 + interest	250,000 + interest	75,000 + interest	NIL	—
Realisations	1,000,000	1,500,000	200,000	1,000,000	
Less: receiver's liabilities incurred to creditors	100,000	200,000	50,000	150,000	
Receiver's expenses	50,000	50,000	25,000	50,000	
Preferential creditors	150,000	350,000	75,000	200,000	
Total deductions	300,000	600,000	150,000	400,000	
Net realisations	£700,000	£900,000	£50,000	£600,000	

Properties valued approx £100,000 but unrealised

Property valued approx £50,000 subject to standard security but unrealised

8.40 After providing for some contingencies, the receiver wishes to make a payment to account from the realised assets of Galaxy, Rococo and Orinoco in respect of the aggregate indebtedness to the lender. It is suggested that the correct starting point in relation to any repayments to the lender should be that each company in the group should first of all repay its own indebtedness to the lender. As a result, Rococo's debt on its own account, after paying the lender's preferred claim, is extinguished in respect of its own indebtedness.

8.41 Orinoco had, in fact, no indebtedness of its own to the lender but had instead a credit balance of £50,000 as at the date of the receiver's appointment and in terms of the letter of set-off, the lender is entitled to take such credit balance to extinguish any other liabilities of Galaxy and Rococo. To that extent, Orinoco can be said to have already paid to the lender in respect of its liability to do so under the joint and several unlimited guarantee.

8.42 In view of the order of priorities of payments laid down under section 60 of the Insolvency Act 1986, it is suggested that the receiver's own fees and those of his agents should be apportioned between Galaxy, Rococo, Rococo (Scotland) and Orinoco, rather than charging them entirely to Galaxy.

8.43 In terms of the unlimited guarantees, each of the companies in the group has undertaken jointly and severally to guarantee payment on demand of all sums for which any of those companies and others were or would become liable to pay to the lender. Although it is assumed that the lender will have made formal demands under and in terms of such unlimited guarantees, this should be specifically checked with the receiver as, normally, it would be necessary for the lender, at some stage, to make a formal demand to each guarantor to enable it to recover the balance of Galaxy's indebtedness not satisfied from that company's assets. Formal demands for payment under the guarantees may not, however, be strictly necessary if, for example, the lender at any time prior to the appointment of the receiver, applied the terms of the letters of set off and consolidated all the accounts leaving only Galaxy with any indebtedness to the lender. The formal demand on the other companies in the group will be necessary only if Galaxy's realised assets are less than Galaxy's aggregate indebtedness to the lender.

8.44   The following points should be kept in mind. Firstly, the unlimited guarantees are joint and several, ie the lender at its option could look to any of the companies in the group for payment of the total indebtedness.

8.45   Secondly, the companies who contribute under the unlimited guarantees are entitled to recover their contributions from the principal debtor, ie Galaxy. As Galaxy does not have sufficient funds to meet its indebtedness to the lender, this will not be possible.

8.46   Thirdly, any of the companies which contributes more than its share is entitled to relief from the others. There are, however, two important exceptions to this principle. If any of the co-guarantors are insolvent and unable to contribute their share of the aggregate indebtedness, then the shares of any such co-guarantors are redistributed amongst the remaining co-guarantors. The second exception covers the position where the co-guarantors are in reality guaranteeing the obligations of a principal debtor and, at least in theory, are entitled to recover in full any amounts paid out to a creditor in respect of the obligations of the principal debtor. However, in practice, most forms of joint and several unlimited guarantee currently used by lenders make it clear that all the co-guarantors are liable both as principal debtors and as co-guarantors. It is, of course, still possible to establish the precise principal and guarantee obligations of each co-guarantor.

8.47   Fourthly, in terms of the unlimited guarantees, none of the companies is entitled in respect of any payments made by it thereunder to require any assignation of the debts or any part thereof until the whole sums due to the lender by all such companies have been paid. As the lender will be paid in full, the lender could be approached by a future liquidator of Rococo or Orinoco (being companies liable to contribute substantially under the terms of the unlimited guarantees) and an assignation of the moneys paid under such contribution be requested to enable Rococo and/or Orinoco to enforce its right of relief against other co-guarantors if these companies had assets from which a right of relief could be satisfied. It is a general principle of the law of cautionary obligations that where a cautioner obtains an assignation of a debt, he also obtains the benefit of any security held for such debt. Therefore, any contributing guarantor would enjoy the status of a floating charge creditor and would clearly rank in front of ordinary creditors, for example, of the company for whom the guarantor had to contribute towards the overall indebtedness. A style of assignation in these circumstances is given in Appendix 18.

8.48 It is thought that if the same person is receiver of the various companies in the group (which would usually be the case) he should not be subject to criticism provided that the scheme of division necessary in view of the unlimited guarantees is arranged on a fair and equitable basis with each of the guaranteeing companies (in so far as it is in a position to do so) bearing its rateable share of Galaxy's indebtedness to the lender.[1]

1 *Gloag on Contract* (2nd edn) pp 206–208.

8.49 Working through the example of the Galaxy companies whose particulars are set out in paragraphs 8.36–8.39 the receiver should proceed as follows (and for present purposes ignoring interest liabilities):

Galaxy indebtedness	–	1,500,000
Net realisations to date	–	700,000
		(800,000)
Unrealised properties	–	100,000
Rococo indebtedness	–	250,000
Net realisations to date	–	900,000
		650,000
		£
Rococo (Scotland) indebtedness	–	75,000
Net realisations to date	–	50,000
		(25,000)
Orinoco indebtedness	–	Nil
Realisations to date	–	600,000
Unrealised properties	–	50,000

Rococo should pay off its own indebtedness to the lender and each of Galaxy and Rococo (Scotland) should make a payment to account for their own indebtedness from their respective realisations. Galaxy is still liable to pay £800,000 and Rococo (Scotland) is still liable to pay £25,000. The unrealised properties for present purposes must be ignored and should be part of the final settlement of liability amongst the co-guarantors when all realisations have been completed.

8.50 The allocation from this stage should be based on the number of co-guarantors able to contribute rather than the amount of their respective funds. Such a course follows the joint and several argument previously discussed and is on the whole a fair and equitable method of settling the liability of each co-guarantor who is able to contribute. The net result is that, from the example above, it will be necessary for Rococo and Orinoco to pay off in equal shares the balance of indebtedness due by Galaxy and Rococo (Scotland) save that Orinoco will be entitled to be reimbursed by Rococo to the extent of £50,000 being the amount already appropriated by the lender in terms of the letters of set-off.

8.51 The receiver has, as previously noted, no specific statutory duty to ordinary creditors. As soon as the remaining assets of Galaxy and Orinoco are realised, the final payment to the lender and any adjustments can be made to give effect to a final division on the basis set out above. However, this is very much subject to the receiver still acting as receiver and not having repaid the total group indebtedness to the floating charge creditor. If full payment has been made, the receiver has no *locus standi* to deal with ordinary creditors and a final division should in these circumstances be left to a liquidator. Unless there is an obvious conflict of interest, it would be normal for the same person to be appointed as liquidator of each of the companies on petitions to the court by the receiver under section 55 of and Schedule 2 to the Insolvency Act 1986.

Proper division of guarantee liability

8.52 Another problem can arise where, for example, four companies have each been placed in receivership by the same floating charge creditor, and the respective receiverships have been completed with full payment to the holder of the floating charges and the surplus proceeds in each case passed over to a liquidator. The holder of the floating charges as well as holding such a charge from each individual company in respect of its own indebtedness, may also hold a joint and several unlimited guarantee executed by each company in the group. On the appointment of a receiver to each of the four companies the bank accounts of two of the companies could be in credit and the bank accounts of the other two be overdrawn. On the appointment of the receiver the bank (in exercise of its rights under the floating charges and joint and several unlimited guarantees) could immediately freeze the two credit balances but allow compensating interest to be offset on the overdrawn accounts based on the amount standing to the credit of the other two accounts.

8.53 On completion of each of the receiverships, the bank would have recovered all amounts due to it without recourse to the unlimited guarantee. The question which might exercise the mind of the liquidator is whether the result of the arrangement effected by the bank has been to benefit the ordinary creditors of the two companies whose accounts were overdrawn at the commencement of the receiverships in that these companies did not require to pay overdraft interest on the full amount of the overdrafts in view of the offsetting arrangement operated by the bank to the detriment of the creditors of the two companies with credit balances which suffered some loss in that they were unable to earn interest on the amounts standing to the credit of their accounts until such time as the bank's claims against the other two companies had been satisfied, thus releasing these credit balances.

8.54 As already mentioned, a guarantor is entitled on making payment in full to obtain from the creditor an assignation of the debt and any security held for it. However, in this instance, far from making payment in full the guarantor has made no payment whatsoever under the guarantee. Accordingly, there is no debt to be assigned. The possibility of course of the bank calling up the joint and several unlimited guarantees and freezing the credit balances was a foreseeable consequence of each of the companies agreeing to execute joint and several unlimited guarantees. Another possible ground for basing a claim might be that the companies with credit balances were entitled to recompense, the claim being based on quasi contract. Any such claim, of course, would only be entitled to an ordinary ranking.

8.55 It is thought that the two companies whose bank accounts were in credit at the time when the receiver was appointed are entitled to compensation from the two companies whose bank accounts were over-drawn. The two companies with credit balances have suffered loss in that the balances of their bank accounts were frozen and consequently, they were unable to put those sums to use by earning interest on them. The bank would of course normally have no right to freeze these balances were it not for the existence of joint and several unlimited guarantees. The principal debtors, ie the companies with credit balances benefited since the overdraft interest was only charged on the balance of the overdraft over the sums at credit of the other two companies. However, any such claim if upheld would only be given an ordinary ranking in the liquidations of the other two companies.

8.56 One possibility, it is thought, would be an action against the holder of the floating charges challenging the validity of its actions. The challenge would be based on the fact that the bank by not calling up the joint and several unlimited guarantees, took other action which was injurious to the two companies with credit balances with the consequence that the guarantor thereby prejudiced was free from any further liability under the guarantee. Another possibility, it is thought, would be an argument that by its action in freezing the two credit balaces, the bank would be bound to compensate the two companies with credit balances for all loss sustained. In such circumstances, the banks normally rely on the letters of set-off which, it can be argued, are an attempt to create a security. In this context many banks register letters of set-off with the Registrar of Companies in terms of Part XII of the 1985 Act.

Avoidance of certain floating charges

8.57 The statutory provisions under which certain floating charges may be avoided have already been referred to in so far as a receiver's appointment may be affected.[1] These provisions are, however, frequently of more relevance to a receiver when considering the extent of the security afforded by the floating charge by virtue of which his appointment was made and any other floating charges created by the company, as it is a rare occurrence for the floating charge under which he was appointed to be rendered completely invalid by these provisions.

1 See Chap 1 paras 1.42 to 1.51.

8.58   These statutory provisions, previously contained in section 617 of the 1985 Act, are now to be found in section 245 of the Insolvency Act 1986. There are, however, saving provisions in paragraph 9 of Schedule 11 to the Insolvency Act 1986, which replace the equivalent provisions in paragraph 10 of Schedule 9 to the Insolvency Act 1985. The effect of these is that a floating charge created before the coming into effect of section 245 shall not be set aside (nor be subject to an order varying or reversing any of its effects) under that section except to the extent that it could have been set aside under the provisions of section 617 of the 1985 Act. It is assumed for this purpose that any relevant administration order had been a winding-up order. It is accordingly necessary to consider both the old and new provisions in relation to floating charges created before the date on which section 245 came into effect.

8.59   The effect of section 617 of the 1985 Act was to render invalid on the liquidation of a company a floating charge created by it, when insolvent, within twelve months of its winding up except to the extent of cash paid to the company at or subsequent to and in consideration for the charge. If it could be proved that the company immediately after the creation of such a charge was solvent, then the charge was not open to challenge under that section. Furthermore, in the case of a company being wound up in Scotland, a floating charge created by it was not challenge-able as a fraudulent preference either under statute or common law.[1]

1 CA 1985, s 617(3).

8.60   The solvency qualification in section 617 has been replaced in section 245 of the Insolvency Act 1986 by a qualification related to ability to pay debts and then only in the case of a floating charge created in favour of an unconnected person[1] within twelve months of either winding up or the presentation of a petition for an administration order on which such an order has been made. Such a charge is not avoided under section 245 unless the company:

(a)   is unable at the date of creation of the charge to pay its debts within the meaning of section 123 of the Insolvency Act 1986; or

(b)   becomes unable to pay its debts within such meaning in consequence of the transaction under which the charge is created.

1 For definition see Chap 8 para 8.64.

8.61   A company in Scotland is deemed unable to pay its debts in terms of section 123 of the Insolvency Act 1986 if:

(a)   a creditor for over £750 having served a three week demand has not received payment or other satisfaction; or

(b)   the induciae on a charge, decree or extract has expired without payment; or

(c)   it is proved to the satisfaction of the court that the company is either unable to pay its debts as they fall due or that the value of the company's assets is less than the amount of its liabilities, taking into account its contingent and prospective liabilities.

8.62   Solvency for the purpose of section 617 was considered by some authorities[1] to require the satisfaction of two tests, namely:

(a)   the company's assets had to exceed its liabilities; and

(b) the company had to be able to pay its debts as they fell due.

On the other hand it was suggested in the Cork Report[2] that only the second test was applicable. Inability to pay debts within the meaning of section 123, bearing in mind that any challenge of a floating charge under these statutory provisions always relates to a time in the past, will in almost every case require to be established by proving the same to the court's satisfaction and while either test is now applicable the easier to satisfy may well be that of absolute insolvency: namely proving that the value of the company's assets was less than the amount of its liabilities (including contingent prospective liabilities). To avoid challenge it is, however, now necessary to satisfy both tests. In the case of a floating charge created before section 245 came into effect it is thought unlikely that such a charge will avoid challenge if notwithstanding the company fails the test of absolute solvency it shows it was able at the time to pay its debts as they fell due.

1 *Re Patrick and Lyon Ltd* [1933] Ch 786.
2 Report of the Review Committee on Insolvency Law and Practice (Cmnd 8558) paragraph 1558.

8.63 The onus of proving that the company was able to pay its debts or was solvent at the relevant time rests on the holder of the floating charge. For this reason, particularly where no cash is being paid (and also presumably now where no goods or services are being supplied) it has been the practice of parties taking floating charges from companies to request certificates signed by at least two directors to the effect that the company is solvent and will remain so immediately after the creation of the charge. Such circumstances arise, for example, where subsidiaries are asked to grant floating charges in security of guarantees of the parent company's borrowings. Such a certificate only affords a possible remedy, of course, to the holder of the floating charges and is not in any way conclusive evidence of the company's solvency or ability to pay its debts.

8.64 In addition to floating charges created in favour of unconnected persons within twelve months of the relevant date, the following other floating charges are open to avoidance under section 245 of the Insolvency Act 1986:

(a) a floating charge in favour of a person connected with the company within two years of the relevant date; and

(b) a floating charge in favour of any person whether connected or not at a time between the presentation of a petition for the making of an administration order in relation to the company and the making of such an order on that petition.

The relevant date for the purposes of (a) above is either:

(i) the date of presentation of a petition for and on which an administration order is subsequently made; or

(ii) the date of commencement of winding up.

A connected person[1] is a director or shadow director (ie a person in accordance with whose directions or instructions the directors are accustomed to act) of the company or an associate of either as defined in section 435 of the Insolvency Act 1986.

1 Insolvency Act 1986, s 249.

8.65   The exclusion of the avoidance provisions of section 245 by proving ability to pay debts only applies in the case of a floating charge created within the relevant twelve month period in favour of an unconnected person. In the cases of such charges created within two years of the relevant date in favour of connected persons or in favour of any person whether connected or not in the period between the presentation of a petition for and the making of an administration order, they do not escape challenge by proving ability to pay debts.

8.66   As already mentioned, unless the company was solvent at the time, a floating charge was rendered invalid by section 617 of the 1985 Act if created within twelve months of the company's winding up except to the extent of cash paid to the company at or subsequent to and in consideration for the charge together with interest thereon. The exception related only to cash paid to the company whereas under section 245 of the Insolvency Act 1986 this exception has been expanded to include the value of goods and services.

8.67   Section 245 of the Insolvency Act 1986 invalidates floating charges created within the periods mentioned (except in the circumstances mentioned where ability to pay debts is proved) except to the extent of the aggregate of:
(a) the value of so much of the consideration for the creation of the charge as consists of money paid, or goods or services supplied, to the company at the same time as, or after, the creation of the charge;
(b) the value of so much of that consideration as consists of the discharge or reduction, at the same time as, or after, the creation of the charge, of any debt of the company; and
(c) the amount of such interest (if any) as is payable on the foregoing amount in pursuance of any agreement under which the money was paid on the goods or services supplied.
For the purposes of section 245(2)(a), the value of any goods or services supplied by way of consideration for a floating charge shall be the amount in money which at the time of their supply could reasonably have been expected to be obtained for supplying them in the ordinary course of business and on the same terms (apart from the consideration) as those on which they were supplied to the company.

8.68   Whether or not under section 617 of the 1985 Act there was any cash paid to the company or under section 245 of the Insolvency Act 1986 the consideration consisted of money paid or goods or services supplied to the company will depend in each case on the facts.[1] In one case Lord Hanworth MR in considering equivalent provisions in the Companies Act 1929 said 'one has therefore to look at the facts and see whether or not in substance there was cash paid to the company'. That case and two other English cases[2] were considered by Lord Kincraig in a Scottish case[3] where he expressed the view that in considering the applicability of these statutory provisions the court is not bound to accept that cash payments to the company are within the exception if in substance the payments were made, and the floating charge granted, in order to give a preference to an existing creditor and that the court will look at the facts in each case in order to discover whether the payments were made truly for the benefit of the company, even if also securing a benefit to an existing creditor. In that case certain payments, claimed to be secured by a floating charge created within twelve months of liquidation, were made not to the company but direct to certain of its creditors and Lord Kincraig held that the exception for cash paid to the company was applicable only to cash so paid and not to any other person albeit on behalf of the company. Had the cash been paid to the company on condition that it was used to pay the debts due to such creditors and there was good reason for holding that this was done for the benefit of the company, the floating charge in Lord Kincraig's view might not have been rendered invalid to the extent of the respective amounts advanced.

1 *Re Matthews Ellis Ltd* [1933] Ch 458.
2 *Re Orleans Motor Co Ltd* [1911] 2 Ch 41 and *Re Destone Fabrics Ltd* [1941] Ch 319.
3 *Libertas–Kommerz GmbH* 1978 SLT 222.

8.69 The decision in the *Libertas–Kommerz* case[1] does not, it is thought, mean that a payment to qualify as cash paid to the company for the purposes of the statutory provisions in question must always go directly to the company to swell its assets. Where, for example, a bank holding a floating charge, at the company's request, makes a payment direct to another creditor of the company (without the money being paid to the company to enable it to make the payment) such a payment constitutes cash paid to the company provided the bank has no liability to such creditor in respect of the debt in question. In the *Thomas Mortimer* case[2] Romer J in considering cheques honoured by the bank after the granting of a debenture in its favour by the company expressed the view that this amounted to the bank paying cash at the request of the company to persons who were creditors of the company, the bank not being liable itself to such creditors. He then went on to say – 'Again, if I may say so with all respect to the argument which has been addressed to me, why that is not a payment in cash by the bank to the company for the purposes of this section passes my comprehension.'

1 *Libertas–Kommerz GmbH* 1978 SLT 222.
2 *Re Thomas Mortimer Ltd* [1965] Ch 186; *Re Yeovil Glove Co Ltd* [1965] Ch 148.

8.70 Companies do from time to time change their bankers and it is not unusual for the new bank in consideration for a floating charge to allow the company to pay off its total indebtedness to the old bank by one cheque drawn on its new account or even for the new bank to telegraphically transfer to the old bank at the company's request the amount necessary to clear such indebtedness. It is thought that on the basis of the two English decisions mentioned above this would qualify as cash paid to the company for the purposes of these statutory provisions.

8.71 The cash paid or goods or services supplied to the company must be so paid or supplied in terms of section 617 of the Companies Act 1985 'at the time of or subsequently to' the creation of the charge and in terms of section 245 'at the same time as, or after' the creation of the charge. These words in section 617 of the 1985 Act have been interpreted as not necessarily meaning at the same moment but in reasonable proximity looking in each case at the circumstances and nature of the transaction. Whether by the introduction in section 245 of the word 'same' in relation to time will lead to a stricter interpretation by the courts remains to be seen.

8.72   Section 617 of the 1985 Act required the cash paid to be in consideration for the charge and again in section 245 of the Insolvency Act 1986 the extent to which a floating charge in question may be valid is related to the value of the consideration for the creation of the charge. It has been held[1] that these words are not used in a strict contractual sense and can be applied to payments made in reliance upon and because of the existence of the charge.

1 *Re Yeovil Glove Co Ltd* [1965] Ch 148 at 178.

8.73   It is often the case that when a bank requests a floating charge from a company its account with the bank is already in overdraft. The bank in these circumstances, if it allows the account to run on in the normal course, is entitled to apply the rule in *Clayton*'s case.[1] This means any credits after the creation of the charge can be applied against pre-charge indebtedness until such time as this indebtedness is extinguished with the result that all post-charge debts are cash payments in consideration for the charge and so secured by the floating charge.[2] The Cork Committee[3] recommended that the decision in *Re Yeovil Glove* should be reversed but this recommendation has not to date been implemented.

1 *Devaynes v Noble* (1816) 1 Mer 572.
2 *Re Yeovil Glove Co Ltd* [1965] Ch 148.
3 Report of the Review Committee on Insolvency Law and Practice (Cmnd 8558) paragraph 1562.

8.74   Finally, section 617(3) of the 1985 Act contained provisions to the effect that where a company was being wound up in Scotland, a floating charge created by it was not to be challengeable as an alienation or preference voidable by statute (other than under that section) or at common law on the ground of insolvency or notour bankruptcy. This saving from challenge other than under the provisions of section 617 has not been included in section 245 of the Insolvency Act 1986 and so it appears that a floating charge may now be challenged not only under section 245 but also as a gratuitous alienation or unfair preference either under section 242 or 243 of the Insolvency Act 1986 or at common law.

Chapter 9

Payments and distributions

Provisions of section 60

9.01 Section 60(1) of the Insolvency Act 1986 provides that subject to section 61 of that Act (power of court to authorise a disposal of an interest in property) and to the rights of the following categories of persons (which rights shall, except to the extent otherwise provided in any instrument, have the following order of priority) namely:

(a) the holder of any fixed security which is over property subject to the floating charge and which ranks prior to, or *pari passu* with, the floating charge;

(b) all persons who have effectually executed diligence on any part of the property of the company which is subject to the charge by virtue of which the receiver was appointed;

(c) creditors in respect of all liabilities, charges and expenses incurred by or on behalf of the receiver;

(d) the receiver in respect of his liabilities, expenses and remuneration and any indemnity to which the receiver is entitled out of the property of the company; and

(e) the preferential creditors entitled to payment under section 59 of the Insolvency Act 1986,

the receiver shall pay moneys received by him to the holder of the floating charge by virtue of which the receiver was appointed in or towards satisfaction of the debt secured by the floating charge. Thus both the category of claimants having rights in priority to that of the floating charge creditor over the assets subject to the charge and the order in which these claimants so rank are clearly defined. The statutory order of ranking of such claimants is, however, now subject to any contrary ranking provided in any instrument.

9.02 Section 60(2) of the Insolvency Act 1986 provides that any balance of moneys remaining after the provisions of sections 60(1) and 61 of that Act have been satisfied shall be paid in accordance with their respective rights and interests to the following persons, as the case may require, namely:

(a) any other receiver;

(b) the holder of a fixed security which is over property subject to the floating charge;

(c) the company or its liquidator, as the case may be.

The most normal occurrence is for a receiver to hand over any surplus funds, after satisfaction of the floating charge creditor's claim, to a liquidator.

9.03   In terms of section 60(3) of the Insolvency Act 1986 where any question arises as to the person entitled to a payment under section 60, or where a receipt or a discharge of a security cannot be obtained in respect of any such payment, the receiver shall consign the amount of such payment in any joint stock bank of issue in Scotland in name of the Accountant of Court for behoof of the person or persons entitled thereto.

9.04   In the case of receivership where the sole asset is a heritable property subject to a standard security as well as the floating charge, a number of problems may arise. Firstly, whatever the ranking of the charges, if the property is to be sold by the receiver, he should, obtain the prior approval of the standard security holder as well as the floating charge holder (if these are different persons) to the price at which he proposes to sell the property. In most cases where the receiver has adequately advertised the property, such secured creditors will normally accept that the property should be sold to the highest bidder even though a shortfall will ensue and either or both such creditors will not receive the full amount (or any) of the indebtedness due by the company.

9.05   Secondly, where the standard security ranks in priority to the floating charge in the event of no other assets being available the receiver may experience difficulty in recovering his costs. In such circumstances, the receiver will seek to reach an agreement with a standard security holder whereby the reasonable expenses of realisation (including incidental receivership expenses) will be deducted from the proceeds of sale before accounting to such standard security holder.

9.06   Thirdly, if the receiver should be successful in clearing off the whole indebtedness due to a floating charge creditor who also holds a prior ranking standard security over the sole asset of the heritable property, simply by advantageously realising such heritable property, there was at one time a school of thought to the effect that he should either resign office having so paid off the floating charge creditor or he should retain a small amount of indebtedness to the floating charge creditor pending payment of the preferential creditors and completion of the other remaining matters in the receivership. However, on the basis of the decision in *Manley Petitioner*[1] in so far as it was held that a receiver was obliged to pay the preferential creditors, it is thought that a receiver in these circumstances should carry on and complete the receivership.

1 1985 SLT 42.

9.07   Fourthly, a standard security holder may not be willing to discharge such security if the full amount of the company's indebtedness is not paid. In these circumstances, if the receiver is satisfied that he has adequately advertised the property, he should apply to the court for authority to sell the property under and in terms of section 61 of the Insolvency Act 1986.

9.08   As in the case of the powers of the receiver under section 55 of, and Schedule 2 to, the Insolvency Act 1986 so also in terms of section 60(1)(b) the distribution of moneys is subject to the rights of any persons who have 'effectually executed diligence'. On the basis of the law as it stands at present it is, therefore, clear that an arrestment not followed by a decreee of furthcoming is not effectually executed diligence:[1] It is also possible that an inhibiting creditor who does not succeed in obtaining a decree of adjudication before the appointment of a receiver has not effectually executed diligence.[2] In the case of creditors who have done diligence, only those who have effectually executed diligence are entitled to rank in priority to the floating charge creditor.

1 *Lord Advocate v Royal Bank of Scotland Ltd* 1978 SLT 38.
2 *Armour and Mycroft Petitioners* 1983 SLT 453.

9.09   Section 60(1)(c) of the Insolvency Act 1986 requires the claims of all creditors in respect of liabilities incurred by the receiver to rank in priority to the claim of the floating charge creditor. In any case, where the receiver hopes to dispose of the business of the company on a going concern basis, even on the basis of an orderly running down of the business, it will be necessary for liabilities to suppliers, for example, to be incurred and it is perfectly appropriate that any such liabilities should be settled in full prior to any payment to the holder of the floating charge.

Liabilities, expenses and remuneration of receiver

9.10   Section 60(1)(d) of the Insolvency Act 1986 recognises that the receiver's own liabilities, expenses and remuneration rank before the floating charge creditor. The receiver will have incurred certain professional fees (eg to his solicitor or surveyor or other agents) and prima facie the receiver is liable personally to settle such professional fees. Although, in practice, it occurs very rarely, the solicitor's fees may be subject to taxation by the Auditor of the Court of Session at the instance of the receiver. If the receiver is unfortunate enough to have become liable for some obligation or other matter for which monetary compensation has to be paid, then section 57(3) together with section 60(1)(d) allow him to include such liability within this head.

9.11   Section 58 of the Insolvency Act 1986 deals principally with the remuneration of the receiver and it states that the remuneration to be paid to a receiver shall be determined by agreement between the receiver and the holder of the floating charge by virtue of which he was appointed. Most receivers, as partners of firms of chartered accountants, operate time recording and time costing systems and such a basis for fixing the remuneration of a receiver is widely used in discussions with floating charge holders. If the receiver's remuneration cannot be determined in accordance with section 58(1) or where it is so determined but is disputed by the holder of any floating charge or fixed security over all or any part of the property of the company, the company or the liquidator of the company, such remuneration may on the application of the receiver or of any such other persons be fixed by the Auditor of the Court of Session.[1] In certain cases (eg the work involved being out of proportion to the value of the assets), there may be some merit in any event in the receiver formally submitting his account to the Auditor for approval. It is, however, unusual for such a course to be taken in a receivership.

1 Insolvency Act 1986, s 58(2).

9.12   Under the provisions of section 58(3) of the Insolvency Act 1986, where the receiver has been paid or retained for his remuneration for any period before the remuneration has been fixed by the Auditor any amount in excess of the remuneration so fixed for that period, the receiver or his personal representatives shall account for the excess.

Priority of debts

9.13   Section 59(1) of the Insolvency Act 1986 provides that where a receiver is appointed and the company is not at the time of the appointment in course of being wound up,[1] the debts which fall under section 59(2) shall be paid out of any assets coming to the hands of the receiver in priority to any claim for principal or interest by the holder of the floating charge by virtue of which the receiver was appointed.

1 But see *Manley, Petitioner* 1985 SLT 42.

9.14   The debts referred to in section 59(1) of the Insolvency Act 1986 are in terms of section 59(2) debts which satisfy the following conditions, that is to say, they are debts:
(a)   which are preferential debts within the meaning of section 386 of the Insolvency Act 1986 and Schedule 6 thereto (read with Schedule 3 to the Social Security Pensions Act 1975); and
(b)   which, by the end of a period of six months after advertisement by the receiver for claims in the Edinburgh Gazette and in a newspaper circulating in the district where the company carries on business, either
(i)   have been intimated to him; or
(ii)   have become known to him.
Preferential creditors in a receivership are thus those who would have a similar right on the liquidation of the company and have become known to the receiver by intimation or otherwise in the six month period following his advertisement for such claims. The effect of this is that the receiver is obliged to advertise for such claims as provided in section 59(2).

9.15   Section 387(4)(b) of the Insolvency Act 1986 provides that, for the purposes of Schedule 6 to that Act (the provisions relating to preferential creditors in a liquidation) the relevant date is the date of appointment of the receiver under section 53(6) or 54(5) of the Insolvency Act 1986. Section 59(3) of the Insolvency Act 1986 further provides that any payments made under the provisions of section 59 shall be recouped as far as may be out of the assets of the company available for payment of ordinary creditors.

9.16 For a proper understanding of what now constitute preferential debts, it is necessary to examine the provisions of sections 175 and 386 of and Schedule 6 to the Insolvency Act 1986 which contain definitions of preferential debts which no longer include local rates and taxes on profits. The referable period for value added tax has also been reduced to six months. Section 175(1) of the Insolvency Act 1986 provides that in a winding up the preferential debts listed in section 386 of, and Schedule 6 to, that Act shall be paid in priority to all other debts. Schedule 6 lists the preferential debts as follows.

Debts due to Inland Revenue

1 (1) Sums due at the relevant date from the debtor on account of deductions of income tax from emoluments paid during the period of twelve months next before that date, being deductions which the debtor was liable to make under section 204 of the Income and Corporation Taxes Act 1970 (pay as you earn) less the amount of the repayments of income tax which the debtor was liable to make during that period.

(2) Sums due at the relevant date from the debtor in respect of such deductions as are required to be made by the debtor for that period under section 69 of the Finance (No 2) Act 1975 (sub-contractors in the construction industry).

No longer included in preferential debts are income tax, corporation tax, capital gains tax and other taxes assessed on the company.

Debts due to Customs and Excise

2 (1) Any value added tax which is referable to the period of six months next before the relevant date. This period was previously twelve months.

(2) The amount of any car tax which is due at the relevant date from the debtor and which became due within a period of twelve months next before that date.

(3) Any amount which is due:

(a) by way of general betting duty or bingo duty; or

(b) under section 12(1) of the Betting and Gaming Duties Act 1981 (general betting duty and pool betting duty recoverable from agent collecting stakes); or

(c) under section 14 of, or Schedule 2 to, that Act (gaming licence duty),

from the debtor at the relevant date and which became due within the period of twelve months next before that date.

Social security contributions

3 (1) All sums which on the relevant date are due from the debtor on account of Class 1 or Class 2 contributions under the Social Security Act 1975 or the Social Security (Northern Ireland) Act 1975 and which became due from the debtor in the twelve months next before the relevant date.

(2) All sums which on the relevant date have been assessed on and are due from the debtor on account of Class 4 contributions under either of the said Acts of 1975, being sums which:

(a) are due to the Commissioners of Inland Revenue (rather than to the Secretary of State or a Northern Ireland department); and

(b) are assessed on the debtor up to 5 April next before the relevant date,

but are not exceeding, in the whole, any one year's assessment.

Contributions to occupational pension schemes etc

4 Any sum which is owed by the debtor and is a sum to which Schedule 3 to the Social Security Pensions Act 1975 (contributions to occupational pension scheme and state scheme premiums) applies.

Remuneration of employees etc

5 (1) So much of any amount which:

(a) is owed by the debtor to a person who is or has been an employee of the debtor; and

(b) is payable by way of remuneration in respect of the whole or any part of the period of four months next before the relevant date,

as does not exceed such amount as may be be prescribed by order made by the Secretary of State. The current prescribed amount is £800 in the case of any one employee.

(2) An amount owed by way of accrued holiday remuneration, in respect of any period of employment before the relevant date, to a person whose employment by the debtor has been terminated, whether before, on or after that date.

(3) So much of any sum owed in respect of money advanced for the purpose as has been applied for the payment of a debt which, if it had not been paid, would have been a debt falling within sub-paragraph (1) or (2) above.

6 So much of any amount which:

(a) is ordered, whether before or after the relevant date, to be paid by the debtor under the Reserve Forces (Safeguard of Employment) Act 1985; and

(b) is so ordered in respect of a default made by the debtor before that date in the discharge of his obligations under that Act,

as does not exceed such amount as may be prescribed by order made by the Secretary of State.

9.17   As already mentioned in the interpretation of Schedule 6 to the Insolvency Act 1986, in the context of receivership, the relevant date means the date of the appointment of the receiver. The debtor in such context means the company in receivership.

Periods to which value added tax referable

9.18   For the purposes of paragraph 3 of Schedule 6:
(a) where the whole of the prescribed accounting period to which any value added tax is attributable falls within the period of six months next before the relevant date (the relevant period), the whole amount of that tax shall be referable to the relevant period; and
(b) in any other case the amount of any value added tax which shall be referable to the relevant period shall be the proportion of the tax which is equal to such proportion (if any) of the accounting reference period in question as falls within the relevant period;
and in that paragraph 'prescribed' means prescribed by regulations under the Value Added Tax Act 1983.

Amounts payable by way of remuneration

9.19
(1) For the purposes of paragraph 13(1) of Schedule 6, a sum is payable by the debtor to a person by way of remuneration in respect of any period if:
  (a) it is paid as wages or salary (whether payable for time or for piece work or earned wholly or partly by way of commission) in respect of services rendered to the debtor in that period; or
  (b) it is an amount falling within sub-paragraph (2) of paragraph 13 of Schedule 6 and is payable by the debtor in respect of that period.
(2) Sub-paragraph (2) of paragraph 13 of Schedule 6 provides that an amount falls within that sub-paragraph if it is:
  (a) a guarantee payment under section 12(1) of the Employment Protection (Consolidation) Act 1978 (employee without work to do for a day or part of a day);
  (b) remuneration on suspension on medical grounds under section 19 of that Act;
  (c) any payment for time off under section 27(3) (trade union duties), section 31(3) (looking for work, etc) or section 31A(4) (ante-natal care) of that Act;
  (d) statutory sick pay under Part I of the Social Security and Housing Benefits Act 1982; or
  (e) remuneration under a protective award made by an industrial tribunal under section 101 of the Employment Protection Act 1975 (redundancy dismissal with compensation).
(3) For the purposes of paragraph 14 of Schedule 6 holiday remuneration shall be deemed, in the case of a person whose employment has been terminated by or in consequence of his employer going into liquidation or being adjudged bankrupt, to have accrued to that person in respect of any period of employment if, by virtue of that person's contract of employment or of any enactment (including an order or

185

direction made under any enactment), that remuneration would have accrued in respect of that period if that person's employment had continued until he became entitled to be allowed the holiday.

(4) Without prejudice to the preceding provisions of paragraphs 13 and 14 of Schedule 6:

   (a) any remuneration payable by the debtor to a person in respect of a period of holiday or of absence from work through sickness or other good cause is deemed to be wages or, as the case may be, salary in respect of services rendered to the debtor in that period; and

   (b) references in paragraphs 13–15 to remuneration in respect of a period of holiday include references to any sums which, if they had been paid, would have been treated for the purposes of the enactments relating to social security as earnings in respect of that period.

Orders

9.20

(1) An order under paragraph 9 or 12 of Schedule 6 may contain such transitional provisions as may appear to the Secretary of State necessary or expedient.

(2) An order under the said paragraph 9 or 12 shall be made by statutory instrument which shall be subject to annulment in pursuance of a resolution of either House of Parliament.

Money advanced for the purpose of remuneration or accrued holiday remuneration

9.21 Paragraph 11 of Schedule 6 to the Insolvency Act 1986 has preserved the old rule that money advanced by a third party for the purpose of payment of remuneration to employees of the company and so used is preferential although now expressed in much simpler terms. Paragraph 11 provides that so much of any sum owed in respect of money advanced for the purpose as has been applied for the payment of a debt which, if it had not been paid, would have been preferential as employees' remuneration or accrued holiday remuneration will be preferential.

9.22 This provision can be of benefit to a floating charge holder where such holder is a clearing bank which has provided funds to enable the company to pay its employees. In these circumstances certain conditions must be met, however, before a preferential ranking can be admitted. In considering the equivalent provisions in the Companies Act 1929 Mr Robert Finlayson in his *Law Lectures to Bankers*,[1] at page 152, states as follows:

'The money must be advanced "for that purpose" – that is, for the purpose of paying wages or salaries – and it is accordingly necessary to preserve evidence that the advances in question were so made. The simplest method of doing that is to have the cheques which are drawn for the purpose specially marked by the customers as being for wages. They may, for example, be made payable to "Selves for Wages" or as employees' "Wages or bearer". It is not sufficient if the cheques have merely a marking on the back to show numbers and denominations of the notes and coins drawn from the bank or that the banker assumed or understood that the money was required to meet wages. The money, according to the Act, must have been advanced for the specific purpose, and this involves definiteness.'

1 Published by William Blackwood & Sons Limited in 1939 but now out of print.

9.23 In terms of the previous statutory provisions entitlement to the preference only arose in so far as the employees' priority claims had been diminished by reason of the advances in question having been made. The terms of paragraph 11 of Schedule 6 appear to have the same effect. Mr Finlayson[1] goes on to state:

'If the money, although specially borrowed for the purpose, is not actually applied in paying the wages, the position would be that the employees' claim in the liquidation would not have been diminished and they, themselves, would be entitled to a preferential ranking in full. Consequently, the bank, in a case of that kind, could not also obtain a preferential ranking and would require to be satisfied with an ordinary ranking. No doubt, however, any director or officer of the company who obtained advances from a bank for the specific purpose of paying wages, and instead of doing so, applied the money otherwise, would lay himself open to a charge of fraud.'

1 *Law Lectures to Bankers* published by William Blackwood & Sons Limited in 1939 but now out of print.

9.24 It is accordingly essential that a receiver in considering a claim to a preferential ranking under this head should be satisfied both that the money was advanced and was used for the purposes in question. The claim is of course restricted to the aggregate claims of the employees who received the money advanced which would have been preferential had they not received such money.

9.25 It can arise that even though a designated wages account has not been opened, a bank can establish that moneys were advanced for the payment of wages, in which event it is entitled to claim a ranking. However, in these circumstances, the bank faces the difficulty of the operation of the rule in *Clayton*'s case[1] to the effect that any credit received must first be applied in discharging the earliest debit on the account which may have the effect of reducing its potential preferential claim. One of the difficulties of proving in such circumstances that all moneys advanced by the bank in a particular payment are truly for the purposes of paying wages is that there may, for example, be sums included for other expenses and petty cash. Such sums must be clearly excluded in a calculation of the bank's wages preference.

1 *Devaynes v Noble* (1816) 1 Mer 572.

9.26 In his *Law Lectures to Bankers*,[1] Mr Robert Finlayson at page 121 refers to the unreported case of *National Provincial Bank Ltd v Freedman* where no separate wages account was opened. Shortly before a company went into liquidation, the bank insisted that the debit on the sole account with the company should not exceed a fixed limit. The company required money to pay wages each week and the bank refused to cash wages cheques in favour of the company until it was satisfied that either at the same time or within a few hours cheques in favour of the company would be lodged to reduce the overdraft to such an extent that the wages cheques when drawn would not increase the overdraft beyond the prescribed limit. On the liquidation of the company, the liquidator argued that the bank had advanced no money to meet wages because the cash it had paid out on the wages cheques was merely the same cash which had been lodged around the same time to the credit of the account. The court held, however, that these cheques did not provide the wages but simply reduced the overdraft: the wages cheques were paid by money which was advanced by the bank for that purpose.

1 Published by William Blackwood & Sons Limited in 1939 but now out of print.

9.27 On the other hand in the *E J Morel* case[1] the normal trading account (the No 2 account) of a company was maintained in credit in excess of the amount to which the wages account was in debit. Wages were drawn monthly and as soon as a debit to the wages account was more than four months old, it was transferred to the wages account from the No 2 account. Buckley J said at 32:

'. . . and I think that those two accounts were truly interdependent, so that the bank would never have met a cheque drawn on either one or the other without considering the combined position of those two accounts taken together and, if one reaches that conclusion, the sensible and the right way to regard the matter is to treat those two accounts as though they were in reality one. If that is right, then I think that there is substance in the contention that the bank never did in fact make advances to meet the wages cheques; the company when it drew on its wages account was really drawing its own moneys standing to the credit of the No 2 account . . .'

1 *Re E J Morel (1934) Ltd* [1962] Ch 21.

Right to combine accounts

9.28 The right to combine the bank accounts of a company in receivership or liquidation depends on the person who wishes to apply such right, the nature of each account and impinges upon the principles of the law of set-off.[1] In many of the cases to which reference is made in the succeeding paragraphs, the extent of a bank's preferred ranking for 'sums advanced for the purpose' depended to some extent on whether or not accounts could be combined and also arose as a separate issue.

1 See Chap 4 paras 4.67 to 4.79.

9.29 It has been generally established that a bank is entitled to combine current accounts of a customer in any way it wishes[1] and in a subsequent case[2] combination of a current account and a frozen account of the same customer has been approved. What appears, however, clear is that a receiver or liquidator of a company is not entitled to combine two accounts.[3]

1 In *Re E J Morel (1934) Ltd* [1962] Ch 21; *Garnett v McKewan* (1872) LR 8 Exch 10.
2 *National Westminster Bank Ltd v Halesowen Presswork and Assemblies Ltd* [1972] AC 785.
3 *Bank of Scotland v Purvis Industries Ltd* (unreported) – opinion of Lord Hill Watson dated 21 July 1954.

9.30 The facts in the *E J Morel* case[1] were that at one stage a company had one bank account which was overdrawn. It was agreed between the company and its bankers that the first account be frozen, a No 2 account be opened to deal with normal business transactions and a No 3 account be opened as a wages account. Thereafter, the No 2 account was maintained in credit in excess of the amount to which the wages account was in debit. Wages were drawn on a monthly basis and as soon as a debit to the wages account was more than four months old, it was transferred to the wages account from the No 2 account. On the winding up of the company, the No 1 account was in debit to the extent of £1,839, the No 2 account was in credit to the extent of £1,544 and the No 3 account was in debit to the extent of £1,623. The bank applied a set-off to the debit and credit balances of the No 1 and No 2 accounts and added the balance of the small debit arising to the debit on the No 3 account. The liquidator argued that only the No 2 and No 3 accounts should be adjusted in this way, no account being taken of the frozen No 1 account. The court held that while the bank could combine several current accounts of a customer as it might choose, it was inappropriate to do so where the accounts were of a different character, such as the frozen No 1 account. As was noted by Buckley J in the course of his judgment[1] at 30, the case of *Garnett v McKewan*[2] where the bank transferred one account to another branch where the customer also had an account, is authority for the proposition that current accounts of a customer may be combined.

1 *Re E J Morel (1934) Ltd* [1962] Ch 21.
2 (1872) LR 8 Exch 10.

9.31 The facts in *National Westminster Bank Ltd v Halesowen Presswork and Assemblies Ltd*[1] were that as a result of concern by the bank, the No 1 account of the company was frozen and a new No 2 account was opened for the normal trading business of the company, it being understood that the No 2 account should always be kept in credit. These arrangements were to subsist for a period of four months pending the sale of the company as a going concern and in the absence of materially changed circumstances in the meantime. Within the period of four months the company gave the bank notice of a meeting of creditors for the purpose of appointing a liquidator. On the day of such meeting of creditors, the company paid into the No 2 account a cheque for £8,611 prior to the resolution to wind up the company. The cheque was cleared two days later and the bank claimed to be able to set off the credit of £8,611 against the company's indebtedness on the No 1 account. The bank relied on the terms of section 31 of the Bankruptcy Act 1914 as extended by section 317 of the Companies Act 1948[2] (these sections being applicable only in England), the effect of which was that an account be taken of what is due from the one party to the other in respect of mutual dealings and the balance of the account only should be claimed or paid on either side respectively. The House of Lords held that the terms of section 31 as extended were mandatory and that the bank was entitled to combine a current credit account with a frozen account since the debit on the one account and the credit on the other account amounted to mutual dealings under the section. The arrangements agreed between the bank and the company a few months prior to the appointment of the liquidator ceased on liquidation.

1 [1972] AC 785.
2 Re-enacted as CA 1985, s 612.

9.32 One further aspect of the *Halesowen* case[1] should be mentioned from the standpoint of the law of Scotland. At 822 of the report Lord Kilbrandon stated:

'An interesting feature of this controversy is that, while by section 318 of the Companies Act 1948 the provisions of the Bankruptcy (Scotland) Act 1913 relating to ranking of claims are imported into the Scottish liquidation code, there is no equivalent to section 31 to be found in the latter Act. The right of set off, or, as Bell calls it in his Commentaries on the Laws of Scotland, 5th ed (1826), vol II, p 124, "the balancing of accounts in bankruptcy," stands on the common law of compensation or retention, expanded in cases of bankruptcy to include debts which would not be susceptible of set off in the case of a solvent creditor. For example, in bankruptcy, the debts need not be of the same nature, or both due at the same time, or both liquid. Bell's Commentaries, vol II, pp 119–121, supply an illuminating account of the parallel development of the law in England and Scotland respectively. It would hardly be possible to maintain in Scotland that set off is mandatory, and independent of the act or agreement of parties, since "it must be pleaded by the debtor who wishes to take advantage of it," and, again:

"Compensation may be pleaded not only by the primary debtor, but even *illo tacente vel negante*, by anyone having an interest, as a cautioner in a bond, or an indorser of a bill of exchange" (Goudy on Law of Bankruptcy, 4th ed (1914), pp 551, 552).

So, if set off be mandatory in England, this seems to be one of the fields in which the law relating to companies varies according as they are registered in England or in Scotland.'

1 *National Westminster Bank Ltd v Halesowen Presswork and Assemblies Ltd* [1972] AC 785.

9.33 The case of *Bank of Scotland v Purvis Industries Ltd*[1] is instructive from the point of view of calculation of a wages preference and also decided that the liquidators of Purvis were not entitled to combine various accounts. It also makes clear that if it is made a condition that a separate wages account be opened and withdrawals are limited to the payment of wages for the statutory period, the bank should experience no real difficulty in establishing a wages preference.

1 Unreported Opinion of Lord Hill Watson dated 21 July 1954.

9.34 Payments to an employee by way of commission can occasionally cause problems in the context of sums advanced for the purpose of such payments. If an employee is remunerated by the payment of a salary plus a commission based, for example, on the number of products of the company sold by him or based on some other factor clearly linked to the employee's performance, any moneys advanced to the company for the purpose of paying such salary and commission would, it is submitted, be preferential within the usual limits in that payment by way of commission is remuneration. Fees paid to directors do not however qualify as remuneration and so cannot form the basis of a preferential claim by a third party who has advanced the funds to meet such fees.

9.35 In receivership preferential debts rank equally among themselves and are to be paid in full, unless the assets are insufficient to meet them, in which case they abate in equal proportions.[1]

1 Insolvency Act 1986, s 175(2).

'Gross' or 'net'

9.36 There has been prolonged and continuing discussion in relation to both an employee's claim in liquidation or receivership to a preferential ranking for unpaid remuneration and even more so to the subrogated claim of a third party who has advanced funds for the purpose of and which were applied in payment of such remuneration. The discussion has arisen from the fact that there is a monetary limit on an employee's preferential claim for unpaid remuneration, the necessity for the company debtor to make certain statutory deductions from employees' remuneration (such as employees' NIC contributions and PAYE) which if unpaid on liquidation or receivership are themselves within certain limits preferential and the practice of banks to advance in some but not all cases the net amount only of the company's wage bill. The arguments are generally known as the 'gross' and 'net' arguments respectively and the authors have read numerous well-reasoned and persuasive opinions of learned counsel on both sides of the border, some arguing strongly for one view and some for the other, particularly in relation to a third party lender's subrogated claim. The Cork Committee[1] acknowledged the problem and recommended in paragraph 1444 of its Report that the question be resolved by legislation. Paragraph 11 of Schedule 6 to the Insolvency Act 1986 undoubtedly expresses the right to a preferential claim of a third party lender for remuneration payment purposes in much simpler terms but whether the problem is now resolved remains to be seen.

1 Report of the Review Committee on Insolvency Law and Practice (Cmnd 8558).

9.37   It is not intended to set out at length the competing arguments but to put forward, in reasonably succinct terms, the views of the authors which, as will be seen, support the gross view. These are:

(a) In the case of an employee's claim to a preferential ranking, this is for gross remuneration. In making payment, the receiver is required to deduct and account for, PAYE income tax and employees' NIC contributions.

(b) In the case of the claim of a third party who has advanced funds for the purpose of payment of remuneration which have been so applied and such remuneration had it not been paid would have been preferential, such claim is subject to a simple monetary limit being in respect of each employee involved the maximum amount of the employee's claim to a preferential ranking. The third party's claim is not related to either the net amount actually received by each employee nor to the net amounts advanced during the period in question over which the employee's claim for gross wages would have reached the maximum preferential amount.

Chapter 10

Notification and information where receiver appointed

Registration and notification of appointment

Appointment by holder of floating charge

10.01 On the appointment of a receiver by the holder of a floating charge, such holder or person on his behalf must deliver to the Registrar of Companies for registration, within seven days of its execution, a copy (certified in the prescribed manner to be a correct copy) of the instrument of appointment.[1] 'Prescribed' in this context is defined in sections 251 and 411 of the Insolvency Act 1986 as meaning prescribed by the rules made by the Secretary of State. Certification of copies of instruments of appointment are accepted by the Registrar of Companies if certified in the usual way by the appointer or a person on his behalf.

1 Insolvency Act 1986, s 53(1).

10.02 A notice in the prescribed form requires to be delivered to the Registrar of Companies[1] together with a certified copy of the instrument of appointment and such notice should contain the following information:
(a) details of the appointment;
(b) a statement of the circumstances justifying the appointment;
(c) particulars of the floating charge under which the receiver is appointed; and
(d) the name (or the first-named if several) of the person entitled to the benefit of the floating charge.
On receipt of the certified copy of the instrument of appointment the Registrar requires to enter the particulars of the appointment in the Register of Charges.[2] No registration fee is payable.

1 Insolvency Act 1986, s 53(1).
2 Ibid s 53(5).

10.03 The receiver must unless there is already a receiver in office or he has been appointed to replace a deceased or previous receiver who has ceased to act (except where the deceased or previous receiver has not fully complied with the requirements):
(1) forthwith send to the company and publish notice of his appointment;[1] and
(2) within twenty-eight days after his appointment, unless the court

otherwise directs, send such notice of his appointment to all the company's creditors (so far as he is aware of their addresses).

1 Insolvency Act 1986, s 65(1) and (2).

10.04 If the company is being wound up, these provisions apply notwithstanding that the receiver and liquidator are the same person subject to any necessary modifications arising from that fact.[1]

1 Insolvency Act 1986, s 65(3).

10.05 A person who fails without reasonable excuse to comply with these provisions is liable to a fine and, for continued contravention, to a daily default fine.[1]

1 Insolvency Act 1986, s 65(4).

10.06 Prior to the repeal by the Insolvency Act 1985 of section 481 of the 1985 Act (which provided for the information to be given by a receiver on his appointment) it was only necessary for a receiver to notify the company of his appointment and the only public notice of the receiver's appointment (other than its registration with the Registrar of Companies which only came to the attention of persons examining the company file) was the statutory notice for preferential claims under section 475(2)(b) of the 1985 Act (now section 59(2) of the Insolvency Act 1986). Such statutory notice is advertised in the Edinburgh Gazette and a local newspaper. While there is no provision for the advertisement of such notice within a certain period of the receiver's appointment, this is usually done in practice within a few weeks of his appointment.

10.07 The lack of information on the appointment of a receiver resulted in many complaints, particularly from ordinary trade creditors, in respect of the absence of provisions for making known at an early date that a receiver had been appointed and also the likely outcome of the receivership. The Cork Committee[1] in its Report stated: 'the most frequent complaint which we have received is of the lack of information once a receiver has been appointed'. As a result the Cork Committee made certain recommendations[2] intended to remedy the position and these have been implemented in the repeal of sections 481 and 482 of the 1985 Act and their replacement by new provisions incorporating the Cork proposals.

1 Report of the Review Committee on Insolvency Law and Practice (Cmnd 8558) paragraph 438.
2 Ibid paragraphs 476–489.

Appointment by the court

10.08 On the appointment of a receiver by the court, the party who presented the petition or a person on the petitioner's behalf must deliver to the Registrar of Companies for registration, within seven days of its date or such longer period as the court may allow, a copy of the court's interlocutor certified by the clerk of court to be a correct copy together with the prescribed form.[1] As in the case of the appointment of a receiver by instrument of appointment, the Registrar of Companies is required on payment of the prescribed fee to enter particulars of a court appointment in the Register of Charges.[2]

1 54(3) of the Insolvency Act 1986, s 54(3).
2 Ibid s 54(4).

10.09   The receiver in a court appointment, unless there is already a receiver in office or he has been appointed to replace a deceased or previous receiver except where such requirements have not been fully implemented, has the same duty to notify the company and its creditors of his appointment and publish it.[1]

1 Insolvency Act 1986, s 65.

Receiver should seek confirmation of registration

10.10   While it is the duty of the holder of the floating charge or the petitioner to register particulars of his appointment with the Registrar of Companies, it is suggested that in the interests of prompt notification of his appointment the receiver should always seek confirmation from such holder or petitioner that registration has been effected.

Non-registration of appointment

10.11   Failure to deliver to the Registrar of Companies a certified copy of the instrument of appointment or the court interlocutor in the case of a court appointment or the appropriate company form or to notify the company of the appointment does not affect the validity of the receiver's appointment nor the exercise of his powers. The only potential penalty is the imposition of a fine and, for continued contravention, of a daily default fine on any person who without reasonable excuse makes default in complying with the registration requirements[1] and a receiver who fails to notify the company being subject to a similar penalty.[2] There has been criticism of the absence of any other sanctions, particularly as delay or failure to register may result in a party inspecting the Register of Charges being unaware of the appointment. The Cork Committee[3] in considering the effective date of the appointment of a receiver referred to the fact that the Kilbrandon Committee recommended that the appointment of a receiver should take effect only when a duly certified copy of the instrument of appointment had been delivered to the Registrar for registration but the Cork Committee considered that to use the date of registration for filing would introduce an element of uncertainty and would also be unacceptable because speed of appointment is frequently essential. The Cork Committee's own recommendation in relation to the time when a receiver's appointment should run has been implemented by section 53 of the Insolvency Act 1986[4] but does not alter the position that non-registration of the appointment does not affect its validity. However, the increased notification requirements should go some way to meet the criticism of the absence of sanctions for non-registration other than monetary penalties.

1 Insolvency Act 1986, ss 53(2) and 54(3).
2 Ibid s 65(4).
3 Report of the Review Committee on Insolvency Law and Practice (Cmd 8558) paragraphs 471 and 472.
4 See Chap 1 para 1.34.

Other publication of receiver's appointment

10.12   In addition to the increased notification requirements contained in the Insolvency Act 1986, a receiver still also requires to give the statutory notice under section 59(2) of that Act for preferential claims, such notice requiring to be advertised in the Edinburgh Gazette and in one newspaper circulating in the district where the company carries on business. There is no provision for such notice being advertised within a certain period of the receiver's appointment although in practice this is usually done within a few weeks.

Notification of appointment on invoices

10.13   In addition to the registration and notification requirements already mentioned, where a receiver has been appointed, every invoice, order for goods or business letter issued by or on behalf of the company or the receiver or the liquidator of the company on which the company's name appears must contain a statement that a receiver has been appointed.[1] Failure to comply with this requirement can render any officer of the company or any receiver or liquidator who knowingly and wilfully authorises or permits the default liable to a fine.

1 Insolvency Act 1986, s 64(1)

10.14   In addition to letters issued by the receiver himself, every letter issued by an agent either on his behalf or on behalf of a liquidator should, in any reference to the company, state that it is in receivership or that a receiver has been appointed and, if appropriate, that it is also in liquidation. The normal practice in Scotland is for a receiver to overstamp on every letter, invoice, order or other document issued by him a notice both intimating the appointment of a receiver and including a general disclaimer of personal liability on the following lines: 'Receiver appointed.

The receiver contracts only as agent of the company and without personal liability.'

Statement to be made to and returns to be made by a receiver

Statement to be made by officers to receiver

10.15   The Insolvency Act 1985 introduced new provisions governing the information to be supplied to the receiver by the company's management and the information to be disseminated by the receiver to creditors and others, these new provisions (now contained in sections 66–68 of the Insolvency Act 1986) being designed to meet criticisms of the previous provisions.

10.16   On his appointment, a receiver must forthwith require some or all of certain specified persons to make out and submit to him a statement in the prescribed form of the affairs of the company.[1]

1 Insolvency Act 1986, s 66(1) and (3).

10.17   The persons specified[1] as requiring to submit a statement of affairs, who must verify it by affidavit, are those:
(a) who are or have been officers of the company;
(b) who have taken part in the formation of the company at any time within a year of the date of the receiver's appointment;
(c) who are or have been within such period employees of or employed under a contract of services by the company and who, in the receiver's opinion, are capable of giving the required information;
(d) who are or have been within such period officers or employees of or employed under a contract of services by a company which within that period was an officer of the company in receivership.

1 Insolvency Act 1986, s 66(3).

10.18   A statement of affairs,[1] verified by affidavit by the persons required to submit it, must show:
(a) particulars of the company's assets, debts and liabilities;
(b) the names and addresses of the creditors;
(c) the securities held by them respectively;
(d) the dates when the securities were respectively given; and
(e) such further or other information as may be presented.

1 Insolvency Act 1986, s 66(2).

10.19   Where any persons are required by the receiver to submit a statement of affairs to him, they must do so within twenty-two days of being given notice of such requirement[1] unless the receiver, at his discretion, either when giving such notice or subsequently extends such period.[2] The court also has a residual discretionary power to extend the period where the receiver has refused to exercise his power to do so.[2]

1 Insolvency Act 1986, s 66(4).
2 Ibid s 66(5).

10.20 The receiver has a discretionary power to release any person either from the requirement to submit to him a statement of affairs or from the obligation to verify or include in such statement any of the specified information[1] with the court again having a residual discretion to exercise this power in the event of the receiver's refusal to do so.[2]

1 Insolvency Act 1986, s 66(5)(a).
2 Ibid s 66(5).

10.21 Any person who without reasonable cause fails to comply with any of these obligations relating to the giving of a statement of affairs is liable to a fine and, for continued contravention, to a daily default fine.[1]

1 Insolvency Act 1986, s 66(6).

Report by receiver

10.22 Prior to the changes introduced by the Insolvency Act 1985 a receiver only required to supply limited information during the course of the receivership to the Registrar of Companies, the company itself, the holders of fixed and floating charges (including that under which he was appointed) and to debenture holders and any trustee for them. There was no requirement to supply ordinary creditors (other than indirectly by filing limited information with the Registrar of Companies) with any information and this attracted adverse comment. The substitution by the Insolvency Act 1985 of the new sections 482A and B into the 1985 Act (now sections 67 and 68 of the Insolvency Act 1986) is intended to counter such adverse comment in that they require a report to be made available to ordinary creditors which will normally be placed before a meeting of such creditors who may at the meeting establish a committee of creditors.

10.23 On the appointment of a receiver, whether by the holder of a floating charge or by the court, the receiver must within three months (or such longer period as the court may allow) send a report[1] on certain matters to:
(a) the Registrar of Companies;
(b) the holder of the floating charge under which he was appointed;
(c) any trustee for secured creditors (ie creditors holding any security (whether heritable or moveable) any floating charge or any right of lien, retention or preference); and
(d) so far as he is aware of their addresses, all such secured creditors.
The previous obligations of a receiver to send on an annual basis and at the end of the receivership to the Registrar of Companies and others an abstract of receipts and payments were contained in section 481 of the

1985 Act which section was substituted by section 63 of the Insolvency Act 1985 without the inclusion of such obligations.

1 Insolvency Act 1986, s 67(1).

10.24   The matters to be dealt with in such report are:
(a) the events leading up to his appointment, so far as he is aware of them;
(b) actual or proposed disposal of any of the company's property;
(c) the actual or proposed carrying on of the company's business;
(d) the total amounts payable to the holder of the floating charge under which he was appointed;
(e) the amounts payable to preferential creditors; and
(f) the amount, if any, likely to be available for the payment of other creditors.

The report must also include[1] a summary of the statement of affairs submitted to the receiver under section 66 and any comments he may have on it.

1 Insolvency Act 1986, s 67(5).

10.25   In assessing what sum, if any, is likely to be available for other creditors the receiver will require to take account of the claims of any other secured creditors in addition to that of the holder of the floating charge under which he was appointed and also the estimated costs of the receivership.

10.26   Within a like period of three months from his appointment (or such longer period allowed by the court) the receiver[1] must either:
(a) send a copy of the report to all unsecured creditors (ie creditors other than secured creditors) in so far as he knows their addresses; or
(b) publish a notice stating an address to which unsecured creditors should write for copies of the report to be sent to them free of charge. The form of this notice will be prescribed by rules made by the Secretary of State.[2]

In addition, whether copies of the report are sent to creditors or they are notified by advertisement where copies can be obtained, the receiver, unless the court otherwise directs, must summon a meeting of the unsecured creditors on not less than fourteen days' notice and lay before such meeting a copy of his report.

1 Insolvency Act 1986, s 67(2).
2 See Rules, Appendix 19 to this book.

10.27   The court cannot direct[1] that the requirements to lay the receiver's report before a meeting of the unsecured creditors be dispensed with unless:
(a) the receiver states in the report that he intends to apply for a direction to that effect; and
(b) not less than fourteen days before the hearing of the receiver's application for a direction to that effect, either a copy of the report containing such statement is sent to all unsecured creditors or there is published notification of where a copy can be obtained.

1 Insolvency Act 1986, s 67(3).

10.28 If the company is or goes into liquidation the receiver[1] must send the liquidator a copy of his report within seven days of either sending his report to the Registrar of Companies and the secured creditors mentioned in section 67(1) of the Insolvency Act 1986 or, if later, the nomination or appointment of the liquidator and if he does so within the period of three months from his appointment (or such longer period allowed by the court) he is relieved of compliance with the requirements to send or make the report available to ordinary creditors and to lay it before a meeting of such creditors.

1 Insolvency Act 1986, s 67(4).

10.29 There is a saving provision[1] allowing the exclusion from the receiver's report of any information the disclosure of which would seriously prejudice the carrying out by the receiver of his functions.

1 Insolvency Act 1986, s 67(6).

10.30 These obligations on a receiver in relation to the making of a report do not apply[1] where there is already a receiver in office or the receiver has been appointed to replace a deceased or previous receiver who has ceased to act (except where the deceased or previous receiver has not fully complied with the requirements).

1 Insolvency Act 1986, s 67(7).

10.31 Any person who without reasonable excuse fails to comply with these provisions in relation to the making of a report is liable to a fine and, for continued contravention, to a daily default fine.[1]

1 Insolvency Act 1986, s 67(8).

Committee of creditors

10.32 Prior to the Insolvency Act 1985 there were no statutory provisions for the appointment of a committee of creditors although in larger receiverships both in Scotland and in England it is understood that receivers frequently requested the formation of an informal committee. The Cork Committee[1] recommended that the appointment of such a committee should be obligatory.

1 Report of the Review Committee on Insolvency Law and Practice (Cmnd 8558) paragraph 481.

10.33 Section 65 of the Insolvency Act 1985 introduced provisions now contained in section 68 of the Insolvency Act 1986 entitling unsecured creditors in a receivership situation to establish a committee. Where a meeting of such creditors is convened by the receiver under section 67(2) of the Insolvency Act 1986 (it would not be only if the court otherwise directed or in certain circumstances when the company is in liquidation), the meeting may, if it thinks fit, establish a committee to exercise the functions conferred on it by or under the Insolvency Act 1986. In this connection sections 545 to 548 (Committees of Inspection) and Schedule 17 (Proceedings of such Committees) of the 1985 Act were repealed by the Insolvency Act 1985 and the Insolvency Act 1986 appear to be silent on the functions and proceedings of a committee of creditors. As far as Scotland is concerned section 142(1) of the Insolvency Act 1986 provides for the establishment in a court liquidation of such a committee to exercise the functions imposed by the Insolvency Act 1986 which in addition to the powers and duties conferred and imposed on it by both statutes has such of the powers and duties of Commissioners in a sequestration as may be conferred or imposed on such committees by the rules. It is presumably the intention to make rules[1] governing the functions and proceedings of a committee of creditors in a receivership and in a liquidation.

1 See Rules, Appendix 19 to this book.

10.34   If a committee of creditors is established, it may on giving not less than seven days' notice require the receiver's attendance before it at any reasonable time to furnish it with such information as it may reasonably require relating to the carrying out by him of his functions.[1]

1 Insolvency Act 1986, s 68(2).

10.35   The statutory obligations of a receiver in relation to the giving of information do not necessarily relieve him of his duty of accountability to persons to whom he may otherwise be required to account. In an English case[1] decided on the equivalent English provisions prior to the passing of the Insolvency Act 1985 it was held that a receiver appointed under a debenture providing for him to be the agent of the company was answerable to the company for the conduct of its affairs and was, therefore, under a duty to keep fuller accounts than the statutory abstracts of receipts and payments then required to be compiled and to produce these to the company when required to do so. In that case the receiver was successful in discharging the debenture holder's debt thus enabling the company to continue in business.

1 *Smiths Ltd v Middleton* [1979] 3 All ER 842.

Enforcement provisions

10.36   Section 69 of the Insolvency Act 1986 contains provisions enabling any member or creditor of the company, the Registrar of Companies or a liquidator to apply to the court in appropriate circumstances for an order to enforce compliance by a receiver who is in default with any of his obligations as to filing, delivering or making any return account or document or giving any notice, which order may include an award of the costs of the application against the receiver. The form of such application prior to the coming into force of the Insolvency Act 1986 was governed by the Rules of the Court of Session, paragraph 218A(6).

Reports on conduct of directors of insolvent companies

10.37   Administrative receivers (and other insolvency office holders) appointed after 28 April 1986 to companies are obliged to report forthwith to the Secretary of State on the conduct of persons who have been directors or shadow directors[1] of insolvent companies where such conduct makes such persons appear to administrative receivers to be unfit to be concerned in the management of a company.[2] The purpose of such reports is to enable the court on the application of the Secretary of State to make a disqualification order in the appropriate circumstances.

1 For definition see CA 1985, s 741.
2 Company Directors Disqualification Act 1986, ss 6 and 7.

10.38   Rules were first introduced by statutory instrument[1] making provision for the manner in which an administrative receiver (and other insolvency office holders) should make such a report. These Rules have now been replaced by those contained in a subsequent statutory instrument[2] which came into effect on 29 December 1986 and which revokes the earlier Rules[3] except to the extent that Rules 2 and 3 of the earlier Rules continue to apply and have effect in relation to:
(a) any report to which the provisions of such Rule 2 apply, and
(b) any interim return required to be made by such Rule 3.[4]
The report in the case of an administrative receiver is to be made in the manner and to the extent provided in Form D2 (Scot).[5]

1 The Insolvent Companies (Reports on Conduct of Directors) (Scotland) Rules 1986, SI 1986/626 (S 59).
2 The Insolvent Companies (Reports on Conduct of Directors) (No 2) (Scotland) Rules 1986, SI 1986/1916 (S 140).
3 Ibid r 5(1)
4 Ibid r 5(2)
5 Ibid r 2(2)

10.39   Where it appears to an administrative receiver that the company has at any time become insolvent within the meaning of section 6(2) of the Company Directors Disqualification Act 1986,[1] he may, within six months of the date of his appointment, furnish a return[2] to the Secretary of State with respect to every person who:
(a) was, on the date the administrative receiver was appointed, a director or shadow director of the company, or
(b) had been such a director or shadow director at any time in the three years preceding that date.
The six months' period from the date of the receiver's appointment runs from the original appointment and not from that of a successor in office to a receiver who has vacated office.[3]

1 Rule 3(1) of The Insolvent Companies (Reports on Conduct of Directors) (No 2) (Scotland) Rules 1986, SI 1986/1916 (S 140).
2 Ibid r 3(2)
3 Ibid r 3(4)

10.40   The return in the case of an administrative receiver is made in the manner and to the extent provided in Form D4 (Scot).[1] If an administrative receiver without reasonable excuse fails to comply with this Rule, he is liable on summary conviction to a fine not exceeding £400 and, for continued contravention, to a daily default fine not exceeding £40.[2]

1 Rule 3(3) of The Insolvent Companies (Reports on Conduct of Directors) (No 2) (Scotland) Rules 1986, SI 1986/1916 (S 140).
2 Ibid r 3(7).

10.41   It is the duty of an administrative receiver to furnish a return to the Secretary of State no later than six months from the date of his appointment where no return has been so furnished up to one week before the expiry of such period, this duty falling on such receiver in office one week before the expiry of that period or, where none is then in office, on the administrative receiver who vacated office nearest to that time.[1] A return does not need to be provided if the administrative receiver has, since his appointment, made reports to the Secretary of State under section 7(3) of the Insolvency Act 1986 with respect to the person[2] in question.

1 Rule 3(5) of The Insolvent Companies (Reports on Conduct of Directors) (No 2) (Scotland) Rules 1986, SI 1986/1916 (S 140).
2 Ibid r 3(6).

10.42   The Rules[1] enable the Secretary of State to apply to the court to enforce compliance by an administrative receiver with a requirement by the Secretary of State under section 7(4) of the Company Directors Disqualification Act 1986 to furnish information and books, papers and other records relevant to the conduct of a person as a director.

1 Rule 4 of The Insolvent Companies (Reports on Conduct of Directors) (No 2) (Scotland) Rules 1986, SI 1986/1916 (S 140).

Chapter 11

Vacation of appointment of receiver

General

11.01 A receiver, whether appointed by the holder of a floating charge or by the court, vacates office if –

(a) he is removed from office by the court (ie the court having jurisdiction to wind up the company) on cause shown on the application by the holder of the floating charge by virtue of which he was appointed;[1] or

(b) he resigns office by giving notice to that effect in the prescribed manner to such persons as may be prescribed;[2] or

(c) he ceases to be qualified within the meaning of the Insolvency Act 1986 to act as an insolvency practitioner in relation to the company.[3]

1 Insolvency Act 1986, s 62(3).
2 Ibid s 62(1).
3 Ibid s 62(2).

11.02 In the vast majority of receiverships the receiver will vacate office by resignation after disposing of any surplus funds or assets to the party entitled thereto in terms of section 60 of the Insolvency Act 1986.

11.03 While under the statutory provisions the only way in which a receiver can be removed from office is by an application to the court by the holder of the relevant floating charge, it has been suggested[1] that there may be circumstances in which the Court of Session, in the exercise of its *nobile officium*, might entertain a petition for removal presented by a person other than the holder of the charge by virtue of which he was appointed, eg by the company or another creditor. The court on presentation of any such application would presumably order the normal advertisement and service appropriate in the circumstances.

1 *Palmers Company Law* (23rd edn) 48.14.

Remuneration and indemnity

11.04 Where at any time a receiver vacates office he is entitled[1] to be paid from the property of the company subject to the floating charge in accordance with the priority provisions of section 60(1) of the Insolvency Act 1986:

(a) his remuneration and any expenses which he has properly incurred; and

(b) any indemnity to which he is entitled out of the company's property.

1 Insolvency Act 1986, s 62(4).

11.05 Section 60(1) of the Insolvency Act 1986 now provides that the rights of the categories of persons listed in relation to the distribution of moneys by a receiver shall, except to the extent provided in any instrument, have the order of priority as set out in the section and now includes along with the receiver's liabilities, expenses and remuneration any indemnity to which he is entitled out of the company's property.

Notification of cessation of appointment

11.06 The holder of the floating charge by virtue of which a receiver was appointed on the receiver being removed by the court or the receiver himself in a case where the receiver ceases to act as such otherwise than by death must within fourteen days of the event notify the Registrar of Companies.[1] The Registrar must enter the notice in the Register of Charges. For some reason which is not immediately apparent there is no provision for notifying a cessation of appointment arising from a receiver's death.

1 Insolvency Act 1986, s 62(5).

11.07 There is a specific default provision in the subsection to the effect that the receiver or the holder, as the case may require, is liable on default, the penalty being a fine (or a daily default fine in the case of continued contravention).[1]

1 Insolvency Act 1986, s 62(5).

Re-floating of charge

Single receiver

11.08 If on the expiry of one month following upon the removal of the receiver or his ceasing to act as such no other receiver has been appointed, the floating charge by virtue of which he was appointed:

(a) thereupon ceases to attach to the property subject to it; and

(b) again subsists as a floating charge.[1]

In the event of the company subsequently being wound up the floating charge would again crystallise[2] and in the event of such winding up commencing before the end of the one month period the floating charge presumably does not re-float.

1 Insolvency Act 1986, s 62(6).
2 CA 1985, s 463(1).

Joint receivers

11.09   It is competent for either the holder of a floating charge or the court to appoint joint receivers.[1] On one of such joint receivers ceasing to act either through death, resignation or removal the appointment of the other continues and in that event the floating charge by virtue of which they were appointed would not re-float by reason alone of the former receiver not being replaced.

1 Insolvency Act 1986, s 51(1),(2) and (6).

Effect of re-floating of charge

11.10   If the claim of the holder of the floating charge has been fully satisfied then no debt is secured and the charge is fully satisfied. If such claim has not been fully satisfied then in the normal course no assets of the company will remain to further satisfy the claim secured by the charge unless at a later date assets come to light of which there was no previous knowledge. If the company is not then in liquidation and the holder of the floating charge takes the view that these assets would be attached by it on crystallisation, he could presumably reappoint a receiver.

Chapter 12

Administration orders

General

12.01 Prior to the Insolvency Act 1985 if a company was in financial difficulties it could either enter into a scheme of arrangement with its creditors or, if appropriate, a receiver could be appointed over some or all of its assets or it could be put into liquidation by one of the available procedures. The Cork Committee in its Report[1] suggested the introduction of a new insolvency mechanism, which it called the administrator procedure, to facilitate the rehabilitation or reorganisation of companies in serious financial trouble but where there were reasonable prospects of a return to profitability for the whole or parts of the business. As a result of this suggestion the Insolvency Act 1985 introduced an alternative course of action for such companies, namely the making of an administration order.[2] This new procedure is likely to be of value where it is not possible to have an administrative receiver appointed as where this is possible, and such an appointment is made, the holder of the floating charge will not readily consent to the making of such an order. As will be seen, however, notwithstanding that such consent is not forthcoming, the court has power to make such an order where, if it were made, the floating charge would be open to challenge as a fraudulent or unfair preference or gratuitous alienation or would be avoided under section 245 of the Insolvency Act 1986.

1 Report of the Review Committee on Insolvency Law and Practice (Cmnd 8558).
2 See now the Insolvency Act 1986, Pt II (ss 8–27).

12.02 While the purpose of this chapter is primarily to deal with administration orders in so far as they impinge in Scotland on the rights of holders of floating charges and receivers appointed under them, it is necessary at the outset to explain in what circumstances and for what purposes such orders may be made.

Power to make administration orders

12.03 An administration order, that is, an order directing that the company's affairs, business and property be managed by a person called an administrator, may be made by the court[1] if it is satisfied that the company is or is likely to become unable to pay its debts and it considers that the making of such an order would be likely to achieve one or more of the following purposes:[2]

(a) the survival of the company, and the whole or part of its undertaking, as a going concern;

(b) the approval of a composition under the Act in satisfaction of its debts or a scheme of arrangement of its affairs;

(c) the sanctioning of a compromise or arrangement with its creditors or members; and

(d) a more advantageous realisation of the company's assets than would be effected on liquidation.

An administration order cannot be made after the company has gone into liquidation.[3]

1 Insolvency Act 1986, s 8(1).
2 Ibid s 8(3).
3 Ibid s 8(4).

Application for order

12.04 An application for an administration order is by petition to the court[1] presented by all or any of the company, its directors or creditors and notice of such petition[2] must be given immediately to any person who has appointed or is or may be entitled to appoint an administrative receiver, that is a receiver over the whole or substantially the whole of the company's property.[3] The presentation of such a petition, provided no administration order has been made, does not prevent an administrative receiver being appointed or from carrying out his functions[4] but if such an order is made any administrative receiver must vacate office[5] as also must a receiver of part of the company's property if so required by the administrator.[6] During the period an administration order is in force no administrative receiver may be appointed[7] nor may any other steps be taken to enforce any security over the company's property.[8]

1 Insolvency Act 1986, s 9(1).
2 Ibid s 9(2)(a).
3 Ibid s 251.
4 Ibid s 10(2)(b),(c).
5 Ibid s 11(1)(b).
6 Ibid s 11(2).
7 Ibid s 11(3)(b).
8 Ibid s 11(3)(c).

12.05 On an application being made to the court for the appointment of an administrator, it will be necessary to satisfy the court that the company either is or is likely to become insolvent but that there are reasonable prospects of rescuing the whole or part of its business by carrying out some scheme or compromise or alternatively that such an appointment would be likely to be more advantageous for the company's creditors, and perhaps shareholders, than liquidation. An administrator will require to be a qualified insolvency practitioner.

12.06 On hearing a petition for the appointment of an administrator order, if an administrative receiver has been appointed, the court must dismiss the petition unless it is satisfied:

(a) that the person appointing the administrative receiver has consented to the making of the order; or

(b) that, if such an order were made, the floating charge by virtue of which the receiver was appointed would:
   (i) be rendered invalid under section 245 of the Insolvency Act 1986 (avoidance of certain floating charges); or
   (ii) be challengeable either as a gratuitous alienation or an unfair preference under sections 242 or 243 respectively of the Insolvency Act 1986.

12.07 If the holder of a floating charge over the whole or substantially the whole of a company's property receives notice of a petition for the appointment of an administrator, such holder will require to take an early decision whether or not to take steps, if the circumstances so allow, to appoint an administrative receiver. If such an appointment is made it is extremely unlikely that such holder will consent to the making of an administration order unless perhaps it becomes apparent that the floating charge is open to challenge under the statutory provisions mentioned above.

Effect of application for administration order

12.08 During the period between the presentation of a petition for an administration order (or where an administrative receiver is in office at that time, when such receiver consents to the making of an administration order) and either its dismissal or the making of such an order:

(a) no resolution may be passed or order made for the winding up of the company;[1]

(b) no steps may be taken to enforce any security over the company's property or to repossess goods in the company's possession on hire-purchase, lease, conditional sale or subject to retention of title, except with the leave of the court and subject to such terms as it may impose;[2] and

(c) except with such leave and subject to such conditions, no other proceedings and no execution, diligence or other legal process may be commenced or continued against the company or its property.[3]

However, none of these restrictions require the leave of the court for:

(a) the presentation of a winding-up petition;[4]

(b) the appointment of an administrative receiver;[5] or

(c) the carrying out by such a receiver, whenever appointed, of any of his functions.[6]

The result is that there is nothing to stop a creditor during this period from presenting a winding-up petition. Although no order for winding up can be made during such period, the petition will be in place and the preliminary procedure in all probability carried through by the time the court considers the application for an administration order which it might well dismiss. As already mentioned the holder of a floating charge over the whole or substantially the whole of a company's property will require, in the appropriate circumstances, to arrange for the appointment of an administrative receiver if that is the course such holder decides to adopt.

1 Insolvency Act 1986, s 10(1)(a).
2 Ibid s 10(1)(b).
3 Ibid s 10(1)(c).
4 Ibid s 10(2)(a).
5 Ibid s 10(2)(b).
6 Ibid s 10(2)(c).

Effect of administration order

12.09 Once an administration order has been made any petition for winding up is dismissed[1] and, as already mentioned, an administrative receiver vacates office[2] and also a receiver of part of the company's property if so required by the administrator.[3] During the period such an order is in force the company cannot be put into liquidation,[4] no administrative receiver can be appointed[5] and, except with the consent of the administrator or leave of the court on such conditions imposed by it, the same restrictions operate against enforcement of securities, repossession and diligence as apply in the period after the presentation of an application for an order.[6]

1 Insolvency Act 1986, s 11(1)(a).
2 Ibid s 11(1)(b).
3 Ibid s 11(2).
4 Ibid s 11(3)(a).
5 Ibid s 11(3)(b).
6 Ibid s 11(3)(c) and (d).

Receiver vacating office on making of administration order

12.10 Where either an administrative receiver or a receiver of part of the company's property vacates office on the making of an administration order he is entitled to be paid[1] from any property of the company in his custody or under his control, when he vacates office, in priority to any security held by the person appointing him:
(a) his remuneration and any expenses incurred by him; and
(b) any indemnity to which he is entitled out of the assets of the company (eg in respect of personal liability incurred in entering into or adopting a contract).

Where a receiver vacates office in these circumstances, the holder of a floating charge requires to notify the Registrar of Companies in the usual way within fourteen days[2] and the receiver is relieved of any obligation to pay the preferential creditors.[3]

1 Insolvency Act 1986, s 11(4).
2 Ibid s 62(5).
3 Ibid s 11(5).

Notification of order

12.11   When an administration order is in force every invoice, order for goods or business letters issued by the administrator or the company and bearing its name must state the administrator's name and that its affairs, business and property are being managed by the administrator.[1] There are default provisions which apply to the administrator, the company and its officers.[2]

1 Insolvency Act 1986, s 12(1).
2 Ibid s 12(2).

Appointment of administrator

12.12   An administrator is appointed either by an administration order[1] or by the court filling the vacancy in the office caused by death, resignation or otherwise.[2] An application to the court to fill such a vacancy may be made by any continuing administrator, any committee of creditors or, where neither exist, by the company or by its directors or any creditor or creditors.[3]

1 Insolvency Act 1986, s 13(1).
2 Ibid s 13(2).
3 Ibid s 13(3).

12.13   The floating charge by virtue of which a receiver has been appointed attaches on such appointment to the property subject to the charge as if it were a fixed security and in the normal course on a receiver vacating office and no other receiver being appointed within one month, the floating charge ceases to so attach to the property in question and becomes again a floating charge. However, where an administration order is in or comes into force, for the purpose of calculating the one month period from the receiver vacating office no account is taken of any period during which an administration order is in force.[1]

1 Insolvency Act 1986, s 62(6).

Administrator's general powers

12.14   The administrator has power to do everything necessary for the management of the affairs, business and property of the company[1] and, without prejudice thereto, has the same specific powers as an administrative receiver.[2] In addition, an administrator has power to appoint and remove directors of the company[3] and to call meetings of members or creditors.[4] He may apply also to the court for directions in relation to any particular matter arising in connection with the performance of his functions.[5] In exercising his powers the administrator is deemed to be acting as agent of the company[6] and a person dealing with him in good faith and for value is not concerned to inquire whether he is acting within his powers.[7] Finally, except with his consent (given generally or in relation to particular cases) neither the company nor its officers can exercise powers which might interfere with the exercise by the administrator of his powers.[8]

1 Insolvency Act 1986, s 14(1)(a).
2 Ibid s 14(1)(b).
3 Ibid s 14(2)(a).
4 Ibid s 14(2)(b).
5 Ibid s 14(3).
6 Ibid s 14(5).
7 Ibid s 14(6).
8 Ibid s 14(4).

Administrator's power to deal with charged property

12.15 An administrator has power[1] to dispose of or otherwise exercise his powers in relation to any property of the company subject to a floating charge as if such property was not so subject. Where he so disposes of property, however,[2] the holder of the floating charge has the same priority in respect of any property directly or indirectly representing the property disposed of as he would have had under the floating charge. This means that the floating charge continues to have effect as a floating charge in relation to the property representing the property disposed of. The effect of these provisions would accordingly appear to be that where a floating charge exists and an administration order has been made the floating charge remains 'floating' over the property representing that disposed of by the administrator and on the administration order being discharged the holder of such charge can immediately appoint or reappoint a receiver subject always, to any question relating to the validity of such charge under the various relevant statutory provisions.

1 Insolvency Act 1986, s 15(1) and (3).
2 Ibid s 15(4).

12.16 In the case of property of a company subject to any security other than a floating charge or goods in the company's possession subject to hire-purchase, conditional sale, leasing arrangements and retention of title only the court on application by him can authorise the disposal of such property or goods by the administrator[1] on the court being satisfied that such disposal (with or without other assets) would be likely to promote one or more of the purposes specified in the administration order, such authority being given as if the property was not subject to the security or the rights of the owner of the goods were vested in the company.

1 Insolvency Act 1986, s 15(2).

12.17 It is a condition[1] of an order by the court under section 15(2) that the net proceeds of disposal and, where those proceeds are less than the net realisable open market value of the property or the goods as determined by the court, the amount required to make good the deficiency shall be applied towards discharging the sums secured by the security or payable to the owner of the goods. Where such a condition of an order under section 15(5) relates to more than one security,[2] the sums mentioned above are applied towards discharge of the securities in their order of priorities. An office copy of any such order of the court must be filed by the administrator[3] with the Registrar of Companies within fourteen days of it being made, default provisions applying on failure to do so.[4]

1 Insolvency Act 1986, s 15(5).
2 Ibid s 15(6).
3 Ibid s 15(7).
4 Ibid s 15(8).

12.18 There are special provisions relating to the disposal of property or goods under section 15 in its application to Scotland to effect the disencumbering of the property or freeing it from the security and extinguishing the rights of the owner.[1]

1 Insolvency Act 1986, s 16.

12.19 The powers of an administrator to deal with property subject to a floating charge will, it is thought, act as the principal disincentive to the holder of a floating charge over the whole or substantially the whole of the company's property, who has appointed or is in a position to appoint an administrative receiver, giving consent to the appointment of an administrator. In the case of the holder only being in a position to appoint such a receiver on the presentation of an application for an administration order, he will of course require to procure such appointment before the court considers the application.

General duties of administrator

12.20 These include taking custody or control of the company's property[1] and managing its affairs, business and property either in accordance with the directions (if any) of the court or with proposals approved under section 24 of the Insolvency Act 1986.[2] He must also in certain circumstances summon a meeting of the company's creditors.[3]

1 Insolvency Act 1986, s 17(1).
2 Ibid s 17(2).
3 Ibid s 17(3).

12.21 As mentioned previously the purpose of this chapter is primarily to deal with administration orders in so far as they impinge in Scotland on the rights of holders of floating charges and receivers appointed under them. For that reason it is not proposed to deal further with the provisions of the Insolvency Act 1986 relating to applications for discharge or variation of administration orders,[1] vacation of the office of administrator and his release,[2] the detailed provisions relating to the ascertainment and investigation of the company's affairs,[3] the administrator's proposals[4] or committees of creditors.[5]

1 Insolvency Act 1986, s 18.
2 Ibid ss 19 and 20.
3 Ibid ss 21 and 22.
4 Ibid ss 23 and 25.
5 Ibid s 26.

Protection of interests of creditors and members

12.22 There are important provisions to protect the interests of creditors and members when an administration order is in force.[1] Any creditor or member may apply to the court for an order that the company's affairs, business and property are being or have been managed by the administrator in a manner unfairly prejudicial to the interests of its creditors or members generally or of some part of them (including at least himself) or that any actual or proposed act or omission of the administrator is or would be so prejudicial. The court is given wide powers in dealing with such an application.[2]

1 Insolvency Act 1986, s 27(1).
2 Ibid s 27(2) and (4).

Appendix 1

Floating charge

WE, GALAXY PRODUCTS LIMITED, incorporated under the Companies Acts and having our registered office at 10 Heavenly Mansions, Pitlochry DO HEREBY BIND and OBLIGE ourselves to pay or discharge upon demand to BANCO ALBINONI plc, whose registered office is at Corelli Square, Edinburgh ('the Bank') all moneys and liabilities which now are or which may at any time or from time to time be or become due, owing or incurred to the Bank by us and/or for which we now are or may at any time or from time to time be or become liable or responsible to the Bank in any manner of way or in any respect whatsoever, whether alone or jointly with any other person or persons and whether as principal debtors or guarantors or sureties including in particular but without prejudice to the foregoing generality sums of principal, interest, discounts, commissions, charges, costs and expenses, whether on or in connection with or arising out of any current or other account, order, draft, bill, promissory note, letter of credit or guarantee or any one or more of any such or otherwise howsoever; AND IT IS HEREBY PROVIDED AND DECLARED—

First

That a certificate signed by an authorised signatory shall be sufficient to fix and ascertain the whole sums, principal, interest and others, which shall be due by us and/or· for which we shall be liable to the Bank as aforesaid and to constitute a balance and charge against us and no suspension of a charge or of à threatened charge for payment of the balance so constituted shall pass nor any sist of execution thereon be granted except on consignation;

Second

That nothing herein contained shall prejudice or affect any other securities which the Bank already hold or may hereafter hold for any sum or sums due or which may after the date hereof become due by us to the Bank over any other property belonging to us, it being always in the power of the Bank to allow all or any part of such securities or the property to which they relate to be disponed or sold or abandoned without applying the same or the proceeds thereof towards payment of any sum to be hereby secured, and the whole obligations hereby undertaken by us shall remain in full force and effect in the same manner and to the same extent as if no such securities had ever existed; and

Third

That the Bank without prejudice to its rights under these presents and at its discretion, may grant to us or to any other person or persons liable with or for us any time or other indulgence and may compound with us or them, accede to trust deeds and draw dividends, and that all without notice to us or to any other person concerned;
AND IN SECURITY of the said moneys and liabilities mentioned WE DO HEREBY GRANT in favour of the Bank a FLOATING CHARGE over the whole of the property (including uncalled capital) which is or

217

may be from time to time while this Instrument is in force comprised in our property and undertaking DECLARING AS IT IS HEREBY ESPECIALLY PROVIDED AND DECLARED THAT

(Primo)

Except as may be otherwise agreed in writing by the Bank the Floating Charge hereby created shall rank in priority to any fixed security (other than any fixed security in favour of the Bank which shall rank in all respects in priority and in preference to the floating charge hereby created) as defined in section 70 of the Insolvency Act 1986, or any statutory amendment or re-enactment thereof for the time being in force (which Act as so amended is hereinafter referred to as 'the Act') and any other floating charge being a fixed security or floating charge which shall have been granted or created by us after our execution hereof; and

(Secundo)

At any time after any of the sums secured by the Floating Charge hereby created shall have become due and payable or after the Bank shall have been requested by us in writing so to do, the Bank shall have power by Instrument in writing to appoint any person or persons to be a receiver or receivers of our property and assets, and may in like manner appoint any person or persons to be a receiver or receivers in place of any receiver removed by the Court or otherwise ceasing to act. Any receiver so appointed shall have the powers conferred on a receiver by the Act.

(Tertio)

We shall be solely responsible for the acts and defaults of any receiver appointed by the Bank hereunder and for his remuneration, costs, charges and expenses and the Bank shall have no liability or responsibility for or in respect of any act or default of any receiver so appointed or for his remuneration.

(Quarto)

The Bank and every receiver appointed by the Bank hereunder shall be entitled to be indemnified out of the property hereby charged in respect of all liabilities and expenses incurred by them or him in the execution or purported execution of any of the powers, authorities or discretions vested in them or him in pursuance of the Act or these presents and against all actions, proceedings, costs, claims and demands in respect of any matter or thing done or omitted in any way in connection with or relating to the property hereby charged and the Bank and any such receiver may retain and pay all sums in respect of the same out of any moneys received under the powers conferred by the Act or these presents.

(Quinto)

A demand or notice hereunder shall be in writing signed by an authorised signatory of the Bank and may (without prejudice to any other mode of service or delivery) be served on us by delivery thereof to any officer of us at any place or by post addressed to us at our registered office last known to the Bank and a demand or notice so addressed and posted shall be effective twenty four hours after the date and time of such service or delivery notwithstanding that it be returned undelivered;

AND WE UNDERTAKE to procure that while this security is in force—

(A) Without prejudice to the provisions hereinbefore contained, unless with the written consent of the Bank we shall not create or allow to come into being any security or charge upon any part of the property (including heritable, real and leasehold property wherever situated) assets, undertakings or uncalled capital of us which is subject to the security hereby created and no debentures, debenture stock or loan capital shall be created or issued and generally no monies shall be borrowed or raised or the payment thereof secured in any manner of way by us or any of our subsidiaries;

(B) (i) The whole property and corporeal assets belonging to us and our subsidiaries shall be insured and kept insured for their full replacement value against loss by fire and such other risks as the Bank may reasonably require, the relative policy or policies being endorsed or noted with reference to the interest of the Bank as the Bank may reasonably require, and we shall produce to the Bank, if so required, within fifteen days after becoming due and payable receipts for any current premiums, failing which the Bank may at our expense effect or renew any such insurances as the Bank shall deem fit; and

(ii) All monies which may at any time be received or receivable under any such insurance or any other insurance covering any of the property and corporeal assets of us or our subsidiaries against such risks as aforesaid shall be applied in replacing, restoring or reinstating the property or assets destroyed or damaged unless the Bank shall otherwise consent in writing;

(C) Except with the written consent of the Bank no part of our heritable, real or leasehold property shall be sold or otherwise disposed of and no lease or sub-lease for a period exceeding three years shall be granted of any of our heritable, real or leasehold property and no other of our property or assets subject to the security hereby created shall be sold or otherwise disposed of unless in the ordinary course of our business or the business of any of our subsidiaries.

DECLARING that for the purposes of the foregoing undertaking 'subsidiary' shall have the meaning ascribed to it by Section 736 of the Companies Act 1985; And we bind and oblige ourselves for the whole, proper and reasonable expenses of creating and enforcing this security and also for the proper and reasonable expenses of any assignation or discharge thereof; And we warrant these presents at all hands and against all persons; And we consent to the registration hereof and of the aforesaid certificate for preservation and execution

SEALED with the COMMON SEAL of
GALAXY PRODUCTS LIMITED
and subscribed for it and
on its behalf at
on

Director

Director/Secretary

Appendix 2

Extract minute of meeting of directors

EXTRACT from the MINUTES of
MEETING of the DIRECTORS of
GALAXY PRODUCTS LIMITED
held at 10 Heavenly Mansions, Pitlochry on   19

IT WAS RESOLVED that Banco Albinoni plc be asked to appoint a
receiver over the whole property comprised in the Company's property
and undertaking, including uncalled capital, in terms of the floating
charge in their favour dated   and registered with the
registrar of companies on

Certified a true extract

Director/Secretary

Appendix 3

Letter of request
to appoint receiver

On letterhead of Galaxy Products Limited, 10 Heavenly Mansions, Pitlochry

[Date]

Banco Albinoni plc,
Corelli Square,
Edinburgh

Dear Sirs,
In accordance with a resolution passed at a meeting of the directors of the Company held today, a certified copy of which is attached, we hereby formally request you to appoint a receiver over the whole property comprised in the Company's property and undertaking, including uncalled capital.

Yours faithfully,

For and on behalf of
Galaxy Products Limited

Director

Appendix 4

Deed of appointment

WE, BANCO ALBINONI plc, incorporated under the Companies Acts and having our registered office at Corelli Square, Edinburgh, holders of a Bond and Floating Charge granted by GALAXY PRODUCTS LIMITED, incorporated under the Companies Acts and having their registered office at 10 Heavenly Mansions, Pitlochry ('the Company') in our favour dated 3rd August 1982 CONSIDERING that an event has occurred on the occurrence of which we are entitled to appoint a receiver of the property which is subject to the floating charge created by the said Bond and Floating Charge; NOW THEREFORE in pursuance of the powers conferred on us by the said Bond and Floating Charge and as amended by the Insolvency Act 1986 we do hereby appoint FREDER-ICK GALILEO, Chartered Accountant, Saturn House, Pitlochry to be receiver of the whole of the property which is or may be from time to time, while the said Bond and Floating Charge is in force, comprised in the property and undertaking of the Company, including their uncalled capital for the time being.

SEALED with the COMMON SEAL of
BANCO ALBINONI plc at
on   198 and
subscribed for it and on its
behalf by:

                    Director

                    Director/Secretary

Appendix 5

Style of letter to debtor

On letterhead of the company (In Receivership)

[Date]

Dear Sirs,

Rococo Cocoa Co Limited (In Receivership)

I hereby intimate that I was appointed the receiver of the whole assets and undertaking of Rococo Cocoa Co Limited ('the Company') on [198].
From the records of the Company it appears that your company owes the Company an amount equal to [£   ] as specified in the enclosed statement of account.
I shall be obliged if you will please make arrangements to settle the outstanding indebtedness within [   ] days of today's date.

Yours faithfully,

....
Receiver

Note: The Receiver contracts only as agent of Rococo Cocoa Co Limited and without any personal liability.

Appendix 6

Style of letter to creditor

On letterhead of the company (In Receivership)

[Date]

Dear Sirs,

Rococo Cocoa Co Limited (In Receivership)

I hereby intimate that I was appointed the receiver of the whole assets and undertaking of Rococo Cocoa Co Limited ('the Company') on [198].
Any supplies of goods or future orders for such goods to the Company as from the date of my appointment will not be accepted unless the order for such supplies or future orders is authorised by my signature or one of my managers a specimen of whose signatures is given below. Any payment for goods will be strictly on a pro-forma or cash basis unless specific arrangements in any particular case are agreed.
You will no doubt appreciate that I am unable to entertain any form of set-off in respect of monies due by you pre-receivership as against monies due by the Company post-receivership to you or vice versa. Before any transaction can be implemented between us, I require the duplicate copy of this letter to be signed by an authorised officer of your company and returned to me as soon as possible.
If you wish to submit a claim against the Company in respect of a pre-receivership transaction, I shall place any such claim for the attention of a liquidator of the Company (should one be appointed).

Yours faithfully,

....
Receiver

Specimen Signatures

....
Manager

....
Manager

Note: The Receiver contracts only as agent of Rococo Cocoa Co Limited and without any personal liability.

Appendix 6

On Duplicate

To: The Receiver,

Rococo Cocoa Co Limited

[Date]

Dear Sir,
We acknowledge to have received from you a letter dated [   ] of
which the foregoing is a duplicate copy and we hereby confirm our
agreement to its terms.

Yours faithfully,

....
Authorised Signatory

240

Appendix 7

Style of letter to landlord

On letterhead of the company (In Receivership)

Plutocratic Properties Limited,
Golden Egg Lane,
London, EC2

For the attention of [*]*

Dear Sirs,

Rococo Cocoa Co Limited (In Receivership)

I hereby intimate that I was appointed the receiver of the whole assets and undertaking of Rococo Cocoa Co Limited ('the Company') on [198].
I understand that a lease ('the Lease') dated [   ] existed as at the date of my appointment between you, as Landlords, and the Company relating to Unit 3 Silverside Industrial Estate, Glasgow ('the Premises'). I am presently [considering the possibility of selling the business of the Company as a going concern] [making arrangements to dispose of various assets belonging to the Company situated at the Premises] and without in any sense adopting the provisions and obligations of the Lease, I am prepared as agent of the Company to pay rent in respect of the period of my occupation from the date of my appointment to [   ].
I am writing to you on the understanding that during the period of my occupation you will not irritate the Lease by reason of my appointment or of pre-receivership arrears or in respect of any breach of any conditions of the Lease prior to my appointment.
Please confirm your agreement by arranging for an authorised signatory to sign and return to me the duplicate copy of this letter as soon as possible.
You will appreciate that as receiver, I act as agent of the Company and without any personal liability.

Yours faithfully,

....
Receiver

Appendix 7

On Duplicate

To: The Receiver,
Rococo Cocoa Co Limited

[Date]

Dear Sir,

We acknowledge to have received from you a letter dated [   ]
of which the foregoing is a duplicate copy and we hereby confirm our
agreement to its terms.

Yours faithfully,

....
Authorised Signatory

Appendix 8

Caveat

(a) Against Interim Interdict

Sheriffdom of Drumsheugh and West Edinburgh

CAVEAT
for
Rococo Cocoa Co Limited, incorporated in Scotland under the Companies Acts (registered No [   ]) and having its registered office at Baroque House, Louis XV Avenue, Edinburgh

Should any application be presented at the instance of Macbeth Kilts Limited, 3 Shakespeare Way, Macduff or of any other party against Rococo Cocoa Co Limited for interim interdict against (describe activity likely to be complained of) or in respect of any other matter, it is requested that notice be given to the subscriber who will show cause why the application should not be granted.

In Respect Whereof

(b) Against Liquidation

Should any petition be presented for the liquidation of Rococo Cocoa Co Limited by the Court or by order for the supervision of the Court either with or without the appointment of a provisional liquidator, it is requested that notice is given to the subscriber who will show cause why the petition should not be granted.

In Respect Whereof

(c) Against both

Should any petition be presented for the liquidation of Rococo Cocoa Co Limited by the Court or by order for the supervision of the Court with or without the appointment of a provisional liquidator, or any application be made at the instance of any party against Rococo Cocoa Co Limited or interim interdict in respect of any matter, it is requested that notice be given to the subscriber who will show cause why the application or the petition should not be granted.

In Respect Whereof

Appendix 9

Hive down agreement

AGREEMENT
between
GALAXY PRODUCTS LIMITED (1)
(In Receivership)
and
ORINOCO COCOA CO LIMITED (2)

Dated   1986

AGREEMENT
between
GALAXY PRODUCTS LIMITED, incorporated under the Companies Acts and having its registered office at 10 Heavenly Mansions, Pitlochry ('the Vendor') acting by its receiver **FREDERICK GALILEO,** Chartered Accountant, Saturn House, Pitlochry ('The Receiver')

and

ORINOCO COCOA CO LIMITED, incorporated under the Companies Acts and having its registered office at 20 Neo-Classical Lane, Edinburgh, a wholly owned subsidiary of the Vendor ('the Purchaser')

WHEREAS

(A) The Receiver was duly appointed receiver of the Vendor on [   ] pursuant to powers contained in a Bond and Floating Charge dated [   ] and registered with the Registrar of Companies on [   ] executed by the Vendor in favour of Banco Albinoni plc.

(B) The Vendor and the Receiver have agreed to sell to the Purchaser and the Purchaser has agreed to purchase from the Vendor as a going concern the business and assets of the Vendor on the terms and for the consideration set out in this Agreement.

IT IS AGREED as follows:

1. **Definitions**

(1) In this Agreement, unless the context otherwise requires:
'the Business' means the business and undertaking of the Vendor relating to the manufacture, distribution and sale of space invaders and associated products carried on by the Vendor at Pitlochry represented by and including the following:

   (i) the plant and machinery, vehicles, (including all unexpired periods of taxation licences), all office furniture, fixtures, fittings and equipment all more particularly specified in Part [   ] of the Schedule and all other assets owned and used by the Vendor in connection with the Business (but shall exclude assets of the Vendor which are subject to leasing agreements or contract hire or hire purchase or otherwise encumbered);

   (ii) the stock, work-in-progress, raw materials, packaging materials and finished goods of the Business (excluding finished goods manufactured and sold to customers by the Vendor prior to the Transfer Date) and, if required, photocopies of each of the customer list, the order books, all other books and records of the Business and the benefit of all contracts, orders and engagements (insofar as such contracts, orders and engagements are capable of being assigned) relating to the Business current at the Transfer Date;

(iii) the Premises; and

(iv) all patents, designs, copyrights, trade marks, trading names (including the exclusive right for the Purchaser to use the name 'Galaxy'), brand names, symbols, logos, get-up, devices, know-how (including without limitation all technical or confidential information) or similar industrial or intellectual property rights (whether registered or not) used in or necessary to the production, packaging, marketing and sale of products manufactured by the Vendor in connection with the Business;

'the Employees' means the employees who are in the employment of the Vendor in connection with the Business as at the Transfer Date;
'the Premises' means the buildings and adjoining land situated at [   ] more particularly specified in Part [   ] of the Schedule; and
'the Transfer Date' means close of business on [   ].

(2) Each reference to a statute or provision of a statute shall be construed as a reference to that statute or provision as amended, extended or re-enacted by any other statute or provision of a statute.

(3) The headings in the Agreement are for convenience only and shall not affect its interpretation.

2. Sale of business

The Vendor shall sell and the Purchaser shall purchase the Business as a going concern with effect from the Transfer Date.

3. Consideration

The aggregate consideration (exclusive of value added tax and stamp duty, all of which shall be payable by the Purchaser) for the Business shall be such amount as may be agreed between the Vendor and the Purchaser or such amount as Messrs [   ] Chartered Accountants, acting as experts and not as arbiters shall certify to be a fair and proper consideration, the decision of Messrs [   ] being final and binding on the parties.

4. Debtors

For the avoidance of doubt it is expressly declared that the Vendor shall not sell and that the Purchaser shall not purchase any rights (including without prejudice thereto book debts) in respect of any amounts accrued, due and owing to the Vendor or the Receiver as at the Transfer Date.

5. Payment of price

(1)   The price together with any value added tax and any stamp duty payable by the Purchaser in terms of or arising out of this Agreement under and in terms of clause 3 hereof shall be entered in the books of the Vendor and the Purchaser as secured debts repayable on demand to the Vendor.

(2)   By way of security for the price referred to in clause 5(1) the Purchaser shall, at the expense of the Purchaser, forthwith upon the execution of this Agreement create a floating charge over all its whole undertaking and assets in favour of the Vendor.

6. Completion

(1)   Completion of the sale and purchase specified in this Agreement shall take place on the Transfer Date when, unless otherwise agreed between the Vendor and the Purchaser:

   (a)   title to all assets comprised within the Business and sold pursuant to this Agreement which are capable of transfer by delivery thereof and such delivery shall be deemed to have taken place on the Transfer Date;

   (b)   the Vendor will give entry and vacant possession to the Premises [and the Vendor and the Receiver shall implement the provisions of paragraph 4 of Part [   ] of the Schedule]; and

   (c)   the provisions of clause 5 hereof shall be implemented.

(2)   In any case where the consent of any person, firm or corporate body not a party to this Agreement is required to the transfer from the Vendor of any asset hereby agreed to be sold the sale of such asset shall be conditional upon such consent which the Vendor and the Purchaser shall each use its best endeavours to obtain as soon as practicable.

[(3)   The Vendor and the Receiver will use their best endeavours to assist the Purchaser in obtaining transfers or assignations of leased equipment used in the Business and for a period of 30 days from the Transfer Date, the Vendor and the Receiver will use their best endeavours to maintain and fulfil all obligations under such leases subject to the Purchaser reimbursing all rentals and charges thereby incurred by the Vendor and the Receiver provided always that the Vendor and the Receiver will abandon any such lease at the reasonable request of the Purchaser.]

7. Value added tax

The Vendor and the Purchaser will do all acts necessary and file all forms and returns relating to value added tax in connection with and subsequent upon the transfer of the Business and the Purchaser shall indemnify and keep indemnified the Vendor in respect thereof.

8. Liabilities

The Purchaser will not take over or in any way be responsible for any of the debts or liabilities of the Business incurred on or before the Transfer Date for which the Vendor shall remain liable and the Vendor shall indemnify the Purchaser from and against the same and all actions, proceedings, costs, damages, claims and demands in respect thereof.

9. Agreements

(1) Subject to the provisions of clause 8 and to clause 9(2), the Purchaser shall assume and fulfil all debts, liabilities and obligations relating to the Business arising or accruing after the Transfer Date and shall complete (to the extent that it is lawful) all outstanding contracts, engagements and orders relating to the Business at the Transfer Date and shall indemnify the Vendor and the Receiver against all demands, claims, costs, charges and expenses made, suffered or incurred arising out of the Purchaser's failure to fulfil or perform its obligations hereunder.

(2) Without prejudice to the generality of clause 9(1), the Purchaser shall fulfil and perform all contracts for the supply of raw materials to the Business as from the Transfer Date and shall also fulfil and perform all contracts for the supply of raw materials to the Business after the Transfer Date in respect of which early delivery is made by the supplier on or prior to the Transfer Date.

(3) Payments in advance made by the Vendor or the Receiver prior to the Transfer Date in respect of goods to be supplied to the Business but not delivered prior to the Transfer Date and not comprised in the assets of the Business as at the Transfer Date shall be refunded by the Purchaser to the Vendor within 7 days after delivery of such goods.

(4) For the purposes of clause 9(1) an indemnity against liabilities under an agreement shall be deemed to include an indemnity against all demands, claims, costs, charges and expenses made, suffered or incurred by reason of or in any way in connection with that agreement.

10. **Employees**

The Vendor shall retain the services of the Employees and shall sub-contract the same to the Purchaser on the following terms:—

   (i)   the Purchaser shall indemnify the Vendor against the cost of all wages, national insurance, PAYE and pension contributions, holiday pay, employers' liability and third party insurance premiums and against all claims, demands and liabilities (including all employers' liabilities for personal injury or otherwise) in respect of the Employees accruing from and including the Transfer Date and which would otherwise fall to be paid out of funds available in the receivership of the Vendor;

   (ii) payment of the aforesaid items shall:

      (a) in the case of items ascertainable in advance be made not less than three days before the Vendor is liable to make such payment; and

      (b) in the case of all other items be made forthwith upon any amount being agreed or determined;

   (iii) the Vendor shall apply all such payments made by the Purchaser in terms of this clause in paying such wages, national insurance, PAYE and pension contributions and others promptly when due; and

   (iv) neither the Vendor nor the Receiver shall incur any liability to the Purchaser in respect of any failure of the Employees or any negligence on the part of the Employees or in respect of any matter arising out of this clause, provided always that the Vendor and the Receiver shall maintain and pay all premiums relating to current employers' liability insurances.

11. **Inspection of books and records and access**

   (1) For avoidance of doubt it is hereby declared that the Vendor shall retain the beneficial ownership of the customer list, the order books and all other books and records (including all the records of the Business for value added tax which are required pursuant to section 33 of the Value Added Tax Act 1983) relating to the Business but the Purchaser shall be entitled to reasonable access to these documents as may from time to time be required.

   (2) The obligation specified in clause 11(1) shall apply for a period of three years from the Transfer Date except where there is a statutory obligation to retain the documents therein specified for a longer period in which event the period imposed by such statutory obligation shall apply.

12. **Exclusion of warranties**

The Purchaser having inspected the assets comprised in the Business as and where they lie shall take the same in the condition in which they are and no warranty or assurance is given or implied as to the condition, quality or fitness of such assets.

13. Passing the risk

All the assets comprised in the Business will be at the risk of the Purchaser from the Transfer Date, provided always that the Vendor and the Receiver will maintain for a period of three days after the Transfer Date all current insurances and pay all premiums in connection therewith.

14. Receiver's liability

The Purchaser hereby acknowledges and accepts that the Receiver acts only as an agent of the Vendor and accordingly the Purchaser accepts that the Receiver shall incur no personal liability whatsoever hereunder other than to the extent of any free assets in his hands after all categories of persons described (including the holders of the floating charges by virtue of which he was appointed) in section 60 of the Insolvency Act 1986 have been satisfied.

15. Apportionments

This Agreement and the sale and purchase provided therein shall take effect from the Transfer Date and the Purchaser shall account and be indemnified accordingly.

16. Notices

(1) Any notice hereunder may be served by hand or by first class prepaid post through the recorded delivery system addressed to the party to be served at such party's address as hereinbefore appearing.

(2) Any notice served by post shall be deemed to have been served twenty four hours after the same is put into the post.

(3) Any notice requiring to be served on the Vendor and the Receiver shall be sufficiently served by being served on the Receiver.

17. Expenses

All legal expenses together with all stamp duty, value added tax, registration dues and recording dues incidental to the preparation and execution and carrying into effect of this Agreement shall be borne by the Purchaser.

18. Further assurances

[The Vendor and the Receiver shall each use their best endeavours to ensure the Purchaser is provided with all information relating to tax losses of the Vendor as the Purchaser may request and to assist the Purchaser insofar as they are able to obtain a transfer of accrued tax losses from the Vendor to the Purchaser subject to the Purchaser paying all the reasonable expenses and outlays of the Vendor and the Receiver in so doing subject always to the express declaration that the Vendor and the Receiver warrant neither the existence nor the availability of any tax losses and the Purchaser expressly acknowledges that in entering into this Agreement it has placed no reliance whatsoever on the possibility of any tax losses being available for such transfer.]

19. **Proper law**

This Agreement and all documents drafted and executed in pursuance of this Agreement shall in all respects be interpreted in accordance with the law of Scotland.

SEALED with the COMMON SEAL of GALAXY PRODUCTS LIMITED at [   ] on [   ] 198[ ] and subscribed for it and on its behalf by FREDERICK GALILEO as Receiver thereof in the presence of:

Witness

Address

Occupation

Witness

Address

Occupation

SEALED with the COMMON SEAL of ORINOCO COCOA CO LIMITED and subscribed for it and on its behalf at
on [   ] 198[ ] by:

Director

Director/Secretary

SCHEDULE

Part [   ]

Details of Plant and Machinery and Others

Part [   ]

The Premises

Part [   ]

Terms and Conditions for sale of the Premises

1. Vacant possession of the Premises will be given to the Purchaser on the Transfer Date [subject to the lease/rights of occupancy specified in Part [   ] of this Schedule.]

2. The minerals are included in the sale only in so far as the Vendor has right thereto.

3. The Purchaser shall be deemed to have satisfied itself as to the nature and extent of the title to the Premises tendered by the Vendor.

4. At the Transfer Date the Vendor and the Receiver will grant and deliver to the Purchaser (subject to the terms of paragraph 3 hereof) a validly executed Disposition of the Premises, and will deliver or exhibit a valid marketable title to the Premises and will deliver or exhibit either (a) Searches in the Property Register for a period of twenty years and in the Personal Register for the prescriptive period showing no incumbrances or diligences which would preclude the Receiver from granting a good title; or (b) if at the Transfer Date the provisions of section 2(1) or 3(3) of the Land Registration (Scotland) Act 1979 (which together with all amendments thereof and statutory instruments and rules issued there-under are hereinafter referred to as 'the Act') apply to the transfer of the Vendor's interest in the Premises, the Vendor and the Receiver will provide a Form 10 Report brought down to a date as near as practicable to the Transfer Date and showing no entries adverse to the Vendor's and the Receiver's interest (the cost (if any) of said Report being the responsibility of the Purchaser) and, in addition, the Vendor and the Receiver will furnish to the Purchaser such documents and evidence, including a plan as the Keeper may require to enable the Keeper to issue a Land Certificate in name of the Purchaser as the registered proprietor of the Premises and containing no exclusion of indemnity in terms of section 12(2) of the Act.

   The Land Certificate or Certificates to be issued to the Purchaser will disclose no entry, deed or diligence prejudicial to the Purchaser's interest other than such as are created by or against the Purchaser. Notwithstanding delivery of the said Disposition this paragraph will remain in full force and effect and may be founded upon.

   On the Transfer Date letters of obligation will be granted by the Vendor's solicitors and the Receiver's solicitors in usual terms (it being understood that any inhibitions or other diligences disclosed in the personal Searches against the Vendor in respect of the period after the date of appointment of the Receiver shall not be discharged). No Companies Charges Register Search will be produced by the Vendor nor will any obligation whatsoever be given by the Vendor in respect of the Companies Charges Register.

5. In so far as the Receiver will be a party to any Dispositions of the Premises, warrandice from fact and deed only will be given by him and the Vendor will grant warrandice excluding said leases and rights of occupancy.

Agreement for sale of the business

AGREEMENT

between

GALAXY PRODUCTS LIMITED (IN RECEIVERSHIP) (1)

ROCOCO COCOA CO LIMITED (2)

AGREEMENT
between
GALAXY PRODUCTS LIMITED,
incorporated under the Companies Acts and having its registered office at 10 Heavenly Mansions, Pitlochry ('the Vendor') acting by its receiver FREDERICK GALILEO, Chartered Accountant, Saturn House, Pitlochry ('the Receiver')

and

ROCOCO COCOA CO LIMITED
(registered number [   ]) incorporated under the Companies Acts and having its registered office at Baroque House, Louis XV Avenue, Edinburgh ('the Purchaser')

WHEREAS

(A) The Receiver was duly appointed the receiver of the Vendor on [   ] pursuant to powers contained in a Bond and Floating Charge dated [   ] and registered with the Registrar of Companies on [   ] given by the Vendor in favour of Banco Albinoni plc.

(B) The Vendor and the Receiver have agreed to sell to the Purchaser and the Purchaser has agreed to purchase from the Vendor and the Receiver as a going concern the Business (as hereinafter defined) of the Vendor on the terms and for the consideration set out in this Agreement.

IT IS AGREED as follows:

1.   Definitions

(1)   In this Agreement, unless the context otherwise requires:
'the Business' means the business and undertaking of the Vendor relating to the manufacture, distribution and sale of space invaders and associated products carried on by the Vendor at Pitlochry including (without prejudice the the generality of the foregoing) the following:

   (i)   the plant and machinery (fixed and moveable), vehicles, all office furniture, fixtures, fittings and equipment all more particularly specified in Part [   ] of the Schedule and all other assets owned and used by the Vendor in connection with the Business (but shall exclude assets of the Vendor which are subject to leasing agreements or contract hire or hire purchase or otherwise encumbered);

(ii)   the stock, work-in progress, raw materials, packaging materials and finished goods of the Business (excluding finished goods manufactured and sold to customers by the Vendor prior to the Transfer Date) and, if required by the Purchaser, photocopies of each of the customer list, the order books, all other books and records of the Business and the benefit of all contracts, orders and engagements (insofar as such contracts, orders and engagements are capable of being assigned) relating to the Business current at the Transfer Date;

(iii) the Premises; and

(iv) all patents, designs, copyrights, trade marks, trading names (including the exclusive right for the Purchaser to use the name 'Galaxy') brand names, symbols, logos, get-up, devices, know-how (including without limitation all technical or confidential information) or similar industrial or intellectual property rights (whether registered or not) used in or necessary to the production, packaging, marketing and sale of products manufactured by the Vendor in connection with the Business;

'the Completion Date' means [   ];

'the Premises' means the buildings and adjoining land situated at [   ] more particularly specified in Part [   ] of the Schedule; and

'the Transfer Date' means the close of business on [   ].

(2) Each reference to a statute or provision of a statute shall be construed as a reference to that statute or provision as amended, extended or re-enacted by any other statute or provision of a statute.

(3) The headings in this Agreement are for convenience only and shall not affect its interpretation.

2. Sale of business

The Vendor and Receiver shall sell and the Purchaser shall purchase the Business as a going concern as at the Transfer Date.

3. Consideration

(1) The aggregate consideration for the Business shall be [   ] together with any value added tax thereon (if any) which shall be for the account of the Purchaser and such consideration shall be apportioned to the items each forming a part of the Business as follows:

£

(i)   the Premises and the fixed plant and machinery referred to in clause 1(1) (i)

(ii) the moveable plant and machinery and others referred to in clause 1(1) (i)

(iii) the stock, work-in-progress and finished goods and other assets referred to in clause 1(1) (ii)

265

       (iv)   the contracts, orders and engagements
referred to in clause (1) (1) (ii) and the
patents, trade marks, goodwill and others
referred to in clause 1(1) (iv)

                                                                            _____

                                                                             _____

(2)   In ascertaining the value of stock and work-in-progress the Vendor, the Receiver and the Purchaser shall procure that a physical stock-taking is carried out as at the Transfer Date and the value thereof agreed or determined in accordance with clause 3(4) as soon as practicable thereafter.

(3)   The aggregate consideration specified in clause 3(1) shall be increased or decreased (as the case may be) by the amount by which the value of the stock and work-in-progress forming part of the Business as at the Transfer Date exceeds or is less than [   ] as the case may be and the amount of such increase or decrease shall be refunded by the Purchaser to the Vendor or by the Vendor to the Purchaser (as the case may be) within seven days of being agreed or determined in accordance with clause 3(4). The valuation of the stock and work-in-progress shall be ascertained on the basis of lower of cost or net realisable value as at the Transfer Date, using the same principles and methods consistent with those employed over the last three accounting periods by the Vendor in the valuation for the purposes of year end stock valuation excluding for such purposes slow moving or obsolete or damaged stock.

(4)   In the event of the stocktaking and/or the valuation referred to in clause 3(2) not being agreed within 14 days of the Transfer Date the stocktaking and/or valuation shall be referred to a valuer, acting as an expert and not as an arbiter appointed by agreement between the parties or failing agreement as nominated on the application of any party hereto by the President for the time being of the Institute of Chartered Accountants of Scotland whose decision shall be final and binding on the parties.

4.   Books debts, contracts and liabilities

(1)   Notwithstanding any other provision hereof, the Vendor and the Receiver shall not sell and the Purchaser shall not purchase any rights (including without prejudice thereto book debts) in respect of any amounts accrued, due and owing to the Vendor or the Receiver as at the Transfer Date.

(2)   Subject to the provisions of clause 4(3) and to clause 14, the Purchaser will not take over or in any way be responsible for any of the debts and liabilities of the Business which have accrued due on or prior to the Transfer Date, for which the Vendor shall remain liable, and, save for any matters arising

out of the rights and obligations relating to any employees of the Business, the Vendor and the Receiver shall indemnify the Purchaser from and against the same and all actions, proceedings, costs, damages, claims and demands in respect thereof.

(3) Payments in advance made by the Vendor or the Receiver prior to the Transfer Date in respect of goods to be supplied to the Business but not delivered prior to the Transfer Date shall be refunded by the Purchaser to the Receiver within 7 days after delivery of such goods.

(4) Subject to the provisions of clause 4(2) and clause 14, the Purchaser shall assume and fulfil all debts, liabilities and obligations relating to the Business arising or accruing after the Transfer Date and shall complete (to the extent that it is lawful) all outstanding contracts, engagements and orders relating to the Business as at the Transfer Date, and shall indemnify the Vendor and the Receiver against all demands, claims, costs, charges and expenses made, suffered or incurred arising out of the Purchaser's failure to fulfil or perform its obligations under this sub-clause.

(5) Without prejudice to the generality of the foregoing provisions of this clause, the Purchaser shall fulfil and perform all contracts for the supply of goods to the Business as from the Transfer Date as well as fulfil and perform all contracts for the supply of goods to the Business after [   ] in respect of which early delivery is made by the supplier on or prior to the Transfer Date.

(6) For the purposes of clause 4(4) an indemnity against liabilities under an agreement shall be deemed to include an indemnity against all demands, claims, costs, charges and expenses made, suffered or incurred by reason of or in any way in connection with that agreement.

5. Completion

(1) On the Completion Date:
  (1) The Vendor as beneficial and unencumbered owner shall deliver (actually or constructively) to the Purchaser full and free possession of the Business free from all liens, restrictions, options, bills of sale, encumbrances, mortgages and charges of any kind and the Vendor and the Receiver shall implement the provisions of paragraph 4 of Part [ ] of the Schedule.
  (2) The Purchaser shall pay by banker's draft drawn on Banco Albinoni plc [Address] an amount equal to [£
            ] in favour of [   ] Solicitors,
    [   ] as agents for the Vendor and the Receiver whose receipt shall be a sufficient discharge to the Purchaser and such amount shall subject to the provisions of clause 3(3), represent the aggregate of the consideration specified in clause 3(1).

(2) If on the Completion Date, the Vendor or the Receiver, on the

one part, or the Purchaser, on the other part, fail to comply with any provision of clause 5(1) requiring compliance by them, the Vendor or the Receiver (in the case of non-fulfilment by the Purchaser) and the Purchaser (in the case of non-fulfilment by the Vendor or the Receiver) shall be entitled (in addition and without prejudice to any other rights or remedies available to them) to rescind this Agreement.

6. Value added tax

It is the intention of the parties hereto that the provisions of section 33 of the Value Added Tax Act 1983 shall apply to the transfer of the Business hereunder and accordingly:

(a) each of the parties hereto shall on the Completion Date give notice of such transfer to the appropriate office of HM Customs and Excise in accordance with such regulations and requirements as may be applicable; and

(b) notwithstanding the terms of paragraph (a) above, the Vendor shall on completion deliver to the Purchaser all such records as are referred to in the said section 33 unless the Commissioners of HM Customs and Excise, at the request of the Vendor, otherwise direct.

7. Inspection of books and records

(1) For the avoidance of doubt it is hereby declared that the Vendor shall retain the beneficial ownership of the customer list, the order books and all other books, computer data and records (including all the records of the Business for value added tax purposes which are required pursuant to section 33 of the Value Added Tax Act 1983) relating to the Business but the Purchaser and the Receiver shall both be entitled to reasonable access to these documents and to make copies thereof as may from time to time be required.

(2) The entitlement to access and copying specified in clause 7(1) shall apply for a period of three years from the Completion Date except where there is a statutory obligation to retain the documents therein specified for a longer period in which event the period imposed by such statutory obligation shall apply.

8. Exclusion of warranties

The Purchaser having inspected the assets comprised in the Business as and where they lie shall take the same in the condition in which they are and no warranty or assurance is given or implied as to the condition, quality or fitness of such assets.

9. Passing of risk

All the assets comprised in the Business being purchased in terms of this Agreement will be at the risk of the Purchaser from the Transfer Date and title thereto shall pass to the Purchaser when the aggregate consideration for the Business to be paid at the Completion Date has been paid in full.

10. Receiver's liability

The Purchaser hereby acknowledges and accepts that the Receiver acts only as agent of the Vendor and accordingly the Purchaser accepts that the Receiver shall incur no personal liability whatsoever hereunder other than to the extent of any free assets in his hands after all categories of persons described (including the holder of the floating charge by virtue of which he was appointed) in section 60 of the Insolvency Act 1986 have been satisfied.

11. Prior agreements

This Agreement supersedes all previous agreements between the parties in relation to the matters herein specified and represents the entire understanding of the parties in relation thereto.

[12. Change of name

The Receiver shall procure that, in so far as it is competent and legal for him to do so, the name of the Vendor is, at the expense of the Purchaser, changed as soon as practicable after the Completion Date and in any event not later than 28 days after the Transfer Date to a name which does not include the name 'Galaxy' and shall not impede or prevent the Purchaser incorporating a company or companies bearing such names or changing the names of existing companies to a name including the word 'Galaxy'.]

13. Apportionments

(1) Expenses of the Business (including salaries, wages and other emoluments of employees, rent, rates, vehicle licence payments, the costs of telephone, telex and other services and all other normal expenses incidental to the running of the Business) shall to the extent that they relate to any period prior to the Transfer Date, be the liability of the Vendor and the Receiver.

(2) Expenses of the Business incurred prior to the Transfer Date and paid by the Vendor or the Receiver shall, to the extent that they relate to any period after the Transfer Date, be reimbursed to the Vendor and the Receiver by the Purchaser.

[14. Continuance of business

From the date of execution of this Agreement until the Transfer Date, the Vendor and the Receiver shall continue the Business in substantially the same manner as heretofore and they shall not do anything which will or might jeopardise or diminish the goodwill of the Business or any of the property or assets hereby agreed to be sold in any way and without prejudice to the generality of the foregoing they shall maintain the value and type of stock in trade as close as possible to the value and type at the date of execution of this Agreement.]

15. **Announcements**

Neither the Vendor nor the Receiver nor the Purchaser shall make or authorise any announcement or public disclosures concerning the subject matter of this Agreement, either to the press or to shareholders or otherwise, except on terms and in manner mutually agreed between them.

16. **Notices**

(1) Any notice hereunder may be served by hand or by first class prepaid post through the recorded delivery system addressed to the party to be served at such party's address as hereinbefore appearing.

(2) Any notice in terms of this clause served by post shall be deemed to have been served twenty four hours after the same is put into the post.

(3) Any notice requiring to be served on the Vendor and the Receiver shall be sufficiently served by being served on the Receiver.

17. **Expenses**

The Vendor, the Receiver and the Purchaser shall be responsible for their respective expenses incidental to the preparation and execution and carrying into effect of this Agreement.

18. **Arbitration**

In the event of any dispute or difference between the Vendor, the Receiver and the Purchaser arising out of this Agreement, (and subject to the provisions of clause 3(4)) the same shall be referred to the decision of a single arbiter who shall be nominated, failing agreement, by the President of the Law Society of Scotland and the awards of such arbiter, partial, interim or final shall be binding on the Vendor, the Receiver and the Purchaser who agree to exclude the jurisdiction of the Court to give its opinion on any question of law arising in any such arbitration under and in terms of section 3 of the Administration of Justice (Scotland) Act, 1973.

19. **Proper law**

This Agreement and all documents drafted and executed in pursuance of this Agreement shall in all respects be interpreted in accordance with the law of Scotland.

SEALED with the COMMON SEAL of GALAXY PRODUCTS
LIMITED and subscribed for it and on its behalf
at   on
198[   ] by FREDERICK GALILEO
as Receiver thereof in the presence of:

Witness

Address

Occupation

Witness

Address

Occupation

SEALED with the COMMON SEAL of ROCOCO COCOA CO
LIMITED
and subscribed for it and on its behalf at
on   198[   ] by:

Director

Director/Secretary

SCHEDULE

Part [   ]

Details of Plant and Machinery and Others

Part [   ]

The Premises

Part [   ]

Terms and Conditions for sale of the Premises
1.   Vacant possession of the Premises will be given to the Purchaser on
     the Completion Date [subject to the leases/rights of occupancy
     specified in Part [   ] of this Schedule.]
2.   The minerals are included in the sale only in so far as the Vendor has
     right thereto.

3. The Purchaser shall be deemed to have satisfied itself as to the nature and extent of the title to the Premises tendered by the Vendor.

4. At the Completion Date the Vendor and the Receiver will grant and deliver to the Purchaser (subject to the terms of paragraph 3 hereof) a validly executed Disposition of the Premises, and will deliver or exhibit a valid marketable title to the Premises and will deliver or exhibit either (a) Searches in the Property Register for a period of twenty years and in the Personal Register for the prescriptive period showing no incumbrances or diligences which would preclude the Receiver from granting a good title; or (b) if at the Completion Date the provisions of section 2(1) or 3(3) of the Land Registration (Scotland) Act 1979 (which together with all amendments thereof and statutory instruments and rules issued thereunder are hereinafter referred to as 'the Act') apply to the transfer of the Vendor's interest in the Premises, the Vendor and the Receiver will provide a Form 10 Report brought down to a date as near as practicable to the Completion Date and showing no entries adverse to the Vendor's and the Receiver's interest (the cost (if any) of said Report being the responsibility of the Purchaser) and, in addition, the Vendor and the Receiver will furnish to the Purchaser such documents and evidence, including a plan as the Keeper may require to enable the Keeper to issue a Land Certificate in name of the Purchaser as the registered proprietor of the Premises and containing no exclusion of indemnity in terms of section 12(2) of the Act.

    The Land Certificate or Certificates to be issued to the Purchaser will disclose no entry, deed or diligence prejudicial to the Purchaser's interest other than such as are created by or against the Purchaser. Notwithstanding delivery of the said Disposition this paragraph will remain in full force and effect and may be founded upon.

    On Completion Date letters of obligation will be granted by the Vendor's solicitors and the Receiver's solicitors in usual terms (it being understood that any inhibitions or other diligences disclosed in the Personal Searches against the Vendor in respect of the period after the date of appointment of the Receiver shall not be discharged). No Companies Charges Register Search will be produced by the Vendor nor will any obligation whatsoever be given by the Vendor in respect of the Companies Charges Register.

5. In so far as the Receiver will be a party to any Dispositions of the Premises, warrandice from fact and deed only will be given by him and the Vendor will grant warrandice excluding said leases and rights of occupancy.

Form of letter
for collection of book debts

On letterhead of the Purchaser to be typed in duplicate
The Receiver,
Galaxy Products Limited,
10 Heavenly Mansions,
Pitlochry

[Date]

Dear Sir,
We refer to the Agreement ('the Agreement') among Galaxy Products Limited ('Galaxy') you as acting as receiver of Galaxy and us executed or about to be executed by Galaxy, you and us.
Definitions used in the Agreement shall bear the same meanings for the purposes of this letter.
We confirm that an arrangement has been agreed between us whereby we will in consideration of the goodwill of the Business, collect all book debts due to you as at the [Transfer Date] ('the Book Debts') in terms of the List of Debtors ('the List of Debtors') annexed and signed as relative hereto. The terms of the arrangement may be summarised as follows:

(1) We hereby undertake to collect the Book Debts specified in the List of Debtors on your behalf.

(2) Payment of all amounts collected by us shall be made to you within ten days of our receipt of the same and a breakdown of such amounts shall be made by the Purchaser showing the invoices to which such amounts relate.

(3) Subject to paragraph (4) hereof, you hereby reserve the right to recover the Book Debts in any manner you, at your sole discretion, consider appropriate, including without prejudice to the said generality, litigation, sequestration or liquidation.

(4) If we have not collected all or any of the Book Debts within 90 days of the date hereof, you shall be entitled to collect the same in such manner as you, at your sole discretion, may consider appropriate.

(5) We shall not be entitled to issue credit notes or in any other way absolve any debtor from full payment of his debt or grant any indulgence in respect thereof.

(6) We shall maintain separate records for each of the Book Debts which are recovered and make these available to you or your agents at any reasonable time or times.

(7) You shall be responsible for the maintenance of your sales ledgers.

(8) Title to and beneficial ownership of the Book Debts shall at all times remain vested in Galaxy and you respectively.

Yours faithfully,

On Duplicate

[Date]

I acknowledge to have received from you a letter dated [   ] of which the foregoing is a duplicate and as agent of Galaxy Products

Limited and, without in any way accepting personal liability therefor, I confirm my agreement of its terms and conditions.

....

Receiver

Form of letter of indemnity to receiver in the case of early delivery of the business

Form of letter of indemnity to receiver in the case of early delivery of the business

To: The Receiver,
Galaxy Products Limited,
10 Heavenly Mansions,
Pitlochry

[Date]

Dear Sirs,

We refer to the negotiations which are presently being conducted between us relating to the sale of the business of Galaxy Products Limited.

In view of the fact that we anticipate being able to conclude a formal agreement with you very shortly and in consideration of a continuance of such business in the ordinary course, we wish to confirm the following arrangements with you. All obligations and indemnities granted by us shall take effect and continue in full force and effect as from the opening of business on [   ] and shall so continue until the earlier of completion of such sale or the recall in writing by us to you of the terms of this letter ('the period of obligation and indemnity'). Without prejudice thereto, we shall in the event of such recall, honour all obligations and indemnities granted by us arising in respect of the period of obligation and indemnity. During the period of obligation and indemnity, we:

(1) shall, after due and proper consultation with you, order in our name all such raw materials and other supplies as may be reasonably required for the proper continuance of such business and we shall be responsible for payment for all such raw materials and other supplies.

(2) hereby undertake in conjunction with you to use all such raw materials and other supplies in a proper and timeous manner so as to ensure an orderly and efficient continuance of such business and fulfilment of all current contracts to your customers.

(3) hereby undertake to make proper insurance arrangements on a fully comprehensive basis against all normal commercial business risks including without prejudice thereto suitable provisions for the acts or omissions of any of our employees or agents.

(4) shall be responsible for the payment of all salaries and other overheads relating to such business but, as agreed with you, we shall be entitled to retain all profit during the period of obligation and indemnity.

(5) acknowledge and confirm that, notwithstanding the arrangements specified in this letter, title to and the beneficial ownership of such business shall always remain with Galaxy Products Limited.

We hereby indemnify you and we shall keep you indemnified against all liability howsoever arising in respect of any of the matters specified in this letter and in this connection, an indemnity against any such liability shall be deemed to include an indemnity against all demands, claims, costs,

279

charges and expenses made, suffered or incurred by reason of or in connection with any such liability.

Yours faithfully,

[Under Seal of the Purchaser]

Appendix 13

Share purchase agreement

AGREEMENT
between
GALAXY PRODUCTS LIMITED   (1)
(IN RECEIVERSHIP)
ROCOCO COCOA CO LIMITED   (2)

AGREEMENT

between

(1)   GALAXY   PRODUCTS LIMITED incorporated under the Companies Acts and having its registered office at 10 Heavenly Mansions, Pitlochry ('the Vendor') acting by its receiver, FREDERICK GALILEO, Chartered   Accountant,   Saturn House, Pitlochry ('the Receiver')

and

(2)   ROCOCO   COCOA   CO LIMITED incorporated under the Companies Acts and having its registered office at Baroque House, Louis XV Avenue, Edinburgh ('the Purchaser')

1. **Introduction**

   (1)   In terms of an Agreement dated [   ] between the Vendor and the Company (as hereinafter defined) the business and undertaking of the Vendor relating to the manufacture, distribution and sale of space invaders and associated products carried on by the Vendor at Pitlochry was transferred to the Company (as hereinafter defined), the consideration therefor being satisfied by way of an inter-company loan due by the Company (as hereinafter defined) to the Vendor.

   (2)   The Company (as hereinafter defined) (which before the purchase of such business had never traded) was incorporated on [   ] under the Companies Acts as a company limited by shares and has a nominal capital of £100 divided into 100 shares of £1 each two of which have been issued and are in the beneficial ownership of the Vendor.

   (3)   The Vendor has agreed to sell and the Purchaser has agreed to purchase the whole of the issued share capital of the Company (as hereinafter defined) on the terms and conditions set out in this Agreement.

2. **Interpretation**

   (1)   In this Agreement unless the context otherwise requires:
   'the Company' means Orinoco Cocoa Co Limited registered in Scotland number [   ];
   'Completion Date' means [   ]; and 'Shares' means the two issued shares of £1 each in the Company.

   (2)   The headings in this Agreement are inserted for convenience only and shall not affect its interpretation.

3. **Sale of shares**

   The Vendor as the beneficial owner shall sell to the Purchaser and

the Purchaser shall purchase from the Vendor as from
[   ] the Shares being the whole of the issued share
capital of the Company free from all options, liens, charges and
encumbrances and with all rights now or hereafter becoming
attached thereto.

4. **Consideration**

The consideration for the sale of the Shares shall be the sum of
TWO POUNDS (£2).

5. **Completion**
    (1) On the Completion Date the Vendor shall:
        (1) deliver to the Purchaser one copy of the executed engross-
             ment of the Agreement referred to in clause 1(1);
        (2) deliver to the Purchaser in respect of the Shares transfers
             duly executed in favour of the Purchaser and/or its
             nominee(s) together with relative share certificates;
        (3) deliver to the Purchaser the books of the Company duly
             written up and the seal of the Company;
        (4) deliver the title deeds, leases, other documents of title,
             licences and registrations relating to the assets and busi-
             ness of the Company;
        (5) procure that a meeting of the Directors of the Company
             shall be held and that at such meeting:
            (a) such transfers shall, subject to being duly stamped,
                 be approved and registered by the Directors;
            (b) such persons as shall be nominated by notice in
                 writing given by the Purchaser to the Directors of
                 the Company shall be appointed as Directors and the
                 Secretary respectively of the Company; and
            (c) all the Directors of the Company (other than those
                 appointed pursuant to the provisions of clause
                 5(1)(5)(b)) and the Secretary of the Company shall
                 resign office as Directors and the Secretary respecti-
                 vely of the Company and from any other office or
                 employment which they have respectively with the
                 Company and that with immediate effect and with-
                 out payment of compensation for loss of office or any
                 other payment whatsoever and will deliver letters of
                 resignation to that effect; and
        (6) deliver to the Purchaser a duly executed discharge of the
             floating charge by the Company in favour of the Vendor.
    (2) On the Completion Date, the Purchaser shall pay to Messrs
         [   ] Solicitors, [   ] on behalf of
         the Vendor and the Receiver (and as the Purchaser is hereby
         expressly authorised by the Vendor and the Receiver to pay) by
         banker's draft drawn on Banco Albinoni plc [Address] to the
         said   Messrs   [   ])   an   amount   equal   to
         [   ] representing the aggregate consider-

ation for the Shares (£2) and full settlement of the inter-company loan referred to in clause 1(1).

6. **Announcements**

Neither the Vendor nor the Receiver nor the Purchaser shall make or authorise any announcement or public disclosures concerning the subject matter of this Agreement, either to the press or to share-holders or otherwise, except on terms and in manner mutually agreed between them.

7. **Receiver's liability**

The Purchaser hereby acknowledges and accepts that the Receiver acts only as an agent of the Vendor and accordingly the Purchaser accepts that the Receiver shall incur no personal liability whatsoever hereunder other than to the extent of any free assets in his hands after all categories of persons described (including the holders of the floating charges by virtue of which he was appointed) in section 60 of the Insolvency Act 1986 have been satisfied.

8. **Notices**

(1) Any notice hereunder may be served by hand or by first class prepaid post through the recorded delivery system addressed to the party to be served at such party's address as hereinbefore appearing.
(2) Any notice served by post shall be deemed to have been served twenty four hours after the same is put into the post.
(3) Any notice requiring to be served on the Vendor and the Receiver shall be sufficiently served by being served on the Receiver.

9. **Expenses**

The Vendor and the Purchaser shall each be responsible for their respective expenses incidental to the preparation and execution and carrying into effect of this Agreement.

10. **General**

In so far as not implemented on the Completion Date this Agreement shall remain in full force and effect and the undertakings and warranties provided for herein shall be enforceable at the instance of the Vendor, the Receiver and the Purchaser and their respective assignees.

11. **Prior agreements**

This Agreement supersedes all previous agreements between the parties in relation to the matters herein specified and represents the entire understanding of the parties in relation thereto.

12. **Proper law**

This Agreement and all documents drafted and executed in pursuance of this Agreement shall in all respects be interpreted in accordance with the law of Scotland.

> SEALED with the COMMON SEAL of GALAXY PRODUCTS LIMITED and subscribed for it and on its behalf at
> on   198   by FRED-ERICK GALILEO as receiver thereof before these witnesses:
>
> Witness
>
> Address
>
> Occupation
>
> Witness
>
> Address
>
> Occupation
>
> SEALED with the COMMON SEAL of ROCOCO COCOA CO LIMITED and subscribed for it and on its behalf at
> on   198   by:
>
> > Director
>
> > Director/Secretary

Deed of adherence

ADHERENCE
among
[AND OTHERS]
and
GALAXY PRODUCTS LIMITED
and
FREDERICK GALILEO as Receiver thereof
and
ROCOCO COCOA CO LIMITED

DEED OF ADHERENCE
among

[

] the present Trustees of the Scheme hereinafter defined ('the Trustees')

GALAXY PRODUCTS LIMITED, incorporated under the Companies Acts and having its registered office at 10 Heavenly Mansions, Pitlochry ('the Principal Employer') acting by its receiver, FREDERICK GALILEO, Chartered Accountant, Saturn House, Pitlochry ('the Receiver'), the Receiver only acting as agent for the Principal Employer and incurring no personal liability in entering into this deed

and

ROCOCO COCOA CO LIMITED, incorporated under the Companies Acts and having its registered office at Baroque House, Louis XV Avenue, Edinburgh ('the Purchaser')

WHEREAS:
(a) The Trustees are the present Trustees of the Galaxy Products Limited Retirement Benefits Scheme ('the Scheme');
(b) The Scheme is constituted by a Definitive Deed of Trust between [   ] and the Principal Employer dated [   ] and other Supplemental Deeds (the said Definitive Deed, the Supplemental Deeds and the Rules of the Scheme presently in force collectively hereinafter being referred to as 'the Scheme Deeds');
(c) The Purchaser will on [   ] commence to employ certain employees of the Principal Employer all of which employees are members of the Scheme ('the Purchaser's Employees');
(d) The parties are agreed that the Purchaser's Employees should on the commencement of their employment with the Purchaser be and remain members of the Scheme:

THEREFORE it is agreed among the parties as follows:
1. Under Rule [   ] of the said Definitive Deed the Trustees and the Principal Employer agree that as and from [   ] the Purchaser shall become an Employer (as that expression is defined in the Scheme Deeds) of the Scheme and the Purchaser has agreed so to do and undertakes to comply with all the provisions of the Scheme Deeds incumbent upon an Employer.

2. The Purchaser shall pay contributions to the Trustees for the Purchaser's Employees at the rate of [   ] of Pensionable Salary (as defined in the Scheme Deeds) in respect of the continued participation in the Scheme of the Purchaser's Employees.

3. The Trustees and the Principal Employer in so far as interested therein confirm that the Purchaser's Employees shall not leave the Scheme on the commencement of their employment with the Purchaser merely because they have ceased to be employed by the Principal Employer.

4. The Trustees undertake to apply forthwith for Inland Revenue approval for the Purchaser becoming an Employer for a period of not less than [months] from [   ] and during that period undertake to discuss and negotiate with the Trustees of the Purchaser's Pension Scheme with regard to transfer values for the Purchaser's Employees with the intent that within the said period all the Purchaser's Employees will be offered the opportunity to join the Purchaser's Pension Scheme or such other Pension Scheme as is designated by the Purchaser and will be given the opportunity to have a transfer payment made from the Scheme to the Purchaser's Pension Scheme or such other designated Scheme.

5. The Trustees and the Principal Employer and the Receiver for their respective interests confirm that the Scheme Deeds are hereby deemed to be amended in so far as is necessary to give full effect to the terms of this Deed.

6. Notwithstanding the provisions of this Deed, it shall only be given full force and effect to the extent that its implementation does not prejudice Inland Revenue approval of the Scheme.

7. The Receiver consents and agrees to the provisions of this Deed for his whole right, interest and entitlement thereto but enters into the Deed only as agent for the Principal Employer and shall incur no

personal liability whatsoever hereunder.

SIGNED by each of the Trustees at [   ] on [   ] 198[ ]
before these witnesses:

Witness

Address

Occupation

Witness

Address

Occupation

SEALED with the COMMON SEAL of GALAXY PRODUCTS
LIMITED and subscribed for it and on its behalf at [   ] on
[   ] 198[ ] by Frederick Galileo as receiver thereof before
these witnesses:

Witness

Address

Occupation

Witness

Address

Occupation

SEALED with the COMMON SEAL of ROCOCO COCOA CO
LIMITED and subscribed for it and on its behalf at [   ] on
[   ] 198[ ].

                                       Director

                                       Director/Secretary

Appendix 15

Ranking agreement

BANCO ALBINONI plc (1)
GALLIARD INVESTMENTS LIMITED (2)
GALAXY PRODUCTS LIMITED (3)

RANKING AGREEMENT

AGREEMENT
amongst

BANCO ALBINONI plc incorporated under the Companies Acts and having its registered office at Corelli Square, Edinburgh ('the Bank')

and

GALLIARD INVESTMENTS LIMITED, incorporated under the Companies Acts and having its registered office at Bach House, Contrapuntal Row, Edinburgh ('GIL').

and

GALAXY PRODUCTS LIMITED incorporated under the Companies Acts and having its registered office at 10 Heavenly Mansions, Pitlochry ('the Company')

WHEREAS:

(A) the Company has granted in favour of the Bank a Standard Security ('the Bank Fixed Security') over the Company's heritable property at 10 Heavenly Mansions, Pitlochry ('the heritable property') and has also granted a Bond and Floating Charge ('the Bank Floating Charge') over the whole of its undertaking and property ('the floating property');

(B) the Company has granted in favour of GIL a Standard Security ('the GIL Fixed Security') over the heritable property and has also granted a Bond and Floating Charge ('the GIL Floating Charge') over the floating property; and

(C) the parties have agreed that the securities constituted by the said respective documents should rank as follows.

NOW IT IS HEREBY AGREED as follows:

(1) Notwithstanding the terms of the said respective documents and the dates of their constitution or registration it is agreed that the sums secured or to be secured (including the interest due thereon and all costs, charges and expenses for which the Company is liable in connection therewith) ('the interest and expenses') by the Bank Fixed Security and the GIL Fixed Security shall rank and be preferred in the event of a sale of the property thereby secured or any part thereof prior and preferably to the sums secured or to be secured (including the interest and expenses) respectively by the Bank Floating Charge and the GIL Floating Charge.

(2) Notwithstanding the terms of the said respective documents and the dates of their constitution or registration it is agreed that the Bank Fixed Security and the GIL Fixed Security will rank *pari passu* in point of security to the intent that if the security created by the Bank Fixed Security or the GIL Fixed Security shall become enforceable but the proceeds of realisation thereof of the heritable property (after payment of all

expenses) shall be insufficient to satisfy in full the amounts owing by the Company to the Bank (limited to the extent of [   ] plus interest and expenses in the case of the Bank Fixed Security) and to GIL (limited to the extent of [   ] plus interest and expenses in the case of the GIL Fixed Security) the Bank and GIL shall be entitled to payment *pro rata* according to the proportion which the amount (so limited) owing by the Company to each of them bears to the aggregate of all such amounts (so limited) owing provided that after satisfaction in full of the amounts (so limited) any amounts owing by the Company to the Bank and GIL in excess of the amounts limited as aforementioned shall rank *pari passu* according to the proportion which each such amount in excess bears to the aggregate of the amounts in excess.

(3)   Notwithstanding the terms of the said respective documents and the dates of their constitution or registration it is agreed that the Bank Floating Charge and the GIL Floating Charge will rank *pari passu* in point of security to the intent that if the security created by the Bank Floating Charge and the GIL Floating Charge shall become enforceable but the proceeds of realisation thereof (after payment of all expenses) shall be insufficient to satisfy in full the amounts owing by the Company to the Bank (limited to the extent of [   ] plus interest and expenses) in the case of the Bank Floating Charge and GIL (limited to the extent of [   ] plus interest and expenses in the case of the GIL Floating Charge) the Bank and GIL shall be entitled to payment *pro rata* according to the proportion which the amount (so limited) owing by the Company to each of them bears to the aggregate of all such amounts (so limited) owing provided that after satisfaction in full of the amounts (so limited) any amounts owing by the Company to the Bank and GIL in excess of the amounts limited as aforementioned shall rank *pari passu* according to the proportion which each such amount in excess bears to the aggregate of the amounts in excess.

(4)   The Bank and GIL hereby consent to the creation and subsistence of each of the Bank Floating Charge and the GIL Floating Charge respectively and to the creation and subsistence of each of the Bank Fixed Security and the GIL Fixed Security and to such charges and securities ranking as regards security and priority as herein provided notwithstanding anything to the contrary contained in such charges and securities or any of them or of the dates of execution or the dates of registration thereof in the Register of Sasines or Register of Charges.

(5)   The charges created by the respective charges and securities of the Bank and GIL shall rank subject as hereinbefore provided as continuing securities for repayment of the respective amounts owing and shall not be affected by any fluctuation in such amounts or by the existence at any time of a credit balance

299

on any current or other account.

SEALED with the COMMON SEAL of
BANCO ALBINONI plc at
on   198   and subscribed for
it and on its behalf by:

Director

Director/Secretary

SEALED with the COMMON SEAL of
GALLIARD INVESTMENTS
LIMITED   at   on
                    198   and subscribed
for it and on its behalf by:

Director

Director/Secretary

SEALED with the COMMON SEAL of
GALAXY PRODUCTS LIMITED at
                                       on
                    198   and subscribed
for it and on its behalf by:

Director

Director/Secretary

REGISTER on behalf of the within named
BANCO ALBINONI plc in the Register of
the County of [   ]

Solicitors [   ]
Agents
REGISTER on behalf of the within named
GALLIARD   INVESTMENTS
LIMITED in the Register of the County of
[   ]

Solicitors [   ]
Agents
REGISTER on behalf of the within named
GALAXY PRODUCTS LIMITED in the
Register of the County of [   ]

Solicitors [   ]
Agents

Appendix 16

Unlimited guarantee

UNLIMITED GUARANTEE
by
GALAXY PRODUCTS LIMITED AND OTHERS
in favour of
BANCO ALBINONI plc

To: BANCO ALBINONI plc

WE, GALAXY PRODUCTS LIMITED, incorporated under the Companies Acts and having our registered office at 10 Heavenly Mansions, Pitlochry, ROCOCO COCOA CO LIMITED and ROCOCO COCOA CO (SCOTLAND) LIMITED, both incorporated under the Companies Acts and having our registered offices at Baroque House, Louis XV Avenue, Edinburgh, ORINOCO COCOA CO LIMITED and ORINOCO COCOA CO (SCOTLAND) LIMITED, both incorporated under the Companies Acts and having our registered offices at 20 Neo-Classical Lane, Edinburgh all jointly and severally hereby guarantee you payment on demand of all sums for which we or any one or more of us ('the Companies') are now or may become liable to you in any manner of way whatsoever with interest thereon at such rate as may be charged by you to the Companies at the time from the date of your last annual balance preceding application by you to us for payment: AND WE FURTHER DECLARE that you shall be entitled to make calls on us from time to time at your discretion for such sums as you may fix, to account of our liabilities hereunder: AND ALSO that without prejudice to your rights under this guarantee and at your discretion, you may grant to the Companies or to any persons liable with or for them, any time or other indulgence, and may compound with them, accede to trust deeds and draw dividends, all without notice to us: AND WE ALSO DECLARE that this guarantee shall be a security to you to the above extent for any balance which may remain due to you after applying any dividends, compositions or payments which you may receive from the Companies or from any person liable with or for them and that we shall not be entitled to require any assignation of the debts hereby guaranteed or any part thereof or to rank on the estates of the Companies in respect of any payments made by us hereunder, or to have the benefit of any securities or any claims against third parties held by you until the whole sums due to you by the Companies have been paid in full: AND DECLARING that our liability hereunder shall not depend upon, or be affected by the powers of the Companies or their directors or other agents in regard to borrowing as contained in their respective Memoranda and Articles of Association or otherwise, or the validity or invalidity of any security given by the Companies, but the obligation hereby undertaken shall be binding upon us: AND DECLARING ALSO that this guarantee is a continuing obligation and shall remain in force until recalled by us or our respective successors in writing and is without prejudice to any further or other guarantees granted or to be granted by us or any of us to you on behalf of the Companies.

SEALED with the COMMON SEAL of
GALAXY PRODUCTS LIMITED at
         on   198 and subscribed
for it and on its behalf by:

                Director

                Director/Secretary

SEALED with the COMMON SEAL of
ROCOCO COCOA CO LIMITED at
         on   198 and subscribed
for it and on its behalf by:

                Director

                Director/Secretary

SEALED with the COMMON SEAL of
ROCOCO COCOA CO (SCOTLAND)
LIMITED at   on
            198   and subscribed
for it and on its behalf by:

                Director

                Director/Secretary

SEALED with the COMMON SEAL of
ORINOCO COCOA CO LIMITED at
         on   198[ ] and subs-
cribed for it and on its behalf by:

                Director

                Director/Secretary

SEALED with the COMMON SEAL of
ORINOCO COCOA CO (SCOTLAND)
LIMITED at   on
            198   and subscribed
for it and on its behalf by:

                Director

                Director/Secretary

Appendix 17

Letter of set-off

LETTER OF SET-OFF
by
GALAXY PRODUCTS LIMITED AND OTHERS
in favour of
BANCO ALBINONI plc

To: BANCO ALBINONI plc

WE, GALAXY PRODUCTS LIMITED, incorporated under the Companies Acts and having our registered office at 10 Heavenly Mansions, Pitlochry, ROCOCO COCOA CO LIMITED and ROCOCO COCOA CO (SCOTLAND) LIMITED, both incorporated under the Companies Acts and having our registered offices at Baroque House, Louis XV Avenue, Edinburgh, ORINOCO COCOA CO LIMITED and ORINOCO COCOA CO (SCOTLAND) LIMITED, both incorporated under the Companies Acts and having our registered offices at 20 Neo-Classical Lane, Edinburgh do hereby request and authorise you to hold all sums standing or that may stand to the credit of any of the current accounts in our names in your books in security and for payment of any advances made or to be made by you to any one or more of us and of all interest and charges accrued and to accrue thereon and of any other obligations for which any one or more of us now or may hereafter become liable to you in any way whatever: Declaring that you shall have full power at any time and in your discretion, without notice to us or any of us to apply all sums standing or that may stand to the credit of any of such accounts, or any part thereof, in payment or in reduction of such advances and obligations and interest and charges thereon: And we also declare that all sums standing or that may hereafter stand to the credit of any of such accounts shall be held by you in addition and without prejudice to any other security which you now or may hereafter hold for such advances and obligations and interest and charges thereon and that we shall not be entitled to rank on the estates of any of the other companies executing these presents in respect of any sums applied by you until the whole sums due to you by any one or more of us shall have been paid in full.

SEALED with the COMMON SEAL of
GALAXY PRODUCTS LIMITED at
        on   198[ ] and subscribed
for it and on its behalf by:

                Director

                Director/Secretary

SEALED with the COMMON SEAL of
ROCOCO COCOA CO LIMITED at
        on   198[ ] and subscribed
for it and on its behalf by:

                Director

                Director/Secretary

SEALED with the COMMON SEAL of
ROCOCO COCOA CO (SCOTLAND)
LIMITED at   on
        198[ ] and subscribed
for it and on its behalf by:

                Director

                Director/Secretary

SEALED with the COMMON SEAL of
ORINOCO COCOA CO LIMITED at
        on   198[ ] and subscribed
for it and on its behalf by:

                Director

                Director/Secretary

SEALED with the COMMON SEAL of
ORINOCO COCOA CO (SCOTLAND)
LIMITED at   on
        198[ ] and subscribed
for it and on its behalf by:

                Director

                Director/Secretary

Appendix 18

Assignation

ASSIGNATION
by
BANCO ALBINONI plc
in favour of
ROCOCO COCOA CO LIMITED

WE, BANCO ALBINONI plc, having our registered office at Corelli Square, Edinburgh Considering that by unlimited guarantee dated [   ] and executed by ROCOCO COCOA CO LIMITED, having its registered office at Baroque House, Louis XV Avenue, Edinburgh ('Rococo') Rococo guaranteed payment to us of all sums due or to become due on an account kept in our books *inter alia* in name of GALAXY PRODUCTS LIMITED ('Galaxy') having its registered office at 10 Heavenly Mansions, Pitlochry and that whenever required by us; Further Considering that Rococo has in full and final implement of such unlimited guarantee made payment to us of the sum of [   ] due by Galaxy on its account with us and has required us to grant these presents; Therefore we hereby assign to Rococo and its assignees whomsoever (1) the said sum of [   ] of principal and interest respectively and the liability of Galaxy therefor with all our right, title and interest in and to the premises; and (2) the Bond and Floating Charge granted by Galaxy dated [   ] and our right, title and interest, present and future therein to the extent of [Ratio of Debt Paid/Aggregate Amount paid by Guarantors] thereof; And that to the effect of enabling Rococo and its foresaids to operate any claim of relief they may have against Galaxy; And we warrant the foregoing assignation from our own facts and deeds only; And we have herewith delivered up to Rococo such unlimited guarantee.

SEALED with the COMMON SEAL of
BANCO   ALBINONI   plc   at
on [198] and subscribed
for it and on its behalf by:

Director

Appendix 19

Rules and Regulations

The Receivers (Scotland) Regulations 1986
SI 1986/1917 (S 141)

Made – – – – – – *10 November 1986*

Coming into Operation   *29 December 1986*

The Secretary of State, in exercise of the powers conferred upon him by sections 53(1) and (6), 54(3), 62(1) and (5), 65(1)*(a)*, 66(1), 67(2)*(b)*, 70(1) and 71 of the Insolvency Act 1986 and of all other powers enabling him in that behalf, hereby makes the following regulations:

Citation and commencement

1. These regulations may be cited as the Receivers (Scotland) Regulations 1986 and shall come into operation on 29 December 1986.

Interpretation

2. In these regulations, 'the Act' means the Insolvency Act 1986.

Forms

3. The forms set out in the Schedule to these regulations, with such variations as circumstances require, are the forms prescribed for the purposes of the provisions of the Act which are referred to in those forms.

Instrument of appointment

4. The certified copy instrument of appointment of a receiver which is required to be submitted to the registrar of companies by or on our behalf of the person making the appointment under section 53(1) of the Act shall be certified to be a correct copy by or on behalf of that person.

Joint receivers

5. Where two or more persons are appointed joint receivers by the holder of a floating charge under section 53 of the Act, subsection (6) of that section shall apply subject to the following modifications:
  (a) the appointment of any of the joint receivers shall be of no effect unless the appointment is accepted by all of them in accordance with paragraph *(a)* of that subsection and Rule 3.1 of the Insolvency (Scotland) Rules 1986; and
  (b) their appointment as joint receivers shall be deemed to be made on the day on and at the time at which the instrument of appointment is received by the last of them, as evidenced by the written docquet required by paragraph *(b)* of that subsection.

Resignation

6. For the purposes of section 62(1) of the Act, a receiver, who wishes to resign his office, shall give at least 7 days' notice of his resignation to:-

(a) the holder of the floating charge by virtue of which he was appointed;

(b) the holder of any other floating charge and any receiver appointed by him;

(c) the members of any committee of creditors established under section 68 of the Act; and

(d) the company, or if it is then in liquidation, its liquidator,

and the notice shall specify the date on which the resignation takes effect.

Report to creditors

7. Where the receiver determines to publish a notice under paragraph *(b)* of section 67(2) of the Act, the notice shall be published in a newspaper circulating in the area where the company has its principal place of business or in such other newspaper as he thinks most appropriate for ensuring that it comes to the notice of the unsecured creditors of the company.

SCHEDULE   Regulation 3

FORMS

Form 1 (Scot)	Notice of appointment of a receiver by the holder of a floating charge.
Form 2 (Scot)	Notice of appointment of a receiver by the court.
Form 3 (Scot)	Notice of the receiver ceasing to act or of his removal.
Form 4 (Scot)	Notice of appointment of receiver.
Form 5 (Scot)	Statement of affairs.

The Insolvency (Scotland) Rules 1986
SI 1986/1915 (S 139)

Made – – – – – –	*10 November 1986*
Laid before Parliament	*26 November 1986*
Coming into Operation	*29 December 1986*

The Secretary of State, in exercise of the powers conferred on him by section 411 of the Insolvency Act 1986 and of all other powers enabling him in that behalf, hereby makes the following Rules:

PART 3

RECEIVERS

CHAPTER 1

APPOINTMENT

Acceptance of Appointment

3.1.—(1) Where a person has been appointed a receiver by the holder of a floating charge under section 53, his acceptance (which need not be in writing) of that appointment for the purposes of paragraph *(a)* of section 53(6) shall be intimated by him to the holder of the floating charge or his agent within the period specified in that paragraph and he shall, as soon as possible after his acceptance, endorse a written docquet to that effect on the instrument of appointment.

(2) The written docquet evidencing receipt of the instrument of appointment, which is required by section 53(6)*(b)*, shall also be endorsed on the instrument of appointment.

(3) The receiver shall, as soon as possible after his acceptance of the appointment, deliver a copy of the endorsed instrument of appointment to the holder of the floating charge or his agent.

(4) This Rule shall apply in the case of the appointment of joint receivers as it applies to the appointment of a receiver, except that, where the docquet of acceptance required by paragraph (1) is endorsed by each of the joint receivers, or two or more of them, on the same instrument of appointment, it is the joint receiver who last endorses his docquet of acceptance who is required to send a copy of the instrument of appointment to the holder of the floating charge or his agent under paragraph (3).

CHAPTER 2

STATEMENT OF AFFAIRS

Notice requiring statement of affairs

3.2.—(1) Where the receiver decides to require from any person or persons a statement as to the affairs of the company to be made out and submitted to him in accordance with section 66, he shall send to each of those persons a notice in the form required by Rule 7.30 and Schedule 5 requiring him to make out and submit a statement of affairs in the form prescribed by the Receivers (Scotland) Regulations 1986.

(2) Any person to whom a notice is sent under this Rule is referred to in this Chapter as 'a deponent'.

321

(3) The receiver shall insert any statement of affairs submitted to him in the sederunt book.

Expenses of statement of affairs

3.3.—(1) A deponent who makes up and submits to the receiver a statement of affairs shall be allowed and be paid by the receiver, as an expense of the receivership, any expenses incurred by the deponent in so doing which the receiver considers to be reasonable.

(2) Any decision by the receiver under this Rule is subject to appeal to the court.

(3) Nothing in this Rule relieves a deponent from any obligation to make up and submit a statement of affairs, or to provide information to the receiver.

CHAPTER 3

THE CREDITORS' COMMITTEE

Constitution of committee

3.4.—(1) Where it is resolved by the creditors' meeting to establish a creditors' committee under section 68, the committee shall consist of at least 3 and not more than 5 creditors of the company elected at the meeting.

(2) Any creditor of the company who has lodged a claim is eligible to be a member of the committee, so long as his claim has not been rejected for the purpose of his entitlement to vote.

(3) A body corporate or a partnership may be a member of the committee, but it cannot act as such otherwise than by a representative appointed under Rule 7.20, as applied by Rule 3.6.

Functions of the committee

3.5. In addition to the functions conferred on it by the Act, the creditors' committee shall represent to the receiver the views of the unsecured creditors' and shall act in relation to him in such manner as may be agreed from time to time.

Application of provisions relating to liquidation committee

3.6.—(1) Chapter 7 of Part 4 (The liquidation committee) shall apply with regard to the creditors' committee in the receivership and its members as it applies to the liquidation committee and the creditor members thereof, subject to the modifications specified below and to any other necessary modifications.

(2) For any reference in the said Chapter 7 to —
(a) the liquidator or the liquidation committee, there shall be substituted a reference to the receiver or to the creditors' committee;
(b) to the creditor member, there shall be substituted a reference to a creditor,
(and any reference to a contributory member shall be disregarded.

(3) In Rule 4.42(3) and 4.52(2), for the reference to Rule 4.41(1), there shall be substituted a reference to Rule 3.4(1).

(4) In Rule 4.57,
(a) for the reference to an expense of the liquidation, there shall be substituted a reference to an expense of the receivership;
(b) at the end of that Rule there shall be inserted the following:

'This does not apply to any meeting of the committee held within 3 months of a previous meeting, unless the meeting in question is summoned at the instance of the receiver.'.

(5) The following Rules shall not apply, namely —
Rules 4.40, 4.41, 4.43, to 4.44, 4.53, 4.56, 4.58 and 4.59.

Information from receiver

3.7.—(1) Where the committee resolves to require the attandance of the receiver under section 68(2), the notice to him shall be in writing signed by the majority of the members of the committee for the time being or their representatives.

(2) The meeting at which the receiver's attendance is required shall be fixed by the committee for a business day, and shall be held at such time and place as he determines.

(3) Where the receiver so attends, the members of the committee may elect any one of their number to be chairman of the meeting, in place of the receiver or any nominee of his.

Members' dealings with the company

3.8.—(1) Membership of the committee does not prevent a person from dealing with the company while the receiver is acting, provided that any transactions in the course of such dealings are entered into on normal commercial terms.

(2) The court may, on the application of any person interested, set aside a transaction which appears to it to be contrary to the requirements of this Rule, and may give such consequential directions as it thinks fit for compensating the company for any loss which it may have incurred in consequence of the transaction.

CHAPTER 4

MISCELLANEOUS

Abstract of receipts and payments

3.9.—(1) The receiver shall —

(a) within 2 months after the end of 12 months from the date of his appointment, and of every subsequent period of 12 months, and

(b) within 2 months after he ceases to act as receiver,

send the requisite accounts of his receipts and payments as receiver to —

> (i) the registrar of companies,
> (ii) the holder of the floating charge by virtue of which he was appointed,
> (iii) the members of the creditors' committee (if any),
> (iv) the company or, if it is in liquidation, the liquidator.

(2) The court may, on the receiver's application, extend the period of 2 months referred to in paragraph (1).

(3) The accounts are to be in the form of an abstract showing—

(a) receipts and payments during the relevant period of 12 months, or

(b) where the receiver has ceased to act, receipts and payments during the period from the end of the last 12-month period to the time when he so ceased (alternatively, if there has been no previous abstract, receipts and payments in the period since his appointment as receiver).

(4) This Rule is without prejudice to the receiver's duty to render proper accounts required otherwise than as above.

(5) If the receiver makes default in complying with this Rule, he is liable to a fine and, for continued contravention, to a daily default fine.

Receiver deceased

3.10. If the receiver dies, the holder of the floating charge by virtue of which he was appointed shall, forthwith on his becoming aware of the death, give notice of it to—

(a) the registrar of companies,

(b) the members of the creditors' committee (if any),

(c) the company or, if it is in liquidation, the liquidator,

(d) the holder of any other floating charge and any receiver appointed by him.

Vacation of office

3.11. The receiver, on vacating office on completion of the receivership or in consequence of his ceasing to be qualified as an insolvency practitioner, shall, in addition to giving notice to the registrar of companies under section 62(5), give notice of his vacating office, within 14 days thereof, to—

(a) the holder of the floating charge by virtue of which he was appointed,

(b) the members of the creditors' committee (if any),

(c) the company or, if it is in liquidation, the liquidator,

(d) the holder of any other floating charge and any receiver appointed by him.

CHAPTER 5

VAT BAD DEBT RELIEF

Issue of certificate of insolvency

3.12.—(1) In accordance with this Rule, it is the duty of the administrative receiver to issue a certificate in the terms of paragraph *(b)* of section 22(3) of the Value Added Tax Act 1983 (which specifies the circumstances in which a company is deemed insolvent for the purposes of that section) forthwith upon his forming the opinion described in that paragraph.

(2) There shall in the certificate be specified—

(a) the name of the company and its registered number;

(b) the name of the administrative receiver and the date of his appointment; and

(c) the date on which the certificate is issued.

(3) The certificate shall be entitled 'CERTIFICATE OF INSOLVENCY FOR THE PURPOSES OF SECTION 22(3)*(b)* OF THE VALUE ADDED TAX ACT 1983'.

Notice to creditors

3.13—(1) Notice of the issue of the certificate shall be given by the administrative receiver within 3 months of his appointment or within 2 months of issuing the certificate, whichever is the later, to all of the company's unsecured creditors of whose address he is then aware and who have, to his knowledge, made supplies to the company, with a charge to value added tax, at any time before his appointment.

(2) Thereafter, he shall give the notice to any such creditor of whose address and supplies to the company he becomes aware.

(3) He is not under obligation to provide any creditor with a copy of the certificate.

Preservation of certificate with company's records

3.14.—(1) The certificate shall be retained with the company's accounting records, and section 222 of the Companies Act (where and for how long records are to be kept) shall apply to the certificate as it applies to those records.

(2) It is the duty of the administrative receiver, on vacating office, to bring this Rule to the attention of the directors or (as the case may be) any successor of his as receiver.

Chapter 7 of Part 4 of The Insolvency (Scotland) Rules 1986 as applied to the creditors' committee in the receivership and its members

THE CREDITORS' COMMITTEE

Formalities of establishment

4.42.—(1) The creditors' committee shall not come into being, and accordingly act, until the receiver has issued a certificate of its due constitution.

(2) If the chairman of the meeting which resolves to establish the committee is not the receiver, he shall forthwith give notice of the resolution to the receiver (or, as the case may be, the person appointed as receiver by the same meeting), and inform him of the names and addresses of the persons elected to be members of the committee.

(3) No person may act as a member of the committee unless and until he has agreed to do so; and the receiver's certificate of the committee's due constitution shall not be issued until at least the minimum number of persons in accordance with Rule 3.4(1) who are to be members of it have agreed to act, but shall be issued forthwith thereafter.

(4) As and when the others (if any) agree to act, the receiver shall issue an amended certificate.

(5) The certificate (and any amended certificate) shall be sent by the receiver to the Registrar of Companies.

(6) If after the first establishment of the committee there is any change in its membership, the receiver shall report the change to the registrar of companies.

Meetings of the committee

4.45.—(1) Subject as follows, meetings of the creditors' committee shall be held when and where determined by the receiver.

(2) The receiver shall call a first meeting of the committee to take place within 3 months of his appointment or of the committee's establishment (whichever is the later); and thereafter he shall call a meeting—

(*a*) if so requested by a creditor member of the committee or his representative (the meeting then to be held within 21 days of the request being received by the receiver), and

(*b*) for a specified date, if the committee has previously resolved that a meeting be held on that date.

(3) The receiver shall give 7 days' written notice of the time and place of any meeting to every member of the committee (or his representative, if designated for that purpose), unless in any case the requirement of the notice has been waived by or on behalf of any member. Waiver may be signified either at or before the meeting.

The chairman at meetings

4.46.—(1) The chairman at any meeting of the creditors' committee shall be the receiver or a person nominated by him to act.

(2) A person so nominated must be either—

(*a*) a person who is qualified to act as an insolvency practitioner in relation to the company, or

(*b*) an employee of the receiver or his firm who is experienced in insolvency matters.

Quorum

4.47. A meeting of the committee is duly constituted if due notice of it has been given to all the members, and at least 2 creditors are present or represented.

Committee members' representatives

4.48.—(1) A member of the creditors' committee may, in relation to the business of the committee, be represented by another person duly authorised by him for that purpose.

(2) A person acting as a committee-member's representative must hold a mandate entitling him so to act (either generally or specially) and signed by or on behalf of the committee-member.

(3) The chairman at any meeting of the committee may call on a person claiming to act as a committee-member's representative to produce his mandate and may exclude him if it appears that his mandate is deficient.

(4) No member may be represented by a body corporate or by a partnership, or by an undischarged bankrupt.

(5) No person shall—

(*a*) on the same committee, act at one and the same time as representative of more than one committee-member, or

   (b) act both as a member of the committee and as representative of
another member.

(6) Where a member's representative signs any document on the
member's behalf, the fact that he so signs must be stated below his
signature.

Resignation

4.49. A member of the creditors' committee may resign by notice in
writing delivered to the receiver.

Termination of membership

4.50. Membership of the creditors' committee of any person is automatically terminated if—
   (a) his estate is sequestrated or he becomes bankrupt or grants a trust
deed for the benefit of or makes a composition with his creditors, or
   (b) at 3 consecutive meetings of the committee he is neither present
nor represented (unless at the third of those meetings it is resolved
that this Rule is not to apply in his case), or
   (c) that creditor being a creditor, he ceases to be, or is found never to
have been a creditor.

Removal

4.51 A creditor of the committee may be removed by resolution at a
meeting of creditors.

Vacancy (creditors)

4.52.—(1) The following applies if there is a vacancy among the
creditors of the committee.

(2) The vacancy need not be filled if the receiver and a majority of the
remaining creditors so agree, provided that the total number of members
does not fall below the minimum required by Rule 3.4(1).

(3) The receiver may appoint any creditor, who is qualified under the
Rules to be a member of the committee, to fill the vacancy, if a majority of
the other creditors agree to the appointment, and the creditor concerned
consents to act.

(4) Alternatively, a meeting of creditors may resolve that a creditor be
appointed (with his consent) to fill the vacancy. In this case, at least 14
days' notice must have been given of the resolution to make such an
appointment (whether or not of a person named in the notice).

(5) Where the vacancy is filled by an appointment made by a creditors' meeting at which the receiver is not present, the chairman of the meeting shall report to the receiver the appointment which has been made.

Voting rights and resolutions

4.54.—(1) At any meeting of the committee, each member of it (whether present himself, or by his representative) has one vote; and a resolution is passed when a majority of the creditors present or represented have voted in favour of it.

(2) Every resolution passed shall be recorded in writing, either separately or as part of the minutes of the meeting. The record shall be signed by the chairman and kept as part of the sederunt book.

Resolutions by post

4.55.—(1) In accordance with this Rule, the receiver may seek to obtain the agreement of members of the creditors' committee to a resolution by sending to every member (or his representative designated for the purpose) a copy of the proposed resolution.

(2) Where the receiver makes use of the procedure allowed by this Rule, he shall send out to members of the committee or their representatives (as the case may be) a statement incorporating the resolution to which their agreement is sought, each resolution (if more than one) being set out in a separate document.

(3) Any creditor of the committee may, within 7 business days from the date of the receiver sending out a resolution, require him to summon a meeting of the committee to consider the matters raised by the resolution.

(4) In the absence of such a request, the resolution is deemed to have been passed by the committee if and when the receiver is notified in writing by a majority of the creditors that they concur with it.

(5) A copy of every resolution passed under this Rule, and a note that the committee's concurrence was obtained, shall be kept in the sederunt book.

Expenses of members, etc.

4.57 The receiver shall defray any reasonable travelling expenses directly incurred by the members of the creditors' committee or their representatives in respect of their attendance at the committee's meetings, or otherwise on the committee's business, as an expense of the receivership. This does not apply to any meeting of the committee held within 3 months of a previous meeting, unless the meeting in question is summoned at the instance of the receiver.

PART 7

PROVISIONS OF GENERAL APPLICATION

CHAPTER 1

MEETINGS

Scope of Chapter 1

7.1.—(1) This Chapter applies to any meetings held in insolvency proceedings other than meetings of a creditors' committee in administration or receivership or of a liquidation committee.

(2) The Rules in this Chapter shall apply to any such meeting subject to any contrary provision in the Act or in the Rules, or to any direction of the court.

Summoning of meetings

7.2.—(1) In fixing the date, time and place for a meeting, the person summoning the meeting ('the convenor') shall have regard to the convenience of the persons who are to attend.

(2) Meetings shall in all cases be summoned for commencement between 10.00 and 16.00 hours on a business day, unless the court otherwise directs.

Notice of meeting

7.3.—(1) The convenor shall give not less than 21 days' notice of the date, time and place of the meeting to every person known to him as being entitled to attend the meeting.

(2) In paragraph (1), for the reference to 21 days, there shall be substituted a reference to 14 days in the following cases:
  (a) any meeting of the company or of its creditors summoned under section 3 (to consider directors' proposal for voluntary arrangement);
  (b) a meeting of the creditors under section 23(1)*(b)* or 25(2)*(b)* (to consider administrator's proposals or proposed revisions); and
  (c) a meeting of creditors under section 67(2) (meeting of unsecured creditors in receivership).

(3) The convenor may also publish notice of the date, time and place of the meeting in a newspaper circulating in the area of the principal place of business of the company or in such other newspaper as he thinks most appropriate for ensuring that it comes to the notice of the persons who are entitled to attend the meeting. In the case of a creditors' meeting summoned by the administrator under section 23(1)*(b)*, the administrator shall publish such a notice.

(4) Any notice under this Rule shall state—

(a) the purpose of the meeting;

(b) the persons who are entitled to attend and vote at the meeting;

(c) the effects of Rule 7.9 or, as the case may be, 7.10 (Entitlement to Vote) and of the relevant provisions of Rule 7.12 (Resolutions);

(d) in the case of a meeting of creditors or contributories, that proxies may be lodged at or before the meeting and the place where they may be lodged; and

(e) in the case of a meeting of creditors, that claims may be lodged by those who have not already done so at or before the meeting and the place where they may be lodged.

Where a meeting of creditors is summoned specially for the purpose of removing the liquidator in accordance with section 171(2) or 172(2), or of receiving his resignation under Rule 4.28, the notice summoning it shall also include the information required by Rule 4.23(2) or, as the case may be, 4.28(2).

(5) With the notice given under paragraph (1), the convenor shall also send out a proxy form.

(6) In the case of any meeting of creditors or contributories, the court may order that notice of the meeting be given by public advertisement in such form as may be specified in the order and not by individual notice to the persons concerned. In considering whether to make such an order, the court shall have regard to the cost of the public advertisement, to the amount of the assets available and to the extent of the interest of creditors or contributories or any particular class of either.

Additional notices in certain cases

7.4.—(1) This Rule applies where a company goes, or proposes to go, into liquidation and it is—

(a) a recognised bank or licensed institution within the meaning of the Banking Act 1979, or

(b) an institution to which sections 16 and 18 of the Act apply as if it were a licensed institution.

(2) Notice of any meeting of the company at which it is intended to propose a resolution for its voluntary winding up shall be given by the directors to the Bank of England ('the Bank') and to the Deposit Protection Board ('the Board') as such notice is given to members of the company.

(3) Where a creditors' meeting is summoned by the liquidator under section 95 or 98, the same notice of meeting must be given to the Bank and Board as is given to the creditors under this Chapter.

(4) Where the company is being wound up by the court, notice of the first meetings of creditors and contributories within the meaning of Rule 4.12 shall be given to the Bank and the Board by the liquidator.

(5) Where in any winding up a meeting of creditors or contributories is summoned for the purpose of—
(*a*) receiving the liquidator's resignation, or
(*b*) removing the liquidator, or
(*c*) appointing a new liquidator,
the person summoning the meeting and giving notice of it shall also give notice to the Bank and the Board.

(6) The Board is entitled to be represented at any meeting of which it is required by this Rule to be given notice; and Schedule 3 has effect with respect to the voting rights of the Board at such a meeting.

Chairman of meetings

7.5.—(1) The chairman at any meeting of creditors in insolvency proceedings shall be the responsible insolvency practitioner, or a person nominated by him in writing.

(2) A person nominated under this Rule must be either—
(*a*) a person who is qualified to act as an insolvency practitioner in relation to the company, or
(*b*) an employee of the administrator, receiver or liquidator, as the case may be, or his firm who is experienced in insolvency matters.

(3) This Rule also applies to meetings of contributories in a liquidation.

(4) At the first meeting of creditors or contributories in a winding up by the court, the interim liquidator shall be the chairman except that, where a resolution is proposed to appoint the interim liquidator to be the liquidator, another person may be elected to act as chairman for the purpose of choosing the liquidator.

(5) This Rule is subject to Rule 4.23(3) (meeting for removal of liquidator).

Meetings requisitioned

7.6.—(1) Subject to paragraph (8), this Rule applies to any request by a creditor or creditors for a meeting of creditors—
(*a*) to an administrator under section 17(3), or
(*b*) to a liquidator under section 142(3), 171(3) or 172(3),

or under any other provision of the Act or the Rules.

(2) Any such request shall be accompanied by—
(*a*) a list of any creditors concurring with the request, showing the amount of the respective claims against the company of the creditor making the request and the concurring creditors;
(*b*) from each creditor concurring, written confirmation of his concurrence; and
(*c*) a statement of the purpose of the proposed meeting.

(3) If the administrator or, as the case may be, the liquidator considers the request to be properly made in accordance with the Act or the Rules, he shall summon a meeting of the creditors to be held on a date not more than 35 days from the date of his receipt of the request.

(4) Expenses of summoning and holding a meeting under this Rule shall be paid to the creditor or creditors making the request, who shall deposit with the administrator caution for their payment.

(5) The sum to be deposited shall be such as the administrator or, as the case may be, the liquidator may determine and he shall not act without the deposit having been made.

(6) The meeting may resolve that the expenses of summoning and holding it are to be payable out of the assets of the company as an expense of the administration or, as the case may be, the liquidation.

(7) To the extent that any caution deposited under this Rule is not required for the payment of expenses of summoning and holding the meeting, it shall be repaid to the person or persons who made it.

(8) This Rule applies to requests by a contributory or contributories for a meeting of contributories, with the modification that, for the reference in paragraph (2) to the creditors' respective claims, there shall be substituted a reference to the contributories' respective values (being the amounts for which they may vote at any meeting).

(9) This Rule is without prejudice to the powers of the court under Rule 4.67(2) (voluntary winding up succeeded by winding up by the court).

Quorum

7.7.—(1) Subject to the next paragraph, a quorum is—
  (*a*) in the case of a creditors' meeting, at least one creditor entitled to vote;
  (*b*) in the case of a meeting of contributories, at least 2 contributories so entitled, or all the contributories, if their number does not exceed 2.

(2) For the purpose of this Rule, the reference to the creditor or contributories necessary to constitute a quorum is not confined to those persons present or duly represented under section 375 of the Companies Act but includes those represented by proxy by any person (including the chairman).

Adjournment

7.8.—(1) This Rule applies to meetings of creditors and to meetings of contributories.

(2) If, within a period of 30 minutes from the time appointed for the commencement of a meeting, a quorum is not present, then, unless the chairman otherwise decides, the meeting shall be adjourned to the same time and place in the following week or, if that is not a business day, to the business day immediately following.

(3) In the course of any meeting, the chairman may, in his discretion, and shall, if the meeting so resolves, adjourn it to such date, time and place as seems to him to be appropriate in the circumstances.

(4) Paragraph (3) is subject to Rule 4.23(3) where the liquidator or his nominee is chairman and a resolution has been proposed for the liquidator's removal.

(5) An adjournment under paragraph (1) or (2) shall not be for a period of more than 21 days.

(6) Where a meeting is adjourned, any proxies given for the original meeting may be used at the adjourned meeting.

Entitlement to vote (creditors)

7.9.—(1) This Rule applies to a creditors' meeting in any insolvency proceedings.

(2) A creditor is entitled to vote at any meeting if he has submitted his claim to the responsible insolvency practitioner and his claim has been accepted in whole or in part.

(3) Chapter 5 of Part 4 (claims in liquidation) shall apply for the purpose of determining a creditor's entitlement to vote at any creditors' meeting in any insolvency proceedings as it applies for the purpose of determining a creditor's entitlement to vote at a meeting of creditors in a liquidation, subject to the modifications specified in the following paragraphs and to any other necessary modification.

(4) For any reference in the said Chapter 5, or in any provision of the Bankruptcy Act as applied by Rule 4.16(1), to—
  (a) the liquidator, there shall be substituted a reference to the supervisor, administrator or receiver, as the case may be;
  (b) the liquidation, there shall be substituted a reference to the voluntary arrangement, administration or receivership as the case may be;
  (c) the date of commencement of winding up, there shall be substituted a reference—
     (i) in the case of a meeting in a voluntary arrangement, to the date of the meeting or, where the company is being wound up or is subject to an administration order, the date of its going into

liquidation or as the case may be, of the administration order; and

    (ii) in the case of a meeting in the administration or receivership, to the date of the administration order or, as the case may be, the date of appointment of the receiver;

(5) In the application to meetings of creditors other than in liquidation proceedings of Schedule 1 to the Bankruptcy Act, paragraph 5(2) and (3) (secured creditors) shall not apply.

(6) This Rule is subject to Rule 7.4(6) and Schedule 3.

Entitlement to vote (members and contributories)

7.10.—(1) Members of a company or contributories at their meeting shall vote according to their rights attaching to their shares respectively in accordance with the articles of association.

(2) In the case of a meeting of members of the company in a voluntary arrangement, where no voting rights attach to a member's share, he is nevertheless entitled to vote either for or against the proposal or any modification of it.

(3) Reference in this Rule to a person's share include any other interests which he may have as a member of the company.

Chairman of meeting as proxy holder

7.11.—(1) Where the chairman at a meeting of creditors or contributories holds a proxy which requires him to vote for a particular resolution and no other person proposes that resolution—
    (a) he shall propose it himself, unless he considers that there is good reason for not doing so, and
    (b) if he does not propose it, he shall forthwith after the meeting notify the person who granted him the proxy of the reason why he did not do so.

(2) At any meeting in a voluntary arrangement, the chairman shall not, by virtue of any proxy held by him, vote to increase or reduce the amount of the remuneration or expenses of the nominee or the supervisor of the proposed arrangement, unless the proxy specifically directs him to vote in that way.

Resolutions

7.12.—(1) Subject to any contrary provision in the Act or the Rules, at any meeting of creditors, contributories or members of a company, a resolution is passed when a majority in value of those voting, in person or by proxy, have voted in favour of it.

(2) In a voluntary arrangement, at a creditors' meeting for any resolution to pass approving any proposal or modification, there must be at least three quarters in value of the creditors present or represented and voting, in person or by proxy, in favour of the resolution.

(3) In a liquidation, in the case of a resolution for the appointment of a liquidator—

(a) if, on any vote, there are two nominees for appointment, the person for whom a majority in value has voted shall be appointed;

(b) if there are three or more nominees, and one of them has a clear majority over both or all the others together, that one is appointed; and

(c) in any other case, the chairman of the meeting shall continue to take votes (disregarding at each vote any nominee who has withdrawn and, if no nominee has withdrawn, the nominee who obtained the least support last time), until a clear majority is obtained for any one nominee.

The chairman may, at any time, put to the meeting a resolution for the joint appointment of any two or more nominees.

(4) Where a resolution is proposed which affects a person in respect of his remuneration or conduct as a responsible insolvency practitioner, the vote of that person, or of his firm or of any partner or employee of his shall not be reckoned in the majority required for passing the resolution. This paragraph applies with respect to a vote given by a person either as creditor or contributory or member or as proxy for a creditor, contributory, or member.

Report of meeting

7.13.—(1) The chairman at any meeting shall cause a report to be made of the proceedings at the meeting which shall be signed by him.

(2) The report of the meeting shall include—

(a) a list of all the creditors or, as the case may be, contributories who attended the meeting, either in person or by proxy;

(b) a copy of every resolution passed; and

(c) if the meeting established a creditors' committee or a liquidation committee, as the case may be, a list of the names and addresses of those elected to be members of the committee.

(3) The chairman shall keep a copy of the report of the meeting as part of the sederunt book in the insolvency proceedings.

CHAPTER 2

PROXIES AND COMPANY REPRESENTATION

Definition of 'proxy'

7.14.—(1) For the purposes of the Rules, a person ('the principal') may authorise another person ('the proxy-holder') to attend, speak and vote as his representative at meetings of creditors or contributories or of the company in insolvency proceedings, and any such authority is referred to as a proxy.

(2) A proxy may be given either generally for all meetings in insolvency proceedings or specifically for any meeting or class of meetings.

(3) Only one proxy may be given by the principal for any one meeting; and it may only be given to one person, being an individual aged 18 or over. The principal may nevertheless nominate one or more other such persons to be proxy-holder in the alternative in the order in which they are named in the proxy.

(4) Without prejudice to the generality of paragraph (3), a proxy for a particular meeting may be given to whoever is to be the chairman of the meeting.

(5) A proxy may require the holder to vote on behalf of the principal on matters arising for determination at any meeting, or to abstain, either as directed or in accordance with the holder's own discretion; and it may authorise or require the holder to propose, in the principal's name, a resolution to be voted on by the meeting.

Form of proxy

7.15.—(1) With every notice summoning a meeting of creditors or contributories or of the company in insolvency proceedings there shall be sent out forms of proxy.

(2) A form of proxy shall not be sent out with the name or description of any person inserted in it.

(3) A proxy shall be in the form sent out with the notice summoning the meeting or in a form substantially to the same effect.

(4) A form of proxy shall be filled out and signed by the principal, or by some person acting under his authority and, where it is signed by someone other than the principal, the nature of his authority shall be stated on the form.

Use of proxy at meeting

7.16.—(1) A proxy given for a particular meeting may be used at any adjournment of that meeting.

(2) A proxy may be lodged at or before the meeting at which it is to be used.

(3) Where the responsible insolvency practitioner holds proxies to be used by him as chairman of the meeting, and some other person acts as chairman, the other person may use the insolvency practitioner's proxies as if he were himself proxy-holder.

Retention of proxies

7.17.—(1) Proxies used for voting at any meeting shall be retained by the chairman of the meeting.

(2) The chairman shall deliver the proxies forthwith after the meeting to the responsible insolvency practitioner (where he was not the chairman).

(3) The responsible insolvency practitioner shall retain all proxies in the sederunt book.

Right of inspection

7.18.—(1) The responsible insolvency practitioner shall, so long as proxies lodged with him are in his hands, allow them to be inspected at all reasonable times on any business day, by—
 (*a*) the creditors, in the case of proxies used at a meeting of creditors.
 (*b*) a company's members or contributories, in the case of proxies used at a meeting of the company or of its contributories.

(2) The reference in paragraph (1) to creditors is—
 (*a*) in the case of a company in liquidation, those creditors whose claims have been accepted in whole or in part, and
 (*b*) in any other case, persons who have submitted in writing a claim to be creditors of the company concerned,
but in neither case does it include a person whose claim has been wholly rejected for purposes of voting, dividend or otherwise.

(3) The right of inspection given by this Rule is also exercisable, in the case of an insolvent company, by its directors.

(4) Any person attending a meeting in insolvency proceedings is entitled immediately before or in the course of the meeting, to inspect proxies and associated documents to be used in connection with that meeting.

Proxy-holder with financial interest

7.19.—(1) A proxy-holder shall not vote in favour of any resolution which would directly or indirectly place him, or any associate of his, in a position to receive any remuneration out of the insolvent estate, unless the proxy specifically directs him to vote in that way.

(2) This Rule applies also to any person acting as chairman of a meeting and using proxies in that capacity; and in its application to him, the proxy-holder is deemed an associate of his.

Representation of corporations

7.20.—(1) Where a person is authorised under section 375 of the Companies Act to represent a corporation at a meeting of creditors or contributories, he shall produce to the chairman of the meeting a copy of the resolution from which he derives his authority.

(2) The copy resolution must be executed in accordance with the provisions of section 36(3) of the Companies Act, or certified by the secretary or a director of the corporation to be a true copy.

CHAPTER 3

MISCELLANEOUS

Giving of notices, etc.

7.21.—(1) All notices required or authorised by or under the Act or the Rules to be given, sent or delivered must be in writing, unless it is otherwise provided, or the court allows the notice to be sent or given in some other way.

(2) Any reference in the Rules to giving, sending or delivering a notice or any such document means, without prejudice to any other way and unless it is otherwise provided, that the notice or document may be sent by post, and that, subject to Rule 7.22, any form of post may be used. Personal service of the notice or document is permissible in all cases.

(3) Where under the Act or the Rules a notice or other document is required or authorised to be given, sent or delivered by a person ('the sender') to another ('the recipient'), it may be given, sent or delivered by any person duly authorised by the sender to do so to any person duly authorised by the recipient to receive or accept it.

(4) Where two or more persons are acting jointly as the responsible insolvency practitioner in any proceedings, the giving, sending or delivering of a notice or document to one of them is to be treated as the giving, sending or delivering of a notice or document to each or all.

Sending by post

7.22.—(1) For a document to be properly sent by post, it must be contained in an envelope addressed to the person to whom it is to be sent, and pre-paid for either first or second class post.

(2) Where the first class post is used, the document is to be deemed to be received on the second business day after the date of posting, unless the contrary is shown.

(3) Where second class post is used, the document is to be deemed to be received on the fourth business day after the date of posting, unless the contrary is shown.

Certificate of giving notice, etc.

7.23.—(1) Where in any proceedings a notice or document is required to be given, sent or delivered by the responsible insolvency practitioner, the date of giving, sending or delivery of it may be proved by means of a certificate signed by him or on his behalf by his solicitor, or a partner or an employee of either of them, that the notice or document was duly given, posted or otherwise sent, or delivered on the date stated in the certificate.

(2) In the case of a notice or document to be given, sent or delivered by a person other than the responsible insolvency practitioner, the date of giving, sending or delivery of it may be proved by means of a certificate by that person that he gave, posted or otherwise sent or delivered the notice or document on the date stated in the certificate, or that he instructed another person (naming him) to do so.

(3) A certificate under this Rule may be endorsed on a copy of the notice to which it relates.

(4) A certificate purporting to be signed by or on behalf of the responsible insolvency practitioner, or by the person mentioned in paragraph (2), shall be deemed, unless the contrary is shown, to be sufficient evidence of the matters stated therein.

Validity of proceedings

7.24. Where in accordance with the Act or the Rules a meeting of creditors or other persons is summoned by notice, the meeting is presumed to have been duly summoned and held, notwithstanding that not all those to whom the notice is to be given have received it.

Evidence of proceedings at meetings

7.25. A report of proceedings at a meeting of the company or of the company's creditors or contributories in any insolvency proceedings, which is signed by a person describing himself as the chairman of that meeting, shall be deemed unless the contrary is shown, to be sufficient evidence of the matters contained in that report.

Right to list of creditors and copy documents

7.26.—(1) Paragraph (2) applies to—
(a) proceedings under Part II of the Act (company administration), and
(b) proceedings in a creditors' voluntary winding up, or a winding up by the court.

(2) Subject to Rule 7.27, in any such proceedings, a creditor who has the right to inspect documents has the right to require the responsible insolvency practitioner to furnish him with a list of the company's creditors and the amount of their respective debts.

(3) Subject to Rule 7.27, where a person has the right to inspect documents, the right includes that of taking copies of those documents, on payment of the appropriate fee.

(4) In this Rule, the appropriate fee means 15 pence per A4 or A5 page and 30 pence per A3 page.

Confidentiality of documents

7.27.—(1) Where, in any insolvency proceedings, the responsible insolvency practitioner considers, in the case of a document forming part of the records of those proceedings,—
(a) that is should be treated as confidential, or
(b) that it is of such nature that its disclosure would be calculated to be injurious to the interests of the company's creditors or, in the case of the winding up of a company, its members or the contributories in its winding up,
he may decline to allow it to be inspected by a person who would otherwise be entitled to inspect it.

(2) The persons who may be refused the right to inspect documents under this Rule by the responsible insolvency practitioner include the members of a creditors' committee in administration or in receivership, or of a liquidation committee.

(3) Where under this Rule the responsible insolvency practitioner refuses inspection of a document, the person who made that request may apply to the court for an order to overrule the refusal and the court may either overrule it altogether, or sustain it, either unconditionally or subject to such conditions, if any, as it thinks fit to impose.

Insolvency practitioner's caution

7.28.—(1) Wherever under the Rules any person has to appoint, or certify the appointment of, an insolvency practitioner to any office, he is under a duty to satisfy himself that the person appointed or to be appointed has caution for the proper performance of his functions.

(2) It is the duty—
(*a*) of the creditors' committee in administration or in receivership,
(*b*) of the liquidation committee in companies winding up, and
(*c*) of any committee of creditors established for the purposes of a voluntary arrangement under Part I of the Act,
to review from time to time the adequacy of the responsible insolvency practitioner's caution.

(3) In any insolvency proceedings the cost of the responsible insolvency practitioner's caution shall be paid as an expense of the proceedings.

Punishment of offences

7.29.—(1) Schedule 4 has effect with respect to the way in which contraventions of the Rules are punishable on conviction.

(2) In that Schedule—
(*a*) the first column specifies the provision of the Rules which creates an offence;
(*b*) in relation to each such offence, the second column describes the general nature of the offence;
(*c*) the third column indicates its mode of trial, that is to say whether the offence is punishable on conviction on indictment, or on summary conviction, or either in the one way or the other;
(*d*) the fourth column shows the maximum punishment by way of fine or imprisonment which may be imposed on a person convicted of the offence in the mode of trial specified in relation to it in the third column (that is to say, on indictment or summarily), a reference to a period of years or months being to a maximum term of imprisonment of that duration; and
(*e*) the fifth column shows (in relation to an offence for which there is an entry in that column) that a person convicted of the offence after continued contravention is liable to a daily default fine; that is to say, he is liable on a second or subsequent conviction of the offence to the fine specified in that column for each day on which the contravention is continued (instead of the penalty specified for the offence in the fourth column of that Schedule).

(3) Section 431 (summary proceedings), as it applies to Scotland, has effect in relation to offences under the Rules as to offences under the Act.

Forms for use in insolvency proceedings

7.30. The forms contained in Schedule 5, with such variations as circumstances require, are the forms to be used for the purposes of the provisions of the Act or the Rules which are referred to in those forms.

Fees, expenses, etc

7.31. All fees, costs, charges and other expenses incurred in the course of insolvency proceedings are to be regarded as expenses of those proceedings.

Power of court to cure defects in procedure

7.32.—(1) Section 63 of the Bankruptcy Act (power of court to cure defects in procedure) shall apply in relation to any insolvency proceedings as it applies in relation to sequestration, subject to the modifications specified in paragraph (2) and to any other necessary modifications.

(2) For any reference in the said section 63 to any expression in column 1 below, there shall be substituted a reference to the expression in column 2 opposite thereto:

Column 1	*Column 2*
This Act or any regulations made under it	The Act or the Rules
Permanent trustee	Responsible insolvency practitioner
Sequestration process	Insolvency proceedings
Debtor	Company
Sheriff	The court
Person who would be eligible to be elected under section 24 of this Act	Person who would be eligible to act as a responsible insolvency practitioner

Sederunt book

7.33.—(1) The responsible insolvency practitioner shall maintain a sederunt book during his term of office for the purpose of providing an accurate record of the administration of each insolvency proceedings.

(2) Without prejudice to the generality of the above paragraph, there shall be inserted in the sederunt book a copy of anything required to be recorded in it by provision of the Act or of the Rules.

(3) The responsible insolvency practitioner shall make the sederunt

book available for inspection at all reasonable hours by any interested person.

(4) Any entry in the sederunt book shall be sufficient evidence of the facts stated therein, except where it is founded on by the responsible insolvency practitioner in his own interest.

Index

Note: *All references are to paragraph numbers*